Death

AND

Conversion

IN THE

Andes

D1496381

Death

AND

Conversion

IN THE

Andes

Lima and Cuzco,
1532–1670

GABRIELA RAMOS

UNIVERSITY OF NOTRE DAME PRESS

NOTRE DAME, INDIANA

Library of Congress Cataloging-in-Publication Data

Ramos, Gabriela.
Death and conversion in the Andes : Lima and Cuzco, 1532–1670 /
Gabriela Ramos.
p. cm. — (History, languages, and cultures of the Spanish and
Portuguese worlds)
Includes bibliographical references and index.
ISBN-13: 978-0-268-04028-4 (pbk. : alk. paper)
ISBN-10: 0-268-04028-1 (pbk. : alk. paper)
1. Indians of South America—Peru—Lima—Religion. 2. Indians of
South America—Peru—Lima—Rites and ceremonies. 3. Indians of
South America—Peru—Cuzco—Religion. 4. Indians of South
America—Peru—Cuzco—Rites and ceremonies. 5. Death—Religious
aspects—Christianity. 6. Conversion—Christianity. 7. Ancestor
worship—Andes Region. 8. Andes Region—Religious life and customs.
9. Spain—Colonies—America—America—Administration—History.
I. Title.
F3429.3.R3R36   2010
985'.25—dc22
                                    2010008786

Because nothing in the world is as important or as difficult as dying well.

—Alonso de la Peña y Montenegro,

Itinerario para párrocos de Indios

Nadie nos dice cómo voltear la cara contra la pared y morirnos sencillamente.

—Blanca Varela, *El falso teclado*

CONTENTS

MAPS

ACKNOWLEDGMENTS

Various people and institutions made it possible for me to carry out the research for this book and devote the time necessary to write it. A fellowship from the University of Pennsylvania allowed me to pursue my doctoral studies and develop my interest in the topic. The Center for New World Comparative Studies of the John Carter Brown Library in Providence, Rhode Island, gave me access to its book and document collection in the summer of 1998. I was able to complete the research in Peruvian archives and libraries that serves as the basis for this book and other works that I have published in recent years thanks to Fellowship 6338 of the Wenner-Gren Foundation for Anthropological Research. I wish to thank the staffs of the research room in the Archivo General de la Nación, of the Sala de Investigaciones in the National Library of Peru, of the Archivo Arzobispal de Lima, and of the Archivo Departamental del Cusco for their professional support. Help from the Red para el Desarrollo de las Ciencias Sociales en el Perú during the 2001–2 academic year allowed me to reformulate portions of this work. In the United Kingdom, the support and understanding of colleagues and administrators in the history faculty at the University of Cambridge, Newnham College, and the Centre of Latin American Studies, University of Cambridge, were very important during the composition of the final manuscript. I especially wish to thank Chris Bayly, Alison Burgess, Julie Coimbra, Elizabeth Haresnape, John Hatcher, Melissa Lane, David Lehmann, Michael O'Brien, and Megan Vaughan.

Sabine MacCormack enthusiastically undertook the task of publishing this manuscript in the series she directs and gave me valuable advice. Barbara Hanrahan, director of the University of Notre Dame Press, has been extremely kind and patient. Two anonymous readers for the Press gave me a wealth of useful suggestions. I am deeply grateful to Rebecca DeBoer and to Ann Aydelotte from the University of Notre Dame Press for their editorial work.

I wrote the original version of this book in Spanish, my native language. I wish to thank Anne Pushkal, who translated the first chapter. I also thank Patricia Simonson, who translated chapters 2, 3, and 4, and Michael Kidd, who undertook the translation of the final chapters as well as the introduction and conclusion. Kate Reeves revised and edited the entire manuscript.

I owe an enormous debt to Nancy M. Farriss for the privilege of her support, friendship, and wise counsel over more than ten years. Steven Feierman and Ann Farnsworth-Alvear read and critiqued early versions of this work and offered useful advice. In Philadelphia, Catherine Bogosian, Joan Bristol, Shefali Chandra, Luli Feliciano, Laura Matthew, Gene Ogle, Anne Pushkal, and Yanna Yannakakis were enthusiastic listeners and excellent friends.

My gratitude goes to the friends and colleagues with whom I share my passion for Peru for their dialogue, help, commentary, and constant support: Susana Aldana, Berta Ares, Betford Betalleluz, Nicanor Domínguez, Juan Carlos Estenssoro, Pedro Guibovich, Marta Irurozqui, César Itier, Natalia Majluf, Cecilia Méndez, Víctor Peralta, Valérie Robin, and Margarita Suárez. In Cuzco, the friendship and support of Donato Amado, Marco Chevarría, Mary Chino, Luis Nieto Degregori, Celia Jaimes, Julia Rodríguez, Miki Suzuki, and Marta Zegarra made my visits and stays in the city and the region pleasant and productive.

I regret that several people are no longer here to receive my thanks and see the result of my work. Their presence was very important at decisive stages in my training as a historian, and the pain of their absence has influenced the reflections underlying this book. Guido Delran, founder of the Centro de Estudios Andinos "Bartolomé de las Casas," gave me the opportunity to carry out research in Cuzco and begin my academic career in Peru. Juan Bautista Lassègue shared his knowledge of Church history and the Cuzco archives in addition to being a close friend. During the years in which I researched and wrote this book, I lost my siblings and my parents. Their deaths made my journey difficult, and as a result of the successive mourning through which I have passed, I have come to a greater understanding of the experience of the men and women about whom I write in this book. I wish to thank Milena Stoynic for helping me to reflect on their memory.

I am grateful to Évelyne Mesclier not only for her affection, companionship, and long hours of discussion in clarifying ideas, reading drafts, visiting many of the sites mentioned in this book, and preparing maps and figures but also for her joy of living, enthusiasm for intellectual work, and unquenchable curiosity about what lies beyond. It is to her that I dedicate this book.

Introduction

This book studies how the conversion of the Andean populations to Catholicism was achieved from a particular perspective: changes in attitudes toward death. Specifically, it investigates how and why the members of a society modify their attitudes toward the sacred to the point of changing not only their ideas and beliefs about, for example, the origin and operation of the world but the way in which they relate to their peers or what arrangements they make for the remains of their dead. The people of the Andes in the sixteenth century had no choice in their conversion to Christianity. Through different routes, men and women of all classes were compelled to receive baptism and to fulfill a series of requirements implied therein, some of which are topics of this book. Several decades later, the spread of Catholicism in the Andes was wide and effective and, despite opinions to the contrary from some observers and scholars, it had deeply permeated the lives of the indigenous population and transformed them completely. Consequently, this is also an investigation into how the conditions were established that made possible a change of this scope: the terrain, the main actors, the methods and instruments employed by missionaries and colonizers, and the reactions and strategies of the men and women who were the target of this assault.

The problem of religious conversion in the context of colonialism forms the general frame within which this study is inscribed. The work of other scholars who have explored this vast field, placing different emphases on themes, space, chronology, and point of view, is thus expanded. The use of the term "conversion" has been and still is the object of disagreement among historians and anthropologists, and it has generated an extensive secondary literature that I shall not summarize here.[1] I would, nonetheless, like to clarify several points. In speaking of conversion, I refer to a multiple, prolonged, and non-linear process that involves an effort to adopt and adapt ideas and practices centered on the sphere of the sacred. These multiple transformations are motivated and accompanied by changes in the living conditions of their agents. In the context of colonialism, the difference between religious traditions and customs that came into contact with one other and the unequal power relationships of those who took part in the process should not necessarily lead us to imagine a scenario divided into two clearly opposing camps, each neatly defined and homogeneous.

In comparison to other times and places, the distinguishing characteristic of religious conversion in the context of Spanish colonialism was its unavoidability. In most of the New World territories occupied by the Spaniards, cooperation between Church and state in the evangelizing mission was also a distinctive feature.[2] In the Andes in particular, the conquest and the establishment of political and social order had a specifically Catholic orientation. It could not have been otherwise, because the prevailing culture and legal order in Spain were informed by that same source.

Moreover, the missionary and colonization process in the Andes was affected by the political, religious, and cultural reforms of the mid-sixteenth-century Council of Trent.[3] In Mexico in the years immediately following the conquest, the mendicant orders were able to put into practice missionary ideas and methods of the period prior to the Catholic reform, with a considerable degree of autonomy, utopianism, original evangelizing materials, and decentralized printing presses established early on. For a while, the religious orders operated to a large extent free from state oversight and a centralized ecclesiastical structure.[4] The later date of the conquest in the Andes and, above all, the period of wars and enormous political instability that followed it resulted in evangelization headed by a Church eager to stake out a clearly institutional role. At the foundation of the Andean colonial project, the ecclesiastical and political authorities were for the most part bound by the dictates of Trent. This is clear not only in doctrinal issues or in the evangelizing role that fell to the secular clergy and to the Society of Jesus but also in such crucial and lasting factors as linguistic policy, control of the printing presses, and the planning of urban centers, crucial spaces from which Christianity was spread. Cooperation and symbiosis between the evangelization and the colonial project were fundamental to the Andes. For these reasons, studying the process of religious conversion involves not only attending to its functions and consequences in the area of ideas, beliefs, and the transmission and expression of doctrinal knowledge articulated in a coherent discourse, but also to the construction of the colonial order. Its course was marked by a diversity of factors, some not doctrinal but very influential, which left their stamp on it and legitimized it.

Some of the most important studies on colonization and religious conversion in the Andes cover very wide geographical and cultural areas as well as very long periods and multiple topics.[5] This study is an analysis of a single theme: death, and attitudes toward it in the context of the conquest and colonization. It is an extensive area that permits an approach to the process of Christianization and colonization in the Andes from different angles. Although indebted to them, this is not a full analysis of death in the vein of the classic studies on the topic, which sought to understand the course of a society or of a "civilization," the development of symbols and traditions, or even changes in the experience of a given social class, city, or particular region.[6]

In considering death, we are led to study the peculiar features that distinguish a society: ways in which the body is treated, specific rituals of mourning and commemoration, methods and sites for placing the remains of the dead, and explanations of what happens to people once they have crossed the threshold of death, among others. Additionally, the study of death brings us face to face with questions with which all human beings are concerned: where we come from, and where we are going; what our ancestors mean to us, and their role in our lives; what we can do in the face of the pain and emptiness brought about by others' deaths and the fear and uncertainty provoked by the idea of our own; what happens to the body; what feelings arise in us from the decomposition of matter, the disintegration of what we are and what we possess; how much importance we ascribe to this dispersion; and how we imagine the living will remember us. Besides its religious significance, death has political repercussions, acting as a unifying or disintegrating force upon groups of humans. It influences the way in which societies distribute the physical space they inhabit: space assigned to the dead will always be in reference to space occupied by the living.[7] The way a society relates to its dead molds its vision of the past and affects the way ties are established between the living.[8] In the Andes, death operated as a force that not only had a destructive momentum but was also fundamental in the formation of colonial society.

This book proposes that the Christianization of death was crucial in the conversion of the Andean peoples to Catholicism and investigates its history from the moment of the Spanish invasion in 1532 to well into the seventeenth century, when colonial control and evangelization were fairly well established and major and lasting changes had come about across the Andes. The Church by that point had developed clear guidelines, materials, and personnel to carry out the missionary project; ecclesiastical and political jurisdictions were outlined, and the territory was thus organized into cities, settlements, and parishes, the majority of whose residents buried the remains of their loved ones in churches. Policies and institutions that sought to extend their reach across the whole of the territory and its settlers show the desire for uniformity characteristic of both reformed Catholicism and the ideals of the Spanish crown in the sixteenth and seventeenth centuries. But this does not mean that those policies and institutions were imposed uniformly or, even less, that the directions and consequences were the same everywhere.

In order to explain the nuances and contrasts that characterize this process, the book offers a comparative study of the two major cities of the Peruvian viceroyalty: Cuzco and Lima. There are two reasons for this choice. First, the cities arose as models of physical, political, and spiritual order and, as such, were the strategic sites from which both evangelization and colonization were spread across the rest of the territory. Second, Cuzco and Lima were urban centers of practically equal hierarchy and importance, but for very different reasons. Cuzco, which had been the region's ancient political and sacred center, was home to the most representative and well-established indigenous elite in the Andes: the descendants of the Incas. Thus, its political and symbolic significance continued to be very great during the colonial period. Because of their power, especially symbolically, the ties that the Incan descendants established with the Spanish population were multiple and long lasting. Both the city and the region it controlled made it through the process of conquest and colonization without suffering great population losses, either numerically or culturally. With the peak of silver mining operations in Upper Peru, Cuzco retained its major-city status, which efficiently connected the southern highlands with the rest of the Peruvian viceroyalty.

Lima, in contrast, was established as the seat of Spanish power. Its native population was seriously weakened by the effects of the Spanish invasion, and the majority of its original leadership was marginalized in terms of both physical location and political significance. Upon becoming a political, economic, and commercial center, Lima turned into a magnet for immigrants of all social strata from abroad and from all points of the viceroyalty. Its indigenous elite had little chance to develop a self-legitimizing discourse that would appeal to its ancient historical roots. In a dynamic socioeconomic setting, there was wide social mobility among the indigenous population. The city maintained a complex relationship with its surroundings, constantly exchanging people, goods, ideas, and customs. In this context, both the installation of the colonial order and the conversion of the native populations to Catholicism were achieved. In terms of ritual and funerary customs, the Christianization of death in both cities followed general patterns that prevailed at that point in the Catholic world, but these patterns nonetheless assumed specific forms as a result of regional differences and the adaptations and appropriations put in place by all parties involved.

Some of the most influential studies of religious life in the colonial Andes have been guided by the content of a historical record of unique interest and importance: the documentation of the religious repression carried out in portions of the Lima diocese in the seventeenth century. Denying the religious repression, destruction, and violence that characterized a significant portion of the colonization and evangelization of the region would be tantamount to silencing key chapters of the history that I am attempting to write here. Nevertheless, to reduce this history to a series of episodes of open, continuous, and exclusive opposition also results in a loss. The men and women on whom this study focuses are those who contributed to the creation of Andean Catholicism: those who, in their attempts to incorporate, understand, and appropriate ideas and practices that would give meaning to their lives, became actors in a major cultural transformation. Consequently, this study is based mainly on a different type of source: wills, which document ordinary, routine aspects of people's lives.

Based on a reading of the archaeological literature, chapter 1 offers an overview of the ideas and practices regarding death in the Andes from the period prior to the conquest, emphasizing the connections between these ideas and their diversity. Through a study of the configuration and location of burials, the link between ancestor worship and control of space is examined. Consideration of the ways that human remains were treated establishes the basis for analyzing perceptions of the body and the self as well as the way in which social hierarchies were constituted. Finally, I use the study of funerary rituals to deduce some of the central ideas on the fate of the dead and the way in which the living understood and conducted their relations with them.

Based on an analysis of different versions of contemporary chronicles, chapter 2 studies the meaning of death during the conquest. The argument is that, in the absence of a common idiom, religion, institutions, or laws, death served as a language among the parties involved and operated as a destructive force as well as one that ordered society in the initial and decisive contacts between Andeans and Europeans.

Policies intended by the Church and state to Christianize death in the Andes are the topic of chapter 3, while chapter 4 is devoted to the study of the methods and instruments created for their implementation. Consequently, these chapters examine the issue of the control and distribution of space for the dead; ideas about the body and self introduced with evangelization; and the establishment of institutions and associations that were fundamental in communicating Christian ideas and practices regarding death to the inhabitants of the Andes.

Chapters 5 and 6 are devoted to studying how the ideas and methods previously analyzed came into play in the lives of indigenous inhabitants in the cities of Lima and Cuzco. In chapter 5, through a close reading of almost five hundred wills,[9] I examine how the use of these documents was introduced and what their impact was on the Andean peoples. I also study the meaning behind the choice of graves and instructions for funerary rituals, proposing that both are a manifestation of the appropriation and redefinition of the two cities' sacred spaces. The fact that ever greater numbers of men and women agreed to bury their relatives' remains in churches signals a definitive Christianization of death, as does the growing adoption of Christian funerary rituals. Also based on an analysis of wills, the final chapter deals with the concerns of many people over what would happen to them after death: who their successors and heirs would be; who would carry out their last requests; who would keep their memory alive, and how. The context in which I raise and attempt to resolve these questions is marked by the circumstances established by colonial power and its legal order; the teachings and dictates of the Church; and the concrete injunctions facing each individual, whether presiding over a *cacicazgo* (chiefdom),[10] a large or small family, or having no relatives at all.

The differences between the ideas, languages, rituals, and social practices regarding death in the pre-Hispanic Andes and those unique to Spanish Catholicism of the sixteenth and seventeenth centuries have appeared to observers to be of such magnitude that any adaptation would be simply impossible. For some, only an overwhelming act of violence could carry it out or explain it, with its counterpart in submission and in a silent—albeit false—acceptance, leading to a clandestine religious life. This book does not dismiss the weight of the violence that permeated the conquest and colonization process, but, claiming that violence was not the only force that gave shape to colonial Andean society, it proposes an interrogation of how existing sociopolitical and cultural patterns were redefined, of the assimilation of new ideas and customs, and of the way in which the people of the Andes resorted to their own creativity to deal with these changes. In short, all that which human beings avail themselves of when, finding themselves surrounded by death, they take on the challenge of surviving.

The Peruvian Andes

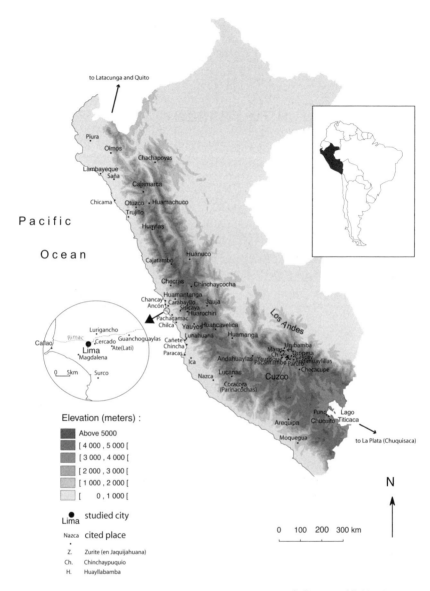

Elevation (meters) :

- Above 5000
- [4 000 , 5 000 [
- [3 000 , 4 000 [
- [2 000 , 3 000 [
- [1 000 , 2 000 [
- [0 , 1 000 [

● **studied city**
Lima

Nazca **cited place**
.

Z.   Zurite (en Jaquijahuana)
Ch.   Chinchaypuquio
H.   Huayllabamba

G. Ramos and E. Mesclier 2007

Source: Penaherrera 1989: 125: Instituto Geografico Nacional, 1997: Blay-Foldex, South America, 1999; Dominguez, 1989.

CHAPTER ONE | # Death in
Pre-Hispanic Peru

Beliefs and practices concerning death were of fundamental importance in the lives of the ancient inhabitants of the Andes. Investigating these beliefs and practices is key to understanding the Andeans'
vision of the world and the sociopolitical organization of their societies. This chapter aims to sketch out some of the characteristics
of experience of death in the Andes at the moment of the Spanish conquest and to explore its diversity and meaning. While this requires
an interdisciplinary focus, I seek also to situate the task historically,
engaging the problem of change, and of the dynamics generated in
pre-Hispanic Peru when diverse cultural practices came into contact
through exchange as well as by means of conquest.

Research on Andean funerary practice in particular, and on the
region's religious practice in general, underscores the significant role
of the cult of the ancestors. Making use of historical and archaeological sources, I will attempt to establish which practices were, in
fact, legitimate manifestations of the cult.[1] To this end, I will consider
those aspects concerned with the process of death: the places of
burial, the placement and positioning of the body, and mourning rituals. Moreover, I wish to understand the place occupied by the dead
and by funerary practices in the processes of competition and political rivalry that characterized the region's history. I believe that this
connection holds the key to understanding the dynamics of conflict
and cultural reproduction that gave rise to diverse political conforma-
tions, both before and after the European conquest.

Ethnographic research has repeatedly shown that death is a phenomenon that involves complex rituals composed of various phases, in which the constitution of society is central. Faced with the loss of one of its members, society redefines its ties, seeking to reestablish its meaning (Hertz 1960). Bloch and Parry (1982) observe that, in the conception and unfolding of their funerary rituals, societies recreate themselves. During this process, forebears, especially those of high social rank, are taken as a point of reference. With them, the living maintain relations that can be ambiguous: the ancestors take the role of protectors of their descendants, but they can also exert a negative influence over them (Bloch and Parry 1982, 43). Whether their influence is for good or for ill, the conviction that the dead are active in the world of the living explains the existence and vigor of the cult of the ancestors in the Andes.[2]

The ancestors' sphere of influence affects practically every aspect of human activity (DeLeonardis and Lau 2004, 78–80).[3] In the rituals conducted in their honor, kin invoked them to ensure the fertility of the earth and an adequate supply of the goods needed for subsistence; they prayed for the health and well-being of their descendants and asked for their ancestors' intercession in order to ensure the political fortunes of the group that fell under their tutelage. The concept of the ancestor implies descent and kinship, and it is directly linked to the representation and exercise of authority, to the unfolding of political life, and to the formation and use of memory. In the Andes, the certainty that a nexus existed between the ancestors, nature, and space explains their decisive role in the appropriation and control of territory by a particular group.[4]

Although Andean societies invoked the ancestors on many kinds of occasions, the activities that ensued when a death took place had special relevance, given that they represented a response to the worries and expectations that emerged with special force in such circumstances. These actions concern the internal order within a given society as well as its relationships with other groups.

The form and meaning of the cult of the ancestors in the Andes has been studied by other researchers, whose work serves me here as a point of departure.[5] What I seek to contribute in the following discussion is a consideration of the regional variations that most directly concern this book, and their possible significance. My sources consist of the reports written in the sixteenth and seventeenth centuries by chroniclers, religious, and functionaries—the majority of them Europeans—about funerary practices and conceptions about death and the hereafter that existed in the Andes up to the moment of conquest, and during the years that followed. I will also make use of examples drawn from archaeological research carried out in different regions of the Andes that bear on the funerary context (whether or not this is their principal theme).[6]

The earliest observers of Andean customs note the amount of work, time, and resources that the living devoted to funerary rituals and to the construction of burial places. The chronicler Pedro de Cieza de León dedicated a remarkable number of pages to the description of the funerary customs of the different Andean peoples that he was able to observe during his extensive travels.[7] Cieza notes that, despite the diversity of customs, in essence the Andeans he encountered shared similar beliefs (1984b [1553], First Part, chap. 63, 197): that there existed a life after death, and that it retained many resemblances to earthly life. In the hereafter, social and political hierarchies persisted, and the dead interacted under the protection of, and near, the divinities to whom they owed their primal origins. Since the bodily needs and the requirements for service and companionship of the most powerful continued in the afterlife, their well-being was sustained by the care that the living provided by means of offerings of food and drink, utensils, clothing, and objects of value as well as the sacrifice of women and servants who accompanied the deceased to his grave (1984b [1553], First Part, chap. 41, 136; chap. 44, 147; chap. 48, 158–59; chap. 51, 165; chap. 62, 193–95). With regard to beliefs, this general model was very widespread in the Andes; and with regard to practices, distinct variations existed, especially with respect to offerings and human sacrifice.

How were these ideas and practices made tangible? Who were the ancestors, and what were they like? Where were they, and how did they interact with the living? In order to address these questions, let us address the places and types of burials, the various ways in which kin prepared the corpse, and the mourning rituals that ensued.

Places

Throughout the region and over different periods of its history, the inhabitants of the Andes chose a wide range of places in which to deposit the remains of their forebears. At the moment of the European conquest, the chroniclers noted the diversity of sites that were chosen for entombment as well as the variety of forms it took, one of the most remarkable signs both of the idea of the sacred and of the spatial manifestation of the political and social order. This has been corroborated by archaeology, and although a significant portion of the available evidence presents certain problems for research,[8] in principle it does not contradict the chroniclers. The matter of burial places is intimately tied to that of funerary architecture or, taking into account the variety of known evidence, to the forms taken by burial places and the spaces where the remains of the dead were placed. For this reason, both aspects will be examined together.

The Jesuit Bernabé Cobo compiled a synthesis of the funerary customs of pre-Hispanic Peru that attempted to cover the greater part of the Andean territory, which we can use as a guide to understanding the conditions and attitudes of the local societies with respect to their neighbors, their surroundings, and their forebears. Cobo explains that among the different funerary structures, two types can be distinguished: subterranean chambers and burials, and surface buildings. These were used in both the highlands and the lowlands. In his opinion, the tombs of the coastal dwellers were considerably more elaborate than those of the highlanders, probably because the former had been constructed in their entirety, whereas the latter showed a tendency to take over natural spaces.[9] On the coast, according to Cobo, the underground sepulchers were hollows, "like vaults" (1956 [1653], 1: Book 14, chap. 18, 272), and their depth and interior finish varied according to the rank of their occupants.[10] The tomb of the highest-ranking dead had a narrow doorway that the kin closed with one or more stone slabs, which could be moved to permit reentry to renew offerings, deposit more bodies, or conduct other rituals. After a certain amount of time, the tomb was sealed, a gesture with which the kin symbolically marked a substantial distance from the dead. This action surely indicates a change in the condition of the dead, who were thus properly converted into ancestors.

Commenting on the funerary monuments that were erected in the coastal valleys, Cobo attributed differences in style and finish, which appeared to be "medium-sized hills," to competition and emulation among different groups (1956 [1653], 1: Book 14, chap. 18, 272). Examining their layout and construction, he concluded that these structures were very similar to the principal residences of the *caciques*. After the conquest, the residents of the new cities, seeking construction materials, demolished these pyramids and burial mounds. Observing the destruction that characterized the era in which he was writing, Cobo attempted to analyze the way they were built. He deduced that, in order to be able to introduce new burials, the structures were filled with earth, which progressively increased their size. The Anonymous Jesuit's description (Anónimo Jesuita 1968, 159–60), written on the basis of observations made in the sixteenth century, suggests that the construction of some of these burial mounds could have been due to the interaction of environmental and political factors. He notes that the backfilling was a response to very severe conditions, since it took place during a period, over a number of years, of bitter warfare, when floods devastated the territory.[11]

In the highlands, mountain caves were used, and hollows were fashioned in the rock; underground chambers were constructed within existing buildings, and structures of various sizes were erected, with access doors like those of houses (Isbell 1997). Although one might think that a given group customarily employed a single, characteristic type of burial, there are indications that in some parts of the central and southern highlands, different ones were used simultaneously (Eaton 1916; MacCurdy 1923; Parsons et al. 2002; Andrushko 2007; Salazar 2007).

What criteria determined the place of the burial? Elucidating the significance of the spaces and places of death (see Silverman 2002; Ashmore and Geller 2005) can offer a means of understanding different social processes. Buikstra (1995) has shown that both funerary rituals and burial sites symbolize the rights that certain social groups claimed over the control and use of resources. Beginning with the assumption that funerary monuments are not just indicators but also instruments of the creation of social spaces, Isbell (1997) has proposed a very suggestive hypothesis about the emergence of funerary structures in different places in the highlands, relating them to processes of territorial appropriation and social organization over a wide area of the central Andes. Additionally, we can credit Isbell (2004) with an interesting exploration of different sequences and forms of burial that predate the domination of the Inca state, suggesting a complex interaction of political and social processes that affected the way in which Andeans organized rituals in homage to their forebears.

The chroniclers attributed the existence of different types of burials to ethnic diversity. For example, Cobo reported that cultivated fields as well as deserts and pastures were chosen, or even inhabited houses (1956 [1653], 1:272), which speaks of a multiplicity of space utilization and of their conception as sacred places, of possible relationships with other groups, and of different decisions about the proximity that the living ought to have among themselves and with the dead. Cieza de León tells us that "each nation sought a new manner of entombing its dead" (1984b [1553], First Part, chap. 63, 196). The chronicler's observation is a sign that strong rivalries existed among different ethnic groups. Nevertheless, it is imperative to corroborate the kinds of burials that the chroniclers distinguish with those that archaeological investigation has recorded.

Cobo's observations indicate still more if we note that the underground structures can be found in different places and have differing significance: some cemeteries on the coast were not always immediately distinguishable from the surrounding landscape. Those who cared for them placed very discreet markers on the graves, such as stakes, carved wooden instruments, or the bones of marine animals. This custom suggests that if these signs served as markers for relatives, their low profile could also be interpreted as a defensive precaution, as Menzel (1976) has noted, based on her excavations in Ica.[12] This raises doubts about the thesis that burials represent a way of claiming possession over a territory.[13] Possibly it indicates some form of legitimation, which would have to be examined, taking into account the offerings that were placed there and the rituals that were enacted. We will return to this point below when we address the significance of the burials and their role in interethnic relations. In some cases, the placement of the cemeteries is more comprehensible to the contemporary observer, since they are found in the immediate area of what can be identified as administrative or religious centers. The persons interred there devoted themselves to activities of different kinds: artisanal, service, and cultic. Examples of this type can be found in the ceremonial centers of Pachacamac and Chincha, and the sites of Sacsahuaman and Kusicancha in Cuzco (Menzel 1959, 138; Julien 1987–1989; Eeckhout 1999; Conlee et al. 2004, 222–24; Shimada 2005; Andrushko et al. 2006, 65; Andrushko 2007, 59).[14] Where the placement of cemeteries cannot be associated with some prominent center, other hypotheses are needed. Ancón, an extensive cemetery located in a desert zone with access to a bay to the north of present-day Lima, was used over the course of successive periods, including that of Inca domination (Ravines 1977; 1981; Kaulicke 1997). Moreover, the area was inhabited, although no notable constructions existed there. What brought about the formation of so extensive a funerary site in this place, over so extended a period?[15] How far were the living kept from the dead in Ancón, and why?[16]

We encounter a more intelligible image in the burials associated with architectural complexes in areas commanding important strategic spaces, such as irrigation canals or vantage points. Their variety, placement, and relation to their surroundings suggest an active relation between inhabitants of these sites and visitors to them, and the dead, denoting a high degree of social complexity (Conrad 1982).[17] The remains of the dead were not relegated to a distant place; rather, the cemeteries were integrated with the architectural grouping. The social hierarchies that governed the world of the living also expressed themselves in the burials.[18] Several examples of this type can be found on the central coast and within the limits of present-day Lima. For example, Cornejo (2004) has studied a cemetery adjoining a tumulus or *guaca* (sacred place) contiguous to Guadtca, one of the vital canals that irrigated the lands of the principal *cacicazgos* of the Valley of Lima,[19] and suggests that not only are social hierarchies and occupations manifested in the burials, but also the geographic origins and ethnic identities of the deceased.[20] The important cemetery found near the site of Puruchuco,[21] which gives privileged access to a sector of the Rímac valley, also shows the confluence of social hierarchies, cultural traditions, and, very possibly, the labor specialization of its inhabitants (Cock 2002; Murphy 2003).

The Incas are known to have occupied some highly strategic sites on the coast and to have established cemeteries as well as taking over existing ones. In his study of the site of Incahuasi, in the Cañete River valley, Hyslop (1985) observes that the military forays of conquest that were deployed from there explain the formation of a cemetery. Incahuasi had a privileged location, controlling the valley and access to the various roads that linked the highland to the coast. Hyslop infers that the occupants laid out the site on a plan analogous to that of the city of Cuzco, which gave it high political rank and a special religious dimension. The burial site, accordingly, participated in Cuzco's prestige and significance.[22]

Another example is the site of Armatambo, to the south of present-day Lima, which served as a port and a point of exchange between the north coast and Pachacamac, thus making possible the supplying of objects that held great importance for the cult, such as the *mullo* (spondylus), to the most important ceremonial center of the central coast. It is known that even when the Incas took control of the area, Armatambo retained its original leadership. As in other zones they occupied, the Incas made use of the local cemetery, which surely helped mark their establishment in this strategic zone.[23] Based on her examination of the funerary contexts of Armatambo, Díaz Arriola (2004) affirms that while the local funerary customs were maintained there, they were also progressively influenced by Inca cultural patterns. As indicated above, in addition to Cobo, other chroniclers such as the Anonymous Jesuit (1968, 158) have noted that in different areas of the coast, the burials of ethnic authorities were found in mounds that stood out in the landscape.[24]

Based on his investigations in the Lurín valley, to the south of Lima and at the sites of Pachacamac and Pampa de las Flores, Eeckhout (1999; 2004, 43) has proposed that the residences of the *caciques* became tombs when their owners died. Whoever succeeded the deceased in the position of *cacique* built his house beside or on top of the tomb of his predecessor. The construction must have required a great deal of labor and resources. This pattern, which resembles that on the north coast during the contemporaneous Chimú rule[25] (Donnan 1978; Conrad 1982; Shimada 2005), suggests the ambition to claim control of a territory by means of the ascendancy of one particular lineage.[26] The social hierarchies and possible ethnic differences that divided inhabitants were manifested spatially, for example, in the cemetery adjacent to the architectural complex of Pampa de las Flores, in the Lurín valley. Here, Eeckhout (1999, 196–210) has observed that some large mounds of refuse mark a kind of "frontier" between the cemetery, where the overwhelming majority of tombs belong to commoners, and the pyramids, where one finds the graves of those of high rank. Similarly, some cemeteries and groups of tombs found in Junín, in the central highlands, were situated at the edges of the walls erected around the settlements (Parsons et al. 2000, 168), which, in addition to their defensive purpose, very clearly evoke the idea of a boundary.[27] It is important to note here that the re-use of graves, and intrusion into them by invading groups or upstarts, was a common phenomenon with a long history on the coast as well as in the highlands (DeLeonardis and Lau 2004, 96, 114; Andrushko 2007, 32, 64), alerting us to the dynamics of competition and occupation that at times could have represented very violent incursions.

The use of caves as graves, known as *machayes*, is well known to us from the colonial sources (Doyle 1988; Salomon 1995; Duviols 2003). Although one could assume that in these natural formations (Hrdlicka 1914) the investment of energy on the part of the kin of the deceased was minimal, Isbell (1997, 183) reports that in some cases the interior walls were stuccoed or even painted. In other cases, the stone of the tombs was worked, with the attendant expenditures of time and labor (Squier 1877, 531–32; Eaton 1916; Isbell 1997, 179–80; Andrushko 2007, 72). Situated at high elevations, with difficult access, they could have complemented the protection and surveillance functions of these places, as in Huarochirí, in the sierra of Lima (Hrdlicka 1914, 10), in Ollantaytambo (Protzen 1993), and at Machu Picchu, in Cuzco (Eaton 1916; Andrushko 2007, 74). This also seems to have been the case with the funerary cave of Molino-Chilacachi, a site under the Lupaqa hegemony,[28] in the environs of Lake Titicaca (De la Vega et al. 2002).[29] The social rank of those who occupied these tombs is uncertain, although it could have varied according to place and local circumstances. For example, Murúa (2001 [1613], 402) reports that the caves were designated for the common people, although he does not specify in what region; Guaman Poma (1989 [1615], 296) relates that the Condesuyos deposited the bodies of some of their dead in caves situated in craggy places that sheltered the remains of the most ancient ancestors, the *uariuiracocharuna;* while Cieza de León (1984b [1553], First Part, chap. 57, 181) notes that in Loja (in present-day Ecuador), when the Spaniards were already established there, the old people asked their relatives to place their bodies in caves in far-away, inaccessible places.[30]

The structures known as *chullpas*,[31] made of stone or adobe with an access door, are found throughout the central Andes. Isbell (1997, 156), who calls the *chullpas* open sepulchers, has specified the criteria for their identification. He connects them directly to the cult of the ancestors represented by the human remains that usually were placed within these structures. Ideally, they form part of an architectural complex adapted to the celebration of public ceremonies, but Isbell and others have identified and described *chullpas* with varied characteristics of volume and construction, which are not adapted to these functions, since they are located on craggy terrain and in some cases form complexes that resemble villages (Thompson 1972; Gasparini and Margolies 1980, 147–57; Protzen 1993; Isbell 1997, 176; Parsons et al. 2000; Sillar and Dean 2002). Some of these structures served strictly as tombs, such as those that Cieza de León described for the Collao region (1984b [1553], First Part, chap. 100, 275) in the environs of Lake Titicaca. Others sheltered the bodies of the dead at the same time as they served as dwellings, as has been noted in examples found in the Lima sierra, in Jauja, in the central highlands, and in Cuzco (Andrushko et al. 2006; Andrushko 2007, 65; Owen and Norconk 1987; Isbell 1997, 189, 194; Gutiérrez Noriega 1937; Hiltunen and McEwan 2004, 245); or as storehouses for provisions and foodstuffs (Parsons et al. 2000, 157; Sillar 1996). In both cases, these structures were designed to maintain contact between the living and the dead. The precise moment that these funerary monuments began to appear is still the subject of debate (Niles 1999b), but Isbell (1997) very convincingly maintains that they originated well before the Inca state and that they signaled very profound processes of political change throughout the Andes.[32]

Finally, the practice of placing the bodies of the dead under the floors of dwellings is documented in the Andes very early. The oldest evidence has been found in the pre-ceramic site of La Paloma (5000

BC), on the central coast, where Quilter (1989, 54) has observed that they constituted a funerary pattern that possibly indicates the continuation of the life of the family unit after death. Despite these antecedents, it has been suggested that traces of this practice are most numerous in the highlands (Isbell 1997, 161). Its use can also be explained by significant changes in the control of territory exercised by a group, the frequency and character of rituals, and the rank of those responsible for the rituals conducted in homage to the ancestors. Isbell (2004) reports that at the site of Conchopata, a Wari settlement,[33] over the Middle Horizon (AD 500–1000) and the Late Intermediate (AD 1000–1450) periods, a change occurred in the type of burial. From the use of open cemeteries, the practice shifted to burials beneath dwellings and patios, possibly signaling the power that this privilege implied.

Similar changes from cemeteries to dwellings have also been identified in zones such as Chokepukio, a multiethnic site south of the city of Cuzco under Wari and Inca rule (Andrushko et al. 2006, 66; Andrushko 2007, 50), the Mantaro valley (Owen and Norconk 1987), and Moquegua (Buikstra 1995, 266), although in this last case one cannot be sure that the reasons are the same. In other regions, such as Lambayeque, on the north coast, the practice appears to have been associated with the separation between groups and individuals determined by the strongly hierarchical societies that prevailed there. Thus, while the elite were interred in pyramids, some common people had their graves in peripheral areas or beneath the floors of dwellings and workshops (Shimada et al. 2004, 374). Stumer (1954, 141), who studied different pre-Hispanic settlements in the Lima valley more than fifty years ago, observed at the site of Cajamarquilla tombs scattered among the areas that had been used as dwellings, although the pattern of, and reasons for, this everyday contact with the dead could have obeyed a logic both ritual and defensive.[34] Cieza (1984b [1553], First Part, chap. 63, 196) writes that the residents of Jauja kept the bodies of the dead in their houses. His description, which adds that the bodies were wrapped in animal skins, would suggest that they were not placed underground but rather were put within reach of their kin. Possibly this refers to the open sepulchers that have been described for this region. It is difficult to speculate on the reasons for this custom, but we may suppose that under conditions of frequent warfare and rivalries, certain groups such as the central highlanders opted to keep the bodies of their forebears inside their dwellings to ensure mutual protection (Silverman 2002, 4). The pre-Hispanic settlements in the region were characterized by dense populations, and the mobility of its inhabitants was limited (Hastorf 2001), which could also explain the practice.[35]

Based on the examination of these different regional examples, it is possible to suggest that those in power judged it necessary to exercise some control over burials. In situations of potential political conflict, burials in homes could have been viewed with mistrust, not so much for "civilizing" reasons as for motives of political order. Although the chronology of these developments is still not sufficiently clear, Guaman Poma's passage (1989 [1615], 186)—relating how the Incas, while permitting their subjects to continue using their respective funerary customs, prohibited kin from keeping the bodies of their dead in their houses—could be interpreted as an initiative of a centralizing, expanding state that sought to contain the sources of power that were maintained by some provincial groups.

We have seen thus far that in the Andes, the places of burial and the kinds of entombments were multifarious. This diversity corresponded to the ethnic and political fragmentation that prevailed in the region's history. These places were intimately linked to the subsistence activities and political life of their inhabitants: they were indicators of the control of a territory and its resources, of the ties that united society, of internal hierarchies, and of the relations among neighboring groups. This speaks as much of spaces of contact as of spaces of dispute. The diversity of burial places was associated, too, with the creation of sacred spaces that contained and symbolized the past of the groups that watched over and cared for them. The bodies of the ancestors placed in these graves were the material expression of the past and represented the moral base of those who identified themselves with them.

Bodies

The image of mummies, and especially that of Inca mummies, almost completely dominates the perception of the role that the body played in Andean funerary customs of the pre-conquest period and into the colonial period. There can be no doubt as to its political and religious importance among the Incas (MacCormack 1991, 118–37; Riva Agüero 1966; Alonso Sagaseta 1989). The impressive testimonies of the conquistadors who, just after their arrival in Cuzco, managed to see the mummies; the inquiries that culminated in the discovery of some of them, their subsequent transfer to the city of Lima, and their final interment in the capital of the viceroyalty, are milestones in an elusive, complex trajectory that concerns the way they were cared for as well as the identities of the rulers and families whom these bodies represented or to which they belonged (Guillén 1983; Hampe 1982).

According to chroniclers such as Acosta, Cobo, and Garcilaso, the bodies of the Inca rulers were embalmed by means of a careful treatment that, following these same authors, conserved an appearance very much as in life.[36] They were dressed in clothing and insignias designating their rank and were placed not in tombs but in temples or their own homes, where their kin could provide them with the care and attention that befitted their status (Rowe 1995). The Inca mummies participated actively in public affairs; they were brought to temples and houses to carry out functions that, to all appearances, were of a political character, and they were regularly borne on litters during the most important ceremonies that took place in Cuzco's plaza.[37] This image has deeply marked our understanding of the place occupied by the remains of the dead, both in the lives of those who were not members of the Inca elite and in the lives of those who resided in the provinces (Isbell 1997; 2004; Salomon 1995). It has also conditioned our perception of the methods that were used to preserve the bodies and thus has influenced our notion of the way that Andean societies perceived the human body and its representations before the conquest. The recurrent and surely impressive presence of mummified bodies in different places in the Andes, and the rituals organized around them, led the chroniclers to suppose that the inhabitants worshipped the bodies of their ancestors.

At the moment of the conquest, funerary patterns featuring, most notably, the desiccation of the body, were widespread in various regions of the Andes (Rakita and Buikstra 2005, 99–100). This practice, favored because the extremely dry conditions made possible both the mummification of human remains and the preservation of organic materials, has a very long history in Peru.[38] The reasons why the ancient populations of the Andes preserved the bodies of their forebears cannot be determined with certainty, although the rituals that took place before, during, and after the funeral provide clues that enable us to come close. Referring to the oldest examples found in Chinchorro, in the zone that today encompasses the extreme south of Peru and the extreme north of Chile, Arriaza et al. (1998, 190–97) point out that the preservation of bodies was a way in which the inhabitants of this region expressed their spiritual beliefs as well as mitigated the pain of their loss. In increasingly complex societies, the social hierarchies, political conditions, and interactions with other groups added to this dense weave, as we have seen in our examination of the places and forms of burial. Vreeland (1978, 213; 1998, 181–83) suggests that observation of the effects of the natural mummification caused by environmental conditions could have led some Andean groups to experiment with methods that induced it artificially.[39] The chroniclers agree that Andeans intentionally mummified the bodies of their forebears in order to worship them, which led José de Acosta to develop part of his argument about the origin of idolatry in the Andes: the embalming of a body would be the equivalent of making what the Spanish missionaries deemed a "false" religious image, or idol.[40]

Determining the methods followed to preserve bodies is difficult, and over many years a number of competing hypotheses have been proposed in this regard.[41] The weight of ethnohistorical inquiry, which asserts that the bodies were always submitted to complex mummification procedures, has conditioned what some researchers have seen when examining a mummy.[42] Understanding the methods of conserving bodies practiced in pre-Hispanic Peru is of more than purely technical interest. Elucidating the matter permits us to glimpse the objectives that were being pursued, whether religious, political, or even aesthetic. Likewise, we can better understand how and where the rituals described in the written sources were performed as well as gain a more precise understanding of how the living and the dead interacted, appreciate the attention and energy that the former dedicated to the latter, and perceive what was expected of the dead. We possess more written information about the Inca mummies, but since the physical evidence is no longer available, unfortunately the assertions of the chronicles cannot be corroborated. Given the descriptions both of the conditions in which the mummies usually were found and the rituals in which they participated, it would appear that these bodies did, in fact, need careful, prolonged treatment in order for them to be exhibited and moved about, sporadic though this may have been. It is possible, then, that the bodies of the Inca rulers would have undergone processes somewhat more effective than those that predominated in the Andes.[43]

Although the funerary rituals devoted to the Incas usually were taken as the model for the customs of diverse Andean groups, as we have seen, the ethnohistorical record has underscored the coexistence of different practices. Guaman Poma (1989 [1615], 288–97) was quite forceful in stating that the inhabitants of different regions had their own funerary rituals and methods of treating the body. While not all of his data can be corroborated, diverse examples studied via archaeological means confirm the existence of these differences and of some of the procedures he describes. Due to the breadth as well as the uneven quality of the record, it is not possible to make a detailed study of all the variations in the ethnohistorical record. However, examination has demonstrated that the bodies were not eviscerated (Dwyer and Dwyer 1975, 152; Fleming 1986, 43; Vreeland 1998, 168; Guillén 2005, 144).[44] While, as we have seen, the treatment of the bodies of the Inca rulers cannot be verified, in most other cases the desiccation and consequent preservation were achieved by wrapping the corpse with a variety of absorbent materials: large quantities of cotton batting or leaves, animal skins, or fabric and baskets made of straw. By placing the prepared bodies in a dry environment, insulated from the air, Andeans succeeded in altering the process of decomposition.[45]

In the period preceding the Spanish conquest, the custom of placing bodies in graves in a crouching or squatting position was widespread across Peru, even in places such as the north coast, where over centuries different patterns have been followed (Donnan 1978, 379–80; 1995). Menzel (1976, 222) and Rowe (1995, 28) have suggested that this custom was introduced not by the Incas but by their predecessors, the Wari, in what appears to be a toughening of their policy toward the populations that they ruled (AD 600–1000). Other examples show that although it was predominant, this practice did not appear uniformly: the social hierarchies, local customs, and rituals enacted during secondary funerals introduced a certain flexibility in what at first would suggest a rigid protocol. All this indicates that there was a relationship between the social status of the individual, his or her age, and the manner in which his or her body was placed in the tomb (Andrushko et al. 2006, 68, 85–87; Julien 1987–1989). In many cases, the bodies of adults were arranged in a seated position, while those of children were extended on cots[46] (Béjar 1976; Cornejo 2004; Eeckhout 1999, 342–68; Cock 2002, 73; Díaz Arriola 2004, 588; Fleming 1986; Frame et al. 2004; Kaulicke 1997, 34–48; Ravines 1981; Stothert 1979).[47] The differences become more obvious with those burials in which one or more principal figures were accompanied by wives and servants. Here, the secondary bodies have been disposed in such a way as to demonstrate their subordination: unlike the principal corpses, they are laid on their sides and deprived of clothing, wrappings, or offerings.[48]

As I have indicated, the wrapping of the body with various materials protects and preserves the cadaver. These layers and the disposition of the offerings can also be interpreted as a language that contains references to the life of the deceased, whether to the circumstances actually lived or to how he or she aspired to live, as well as allusions to an order of what might await him or her in the life beyond death. The quantity and quality of clothing and textiles as well as their disposition are indications of the rank of the persons whose bodies were found in the bundles.[49] The amount of energy and resources that the creation of these wrappings represents (in some cases a single bundle could exceed 100 kilos in weight) demonstrates the importance assigned to a person's rank.[50] The ways of adorning the body varied, but in certain details it would appear that some conventions had been established for the objects that the deceased would have on his or her journey. It was customary to place skeins of thread around the hands and a sheet of silver, copper, or spondylus inside the mouth (Donnan 1978, 381; Frame et al. 2004, 858; Segura et al. 2002). In some cases the face was painted red, with cinnabar (Segura et al. 2002), and the body was covered with objects that not only had a practical purpose but were also indicators of the social status of the deceased, such as a cloth, shards, a cotton cape, a gourd, a ceramic vessel, or a metal mask. Items placed between the layers of cloth and other materials that wrapped the body included those that indicated the occupation of the deceased, such as balls of wool or cotton, weaving implements, or fishing gear (Stothert 1979; Fleming 1986; Squier 1877, 74–75); weapons or insignia of war, such as slings, or emblems of social distinction, such as feathers and sheets of silver (Segura et al. 2002; Frame et al. 2004, 845–46; Eeckhout 1999, 358–60); offerings arranged in a singular manner, consisting of foodstuffs, utensils, and articles of personal adornment, such as ears of corn, coca leaves, guinea pigs, gourds, woven bags or *chuspas*, bracelets, combs, and tweezers. There were bundles containing objects that were apparently simple but were of great importance both practically and symbolically, such as seeds (Squier 1877, 77–78; Stothert 1979, 12); sets of more elaborate objects such as miniature articles of clothing or scraps of cloth (Frame et al. 2004, 857); human hair and animal and vegetable fibers (Segura et al. 2002; Eeckhout 1999, 351); or implements for the ingestion of hallucinogens (De la Vega et al. 2002, 130–31).

The final layer of the bundle varied according to region as well as over time. Especially remarkable are the cases in which an artificial head was added, on which, sometimes, a face was painted or sewn (Menzel 1976; Dawson 1979; Fleming 1986; Kaulicke 1997).[51] In the way these bundles were assembled as much as in their finished aspect, the goal appears to have been, apart from preparing individuals for their journey to the hereafter, to give them the corporeality with which they would be able to participate in the rituals that the living enacted in homage to them. Although important, this was not a common pattern. In some of the bundles found in Ancón the faces of the false heads were covered. Late examples discovered on the central coast seem to communicate an abstract, anonymous image of the deceased or of what he or she represented because, even though false heads were added, they lack any adornment or semblance of a face.[52] Some of these bundles contained more than one body.[53] Others, including large ones, only held some human limbs (Vreeland 1978, 212), and yet others contained the dry, disarticulated bones of one individual (Eeckhout 1999, 363; Andrushko et al. 2006, 88–92).[54] Here we are presented with the very interesting problem of possible changes in the forms by which the person was represented in ancient Peru, which will require further research.

The preparation of the body to ensure that the deceased would pass unimpeded to the next life is one of the characteristic features of Andean funerary customs. The occupants of different Andean regions, especially on the coast, invested considerable amounts of resources and effort to procure the necessary materials with which to attire and provision the bodies of the deceased, especially those of the highest rank. Based on the premise that, as the chronicles assert, the objective pursued was to embalm the body, there has been a great deal of conjecture about the methods used for the preservation of the cadaver. However, there is scant evidence that Andeans employed the techniques necessary for embalming. Desiccation was the result, but the care that kin lavished on the bodies of their forebears was not in each instance intended to result in a body that could be seen and touched, as was the case with the Inca mummies. The concept of a funerary bundle and its finished appearance are indicators of the different ways in which Andeans represented and related to the dead. We have seen that some funerary bundles could simulate the appearance of a person, while others—especially the later examples, contemporary with the Inca mummies—do not: they lack faces, and in some cases they contain more than one body.

The preparation of the body was the first step in a long process that continued with its placement in the tomb where it would remain, either permanently or for the time it took to dry out. While this process was taking place, the kin or individual specialists returned to provide additional care, leave more offerings, or even add other bodies. These secondary funerary rituals had distinct variations, the observation of which permits us to understand other aspects of the relationship between the living and the dead.

Rituals

The sources that describe pre-Hispanic funerary rituals for the most part focus on the Incas. Given the extent of the Inca state, and the immense changes that the death of a ruler brought to the many groups affected, funerary rituals marked an important moment. The chroniclers report how the demise of a sovereign could introduce grave social and cosmic disequilibrium and could precipitate profound crises and wars (Pärssinen 2003, 141). MacCormack (1991, 125) proposes, based on an analysis of descriptions of these funerary rituals and the succession ceremonies associated with them,[55] that their length and complexity aimed to mitigate these effects. Niles (1999a, 35–37, 45–56) observes that the funerary rituals of the Inca elite were associated with the formation of sacred spaces, such as the erection of monuments, which served as testimony to the history of the rulers. As for Kaulicke (2001, 26–35), he considers these rituals as ways of constructing historical memory and the meaning of the ancestors in the Andes.

The relative abundance of information about Inca funerary rituals contrasts with the very tenuous vision that we have of their provincial counterparts. Salomon (1995, 329–30) suggests that a connection existed between the Inca rituals and those of the provinces as well as a line of continuity between pre-Hispanic Cuzqueño beliefs and practices and those of the central Andean provinces described in the seventeenth century. He correlates the accounts of the chronicles with the information derived from the *visitas* (inspections) and idolatry proceedings set in the diocese of Lima during the colonial period. The former describe in detail the ceremonies held in the capital of Tahuantinsuyo and among the Inca elite, while the latter contain descriptions of the rituals devoted to the dead among ordinary people. For Salomon, all over the Andes the mummified bodies of the ancestors occupy the center of funerary rituals. Taking into account essential aspects of his studies, I would like to propose that considering Andean funerary rituals and their variants can guide us toward a more nuanced interpretation of the experience of death, the character and nature of the ancestors, and the relationship between the living and the dead. I will support my interpretation with the analysis of burial places and the treatment of the body in the two preceding sections, and in data taken from the ethnographic and archaeological research that deals with funerary rituals.

The rituals that were carried out upon a person's death constituted both the expression of ideas about what would happen in the hereafter and a way of living through profound collective and individual emotions. The chronicles suggest that the funerary rituals in the highlands and on the coast had some features in common, the most meaningful differences appearing in the entombments and the way in which the body was arranged.[56] For about a week the family and close associates demonstrated their sorrow by crying and making speeches in which they remembered the deceased. In these public demonstrations of grief, clothing or facial decoration, for example, made visible the mourning that the kin, intimates, and especially the women were obliged to observe.[57] The emotional blow that the loss occasioned was mitigated by the sacrifice of at least one animal and the sharing of a communal meal, a response perhaps to the immediate need to renew or reinforce the ties that united the group, now threatened by death. In order to prepare for the journey that the deceased would embark upon, as well as to ensure that the tranquility of the living would not be disturbed if, along the way, the deceased should encounter obstacles, offerings were made of food, coca, or blood. The family and close associates would reconstruct the memory of the dead by recounting aloud incidents of their life and visiting the places they had frequented, carrying in their hands some of their belongings.[58] Kin marked the moment in which they took leave of the deceased by, for example, making ablutions, washing the clothing of the deceased, or cleaning his or her house.

The well-known passage by Guaman Poma (1989 [1615], 289–97) concerning regional differences in funerary customs among the Andean peoples offers some interesting clues on which the available ethnographic and archaeological evidence can shed light. He reports (290) that the Chinchaysuyos simply washed the corpse, which was then dressed, richly adorned, and placed in a tomb. The Collas (294), were buried "with many garments" and a considerable quantity of offerings. Once the body was placed in the tomb, it would not be removed, in contrast to the Chinchaysuyos, who took away the cadaver on certain occasions to carry it in procession. The Condesuyos eviscerated the corpse, dressed it, and deposited it in vaults that had been built and decorated for this purpose (296), and the Yungas, or inhabitants of the coast, did something similar (297), painting the bodies and wrapping them in cotton mantles, sewing these wrappings, binding them with cords, and placing them in storerooms that were most probably occupied by members of the same family group.[59] The Antisuyos, or forest dwellers, conducted themselves in a very different manner, with no prolonged or elaborate ceremonies like those of the highlanders or the coastal dwellers. They ate the flesh of the cadaver and placed the remains in the hollow of a tree, which they covered over. Neither men nor women cried. Once this brief funeral ended, the kin left, never to return or remember the deceased (291–92).[60]

We will comment first on the funerary ceremonies of the Antisuyos in light of the ethnographic data.[61] Shepard's penetrating study (2002) of the beliefs and customs surrounding death among the Matsigenka[62] shows that before the Spanish missionaries imposed the obligation to bury the dead, the Matsigenka used to place them in a seated position between the roots of large trees. That the process of decomposition took place in plain sight gave them the assurance that the soul had actually left the body; if it remained within, it could become a danger to the living (Shepard 2002, 209).[63] Shepard has not recorded any indication that cannibalism was practiced by this group,[64] but he has witnessed the suppression of the emotions of kin. In contrast to their neighbors in the highlands and on the coast, for the Matsigenka, the dead lose their human condition, so the living seek to distance themselves from them as soon as possible. This is why, once the strictly delimited three-day mourning period ends, the relatives never again refer to the deceased and suppress all demonstrations of sorrow. The Matsigenka believe that when emotions are not controlled, they can cause illness and even death. Their dead thus are seen not as protectors but as a threat.[65] Guaman Poma found this attitude, so distinct from those of the highland and coastal peoples, incomprehensible, even unacceptable.

If some of the groups that lived in Chinchaysuyo processed with the bodies of their ancestors on special occasions, as Guaman Poma asserts and as Cieza de León's observations in the central highlands suggest, these rituals resemble those enacted by the Incas.[66] In terms of the cadaver's fragility, it is probable that there were some limits. Whatever form the public display of bodies among certain inhabitants of Chinchaysuyo province took, this visibility and corporeality of the dead were neither common nor continual for the majority of Andean peoples. The chronicles, and especially archaeological studies, show a more varied situation that was symbolically complex. The great size of the funerary bundles as well as their weight and the way in which they were laid out at different sites on the central coast suggests that even in those cases where kin returned to add offerings and place other bundles, the bodies were not removed from the tombs.

Inquiries into the funerary contexts of the coastal regions, or Yungas, show that llamas or other animals were sacrificed both at the time of burial and during secondary funerals (Menzel 1976, 224) and that food, drink, coca, and ceramic objects were also offered. The last were broken during the course of, or at the end of, the ceremonies (Shimada 2005). The remains of animals and also food and objects were deposited in the tomb. When the rituals ended, the tombs were sealed, and usually various items were placed in the upper layers, such as ceramics, human skulls and fetuses, or the bodies of children (Menzel 1976; Kaulicke 1997; Ravines 1977; 1981).[67] The full meaning of the offerings in such burials still eludes us.

Isbell's (2004) studies in Ayacucho show that, while tombs were reentered, the objective appears to have differed both from that of the people in Chinchaysuyo and from that of the Inca elite, inasmuch as bodies were not removed to take part in celebrations. In fact, the rituals that took place after the burial did not require direct contact. Some of these underground tombs had an opening that, as Isbell observes (2004, 9), facilitated communication with the living.[68] The chronicler Agustín de Zárate has described something similar (1995 [1555], chap. 12, 54), referring to libations of *chicha* being poured through channels visible from the surface.[69] The discovery of incomplete bodies in the few tombs that have been found intact indicates that the kin and other people who reentered did so not only in order to leave offerings but also to remove parts of the bodies. These examples show that what was sought was not the maintenance of the body of the deceased intact and life-like, as with a mummy. Such secondary funerary rituals point instead to a different understanding of what the bodies of the dead signified. In Ica, the examination of tombs of high-ranking individuals shows that the kin reentered the tomb once the tissues had decomposed and then painted the bones with a red colorant,[70] after which they placed them in funerary urns together with personal ornaments (Menzel 1976, 225). The bones, especially skulls, were then removed and placed over other graves, as though taking on a protective role.[71] Menzel (225–26, 229) suggests that once the deceased had been the object of secondary funerary rituals, the remains acquired—like the person to whom they belonged—a new meaning.[72]

These dismemberments of corpses and possible grave lootings in the pre-Hispanic period are examples of a custom that is widespread in the Andes, both on the coast and in the highlands. The conditions under which they were produced suggest that actions of members of the same group could have been interwoven with the incursions of outsiders. We have seen that in Ica, kinsmen placed bones and skulls on others' tombs but in some cases also removed the stakes that served as markers, apparently to prevent the tombs from being looted. In the funerary cave of Molino-Chilacachi, in Puno, De la Vega et al. (2002) found that the human remains there were distributed on three levels in a distinctive manner. On the upper level, closest to the entrance, were placed desiccated bodies or mummies inside funerary baskets, while on the two lower levels, human remains were found disarticulated and in disorder. Leaving aside the possibility that this displacement resulted from the activities of modern looters, which in this case can be identified, it is clear that the disaggregation of the bodies in pre-Hispanic times was intentional and corresponds to a different understanding of what occurred not only to the body but also to the concept of the person, once the deceased had crossed a certain temporal and spatial threshold delineated by the secondary funeral rituals. Ossuaries found in Cuzco (Llanos 1941; Eaton 1916; MacCurdy 1923; Andrushko 2007), Chincha (Uhle 1924, 90), Huarochirí (Hrdlicka 1914, 9; Salomon 1995, 338, fig. 8) and other sites throughout the Andes may indicate similar beliefs.[73] It is possible to think that the separation of the bones of the dead and their union with those of the rest of the group symbolized their passage into a different condition, that of protective ancestors and givers of life, along with the dissolution of a supposed individuality (Hertz 1960, 70; Bloch and Parry 1982, 7). If such is the case, then those body parts that represented sources of energy and power could have become the guardians of the tombs of their descendants

or, coveted and removed by outsiders, could have been utilized to protect and strengthen their possessors, whether living or dead.[74]

This examination of funerary practices has attempted to offer
some clues to understanding the experience of death in the Andes,
and it leaves us with many questions. As Chapman (2000), Fowler
(2002), and Thomas (2002) have observed, if we turn to other societies to study funerary practices involving the fragmentation of the
body,[75] we will encounter concepts of the person very different from
the individualism in European Christian thought, which maintain
that the person is contained within the body, understood as a unit.
In contrast, what we find in these secondary funerary rituals, in pre-
Hispanic tomb lootings, in ossuaries, and in other practices in which
body parts are displayed, is the idea, as Chapman proposes, that the
body is not only divisible but also shareable, and that its fragmentation may form part of a process that is seen as not only normal but
also as necessary to the continuity and regeneration of life.

Mummies, however, would appear to evoke precisely the opposite principle: the unity of the body and of the person. Nevertheless,
MacCormack (1991), in referring to Inca mummies and the effigies
that they represented, points out that this is not the only way to interpret them. The relationships between people, mummies, and effigies
indicate that the concept of the person and identity is different from
the Christian belief that human beings consist of one body with one
soul. Among the Incas, a person's identity has a social, consensual
aspect (MacCormack 1991, 134) for which a representation—in this
case, an effigy or bundle that contained parts of the body—could stand.
If this representation can be seen as an extension of the person, we
are not necessarily confronted by two opposing extremes. Comparing examples of fragments of bodies or objects and complete bodies
or groups of objects, Chapman (2000) proposes that the fragments
are the vehicle of relations of enchainment: people establish and symbolize their social relations by sharing fragments of the same object,
whether, for example, a ceramic vessel or human bones. In contrast,
both bodies and whole objects could allude to a process of accumu-
lation, which would express the totality of social relations within a
family group, lineage, or community. Similar principles could be useful for explaining the coexistence in ancient Peru of different funerary

practices. In the joining of these practices to the processes of social differentiation and political change that occurred throughout the Andes, and in the rise, expansion, and consolidation of a state such as that of the Incas, we can imagine dynamic, often violent scenarios in which the bonds between the living and the dead played a decisive role in the configuration of society.

In their campaigns of conquest and occupation, the Incas and their predecessors intervened in the cemeteries, burial places, and sacred spaces of their enemies and allies. There is evidence both that they attempted to suppress some of the funerary practices of their subjects, and that they were imitated by their provincial allies. However, the diversity of mortuary customs and of sacred spaces continued in force, perhaps as a concession to conquered provinces, or because it was not considered necessary or possible to impose other practices. The Spanish conquest and missionary policies marked a crucial departure from the past since, by means that are the subject of the chapters that follow, they tried to regularize and make uniform this diverse landscape.

CHAPTER TWO

Death during
the Conquest

The years between the Spaniards' arrival in the Andes in 1532 and the execution of the last rebel Inca in 1572 were dominated by war and violence. The wars of conquest were followed by civil wars between the Spaniards, caused by disputes over the sharing of the booty and control of the former Inca empire, the Tahuantinsuyo, and by the rebellions of the conquistadors against the crown. For four decades, Peru was the scene of continual armed confrontations and public punishments of crimes, not only between the Spanish and Andean populations but also within each faction. The series of cruel episodes that took place during this period made manifest the different ways in which the participants conceived of the body and exteriorized physical and emotional suffering as well as the sense of honor or humiliation that was expressed through the body.

This chapter seeks to study these populations' attitudes toward death and to understand both their meaning and their impact on religious, cultural, and political behavior during this intense phase, which has been diversely and polemically documented. The wars made it necessary to carry out hasty actions, cutting short or omitting the appropriate rituals. This was a transition stage in which there was no system of justice or any established Church recognized by the rival populations; in short, no common codes of any kind existed. We may say that this period represented a mutual learning process. All things considered, it was a seminal epoch in colonial society.

Death, war, and violence were central aspects in the founding of colonial society because of their communicative power, the force they

exerted to generate hegemony, and the key role they played in forming the system of authority together with its judicial and religious
institutions. These forces went hand in hand, and they are crucial for
understanding the history of conversion to Christianity in the Andes.
Their effects were manifold: they sustained the creation of the political order and its normativity; they were behind the definition of ethnic,
social, and gender categories; and, even more important, they provided
the basis on which a common sacred space was constructed, making
it possible for the new order to become gradually intelligible and
even bearable. The following discussion is based on the chronicles of
the conquest, which date for the most part from the sixteenth century,
and on other historical accounts written some years later by Spanish,
Indian, and mestizo authors. I also use information taken from correspondence and administrative reports.

I focus on the accounts of war, deaths, and executions of both
Andean and Spanish victims. My analysis is partially based on Foucault's work (1991) on the political significance of torture and executions before these practices were replaced by more subtle, complex,
and sophisticated forms of discipline. There are many parallels between episodes from the conquest of Peru and several of the examples
that Foucault analyzes. There are, however, two important differences.
First, the episodes of the conquest do not develop over a common
cultural and political substrate. Whereas the use of physical violence
studied by Foucault is directed at the criminal and confirms the power
of a monarch that everyone recognizes, the violence of the conquest—
expressed in extremely summary trials, torture, and executions—
begins with the execution of the Inca sovereign. The violence of this
episode casts a shadow over all the acts that follow and appears as the
only language possible, which, at the same time that it destroys, lays
the foundation for a new order. Second, the sacred is the force that
gives coherence to this new order. In his analysis, Foucault does not
ignore the realm of the sacred, but neither does he grant it a special
status. For Foucault, the brutality with which the bodies of the executed are treated is ultimately aimed at strengthening and elevating
the figure of the sovereign. In the context of the conquest, a more ambitious project is at work: the religious conversion of those invaded.
Consequently, my analysis of violence during the conquest borrows

many ideas from Girard (2005),[1] who argues for identity between violence and the sacred.[2] There is no doubt that during the period of conquest and civil war, the link between the two is particularly noticeable.

Studies on the introduction of justice systems and corporal punishment in the colonial world have called into question Foucault's assumptions regarding the universality of European experience. Moreover, the chronology proposed by Foucault has been criticized at the same time that it has been shown that the modernization of forms of discipline and punishment did not lead to the disappearance of brutal public violence (Pierce and Rao 2006b; Ward 2006). These same studies neglect the significance of the Spanish conquest, describing it only briefly and with such broad brushstrokes that they distort the complex influence that the realm of the sacred had on both the conquest and the development of the colonial process.[3]

I argue that focusing on violence enables us to understand how the religious sphere is constituted, how a common language is created where none existed earlier, and how power is reorganized once the foundations sustaining a given society are dissolved or subjected to extreme pressure—what Girard calls the "sacrificial crisis." Harrowing though the events of the conquest may have been, this is not just another chapter in the story of the vanquished. As we know from other research (Bourget 2006; Isbell 1997; Rostworowski 1988; Arkush and Stanish 2005), and as the previous chapter showed, the Andean societies before the conquest were far from being peaceful or static. The European conquest caused wars, deaths, and violence, with the atrocious consequences that we all know. However, judging from the chronicles and the colonial records and from the increasingly precise findings of archaeologists, this was not without precedent in the region. In contrast, what was new was the desire to impose uniformity on beliefs about the hereafter and funeral customs.

Expressions of violence and attempts to control it—through religious ritual or the exercise of "justice"—recur during this transition period, which witnesses the simultaneous dissolution and reconstruction of the Andean societies.[4] In these exchanges, a language gradually developed in which the body was the main vehicle of communication. As the conquest progressed, the pressure on the victims to convert became inextricable from the violence. In the following pages, I start

out with a consideration of the different accounts of the Inca Atahualpa's execution. This death, which also involved the first conversion, was an act of foundation. The versions of Atahualpa's death
vary according to different criteria: the spatial and temporal distance
between the events and those who wrote about them is crucial. Beliefs held by the different versions' authors about justice, the body,
death, and the afterlife also come into play. As the chroniclers dealt
with these issues, they began to better understand Andean ideas about
death and funerary customs. Moreover, the differing versions of
Atahualpa's death reflect debates about its legitimacy and, in general,
that of the conquest that led to his execution and the events that followed. Analysis of such episodes will allow us to explore the forces
that are unleashed by this special conjunction of violence and the
sacred. In the last section, I examine the role of physical punishment
and executions during the civil wars, in order to study how violence
contributed to the organization of colonial society.[5]

Death of the Inca Atahualpa

The death of Atahualpa in 1533 is the event that symbolizes the Spanish conquest. No document of the period leaves it out. However,
there are differences between the various versions. These differences
can help us to understand the enormous political and symbolic meaning that this event had, or gradually acquired. We are talking here not
only of the fall of the Inca empire but also of the long-term consequences of this fall. The notions of violence and justice, beliefs about
death and the hereafter, and the way in which these notions are communicated through the body, among other issues, are tested in the
accounts concerning the Inca's death.

    After his capture in Cajamarca in November 1532, Atahualpa was
held prisoner for several months. Once he had paid the Spaniards a
fabulous ransom in gold and silver, the Inca was accused of plotting
an attack against them. On Francisco Pizarro's orders, Hernando de
Soto set out to ascertain how close were the Andean troops who were
supposedly on their way to rescue the Inca. However, Pizarro did not
wait for his men to return. He subjected Atahualpa to a hasty trial

and sentenced him to die at the stake. The chronicles give different versions of the charges brought against him, the way in which the sentence was carried out, and, finally, the fate of his body.[6]

Pedro Sancho, one of Pizarro's secretaries, kept the minutes of the trial and execution of Atahualpa.[7] Shortly afterward, he wrote the first official record of the conquest that contains the account of these events (Sancho 1917 [1534]). The Inca was accused of conspiring against the Spaniards, who had received information that an army of "fifty thousand men of Quito and a great number of Caribs" was marching to destroy them. After deliberations that involved Pizarro himself, the Dominican friar Vicente de Valverde, and "a doctor" whom the chronicler does not identify,[8] Atahualpa was condemned to death (Sancho 1917 [1534], 126). Trumpets were sounded, and the Inca, through an interpreter, was told that he must die for betraying the Spaniards, that it was the will of God that he should die "for the sins that he had committed in this world." Valverde accompanied Atahualpa to the place of execution and tried to persuade him to accept baptism, since his sins would thus be forgiven. In these straits, the Inca agreed. The Spaniards then commuted the sentence of death at the stake to the garrote. Sancho states that before his execution, Atahualpa asked Pizarro to take care of his children. Surrounded by the Spaniards, who recited the Credo for the salvation of his soul, the newly converted Inca was finally strangled. The chronicler writes that in order to carry out the original sentence, the Inca's body and clothing were slightly burned. His corpse was left in the open overnight so that the whole community would know of his death. The next day, Atahualpa was given a solemn funeral and buried in the church, "as if," in Sancho's words, "he had been the leading Spaniard in our camp." The chronicler claims that the *caciques* who were present heard with "great satisfaction" the news that the Inca had not been burned alive, and that the conquistadors had honored him by burying him as if he had been one of their own. This is the only source that mentions this supposed reaction of approval on the part of Atahualpa's subordinates, something to be expected in an official report written with the consent of the conquistadors who had witnessed the event.

The chronicle written by Francisco de Xerez (1985 [1534]) agrees for the most part with this version, but it states that following Pizarro's orders, Atahualpa's body was not burned, either partially or totally.[9]

What Xerez highlights, rather than the approval and rejoicing of the *caciques,* is the grief of the women and servants who were present at the funeral. Cristóbal de Mena describes the Inca's death in similar terms, adding that "many Indian women" expressed the desire to be buried alive with Atahualpa (Porras 1937, 99–100).[10] The *Relación Francesa* (1534) (Porras 1937, 74–77; Pease 1995, 20), written at about the same time, agrees with these versions on certain points, such as the commuting of the sentence of death at the stake to the garrote and the subsequent exposure of the body to the fire, although the description suggests that the Inca's body was completely burned. This source does not mention any funeral ceremony.

These early accounts of Atahualpa's execution show an almost complete ignorance of what death meant for the inhabitants of the Andes. The descriptions offered by Sancho, Xerez, Mena, and the author of the *Relación Francesa* illustrate, rather, how the Spaniards understood death, and their concern about the fate of the soul if the body was not correctly treated: the decision as to whether to send Atahualpa to the stake or not implies no knowledge of the way in which the Incas, and especially their rulers, conceived of the importance of preserving the body. Commuting the sentence to the garrote depended entirely on the Inca's final decision to accept baptism. If Atahualpa understood the proposal that his executioners had made to him, then conversion appeared to be the only way to preserve his body and thus to maintain the cohesion of his people.[11] In Pedro Sancho's account, the honor done to Atahualpa in giving him a Spaniard's funeral (because he was baptized before he died) shows a complete ignorance of the ideal way of living and dying for the Incas. Conversion is seen here as an emptying of his identity. For the Spaniards, it was only once dead and stripped of his own personality that the Inca could become one of them. It is worth noting that the Christian name given to Atahualpa at baptism was the conquistador's, Francisco. By way of this mimesis, the victim ceased to be an opponent and became an object of reverence. The act of execution made this transformation possible (Girard 2005, 297). However, we will see that this assimilation was only temporary.

Finally, the accusation of treason appears absurd both from the point of view of Atahualpa and his followers and from the present day. Whom could the Inca have betrayed? In these early versions, the accusation still does not imply, as it will in later versions, the criminalization of the figure of Atahualpa. At this early date, the authors of the accounts appear to be wondering whether the Inca had offended the Spaniards' king or God. We should note that in the sentence with which the hasty trial against him concluded, Atahualpa was condemned for his sins. How serious were they? How much in agreement were those who thought about this death and wrote an account of it? Confused ideas about the nature of his guilt, the authenticity of his conversion, the extent of the Inca's, the king's, and God's sovereignty, and the mutual influence of these figures and of what they represent come to light in these accounts, which differ on the authority invoked to judge him, on the degree to which the Inca's body was consumed by the fire, and on whether Atahualpa had a Christian funeral.

Twenty years after Atahualpa's execution, three chroniclers with fairly broad knowledge of the Andes—Pedro de Cieza de León (1984b [1553]), Juan de Betanzos (2004 [1551]), and Agustín de Zárate (1995 [1555])—each wrote an account of the episode. Cieza de León was motivated by a curiosity that led him to research many aspects of Andean history and customs. Endowed with exceptional literary powers, he traveled extensively throughout Peru collecting testimonies, witnessing crucial events that he expertly pieced together, and interviewing indigenous authorities and experts on Andean language, and culture, such as Fray Domingo de Santo Tomás. His writings not only demonstrate a greater understanding of Andean religion and society, and concomitant ideas about death and the afterlife, but they also provide a more objective judgment of the political impact of Atahualpa's execution and the conquest in general (Pease 1995, 25–28). Betanzos learned the language of Cuzco, thanks to which he gained firsthand access to the histories and narrative forms of the Inca elite, which becomes clear in his *Suma y narración de los incas,* which includes an account of the death of Atahualpa (Domínguez 1993; Julien 2000). Finally, Zárate's history was well known and greatly admired in his time. It contains important information on the history and religion of the inhabitants of pre-Columbian Peru, which he acquired thanks to his own research and to his consultation of exceptionally rich manuscripts (Pease 1995). The work of these three chroniclers is critically important.

Cieza de León's dramatic account (1984a, Third Part, chap. 54, 291–92) includes both the concerns of some Spaniards about the injustice of the Inca's trial and execution, and several Indian versions of the events. Cieza himself did not hesitate to call Atahualpa's execution a "blunder."[12] His narrative supports this position. Cieza de León writes that before dying, Atahualpa addressed the Indians who were present and told them to wait for him in Quito, where he would return in the shape of a serpent. As for the execution, Cieza agrees that the Inca's body was exposed to the fire in order to carry out the original sentence, but, perhaps to ease the offense that might have been made to his body, affirms that only a few of his hairs were burned. He states that the Spaniards wore signs of mourning at the funeral, and he describes in very vivid terms the sorrow of the Inca's wives and maidservants, who begged so vehemently to be buried with him that Pizarro had to intervene to prevent them all from committing suicide.

Cieza de León's skillful account is impressive in its desire to provide the most complete picture possible of these important events. To that end, he includes in his narration a central aspect of European execution ritual: the speech by the condemned.[13] By giving the Inca and his people a chance to speak, Cieza enhances the critical perspective that his story adopts. By putting into Atahualpa's mouth statements that assert his innocence and remind the Spaniards of his favors and gifts to them as well as his submission, the author highlights the injustice of the Inca's execution and makes more vivid to the reader the tears and supplications of the women around him.

The Inca's death caused dismay and turmoil, according to Cieza de León. His property was quickly appropriated by opportunistic lords. People wept for Atahualpa, "calling blessed those Incas who died without having known such a cruel, bloodthirsty and vicious people" (Cieza de León 1984a, Third Part, chap. 55, 293). Many men and women indeed did commit suicide in order to keep him company in the hereafter. As for the Inca's body, the chronicler asserts that it was removed from the grave and taken to Cuzco, where it was placed in a rich tomb. In the years following, the Spaniards searched for this tomb in the hope of plundering its treasures, but they never found it.

The account written by Juan de Betanzos, who had settled in Cuzco and was familiar with Quechua and with Inca history and culture (Pease 1995, 27–28), diverges from Cieza de León's version only in a few details, but they are important ones. Atahualpa, he claims, was already in the place where he was to be burned when he decided to accept baptism. In view of this change of mind, the Spaniards begged Pizarro to have the Inca garroted, a lesser sentence; this was then carried out. However, the original sentence had to be fulfilled, and therefore Atahualpa's body was put into the fire after he was strangled. The Inca was buried in the church of Cajamarca (Betanzos 2004 [1551], chap. 26, 326). Being well acquainted with Inca beliefs about death and funeral rites, Betanzos introduces into his story an important theme: the dispute that took place over Atahualpa's body. Since this body was a power symbol,[14] the Inca's successors engaged in a struggle to obtain possession of it. After the funeral, once the Spaniards had set out from Cajamarca for Cuzco, Cuxi Yupangue, one of Atahualpa's brothers, removed the body from the church and carried it on a bier to Quito.[15] Rumiñahui, one of the Inca's captains who aspired to succeed him, interpreted this gesture as a sign that Cuxi Yupangue cherished similar ambitions, and he prepared an ambush. He met the procession on the outskirts of Quito on the pretense of paying homage to the body. Succeeding in distracting Cuxi Yupangue, he then sent a group of his men to kill him. Rumiñahui then made his entrance into Quito, bearing with him the body of Atahualpa (326–27).[16]

Agustín de Zárate, who also stands out for his intimate knowledge of the Andes (Pease 1995, 23), is, like Cieza de León, critical of his countrymen for executing the Inca (Zárate 1995 [1555], Book 2, chap. 7, 84).[17] Nevertheless, Zárate's account incorporates a matter that was to be more precisely defined in the future: criminalization of the figure of Atahualpa. Zárate says that, as well as treason, Atahualpa was also accused of the death of his brother Huáscar. As in Cieza's story, Zárate includes a speech from the scaffold in which the Inca denies the charge of treason and reminds the Spaniards of his great power. Atahualpa adds in his own defense that had there been troops gathering to rescue him, Pizarro and his men could have cut off his head as soon as these armies appeared on the horizon. This last detail is particularly interesting, since it is the first trace of a version that was to become popular some years later, which claimed that the

Inca had been beheaded.[18] Even though he includes these preliminaries to the execution, Zárate does not describe the way in which the Inca was put to death.

As the years passed, knowledge of Andean customs and debates about the legitimacy of Atahualpa's execution continued to seep into the accounts of the conquest. Details that appear only vaguely in early versions were now clearly outlined: Andean grief rituals and the representation of Atahualpa as a criminal. These issues appear clearly in the *History of the Discovery and Conquest of Peru,* written by the conquistador Pedro Pizarro a number of years after the conquest (Pizarro 1978 [1571], 62–63). To the charges against Atahualpa he adds incest, which justified the sentence of death at the stake. Like other writers, he mentions the commuting of the sentence to the garrote on Atahualpa's agreeing to baptism.

Pizarro also introduces a new element into the speech that Atahualpa made while choosing the way in which he would be executed. According to this account, the Inca announced that if he was not burned, the sun would bring him back to life and he would thus rejoin his people. The conquistador presents the theme of resurrection from another angle, too. He recounts that once Atahualpa had been executed, some women asked for permission to enter the room in which he had spent his captivity. Once inside, they looked for him and called him: a funeral rite that was customary among the Incas and other Andean peoples. On not hearing a reply, the women began to weep, for they believed that this silence meant that the Inca would never return. Pizarro then intervened to explain to the women what he considered to be the real meaning of resurrection, assuring them that the dead would not return until the Day of Judgment (Pizarro 1978 [1571], 70). Pedro Pizarro's version does not constitute a simple justification of the conquest, for it includes a reflection on the injustice of the sentence passed on Atahualpa. Responding to the harsh criticism generated by the latter's death, though, he attempts to clear Francisco Pizarro of all responsibility by affirming that the conquistador ordered the Inca's execution unwillingly.

In considering the accounts of Atahualpa's death written by Indian and mestizo authors, we must realize that we are dealing with texts that would have been impossible to compose and disseminate much earlier. Their structure and details are significantly more complex and incorporate indigenous and European cultural elements. The texts must be read in part as commentaries on the earlier versions of the Inca's death, as responses to the problems raised by the imprecision of the early accounts, but, above all, as commentaries on the current political scene faced by authors such as Garcilaso de la Vega or Guaman Poma. In these versions, they offer their reflections on the course that the events unleashed by the conquest and the colonial enterprise had taken up to that point; and, especially in the case of Guaman Poma, we find a remarkable interpretation of Atahualpa's execution and its repercussions in the realm of the sacred. These versions situate Atahualpa's execution against the backdrop of the political infighting that had consumed the Incan empire at that time. Moreover, discussion of funerary rituals reflects an understanding of their importance in the Andean context that does not appear even in the work of the most knowledgeable chroniclers.

The Andean and mestizo authors express various positions on the justice of Atahualpa's execution, ranging from acceptance of the official version to a reinterpretation of the facts, which may come from Andean sources. An important point in some of these versions is that they discuss the reactions of the victim's followers and family, and the impossibility of carrying out the appropriate funeral rites. In the account written in his rebel stronghold in Vilcabamba, the Inca Titu Cusi Yupanqui (1992 [1570], 12) maintains, as do the Spanish chroniclers, that Atahualpa had plotted a surprise attack on the conquistadors, and this was why he had been accused of treason. He affirms that Francisco Pizarro, "without encountering any opposition," ordered that the Inca be garroted. These claims reveal the political position of the members of the Titu Cusi line, who belonged to the group opposed to Atahualpa. They initially considered the Spaniards as allies and did not, needless to say, lament the execution of the Inca. Thirty years afterward, Titu Cusi recalled the ties that had united his father with Francisco Pizarro (Julien 2006). The Inca Garcilaso de la Vega (1960 [1613], 134: Book 1, chap. 31, 67), describes Atahualpa's trial and execution in similar terms. He claims that after Atahualpa's burial by the Spaniards in the church of Cajamarca, his men disinterred the body because they considered such a grave unworthy of him, and it was taken to Quito without the customary ceremonies. Garcilaso says that Atahualpa had been afraid of ever being taken to Cuzco, for he was sure that his body would be insulted there: he was hated in the city for the cruelty that he had shown to his relatives on his father's side.[19] Once the body of the Inca reached Quito, however, Captain Rumiñahui and his men received it with very solemn ceremonies. Even though the corpse showed signs of decay, they attempted to embalm it. The Inca's funeral was brief. Garcilaso thus agrees with Cieza de León and Betanzos in confirming that Atahualpa's body was disinterred so that it could be given the Inca funeral rites.

These authors emphasize, from different points of view, the central role played by the Inca's body in the political disputes unleashed among his successors. Its disinterment in these later accounts also marks the ephemeral nature of Atahualpa's conversion, and the futility of any treatment as a Spaniard that, according to the earlier chronicles, may have been given him. The controversy over the body's final destination—Quito or Cuzco—also illustrates the importance of this information in understanding the political conflict in which the Inca state was involved at the time of the conquest. Garcilaso's account attempts to correct Cieza de León's version as to the Inca's place of burial. It also emphasizes that his death was followed by failed funeral rites, both from a Christian and from an Andean point of view. This reinforces the sense of incompleteness that marks his term as a sovereign.[20]

At almost the same time of Garcilaso's work, Felipe Guaman Poma de Ayala wrote his *Nueva corónica y buen gobierno* (New chronicle and good government). Guaman Poma approaches the history of the New World and the Andes very differently from the mestizo chronicler. His is the vision of a man from the provincial indigenous nobility, a powerful connoisseur and observer of Andean culture, who was also a zealous Catholic and an avid reader of European documents and images. A harsh critic of the abuses and excesses of colonialism, Guaman Poma tries in his writings to denounce the present in order to correct it, and frequently he also tries to right past wrongs. We shall thus undertake a reading of his version of the events at Cajamarca not so much in search of the truth as with an eye to the enormous interest of his interpretation of the Inca's death.

Guaman Poma (1989 [1615]) introduced some significant variations into the story of Atahualpa's execution. Contrary to all the other accounts, he leaves out the sentence of death at the stake and its commutation to the garrote, and maintains instead that Pizarro ordered that Atahualpa be beheaded. This description is preceded by a drawing that shows the Inca lying on a slab resembling an altar or sacrificial stone, holding a crucifix in his hands (390–91). Four Spanish soldiers surround him: one of them is holding his head, another his body, a third his feet, while the fourth cuts off his head with a knife or saber and a mallet. The violence of the scene is in contrast to the peaceful expression on the Inca's face.[21] Guaman Poma's account is a surprising and intriguing one. He tells how Atahualpa, from his prison, ordered the murder of his brother Huáscar and his family so that there would be no legitimate Inca. The description of the crimes committed in Cuzco by Atahualpa's captains might move the reader to judge him guilty, and his death just. But the chronicler's intentions are more ambitious. He outlines the great commotion caused by Huáscar and Atahualpa's rivalry coinciding with the arrival of the Spaniards, and the subsequent greed that unleashed violent destruction. What he depicts is the sacrificial crisis described by Girard:[22] "the Indians had lost their gods and shrines (guacas) and their kings and great lords and captains, in this time of the conquest there was neither god of the Christians nor king of Spain nor was there any justice" (389).

While agreeing that some Spaniards were critical of the execution, Guaman Poma claims that this was because the sentence raised an obstacle to the delivery of the ransom. It is in his conclusion that Guaman Poma diverges most from other chroniclers: "he died the death of a most Christian martyr in the city of Caxamarca" (1989 [1615], 391). Rolena Adorno (1989, 115–26), in her study of the use of visual elements in the Nueva corónica, explains how Guaman Poma employs illustrations to confront the authority of the chronicles and to include Andean oral traditions, and also a personal interpretation of the situation. The drawing that shows Atahualpa's beheading contradicts what the chronicles affirm and, because of the power of images, does so persuasively. It also constitutes a counterweight to the uncontrolled violence of the moment that Guaman Poma describes so vividly in the text. Is this an "Andean" death?[23]

In his study of the chroniclers, Pease (1995, 368) maintains that while the Spanish accounts of the conquest state that the Inca was garroted, the Andean sources assert that he was beheaded. Referring to Guaman Poma, however, he does mention that the story of the beheading actually appeared for the first time in a Spanish source (390). Though he offers no interpretation of Guaman Poma's text and drawing, Pease is right to question a purely Andean origin for the beheading hypothesis. The chronicler may have known that in Europe, beheading was considered the honorable punishment for men of rank (Spierenburg 1984, 71; Cohen 1989, 410; Merback 1999, 141). The sentence would thus be credible in the eyes of a European reader. Nevertheless, as we saw in the previous chapter, it is also well known that this was a common practice in Andean wars and religious rituals (Benson and Cook 2001), so it could also be understood by the local population. What is certain is that Guaman Poma describes Atahualpa's execution in exactly the correct terms: it was a sacrifice. Moreover, judging from the calmness with which Atahualpa submits to death in the drawing, it was a martyrdom:[24] martyrs were expected to remain expressionless under torture.[25] This reflects a major preoccupation of Guaman Poma's work: the desire to include Andean history in the history of Christianity, and to vindicate the local population's right to recover its political autonomy and its possessions (Adorno 1989, 100).[26] The Inca's conversion is also a crucial incident in this account, which is why Guaman Poma does not discuss either the episode of the choice between the stake and the garrote or, of course, the story of the exhumation of Atahualpa's body.

We have seen so far how the study of the different accounts of Atahualpa's execution, with the varying reasons put forward to justify it, the sentence passed, and the fate of the body, enables us to understand the range of political and religious issues that took shape during the conquest. The charges against the Inca reflect the debates about the justification of the Spanish presence and the legitimacy of Atahualpa's rule. The contradictory accounts of the sentence and the way in which it was carried out are related to ideas about the body, death, and the hereafter that come into conflict at the moment of the conquest. The application of the sentence implies both acceptance of the prevailing modes of administering justice and the extent to which these modes could motivate religious conversion. The uncertain fate of Atahualpa's body highlights the relevance of topics such as the ephemeral character of the Inca's conversion, the power struggle among his successors, and the memory that was preserved of these events.

Wars of Conquest and the Civil Wars

The violence unleashed by the conquest grew during the following decades. It may seem paradoxical to suggest that this prolonged bloodshed might have given rise to a language that could be understood by all those involved: one that might give meaning both to the field of human relations and to the sphere of the sacred. In fact, the study of some episodes of the wars of conquest and of the civil wars will serve to support this hypothesis.

The period following Atahualpa's death is full of punishments and executions carried out in a seemingly indiscriminate way. The episodes recounted in the sources are confused. We find private violence overlapping and switching places with other forms that claim to be public, and both present themselves as "justice." In effect, during the sixteenth century it is difficult to tell the two apart.[27] Guaman Poma's apt description of the atmosphere that predominated at this time is one of generalized violence, absence of law and authority, and religious crisis. In a situation where none of the factions was able to prevail, one's enemies were subjected to a variety of punishments. We will examine the cultural and religious conditions that produced these punishments as well as their impact, the extent to which they may have varied according to the context and the identity of the victims, and how at the same time violence and the application of punishment may have participated in creating a new order.

Studies of the Spanish penal system all mention its rudimentary character. The administration of justice in Castile during the sixteenth century had not undergone any significant changes for centuries, and it was still conditioned by ideas and procedures established in Alphonse X's *Siete Partidas* in the thirteenth century (Burns 2001). Trials tended to be summary, as befitted a system that paid little attention to theoretical concerns about the nature of crime and punishment, or whether the punishment was proportional to the crime. On the other hand, it did pay attention to the relation between the punishment and the social status of the condemned person (Tomás y Valiente 1969, 359). Extracting confessions through torture was common not only in religious cases but also in all penal procedures (Guillaume-Alonso 1997; Escamilla-Colin 1997). The widespread and frequent use of torture in Europe was grounded in the conviction that this practice opened the door to the truth (Cohen 2000, 50; Foucault 1991, 44; Tomás y Valiente 1969, 414–19; Straw 2000, 23). It did not seem strange or out of proportion, since punishments in general usually centered on the body. During the period of the Spanish conquest of America, amputations and capital punishment prevailed in the Castilian courts.[28] Important questions arise, however, concerning what happens when the parties have different ideas about what constitutes crime and punishment, or when, in a situation of war, the cultural conditioning of violence differs from one group to the other.

Death by Fire

It is striking that the conquistadors should have repeatedly burned Indians at the stake during the wars of conquest in the Andes.[29] The death with which Atahualpa was threatened was actually inflicted upon Chalcochima, one of his most prominent military commanders. On charges of plotting an attack against the Spaniards, Pizarro sentenced Chalcochima to die at the stake in a ceremony attended by his relatives and followers. According to one account, Chalcochima was exhorted to convert, which he refused to do, instead calling on the god Pachacamac to come to his aid (Sancho 1917 [1534], 166). Cieza de León claims that Chalcochima was falsely accused of treason, which is why Pizarro hastily sentenced him to die at the stake, although Cieza does not attempt in his account to demonstrate the prisoner's innocence.[30] He does remark, however, that Pizarro's sentence was inappropriate considering the beliefs of the local population, who were "of the opinion that when the bodies are destroyed by fire so are the souls" (Cieza de León 1984a, Third Part, chap. 68, 313).

Of course, this leads to negative consequences for missionary work. The charges brought against the Inca general, in effect, were treason and his refusal to accept baptism. No defense appears in any of the accounts of what happened, probably because a clear and reasoned objection to the charge of treason could be interpreted as complicity. The goal of the sentence was to dissuade the Andeans from conspiring against the conquistadors and to establish, however precariously, both divine and kingly authority.[31]

As well as hasty penal proceedings, we find a whole series of episodes in which the Spaniards used fire as a punishment during the wars of conquest. In Conchucos, the troops who set out under Captain Francisco de Chaves to avenge the death of some of their people burned and impaled a great number of Indians (Cieza de León 1984a, First Part, chap. 82, 108). The soldiers who were disbanded after the battle of Las Salinas committed a multitude of abuses in the provinces of Condesuyo and Chinchaysuyo, including the burning of many Indians (Cieza de León 1985, First Part, chap. 87, 144–45). The *provisor* Luis de Morales,[32] who in 1541 wrote a *Relación* from Cuzco about the state of the land, bears witness to the regular burning of Indians by conquistadors for the sole purpose of robbing them (Lissón 1943, I: no. 3, 62–63, 90).[33]

Death by fire appears as the first, almost spontaneous, mode of punishing the Andean populations. Possibly the conquistadors conceived it to be the "just" way of proceeding against infidels. Since it was the cruelest mode of execution, it was reserved in Europe for the most serious crimes and sins, and given that the state protected the Christian faith, the boundary between crime and sin was very faintly drawn. Transgressions against the authority of the king and against divine authority tended to merge: for this reason, a variety of offenses were punished by death at the stake.[34] In the Spanish penal practice of the period, such a death aimed at destroying the culprit's body and, more important, any memory of the person (Tomás y Valiente 1969, 386). Justifications for this punishment seem diverse, since it was applied to heretics, to sexual acts considered criminal, and to counterfeiters. In fact, all of these offenses were considered crimes of lese majesty, that is, crimes against the civil and divine authorities (278, 359). In the New World, in the context of the Spaniards' missionary undertakings, death by fire had to be rethought: violence that the Andeans believed would destroy their souls was counterproductive to the evangelical aims of the Church as well as to the authority of the state. Even so, it must not be concluded that we are speaking of a great humanitarian advance. There is nothing here of benevolence: the ends pursued are entirely political. Death sentences continued, but death by fire for the native population subsequently appeared to be an act of extreme cruelty rather than an act of justice. Some years later, in 1567, the royal authorities denounced those *encomenderos* who had sent *caciques* to the stake for refusing to deliver the treasures of the Incas to them.[35]

The lack of documents formally recording the principles and rules of any system of penal law among the Incas poses a serious problem for understanding the impact of the sentences applied by the conquistadors during the conquest.[36] We are obliged to rely instead on the more or less detailed descriptions in the chronicles. In some of the more complete, such as those of Garcilaso de la Vega and Guaman Poma, we can find some Christian influences, and possibly an attempt to suggest an analogy between certain aspects of pre-Hispanic Andean justice and the ideas and practices that inspired the behavior of the Spaniards.

Guaman Poma's work (1989 [1615], 301–14) gives us a view of the Incan penal system that has some things in common with the Spanish: the Andean sovereign, for example, had an even greater power to determine sentences than that of the Spanish king, and loyalty to the sovereign and the gods were of paramount importance.[37] Physical punishment, prison, and various modes of death seem to have been characteristic. The short list of crimes that, according to Guaman Poma, entailed severe penalties includes treason, but instead of the death by fire stipulated in the Castilian system, the punishment was beheading, with the skull and other parts of the condemned's body being then brandished as trophies. This achieved the double effect of highlighting the criminal punished, and the triumph of the punisher. Other severe penalties included not only extreme suffering, as in the case of stoning, but also the denial of any funeral rites and the exposure of the body so that wild animals would devour it (307). While the chronicler affirms that there were prisons over which the Inca had exclusive control, the places of execution were natural spaces—possibly sacred ones—such as mountaintops or lakes, which the sovereign had set apart for this purpose (311). Guaman Poma also notes the connection between the social status of the condemned person and the kind of punishment that was assigned.

While Guaman Poma entirely dismisses the use of fire as a means of exterminating enemies within or outside of the community, it is quite possible that it may have been employed in the Andes with the aim of undermining the honor of a kinship group. Among the Incas, the destruction of the ancestors' bodies was possibly the worst affront that could be committed against a lineage. The story of the struggles between Huáscar and Atahualpa reached its height with the annihilation of the former's family and the public humiliation and burning of his forebears' mummies (Murúa 2001 [1613], chap. 57, 192).

Burning as a punishment is recognized by the Inca Garcilaso de la Vega, who assures us that the stake was a part of Incan justice. In his account, this was a punishment that the Incas practiced against other peoples with the aim both of subduing them and "civilizing" them. Garcilaso writes, for example, that during the reign of the Inca Lloque Yupanqui, a military commander named Auqui Tito set out with other generals and their men to conquer the coastal valleys. He returned from his expedition with a report concerning the religion, rites, and secret customs of the valley dwellers. In the course of their inquiries, the Incas discovered that some of the conquered populations practiced sodomy. The Inca then ordered that both those guilty and those suspected of this crime should be publicly burned alive, that their houses should be burned down, and that any trees they might have planted should be torn up by the roots. The Inca passed a law that, from then on, when even a single man should be found guilty of this practice, his entire village and its people should be destroyed (Garcilaso de la Vega 1945 [1609], 1: Book 3, chap. 13, 155).[38] We may question the truth of this assertion, but the story itself is understandable in the context in which the mestizo chronicler was writing: Garcilaso is well known for deliberately showing the Inca state's benevolence and resemblance to Christianity (Duviols 1994; Pease 1995; MacCormack 1991). Here he presents Incan justice reminiscent of the biblical episode of the destruction of Sodom (Genesis 18:20–32;

19:24–25). No doubt he was also attempting to dispel any suspicion that the "unspeakable sin" (of sodomy) was committed among some Andean populations, an accusation leveled by the conquistadors to deny the legitimacy of the native rulers.

The desire for revenge inspired the Andeans to employ fire to destroy their enemies and erase all memory of them. Garcilaso de la Vega relates an episode during the wars of conquest illustrating the crisis that, as we have seen, was not only religious but also judicial. When Manco Inca, the monarch chosen by Pizarro, was murdered by a group of mestizos and Spaniards, his men kindled a circle of fire around the murderers, forcing them to come out of the house in which they were hiding. Once outside, they shot them dead with arrows. Garcilaso recounts that Manco Inca's men discussed what to do with the bodies. Their first impulse was to eat them, so angry were they at the crime committed. Then they considered burning the bodies and casting their ashes into the river so that no memory would remain of them. Finally, they decided to leave the corpses in the open fields, so that "the birds and animals should eat them, for there could be no worse punishment for those bodies" (Garcilaso de la Vega 1960 [1613], 134: Book 4, chap. 7, 234).[39] Whether the story is true or not, it suggests that extreme violence can blind men to the appropriate rituals. In this particular phase of the wars of conquest, although the death of the enemy might be a source of satisfaction for the Andeans, there was no longer any room for sacrifice or public justice.[40]

Stigmas and Trophies

During the wars of conquest, the struggling factions would send each other messages by means of the death and mutilation of their enemies. The chronicles recount that the Incas beheaded the Spaniards, while both sides mutilated the Indians in an attempt to stigmatize individuals considered to be of lower rank and also to intimidate the rest of the population. During the Inca resistance, Cieza de León writes that Manco Inca and his men killed a group of Spaniards, several of whose heads he then sent to his followers in Vitcos, in order to encourage them to support him in the war.[41] As for the Indians who collaborated with the conquistadors, he gave orders that their hands or noses should be cut off, while others had their eyes put out (Cieza de León 1985, First Part, chap. 88, 147). His enemies adopted a similar stance: when Hernando Pizarro and his men captured a large group of Andean warriors near Cuzco, the conquistador gave orders that all of them should have their right hand cut off before being sent to the Inca capital (Pizarro (1978 [1571], 148–49).

The accounts of the wars repeatedly show a similarity between the methods applied by Andeans and Spaniards to punish and execute the enemy. How are we to read these passages? Are they narrative devices used by the chroniclers to suggest an identity between the two sides? Is this the mimesis caused by violence, as described by Girard?[42] Are we dealing here with the immediate results of an apprenticeship in ways of causing pain, humiliation, and death? And are we witnessing the need, spontaneously arising in two different cultures, to desecrate the enemy's body or exhibit a part of it as a sign of superiority?

For Andeans as well as Spaniards, mutilations and beheadings were among the practices of war, though in the case of the Andeans, the precise significance of certain acts remains to be understood. In Europe, mutilation was usually applied as a penalty for crimes such as theft or homicide, in an attempt to reproduce the crime committed on the body of the culprit (Foucault 1991, 45; Merback 1999, 139; Spierenburg 1984, 75–77). In Spain, thieves, scriveners who gave false witness, and poachers who set traps in the mountains, among others, were punished with the cutting off of hands, feet, ears, and noses (Heras 1992; Redondo 1990b, 192–93; Tomás y Valiente 1969, 376, 381 and n.87). The pre-Hispanic Andean peoples practiced beheading and mutilation both in war and in their rituals (Benson and Cook 2001; Arkush and Stanish 2005). Images on a variety of objects such as pieces of pottery or cloth, or in funeral contexts, confirm amputations, beheadings, and trophy heads among the Incas as well as among their contemporaries and predecessors (Bourget 2001; Carmichael 1995; Cordy-Collins 2001; DeLeonardis 2000; Frame 2001; Verano 1995; 2001; Proulx 2001). It is not yet clear to researchers to what extent the victims were individuals outside of the "aggressor" group, or in what specific contexts the sacrifices or executions took place. Telling sacrifices and executions apart would depend not only on discerning certain patterns of violence inflicted on the bodies of the victims (Walker 2001), but also on understanding the purpose that the violence was supposed to serve. How are we to distinguish an offering to the divinity from an act of "justice"?[43]

Civil Wars and the Ordering of Society

With the outbreak of violent dissension among the conquistadors, the Andean populations became both witnesses of, and participants in, the acts of war, some of which were quite new to them. Many joined the forces of one or the other rival faction in the so-called civil wars, which were to last for a decade, as soldiers, artisans, porters, servants, or mere spectators, and they were thus able to observe in detail the Europeans' way of waging war, their rituals of death, and the corresponding codes that directed these rituals.

The violent events unleashed during the civil wars, in which chaos alternated with a tendency to assert ceremony and spectacle, aroused the curiosity of the native inhabitants. It is difficult to discern what conclusions could be drawn from an Andean perspective about concepts such as guilt, revenge, honor, forgiveness, justice, or betrayal, evidenced in the ways the body was treated by the Spaniards. Their behavior in war provided some clues about the way in which the Spaniards administered justice, while at the same time managing, and creating, social and ethnic differences.

In September 1542 in Chupas, a battle took place in which the troops loyal to the crown, under Cristóbal Vaca de Castro, defeated the forces of Diego de Almagro "el Mozo" (the Younger). According to Cieza de León, a large audience, made up of the inhabitants of the surrounding area, posted themselves on the hills around the battlefield in order to watch the encounter and support one faction or the other. The women who were living with some of Almagro's men, foreseeing the unfavorable outcome of the battle, howled and tore their hair. The enthusiasm and excitement among the Andeans were immense, and they showed it by uttering piercing cries. The chronicler adds: "the Indians themselves were astonished at the loud noise issuing from their own mouths, which resounded on all sides, and were greatly rejoiced to see the majesty of the Spaniards fighting among each other out of refusal of their natural vassalage, giving thanks to their sun that such a famous vengeance should be taken for the harm caused to their forefathers" (Cieza de León 1985: Second Part, chap. 77, 255). Those of Almagro's men who managed to flee after their defeat were killed by the Indians in a nearby valley. The wounded and the dead remained lying on the field of battle. During the night, the Indians stripped the clothes and other belongings from the Spaniards, weilding their cudgels to finish off those who were still alive. Those who did not die from their wounds or from these death blows succumbed to the intense cold (Zárate 1995 [1555], Book 4, chap. 19, 176; chap. 21, 179–80). The way in which Cieza de León describes the emotions and gestures of the Andeans, although it recalls classic narratives, nevertheless establishes significant differences between the participants in the events: it is the Andean men and women who scream in a way that does not even seem human, make wild gestures, finish off the wounded, and rob the dead.[44]

The Andeans must have observed the distinctions that the conquistadors made in their treatment of the vanquished. While prisoners were usually executed on the scene of the battle, the leaders of the opposing factions were taken to the principal city to be publicly executed, with all the corresponding ceremony. After his defeat in the battle of Las Salinas in 1538, Diego de Almagro was taken to Cuzco, where he was executed by order of Hernando Pizarro. Almagro had previously claimed jurisdiction over Cuzco, and Manco Inca and his followers had even considered him as a potential ally. This may be why Pizarro decided not to have him put to death in public: after making his will, Almagro was privately garroted. Once dead, his body was carried out on a cloth marked with his coat of arms, while a town crier proclaimed the charge of "seditious agitator" for which he had been executed. His body was placed at the foot of the pillory and beheaded. The story does not indicate whether his head was exhibited or not. His body then was wrapped in shroud, and the funeral took place. Now that the victim had been sacrificed, the behavior of his enemies had to undergo a radical change and give way to veneration: the procession, headed by Hernando Pizarro himself and his principal captains, made its way to the monastery of La Merced, where Almagro was buried "with great honor" (Cieza de León 1985, First Part, chap. 70, 122; Zárate 1995 [1555], Book 3, chap. 12, 128–29).[45]

Respect for the body of the enemy could not always be counted on, and the Andeans certainly witnessed some instances of defamation. The death in Quito of Blasco Núñez Vela, the first viceroy sent by the crown, offers a very clear picture of the social and ethnic differences between the actors involved, both through traditional roles and spontaneous behavior. At the end of the battle of Añaquito, in which the troops loyal to the king were defeated by those of Gonzalo Pizarro, the viceroy lay wounded. He was then recognized by someone who at once attempted to deal him a death blow in revenge for a personal insult, but his companions persuaded him not to commit such a "base" deed. The viceroy was instead killed and beheaded by a black slave, who proceeded to drag his head around the battlefield. Núñez Vela's body was later subjected to mistreatment and humiliation at the hands of Spanish soldiers, and his head was exposed for several days on the pillory. Finally, the body of the viceroy was recovered and buried in a church "with great pomp and ceremony" (Cieza de León 1985, Third Part, chap. 183, 501–2; Fernández de Palencia 1963 [1571], Book 1, chap. 53, 86).

The triumph of the forces representing the crown, headed by Pedro de la Gasca, over Gonzalo Pizarro in Jaquijahuana in April 1548 was followed by severe punishments for the rebels. Once more, the city of Cuzco was the scene of the executions. Pizarro was beheaded there and his head sent to Lima to be displayed with a placard recounting his crimes. In accordance with the penal law in force at the time for cases of treason committed by high-ranking individuals, his houses were razed, their grounds sown with salt, and all his property was confiscated.[46] In the following days, the city was flooded with violence and death. Gasca gave orders that several of Pizarro's followers should be beheaded, hanged, and quartered (Zárate 1995 [1555], Book 7, chap. 8, 373–74). About one hundred Spanish soldiers were flogged. Garcilaso de la Vega, who was a boy at the time, wrote years later that he would go with friends to watch. The Indians, says the chronicler, saw with "the greatest indignation" that "in such an infamous and insulting fashion the Spaniards treated their own countrymen, for until then, although many had been hanged, no Spaniard had yet been flogged" (Garcilaso de la Vega 1960 [1613], 135: Book 6, chap. 1, 8).

Many of those involved were sentenced to the galleys. Tomás y Valiente notes the ignominy of this last punishment, since, in effect,

it amounted to slavery. In this chaotic climate of successive executions, the condemned were afraid of receiving a sentence that might
not fit their social standing. Garcilaso writes that one prisoner, on
learning that some gentlemen had been hanged, begged the *corregidor* that he himself should be beheaded, out of consideration for his
status, for he feared that if he were sent to the gallows, "he would de-
spair of his salvation and condemn himself to hell" (Garcilaso de la
Vega 1960 [1613], 135: Book 6, chap. 16, 36).

These punishments allow us to observe not only how political and
military conflicts were dealt with, but also how, in these conditions of
chaos and legal vacuum, a certain order was gradually imposed on
the social, cultural, religious, and ethnic space, through the administration of sentences that—as we have seen—tended to consider a
person's social standing and ethnic identity. Starting from the first contacts between Andeans and Europeans, when there were no common
codes or institutions, epidemics, executions, war, and physical violence
played a crucial role in establishing the Spanish dominion in the
Andes. Death and physical punishment presented as "justice" served
as a means of communication between the two groups.

Researchers who have reflected on the meaning of physical pain,
war, and violence in the creation and destruction of the world (Foucault 1991; Scarry 1985; Cohen 2000; Girard 2005 [1972]) tend to
base their analysis on the idea of two sides fighting each other on the
same ground. The conquest of the Andes provides a different context, one that presents more complex nuances for the historian who
wishes to understand the meaning of death and its foundational role
in a colonial society. We must explore how the sphere of the sacred,
if indeed it can be isolated from the other jostling fields of human
activity, is controlled by means of the executions and punishments
that took place during this period. While the executions of Spaniards
in the European mode cannot be stripped of their sacred character,
it is worth asking ourselves whether the Andeans could perceive this
character when they witnessed the deaths. The Indians of the ruling
classes were exhorted to convert to Christianity before being executed,
though this threat only served to change the mode of death, never to
avert it. Once the conversion was accepted, or was publicly rejected,
the sphere of the sacred became very problematic for both sides. How

could the Andeans maintain some control over the sacred? And how could the Spaniards appropriate it?

The Andeans gave, or tried to give, a sacrificial character to the executions of Spanish prisoners, but they had to struggle with the ever-increasing restrictions on the public nature of these acts. This, for example, is why Manco Inca sent to his followers the heads of the Spaniards whose execution he had ordered. But there was a serious limitation here. Since only the objectification or reification of the act was available, the unfolding of the ritual was lost. To what extent could a people preserve its cohesion if it had access only to some of its symbols, not to all of them? This is why the Spaniards gradually increased their domination, as they gained greater and greater control over the public space of the executions, even when the victims were themselves Spaniards, and when this scandalized the Indians. This was a way to build colonial order and to spread an awareness of this order among the conquered population. For what the local populations needed, even though the Spaniards did not consciously aim at this, was to become familiar with the greatest possible number of signs of the culture that was now attempting to assert its hegemony: signs such as the justice of the nobles, of the common men, of the slaves, and of the different categories of Indians.

In her study of the rituals of public execution in Europe in the late Middle Ages, Esther Cohen (1989, 413) remarks that

> Rulers—royal, urban, or regional—were anxious to display the power of justice done and order restored to all and sundry. Therefore they took care to stage their public rituals, executions included, in a spectacular manner. But in order to ensure that the public understood the symbolism involved in each stage of this ritual and got the correct message, those same authorities had to rely upon a universal language of justice derived from the common substratum of popular culture.

Since this "common substratum" did not exist in the Andes, we have to explore further the meaning of the sacred, the sacrificial, and the spontaneous (here I deliberately avoid the word "unconscious") and their connections with the material and spiritual goals of the colonial project. Death by fire, which inaugurated the lethal inroads of the conquistadors, was administered according to the rules established in Europe for the death of those who deviated from the authority of God and the king. This kind of death, however, threatened the missionary and colonizing project because of its both cruel and excessively shameful character, and the method of execution had to be reconsidered. In this respect, the role of pain is crucial. In her discussion of the meaning of publicly induced pain, Cohen explains that in late medieval Europe,

> the aim of the authorities in staging long and painful executions was not to avenge themselves by inflicting a maximum of agony upon the criminals. The spectacle was meant as a visual enactment of implemented authority, displaying the full power of the law to all observers, but the cruelty of the penalties was a corollary, not an aim. . . . The infliction of pain upon a condemned criminal, therefore, was anything but a vengeance. In a sense, it was a purgation preparatory to the one expected beyond the grave. Making the criminal suffer achieved the dual purpose of cleansing his soul and warning potential malefactors. (1989, 408–9)

Of course, the purifying effect that pain was believed to have on the individual who experienced it may not have been a matter of particular concern to the Spaniards during the first years of contact. The construction of the common sacred ground where the redemptive function of pain and death could be recognized would become a central problem for the missionary project in the following decades.

CHAPTER THREE | The Conquest
of Death

Inducing the native populations to adopt Christian beliefs and customs concerning death was a crucial part of the Spanish missionary
project in the Andes. This ambitious goal involved becoming familiar with Andean ideas and practices, reducing them to a concise
and intelligible whole, and using what the Spaniards believed they
had learned to create procedures that, while aiming to eradicate the
old ways, would provide guidance in establishing the new ones.

The missionaries and colonial functionaries did not, of course,
conceive such a simple, straightforward program as the sequence described above might suggest. The first details began to appear during
the early explorations, wars, and plundering. The importance of the
ancestors in Andean societies became apparent when contact began
with the native elites. As priests and officials sought to obtain a more
systematic knowledge of the political and economic order prevailing in
the pre-conquest Andes, the place that the forebears occupied became
increasingly intelligible. The Church, in its council documents, formulated a series of guidelines and instruments designed to achieve
the conversion of the native population. These documents paid special
attention to Andean ideas about death and their correlative funeral
customs, since these ideas and customs were considered guides for
everyday existence. The recommendations of the councils on these
points fell into categories much like those considered in this book:
the bishops encouraged the missionaries to identify the local populations' sacred places, particularly tombs and cemeteries; they stressed

the importance of explaining Christian ideas about the body and the individual, and they exhorted the native populations to give up their own conceptions; finally, they familiarized themselves with native funeral rites in order to oppose and eradicate them. A crucial task was to determine who, besides the missionaries, was to play a central role in this undertaking, and also—a very important point—to establish the methods that should be used. The debates on this last point were constant and involved both the ecclesiastical sphere and the state. The violence of the conquest projected an inescapable shadow on the nature and relevance of the methods employed to begin the missionary project.[1]

In this chapter I analyze the itinerary followed in Christianizing death in the Andes. I will deal here primarily with the formulation of policies, not their implementation (which I will discuss later). This analysis is organized chronologically. I examine three main topics: burial places and their location; the concept of the individual and the body; and, finally, the rites of preparation for death.

The Question of the Tombs

The conquistadors' first contacts with Andean ancestor worship coincided with acts of looting. The company of soldiers who reached the Inca capital shortly after Atahualpa had been taken prisoner in Cajamarca walked into a temple where they found the embalmed bodies of two nobles, carefully tended by a woman. Her face was covered by a gold mask, and she held a tool with which she was brushing away the dust and flies from the mummies. She demanded that the soldiers remove their shoes before entering the temple. Although they obeyed her, the impression made on them by the reverence with which the bodies were being treated was quickly overcome by the sight of the rich ornaments they wore, and the soldiers proceeded to strip them of their jewels and adornments.[2] From then on, the looting became more intense and widespread: temples and homes were sacked, and local authorities, custodians of the tombs, and the relatives of the deceased were forced to reveal the places where objects of gold and silver were kept.[3] The identification of the tombs as treasure houses sparked a search that seemed endless.[4] In a report addressed to Charles V from Cuzco in 1540, the *provisor* Luis de Morales complained that in their eagerness to find treasures, the Spaniards "burned the living and dug up the dead" (Lissón 1943, 1: no. 3, 63).

In spite of the alarm that the conquistadors' abuses aroused in priests such as Morales, the fact that the ancestors' graves were places of worship for the local populations made the missionaries consider them a serious obstacle to persuading the Andeans to embrace the Christian faith. In the same document written from Cuzco, Morales discusses the problems that ancestor worship presented for the teaching of the Catholic doctrine. Describing the state of the city's native population, he draws an appalling picture: the majority lived in miserable conditions, and many of them wandered the streets asking for alms, with crucifixes in their hands, no doubt in order to show that they were already Christian and therefore deserved assistance. Those who stole to meet their needs were punished with the gallows. In spite of food shortages, or perhaps because of them, the natives continued to offer abundant sacrifices to their *guacas* and ancestors.[5] Morales argued that it was necessary to suppress these rituals, since not only would this make the work of the preachers easier, but it would also serve to transfer the huge resources used in the sacrifices—cattle, corn, and coca leaves—to instead sustain the Indians.

The *provisor* of Cuzco also discussed the matter of the treasures kept in the *guacas* and proposed a solution. The Indians knew where there were *guacas* and graves, but he believed that they did not dare to take the gold and silver found there for fear of the Spaniards, who were in the habit of robbing them and sometimes even killing them in order to conceal their crime. Morales proposed that the Indians, should they wish to do so, be allowed to remove the treasures from all the *guacas* and graves that they knew of, and that they should turn over half of the proceeds to the king, keeping the other half for themselves. In addition, he suggested that a functionary of the crown, as protector of the province, should be in charge of preventing the Spaniards, by the threat of severe punishments, from robbing the Indians (Lissón 1943, 1: no. 3, 79–87).

In spite of Morales's concern with protecting the Indians from the abuses they habitually suffered, his suggestions at first seem aimed at entirely uprooting local beliefs and customs. It is true that the *provisor* based his statements on the premise that the doctrine could only be effective if "no worship either of *guacas* or of dead bodies" were permitted (Lissón 1943, 1: no. 3, 81).[6] Nevertheless, we can perceive an important note in his proposal: his considerations go beyond the question of how best to use the treasures or who was to take possession of them, to ask why and on the basis of what rights this was to be done. For Morales, these treasures belonged to the Indians and to the king, as their sovereign, not to the conquistadors and their successors. The Indians, in accepting the Christian faith and the sovereignty of the king, as Morales believed they should do, renounced their own religion and political autonomy. Morales's proposal also, however, contains an implicit recognition of the rights accruing from the bonds of blood and political association that connected the Indians to their forebears—bonds that entitled them to appropriate for themselves the goods to be found in the tombs.

This preoccupation with burial treasures continued during the following decades and contributed to the controversy concerning restitution—the act by which the conquistadors were required to restore what they had taken from the Indians during the conquest, because it was not a just war (Lohmann 1966).[7] Restitution, advocated in particular by the Dominican friar Bartolomé de las Casas, concerned, generally speaking, whatever riches the conquistadors had appropriated by violent methods (Las Casas 1992a [1565]; 1992b [1565]). The starting point for his discussion was a question posed by a member of his order who was a missionary in Peru. Talking of the "great and marvelous treasures" to be found in the *guacas,* he says:

> Now, the question is, whether all these treasures belong indifferently to anyone who—whether on their own authority or by license of our kings of Spain or of the governors who, in the name of the kings, rule these regions—seek them, dig them up, find them and carry them away, with the intention of keeping them for themselves, and in this way acquire possession of said precious things or treasures and are able to appropriate them with a clear conscience. (Las Casas 1992a [1565], 13)

This resembles the proposal made twenty years earlier by the *provisor* of Cuzco in his report to the king, but the argument developed from it is radically different. Las Casas asserted the need to understand and acknowledge different peoples' values on the basis of their humanity rather than of the religious principles that inspired them. Thus, he discusses the following essential points: first, honoring graves was a custom only to be found among rational beings (1992a [1565], 17). Second, burying the deceased with their most precious treasures made manifest "the glory, nobility, riches and excellent condition of these dead people" (31), which is why Las Casas argued that the valuables placed in the tombs were in no way inert objects that had lost their significance with the death of their owners. Third, the honor concerned not only the deceased person but also all those who were connected to him (41), which is why it was clear that many people suffered insult when the tombs of their forebears were profaned and robbed. Finally, the elaborate tombs filled with riches were a means of preserving the memory of the person whose remains were deposited there.[8] For this reason, it could not be assumed that the treasures placed in the tombs were objects that had been abandoned, and therefore had no owner and could be appropriated by anyone. The examples given by Las Casas include practices and ideas that, at the time when he was writing, had recently been or still were common in Spain and other places in Europe. He argued that the king of Spain was not entitled to take possession of these goods or grant others permission to do so; this was the prerogative of the Inca, the legitimate king and natural lord of the populations concerned (49). Those who were guilty of violating these graves had not only greatly offended the descendants of the natural lords buried there but, moreover, had also committed a mortal sin. He concluded that whoever had taken treasures from the tombs was under the obligation to restore them to their rightful owners, on pain of damnation.

The Dominican friar's proposal was thus very different from that of the *provisor* Luis de Morales, since it recognized the validity of Andean religious beliefs and practices. As a result, it adopted quite a radical position in the debate concerning the legitimacy of the Spanish crown's sovereignty over the inhabitants of Peru. Indeed, for Las Casas, the fact that the owners of these tombs were unbelievers, something that many Spaniards considered a justification for the spoliations, was no excuse for despising their rituals and offerings (1992a [1565], 65).

The friar argued that the marks of respect shown for their forebears by human beings in various societies and periods have illustrated with sufficient eloquence the significance of these practices, that anyone possessing standards of justice and reason might recognize. By contrast, the Dominican emphasized the unjust circumstances in which the Spaniards had deposed and executed the Inca. This act of taking political power by force, he asserted, disqualified any claim on the part of the Spanish crown to exercise sovereignty over Peru.[9]

Las Casas's vigorous argument had repercussions in the Peruvian Church through his followers, though, it must be admitted, they were not moved to subscribe to the ultimate consequences of his reasoning. In a decision that must have aroused controversy and opposition, the Second Council of Lima, assembled in 1567, adopted his ideas. One of its constitutions (Constitution 113) established that no one had the right to destroy the graves of the local population or to disinter the bodies therein; it emphasized that this decree was to be complied with even if the graves were those of unbelievers. Even though this measure had its origins in the events occurring in Peru at the time, the bishops' arguments in favor of the constitution made no mention of Las Casas or his controversial work. Instead, they chose to invoke a decree of Pope Clement III (1187–1191) ordering excommunication for those who dared to profane graves, thus leaving the bodies at the mercy of dogs and birds. The Second Council disposed that those found guilty would be excommunicated and fined (Vargas Ugarte 1951, 1:255). Although this declaration is certainly important, it proved totally impossible to enforce.

The Second Council's call to respect the graves of non-Christians stands out as unusual if we examine previous references to tombs and sacred places. Some years earlier, in 1545, another Dominican friar, Bishop Jerónimo de Loayza, wrote an *Instrucción* that set forth the first recommendations issued in furtherance of the conversion of the Indians.[10] In this document, Loayza recommended that graves and *guacas* should be searched for, destroyed, and consecrated to the Catholic faith with the cooperation of young, recently converted Indians; however, he did not discuss the question of the ownership of any treasure found at these sites. Six years later, in 1551, the First Council assembled in Lima thought it necessary to separate the unbelievers from those who were already converted. With this decision, the council pursued the double purpose of conforming to the dictates of canon law and making the preaching of doctrine easier. The bishops decided that as long as the old shrines remained intact, the Indians who had recently been baptized would have incentives to return to their old forms of worship. As a result, the council ordered the destruction of the *guacas* and temples and instructed that churches should be built or crosses set up on their ruins.[11]

As for the burial places, the bishops charged the missionaries with ensuring that those Andeans who were already Christian should have their graves in the churches, and they ordered physical punishments for those who put the bodies of the already-baptized in any other place; they also decreed that in cases where attempts had been made to carry corpses to the old tombs, the bodies should be incinerated. The First Council recommended that the old graves be abolished: for those Andeans who had not yet converted to Christianity, it ordered that a site be set apart that would be visible to all so that their bodies could be buried there. Also, bodies that were in any other place were to be moved there, including those that were buried in the homes of relatives.[12] In this way the Church leaders emphasized the ancient precept according to which the remains of Christians should rest only in the company of those who professed the same faith.[13] In the Andes this gave rise to the stipulation that recent converts should be buried only in churches, thus confronting the problem posed by the great number of burial places as well as attempting to undermine the bonds between the Andeans and their sacred spaces, their ancestors, and their old religion. For the time being, the Church seemed to be open to creating public cemeteries for unbelievers, an idea that was unusual in the Andes but solidly rooted in the history of the Old World (Ariès 1977; Rebillard 2003). The council's directive that tombs should not be violated indicates a very different mood among the upper strata of the Church.

The edict of the Second Council of Lima concerning the inviolability of graves was rarely complied with. Las Casas's ideas and the atmosphere of crisis and repentance moved some conquistadors and *encomenderos* to order restitutions before their deaths (Lohmann 1966, 57), and led public figures to denounce the conduct of laymen and priests as the real obstacles to the conversion of the Indians (Falcón 1918 [1567]; Quiroga 1922 [1563?]). However, they were at odds with other initiatives, both within the Church and outside of it. These proposals were inspired by a very different temperament, increasingly hostile to indigenous culture. The actions of the *licenciado* Polo de Ondegardo, *corregidor* of Cuzco, are among the most notable examples. At the request of the government, Ondegardo carried out exhaustive inquiries into the Andean religion (Duviols 1971, 99–107; González Pujana 1993; MacCormack 1985, 186–204). He was in charge, among other things, of administering justice, and he found it necessary to understand the reasons given by the Indians in support of their complaints. He also thought it was important to become familiar with Incan systems of government in order to appropriate as much as possible for the colonial benefit. His research into Incan taxation was of particular interest to the crown, enabling him and his collaborators to unravel the distribution of resources and the contributions made by Andeans to the upkeep of state, regional, local, and private religious institutions.[14] The researchers uncovered a complex of lands and several dozen temples in the vicinity of Cuzco. This system, known as the *ceques,* organized the sacred places and their corresponding traditions and were connected in turn to social hierarchies and kinship groups that, some said, were repeated throughout the territory of the ancient Inca state (Ondegardo 1906 [1561], 184).[15]

Ondegardo's inquiries, during the years in which the rebel stronghold of Vilcabamba was active, led in 1559 to his famous discovery and despoliation of the mummies and effigies of several Incas. The political and ideological returns of this operation were very great, because it weakened the Incas still living in Vilcabamba while providing more effective weapons for subjugating the Inca elite in Cuzco.[16] Ondegardo and his contemporaries sketched out the general picture of Andean religious practices and compiled a wide-ranging catalogue of native deities, rituals, and religious specialists as well as a sacred calendar, which had a far-reaching impact in the civil and ecclesiastical spheres.[17] His inquiries revealed the importance of the tombs and temples to the native population and therefore constituted a powerful argument for their destruction, if the evangelical and colonial missions were to be successful.

Las Casas's ideas concerning the inviolability of graves were most severely criticized by the *oidor* Juan de Matienzo (1967 [1567], 128–31) and by the author of the text called the *Parecer de Yucay* (Pérez Fernández 1995 [1571], 162–71). Matienzo, for example, refuted Las Casas's ideas one after the other, with arguments that acquired ever-greater force in colonial thought and policies: he denied that the Incas had ever been legitimate rulers; rejected the idea that the Indians deserved any consideration, since they had no sense of honor; and maintained that even though the tombs may have been places sacred to the Andeans, they were not sacred to the Spaniards. For Matienzo, the preaching of the doctrine justified the destruction of the sacred places, the looting of their treasures, the enjoyment of these treasures by whoever should find them, and the payment of a small portion of the profits to the king. This position was reinforced a few years later by the policies of the viceroy, Francisco de Toledo, who, in a series of letters to the king, made clear his total commitment to destroying the tombs, not only because it served the struggle against native religious practices but also because it represented potential income for the Royal Treasury. This is why some of Toledo's letters discuss the tombs in the same passages that consider the mining industry.[18] For the viceroy, the most important issue was to organize the search for treasures, which was in a state of chaos at the time, to determine what share of any findings should go to the king, and to clarify what portion (if any) the Church should receive. In an ordinance issued in La Plata in 1574, he mentions a *Real Cédula* (Royal warrant) originally dated 1540 and confirmed by Philip II in 1571, which stated that the crown was entitled to half of the value of the treasures found in the graves (Toledo 1986, 1:287).

Las Casas's writings were finally banned by a *Real Cédula* issued in 1573 (Pereña 1984, 21; Pérez Fernández 1988, 461), and the search for graves, undertaken from the very beginnings of the Spanish presence in the Andes, spread and intensified.[19] Though José de Acosta repeated the earlier condemnation of such practices (1987 [1588], 2:281), the Third Council of Lima does not mention the topic in its constitutions.[20] By means of the didactic materials produced by this Council, such as the *Confesionario* (Treatise of confessions) and the *Tercer Cathecismo por sermones*,[21] as well as extracts from the writings of Ondegardo, the parish priests were charged with ensuring that burials always took place in churches, and with preventing their parishioners from removing the bodies of their relatives from consecrated sites in order to take them to their old burial grounds.[22] This policy went hand in hand with the decision to uproot the Andean populations from their original places of settlement. The worship of the ancestors and of the *pacarinas,* or places of origin of the various ethnic groups, symbolized their bond with the places to which they claimed to belong, over which they exercised dominion and around which their lives were organized. Thus, by separating them from these sacred spaces, the Spaniards were attempting to destroy the cornerstone of their religious life.

Besides the attempt to locate and destroy ancient burial places and to force the Andean populations to bury their dead in churches, a main aim of the doctrine was to communicate Christian ideas about death and refute Andean beliefs and funeral customs. The Council of Trent had stipulated that the doctrine taught by the Church would only be effective if its teachings were consistent, to which end a catechism was written in the years following the assembly (Rodríguez and Lanzetti 1982). The higher echelons of the Church in the Andes responded to this concern, reinforced by the documents of the Councils of Lima (Durán 1982, 187). Since Philip II's *Real Pragmática* (Pragmatic sanction) of July 12, 1564, had proclaimed the Council of Trent a law of the state, the highest-ranking colonial functionaries shared with the Church the obligation of complying with the council's resolutions (Durán 1982, 67–68).[23] A central tenet of Christian doctrine and of Christian ideas about death and the hereafter was the concept of the individual.

The Individual and the Body

In order to teach Christian precepts about death and the hereafter, it was necessary to ascertain how the Andean populations saw the world, and how the individual was conceived in the Andean context.[24] This involved inquiring into their ideas about the origin and destiny of the human being.[25] A variety of sources, some of them at odds with each other, served this purpose: travelers' and missionaries' descriptions of the country and its history; inquiries aimed at organizing the levying of taxes, the distribution of workers, and the administration of justice; analyses of the local languages; and inspection visits carried out to identify sacred places and local religious practices as well as the many actions that intruded violently into the lives and property of the local populations. The examination of Andean funeral practices was a crucial element in this strategy.[26] The sacking of shrines had shown conquistadors, colonists, and missionaries how the bodies of the dead were laid out. The practice of preserving the bodies, the offerings, and especially the sacrifices and ceremonies carried out periodically by the kin, led Churchmen and civil functionaries to conclude that the Andeans were ignorant of essential aspects of the human being's beginning and fate.

Both because this was one of the fundamentals of Christian doctrine and because of Spanish observations of Andean religion, the Church determined that it was crucial to transmit the idea that the individual was made up of a corruptible body and an immortal soul.[27] The *Instrucción* written by Loayza in 1545 exhorted its readers to attack the Andean practices and beliefs observed through action and preaching. We have seen the instructions issued with respect to the graves and shrines, and how they were justified. The parish priests, thanks to the example given by the native leaders, were called on to prevent the chieftains from being buried along with their wives and servants, in the belief that the latter would continue to provide company and service. Confusing native knowledge with ignorance, the missionaries insisted on stressing in their sermons an elementary fact that Andean settlers knew quite well: that in death the body decayed, and nothing remained of it. However, they added, this did not happen to the soul, concerning whose existence the Indians had to be instructed. The preachers went on to explain what happened to the soul: those who had received baptism went "to glory where they know neither hunger nor thirst, but true and eternal rest, and have their fill of seeing and enjoying God; and the souls of those who have been evil go to hell" (Lissón 1943, I: no. 4, 143–44).

In contrast to what is suggested in Loayza's early *Instrucción*, Ondegardo stated that the people of the Andes did have a concept of the soul (1982 [1585], 460), although they believed its existence to be very similar to that of the body.[28] He pointed out the fact that the kin made offerings of food, drink, and clothing to the deceased in the belief that they suffered from hunger, thirst, and cold, and that they wandered around the world. In this way the living appeased the dead and kept off the bad luck that they, the dead, if not properly cared for, would bring down upon their relatives (450). Unlike others who wrote before and after him,[29] Ondegardo interpreted the custom of preserving the bodies of the dead, and the belief that they needed material sustenance, as a sure sign that the resurrection was a totally alien concept for the Indians.

Ensuring that the Andeans accepted the existence of the soul, that it was eternal, and that human beings must be reborn in order to enter this eternal life, was an indispensable step in communicating the fundamentals of the Christian faith. The Spaniards were therefore eager to determine whether the Andeans' existing beliefs contained signs of these concepts. As Taylor (2000a) and Duviols (1978) have made clear, among the Andean populations it was considered certain that the world, and everything in it, including human beings, was animated by a vital force that made it possible for things to be what they were, or to realize their potential (Taylor 2000a, 5). This vital force, *camac* or *camaquen,* was identified by some observers as a possible equivalent of the Christian soul, although they also identified it with the principle that had brought everything into being. The fact that *camac* was also attributed to animals and objects led some Churchmen and functionaries to aver that the Andeans did not recognize the fundamental difference between themselves and animals, another important aspect of the Christian worldview.[30] They noted that the Indians attributed to things faculties that from a Christian point of view were exclusively reserved to animate beings, besides assigning to a variety of objects and natural phenomena an extraordinary, even sacred, character.

For this reason, their view of the universe and their relationship with nature acknowledged a complex group of forces interacting to determine the course of human existence, instead of the single principle or God of Christian thought. As a result, the Church concluded that it was obliged to demonstrate to the Indians that their beliefs were erroneous and superstitious.[31] The explanation of the Christian concept of the individual, understood as a man endowed with a corruptible body and an immortal soul, had to be preceded, accompanied, and reinforced by the idea of a single God who had created the universe. This topic appears consistently in the earliest ecclesiastical writings, and much more forcefully in the didactic material published by the Third Council of Lima in 1585.[32] As Taylor (2000a; 2003) has demonstrated, these writings, and the terms that were finally fixed upon to designate the central concept of "soul," reflect the long and tortuous route that finally, after attempts to accommodate the native notions of a vital force to the Christian idea of the soul, led the Church to abandon all attempts at translation, in order to avoid ambiguities and deviations from orthodox doctrine. It borrowed instead the term *ánima,* which was used from then on in the pastoral texts.[33]

The body and what happens to it after death received less detailed doctrinal treatment, although the subject was perilous because of the ambiguous practices and interpretations that it could generate.[34] The events we are studying here took place at a time when significant changes were occurring in Spain in the attitudes adopted toward the bodies of the highest-ranking dead. This involved occasional tension with central aspects of the doctrine of the resurrection, as it was conceived by certain influential religious sectors. In the Andes the problem became more complicated when Christian ideas concerning the corruption of the flesh and the resurrection came into contact with Andean reverence for the remains of the ancestors, a reverence seen by the Spaniards as idolatry. In Cuzco, however, missionaries and colonial functionaries were able to see and perhaps even to understand the huge importance that the ancestors' bodies had for their descendants. Moreover, the religious beliefs and customs of the Spanish kings were, as we will see below, similarly concerned with establishing their dominion in the sacred and secular spheres.

The accounts that address the topic of where the Andeans considered their life after death to take place are very vague. They speak, rather, of a different time. Resurrection is sometimes described as an individual phenomenon that, in contrast to Christian belief, did not happen at a specific moment, predetermined for all men; other versions, however, do describe it as a collective event. After death there was no radical change: for example, the powerful retained their privileges and property, which explained the lords' desire to be buried with their servants, wives, and most prized possessions. Chroniclers such as Zárate (1995 [1555], chap. 12, 54), Cieza de León (1984b [1553], First Part, chap. 62, 193), and, later, Garcilaso de la Vega describe the material character of this other life. The body was indispensable for life in this other time, hence the Andeans' concern with preserving and keeping safe the parts that were periodically removed, such as hair and nails.[35]

In spite of the Christian overtones that can be perceived in these writings, we can also see significant differences. In Cieza de León's and Zárate's accounts, there is no mention of an end of time, and the idea that at a specific moment a reunion will take place between the body and the life force that animated it is not clearly expressed.[36] Some years later, Garcilaso de la Vega asserted that the Andean notion of the resurrection meant resuming life on earth. This idea of life after death occurring in the same world where the living dwell may indeed express the beliefs of the Andean populations. Though this idea of a resurrection indicates Garcilaso's desire to demonstrate that Andean religion presented some Christian characteristics,[37] he must have known quite well how inseparable the concept of judgment was from the Christian resurrection; he asserted, nevertheless, that the Incas imagined a hereafter devoid of punishments and rewards.

In contrast, when Ondegardo (1906 [1561], 208–9) writes on this subject, he mentions in very vague terms that the good will be rewarded and evildoers will be punished, without indicating where, how, or even why. This not very coherent statement, in fact, contradicts his next: that it was also believed that the powerful, as God's friends, would enjoy glory in the hereafter, which reflected the contempt that, he tries to demonstrate, was heaped on the aged, the sick, and the poor (209). Also, both Ondegardo and the Church, which adopted his position, saw the Andean belief in the material, that a body would need sustenance after death, as a clear indication that they harbored no hopes of a resurrection, that central preoccupation of Christian doctrine.

The firm opinion of Ondegardo and the authors of the documents designed to guide the new converts to a Christian death sat on shifting ground. The treatment of the bodies of powerful and prominent figures in Spain at that time evoked some uncomfortable analogies to the preservation of bodies by the Incas. Up until a century before the European invasion of the New World, it was customary to embalm the bodies of Spanish monarchs and their relatives and to adorn them richly before placing them in the tomb.[38] The funeral arrangements of the Catholic monarchs constituted an eloquent, albeit temporary, deviation from this tradition: they commanded that their bodies should not be embalmed, and that they should only be clothed in the simple habit of a religious order. This lack of interest in the material did not, however, extend to the tomb: their funeral monuments in Granada commemorate their magnificent achievements in the Reconquista (Varela 1990, 18–20). Emperor Charles V shared this disinterest in what would happen to his body. Priests of mystical and ascetic leanings, who attained positions of considerable influence during the sixteenth century, condemned the attachment to material goods and conceived of the body as a prison from which the soul must be freed (Bataillon 1950; Caro Baroja 1985, 65–67; Martínez Gil 1993; Varela 1990, 18).[39] This view had such a powerful impact that one might have expected its influence to grow stronger. There were those, moreover, who stressed the importance of the monarchs' abstaining from all signs of vanity at a time when the soul was facing its most difficult ordeal. The handbooks on dying well that circulated during this period included a warning to Christians against the assault of the devil, who might arouse in the dying person an attachment to his possessions and to his own body. Some of the authors of these handbooks considered that the extraordinary position occupied by the sovereigns and the nobles put them in danger of succumbing to this threat (Caro Baroja 1985, 70; Varela 1990, 40). Also, for approximately three centuries there had been assertions that attempting to induce incorruptibility in the bodies of the dead (for example, by embalming) was a sign of skepticism about the promise of the resurrection as an effect of divine grace.[40]

From the time of Philip II onward, the funeral rites of royalty took a different turn.[41] Arguments were formulated explaining the exceptional character of the king's and nobles' bodies and distinguishing the attentions paid to them from those given by heathens to the remains of their forebears.[42] From the second half of the seventeenth century, we see a partial revival of the custom of embalming important Spaniards and dressing them elaborately, with the aim of making them look as much as possible as they did when alive (Varela 1990, 77–81). To get a more complete idea of this tradition, in which the bodies of prominent persons and saints played a central role in spreading the idea of the monarchs' power and fostering religious piety, we must also acknowledge the power of the worship of saints' relics during the reign of Philip II (Eire 1995; Martínez-Burgos 1990, 124–45; Varela 1990, 66–73). No other European monarch of this period surpassed Philip's devotion to the relics of the saints: he sent delegations abroad in order to acquire them and, in many cases, to protect them from Protestant attacks. Ceremonies of translation multiplied, and the monastery of San Lorenzo de El Escorial, like some immense reliquary, housed the king's private collection (J. Brown 1998, 52; Eire 1995; Mulcahy 1992). The miracles attributed to these relics during the severe illnesses that afflicted the king and his family were matters of public knowledge (Martínez-Burgos 1990, 119–45; Varela 1990). This was also a period during which it was not unusual to discover, on exhuming the bodies of the saints, that they had escaped the indignities of corruption, something that ancient belief had long considered a sign of divine favor (Ariès 1977). During the seventeenth century in Spain, it was found that the bodies of nobles who had led lives of exemplary virtue and devotion had been granted a similar boon.[43]

Both for the modern observer and for contemporaries, the actual funeral practices of the new European arrivals were at odds with what was being said to the natives and demanded of them. Criticism of Andean ancestor worship was in contrast to the concern that the Spaniards and mestizos showed for the bodies and graves of their own people. The funeral honors given by the authorities even to those whom they had once considered their worst enemies; the removal by Cuzco mestizos of the bones of their fathers from their precarious graves on the battlefields, in order to carry them with pomp and ceremony to the churches and hospitals of the Inca capital (Lissón 1943, 1: no. 3, 58–59; Garcilaso de la Vega 1960 [1613], 134: Book 2, chap. 38, 161); the erection by the Dominicans of a lavish altar with relics brought from Rome in the church of their convent in Lima

(Lizárraga 1908 [1591], chap. 24, 33–34): all of these actions sent a contradictory message about the value that Christians assigned to the bodies of the dead. The priests in their sermons condemned the practice of putting offerings in tombs and tending to bodies. As we have seen, they wished to distance themselves from local rituals, stressing that these were at odds with the correct Christian attitude toward death. We can perceive here the echo of the ascetic ideas that had gained influence in certain intellectual and religious circles in Spain (Bataillon 1950; Eire 1995).

To explain the parts of which a person was composed—the soul and the body—it was crucial to ascertain what image the Indians had of themselves as individuals. José de Acosta, whose ideas guided the work of the Third Council of Lima (1582–1583), wrote that first it was necessary to "ensure that the barbarians should learn to be men, and then to be Christians" (1984 [1588], 1:539). The assumption was that the Indians were intrinsically no different from the Spaniards; Acosta argued that it was not their nature, but their customs that made their conversion a challenge (MacCormack 1991, 266–67). This seems a subtle distinction, but it is a very important one. What kind of people were the Indians? What were these customs that kept them from having the proper disposition to receive the Christian message? Others have studied this question closely.[44] I will mention here those points that are relevant for the teaching of Christian ideas about death.

Acosta reasoned that the Indians, because they had remained so long deprived of any possibility of knowing the true faith, were people of limited understanding: fickle, servile in character, with few or no virtues, and inclined to vice. To this unpromising material were added the obstacles represented by the language and the remoteness of the places in which many of them lived (1984 [1588], 1:89–95, 115). This "limited understanding" explained the great difficulties that, according to the Church, the Indians encountered in comprehending spiritual concepts, which undoubtedly included the most delicate notions concerning the salvation of their souls. The spheres of action that this opened were diverse.[45] As we can see from the writings of Acosta and other missionaries, the spreading of the doctrine had to include inducing the Indians to recognize themselves as men or, more exactly, to become men.[46] It was necessary, the Spaniards argued, to begin with the material world, that is, to attend to their living conditions: places, spaces, and ways of life. Only in this manner could the work in the spiritual sphere begin.[47] Other observers reinforced this view: they stressed the eminently sensual nature of the Indians, which showed itself in the religious domain in their taste for external acts and signs (Durán 1982, 158; Vargas Ugarte, 1951, 1:374). For this reason, the role assigned to memory, representation, and art in the doctrine was crucial.[48]

From the Second Council onward, the Church decided that imposing spiritual penalties on the Indians was of little use, since their difficulties in understanding these penalties prevented them from grasping their meaning and purpose (Vargas Ugarte 1951, 1:256). For this reason, physical punishment played an important role in the teaching of the faith. Although a severe critic of those who advocated physical violence as the only language for disciplining the Indians, Acosta was in favor of this kind of punishment, stating that whereas rebukes were of little use, corporal punishment could have positive effects (Acosta 1987 [1588], 2:143–51).[49] The Councils of Lima established various penalties: flogging for those accused of disinterring bodies buried in churches in order to transfer them to the old graves (Vargas Ugarte 1951, 1:20–21), and for those who, in spite of having been baptized, did not go to mass (1:14), or who consulted the native religious specialists.[50] Though, as we have seen, the infliction of physical pain as a pedagogical tool was based on the idea of the Indians' limited ability to understand the negative effects of evil-doing on the soul, it also paved the way for a process that the most virtuous and well-informed considered crucial for the expiation of sins, an essential aspect of the Catholic ritual of death. What connection was there between the Church's recommendations for instructing the Indians in the Christian faith and the form that the practice of this assumed? When we examine the teaching of the Christian ritual of death to the Indians, we will note the central role assigned to bodily and spiritual pain.

The Christian Ritual of Death

Although the Church began from an early date to deal with the problem of burial places, commemorative rites, and sacrifices, the question of how the individual was treated in the last moments of life remained vague for several decades. The *Instrucción* that Bishop Loayza wrote in 1545 gives priority to the initial teaching and to baptism: it indicates in very general terms that the fate of the body and the soul after death had to be explained to the Indians, but it does not mention the administering of the last rites (Vargas Ugarte 1951, 2:147). We find something similar in the decree of the First Council of Lima (1551–1552): it states that the funeral rites for baptized Indians included the same ceremonies as those for all Christians, but it gives very few details (1951, 1:20–21). The decree also stipulates that the parish priests should not allow mourning to be prolonged for more than a day, and that they should ascertain the identity of the deceased by uncovering his or her face (to ensure that the *caciques* did not continue to be buried in the old graves).

Only in the decrees of the Second Council of Lima (1567) is there any attempt to discuss how the priests should attend the dying; here, the authors mention the difficulties that the priests might encounter, particularly because of language barriers, and they give advice on how to proceed. The priests were reluctant to administer the sacraments of communion and extreme unction to the Indians, which is apparent in the insistence with which the bishops exhorted them not to evade their obligation (Vargas Ugarte 1951, 1:228, 248, 249). There are various explanations for this reluctance: among them, the priests' ignorance of the native languages, which, many of them claimed, prevented them from hearing confession and giving absolution; and uncertainty as to whether the dying person had been baptized due to the lack of ecclesiastical organization that still prevailed at the time. The priests also pleaded the great distances and the miserable roads as obstacles to reaching the houses of the dying. Some also considered that the dwellings of the Indians lacked the appropriate decency and cleanliness for them to carry the viaticum there and administer the last rites.[51] Moreover, an absence of precise instructions as to liturgy explains the priests' resistance.

The decrees of the Second Council of Lima exhorted the priests to confront each one of these difficulties, with instructions that must have aroused doubts as to their propriety and effectiveness. First of all, the bishops ordered that the doctrine be very briefly explained to the Indians and that baptism then be given to whoever should need it. They also stipulated that if the priest did not know the dying person's language, then he must use an interpreter to exhort the sick person to show grief for his or her sins and prepare for confession. The priest must then hear the sick person alone and absolve him or her if, in the act of confession, the dying person had sincerely revealed his or her sins.[52] The Second Council urged the priests not to deny the viaticum to the sick,[53] stating that though ideally the afflicted should come to a church to receive it, in situations where they were unable to do so, the priests must take it to their homes after making sure that the environment be made as seemly as possible (Vargas Ugarte 1951, 1:248).[54] Finally, given the importance of the sacrament of extreme unction in ensuring the salvation of souls, the priests were told not to resist administering it to the dying, in order to protect them from the assault of "the devil and sorcerers" (1:249).

It was a fact acknowledged by every Christian that the moment of death was precisely when the devil would try and take possession of one's soul, by tempting one to resist one's fate, reject pain, and hold fast to one's worldly goods and loved ones (Anonymous 1999 [1479?]; Venegas 1911 [1537], 145–46).[55] For this reason, the presence of the priest and of other persons firm in the faith was indispensable in order to help the dying in the difficult struggle with evil (Venegas 1911 [1537], 138). In the decree of the Second Council, it is significant that sorcerers were added to the figure of the devil as the enemies lying in wait for the dying. Though this is not a radical innovation with respect to the European art of dying well,[56] it indicates the Church's determination to incorporate and combat Andean religious practices and beliefs and to explain them as the work of the devil (Estenssoro 2003).

Though these instructions of the Second Council of Lima show us a Church that is better informed and determined to confront both the obstacles it encounters and the resistance of its own agents, proceedings are not yet systematic. The texts offer advice to guide the parish priests in certain difficult situations, but the liturgy still has not been established. Nearly twenty years later, in 1585, the documents of the Third Council of Lima, invoking the decrees of the previous council, are still insisting that priests administer extreme unction to the Indians. Three decrees (19, 28, and 29) mention assistance to be given to Indians and blacks at the point of death (Vargas Ugarte 1951, 1:330–31, 334). Undoubtedly the objections of the local priests, who complained repeatedly that the Indians' instruction was very limited and questioned their ability to express genuine repentance for their sins, continued unabated. The decrees encourage the priests to be indulgent and not to demand perfection under such trying circumstances, urging them to be content with ascertaining that the dying showed a suitable disposition to repent and manifested their faith according to their limitations.

Acosta censured the attitude of the parish priests who refused to administer extreme unction to those Indians who, as Christians, had every right to receive it (1987 [1588], 2:451).[57] The priests' reluctance led many Indians to resort to native religious specialists, who encouraged them to confess according to their own rituals and to offer sacrifices to their ancient gods (ibid.).[58] We do not find repeated in the decrees of the Third Council the solution offered in the previous one to the problem of priests' ignorance of native languages. Confession heard by a priest who had not understood what the penitent had to say was unacceptable to a considerable sector of the clergy. This is clearly illustrated by the assertion of the Franciscan Luis Jerónimo de Oré (1992 [1598], 198), who echoed the position of the Cuzco diocesan synod of 1591.[59] Supported by his solid reputation as a great expert in the Indian languages and invoking the period's most popular writers of treatises on conscience, he stated that those who administered confession without knowing the language of the dying person were committing a deadly sin.[60]

The Third Council of Lima produced a body of pastoral documents and directions for administering confession, the viaticum, and extreme unction to the dying, thus filling the liturgical gap that had characterized the previous period. It thus reasserted one of the objectives established by the Council of Trent concerning the sacramental character of extreme unction and the assistance that the priest must give to the dying (Martínez Gil 1993, 310–14; Rey Hazas 2003b, xx). The Third Council prepared two documents containing advice for dying well: a short one to be used in the more difficult cases, and a longer and more detailed one. They were supplemented by a sermon devoted to explaining the sacrament of extreme unction, and all were published in Spanish, Quechua, and Aymara. They were inspired by the *Ars Moriendi,* which had been circulating in Spain since the fifteenth century, and had multiplied significantly since the Council of Trent (Martínez Gil 1993, 36–40, 643–48; Morel D'Arleux 1993, 727–28). The bishops and theologians of the Third Council wanted to make widely available a similar, simple handbook based on the principles formulated at Trent, which emphasized the sacraments and aimed at unifying beliefs and encouraging reformation.

The *Exhortación breve* (Brief exhortation)[61] starts out by discussing the solitude and danger in which the individual finds him- or herself when facing death. The solitude described is not an absence of people, but rather the awareness that no one can help the dying to change his or her fate: the fate of the soul depends on the individual alone. Here the figure of the priest is crucial, since he acts as an adviser, a doctor, and a representative of God.[62] The priest was expected to urge the dying person to invoke the name of Jesus Christ in an attitude of repentance for any sins committed. Without any allusion to the eternal suffering awaiting those who do not repent, confess, and beg forgiveness for their sins, fear is instilled in the opening pages by the description of the dying person's helplessness in the face of death, and thus the need for the priest's presence. Also included is a brief summary of the Passion of Christ—a topic that every Christian had to consider at the hour of death—and a brief examination of the articles of the faith (*Doctrina Christiana* 1985 [1585], 287). These steps aim to lead the dying to show grief and remorse for their sins, to implore the forgiveness and protection of Christ and the Virgin Mary, and to pledge their service to God, should their life be spared. The *Exhortación breve* closes with the priest's prayer that God may accept the dying person's prayers and bear his or her soul to its place of rest.

This text, intended to serve as a guide in dire circumstances, outlines some elements of the Christian ritual of death, such as confession, but it does not mention extreme unction. For the sick to receive this sacrament, it was essential that they should be in full possession of their faculties; otherwise, the ritual was invalidated, so that at the first sign of loss of consciousness, it had to be suspended (Venegas 1911 [1537], 137).[63] Nor does the *Exhortación breve* contain any reference to the devil or to other figures that usually served to identify the Andean context. In this sense the text resembles those that circulated in Spain for the same purpose, although here there is no mention of angels attending the dying person (Anonymous 1999 [1479?])—the priest, God, and the Virgin Mary are the only help. In such a brief document, there is little space to describe the punishments awaiting those who do not give up their souls to God; repentance, in the *Exhortación breve,* involves showing contrition for sin rather than anticipating the horrors of hell (Delumeau 1990, 57–70).

The *Otra exhortación más larga* (Other, longer exhortation) is a detailed explanation of the steps to follow in preparing for death, and it seeks with great effectiveness to produce the emotions and ideas that Christian Indians were to express in their last moments. Moreover, the care taken in defining the ritual sequence suggests that it was mainly conceived as a guide for the priests in charge of administering the last rites.[64] It begins by explaining confession, emphasizing its necessity and usefulness while warning of the dreadful consequences that can result from leaving any sin unrevealed. Once the dying have settled their accounts with God, they are urged to restore to its rightful owners whatever property they may have taken and to make a will; the text also explains what relatives were entitled to inherit, and it mentions the importance of providing alms for the soul's benefit and for that of the poor. The passage on communion is addressed both to those who receive the sacrament and to the priests who administer it, and the text mentions the latter's objections to carrying the viaticum to the sick, whose home is described as "a vile hut" and its occupant as a "poor little sinner." In spite of their condition, they are visited by "so high a Lord," present in the Blessed Sacrament (*Doctrina Christiana* 1985 [1585], 294). This passage stresses the necessary humility and undeniable littleness of the Indians as well as the condescending and guiding role of the priests.

With extreme unction, the threshold separating the dying from those who remain in this world is effectively crossed. Following the text of the Council of Trent, the Greater Catechism explains that extreme unction is given "in order to cleanse the soul from sin, and strengthen it in its last pangs against the temptations of the enemy, and also to give health to the body, should this be for its good" (*Doctrina*

Christiana 1985 [1585], 124–25).[65] This sacrament, in which the parts of the body representing the five senses liable to sin—eyes, ears, nose, mouth, and hands—are anointed with consecrated oil, is the means by which whatever traces of sin might have remained in the soul after confession are erased. Its originally curative purpose had long been relegated to the background, but it remains in the texts of the sixteenth century in the conditional mode.[66] Sermon 17, for example, states that the recovery of the sick person's health will depend on his or her living in the service of God (539). In contrast with the *Exhortación breve*, the *Otra exhortación más larga* and the sermon that explains extreme unction have been adapted to the cultural reality of the Andes: the confession of faith is accompanied by a rejection of the devil—who fosters the revival of past customs and beliefs—and of the help of *guacas* and sorcerers (298, 544, 547), presented in these texts as sources of deceit.

To draw an effective analogy, the Greater Catechism recounts the Old Testament story of King Ahaziah. Wishing to ascertain whether he would survive an illness afflicting him as the result of a fall, he resorted to an oracle or pagan deity whom the authors of the sermon decide to call *guaca*. For consulting this deity, he was punished with eternal fire (*Doctrina Christiana* 1985 [1585], 547). (The corresponding biblical text is 2 Kings, 1:1–18.) The discussion of the dangers lying in wait for those who find themselves in the throes of death thus takes on a somewhat different coloring from the European texts. Whereas the Spanish arts of dying well showed the moment of death as a battle in which the devil struggles to get possession of the dying person's soul, in the material published by the Third Council of Lima the damnation of the soul takes on a particularly generational,[67] or, we might say, historical dimension, because the return to the past, whether through memory or ritual acts, entails the ruin of the soul.

These three pastoral documents do not explain everything that a Christian needed to know. The texts assure us that with sufficient preparation, the soul's inevitable destination is heaven. For those who do not meet the necessary conditions, there would seem to be no possibility of salvation. The texts that directly discuss the sacrament of extreme unction do not contemplate unfinished or intermediate situations, and for this reason there is no place in them for explanations of purgatory. The Council of Lima left the explanation of the body and soul's final destination to the sermon on death.[68]

The *Sermón 30 de los Novísimos,* or the Four Last Things—death, judgment, hell (or purgatory), and heaven (*Doctrina Christiana* 1985 [1585], 732–53)—insists, from a slightly different angle to the guidance for dying well, on the need for an adequate preparation for death and eternal salvation. The emphasis here is not on the moments that immediately precede death but on life itself, and the sermon brings to bear the Church's whole doctrinal strength.[69] In the first part we find all the great themes of Christianity, particularly purgatory, which is cautiously explained in terms that the local population could understand because they are linked to existing Andean beliefs. The second part uses the parable of the rich man and the beggar Lazarus (Luke 16:19–31) to illustrate how certain ways of life may lead either to glory or to eternal damnation; this continues a very old tradition within the Church when explaining the fate of men after death (Le Goff 1984). The sermon culminates with an exhortation to convert in order to attain salvation.

The *Sermón 30 de los Novísimos* begins by introducing the general topic of death, which comes equally to all human beings,[70] and whose unexpectedness requires that men live in a constant state of preparation (*Doctrina Christiana* 1985 [1585], 734). When the text mentions the vanity of this world and the futility of earthly possessions, it is referring to the funeral offerings that the Andeans placed in the tombs of powerful people; it also emphasizes the admonition that, since bodies decay, souls do not require material sustenance (735–36). After stressing the importance of adequate preparation for death, the sermon warns that if any spot should remain on the soul as a result of its not having fully expiated its sins—something few people could be certain of having done—the soul will then be sent to purgatory, where they are purified with fire in order to meet the conditions for finally entering heaven.[71]

This powerful image very effectively introduces the mutual solidarity that should exist between the dead and the living, since the latter have the critical responsibility of shortening the souls' stay in purgatory. The living have to help the dead with prayers, alms, good works, and especially masses. All of these things, the sermon explains, together with offerings of wheat, rams, and wax, when they are given in the name of the deceased, are received by God "as if the deceased themselves had made these offerings, for by the charity and love of God all Christians are one, and therefore they may help each other" (*Doctrina Christiana* 1985 [1585], 743–44). Thus, the Church expresses the compromise it had reached with the custom—we might even call it the need—of leaving offerings in the tombs. This went hand in hand with the construction of a more unified discourse concerning the fate of the dead. There is ample evidence that the idea of purgatory had been preached in the Andes before the Third Council of Lima,[72] but, as with other aspects of the doctrine, uncertainty and ambiguity prevailed as far as contents and liturgy were concerned. Almost two decades earlier, a decree of the Second Council instructed parish priests not to allow kin to put cooked food on the graves, so as not to foster the idea that the dead actually consumed it (Vargas Ugarte 1951, 1:253);[73] another decree of the same period stated that, while the priests were to encourage their parishioners to make offerings on the feast days of the living and the dead, these offerings must not consist of rams, live oxen, or sacks of wheat, but only wine, wax, and bread (1:230).[74] This compromise is understandable, because in order to encourage people to bury their dead in the churches, they had to be allowed to perform certain rituals on the graves in homage and memory of the deceased. Moreover, any priest imbued with the spirit of the Counter-Reformation was aware that offerings to the dead were an indispensable part of the distinctively Catholic doctrine concerning purgatory.

The sermon proved to be highly effective at presenting principles very dear to Catholic doctrine that could be appropriated by the Andean population; its adaptability was clear from its success in both Europe and the Andes. It emphasized the mutual dependence between the living and the dead while clearly establishing the sacred nature of this bond. It asserted, moreover, that this relationship could give rise to a community with common interests and goals, whose durability depended on the living, but which the dead—the *ánimas* in purgatory—would repay with interest. These circumstances suggest that we are not faced with the clear opposition between "praying to the dead" and "praying for the dead," which would distinguish the pagan attitude from the Christian one (Le Goff 1984), since the relationship between the two groups is more active and complex. Rather than the severe punishments described in the *Sermón 30 de los Novísimos* in abundant detail in its final section about hell, it was very probably the doctrine of purgatory that turned out to be most convincing for the people of the Andes. Unlike Le Goff's argument for Europe (1984, 5), they may not have needed to believe first in the immortality of the soul or in the resurrection of the flesh in order to accept the idea of purgatory.[75]

One point remains: where do the dead go? As we saw before, several sources leave this question open. Cieza de León (1984b [1553], First Part, chap. 101, 126) wrote that dead nobles, richly adorned in their burial clothes, would appear to their people in the fields to tell them that they were living a pleasant life because they had received the proper care—but he does not specify where they went next.[76] The commentaries of Polo de Ondegardo (1982 [1585], 450) indicate that the Andeans believed that souls who had not been cared for by their relatives were obliged to wander throughout this world, but he does not mention the dwelling-place of those who experienced no difficulties. These images are in contrast with the more precise ones we find some years later in the *Manuscript of Huarochirí* (Taylor 1999, 359–63), in the work of Felipe Guaman Poma de Ayala (1989 [1615], 294), and in that of Pablo Josef de Arriaga (1968 [1621], 220), the author of the most detailed treatise on Andean idolatry. The *Manuscript of Huarochirí* tells of the return of the soul, in the guise of a fly, to its *pacarina*, or sacred place of origin (Taylor 1999, 359). According to Guaman Poma, the people of the Andes believed that the dead returned to their places of origin, once their relatives had completed the proper rituals, and enjoyed a period of solace during which they conversed with other dead persons.[77] At the end of this period came a cycle of punishment in which they had to bear "very great labor, hunger, thirst and cold and . . . very great heat," which their relatives alleviated by bringing offerings. Guaman Poma does not say where the dead underwent this period of anguish, so similar to the Christian purgatory. As for Arriaga, he asserts that it was widely believed among the inhabitants of the *sierra* that the dead went to a place called Upamarca, "silent land or land of the silent," and that before arriving there, they had to cross a river by a narrow bridge made of hair. Arriaga adds that other peoples, among them some of the coastal populations, believed that after death, human beings returned to their *guacas* or places of origin.

These accounts, dating from the end of the sixteenth and the early seventeenth centuries, indicate a process of transformation of various local ideas, perhaps because of their interaction with the preaching of Christianity. Without wishing to suggest that there can only be one source for the mention of the bridge, we must remember that this image appears from a very early date in Christian accounts of the soul's journey into the hereafter (Le Goff 1984, 94; Gurevich 1992, 72–73, 79), and that it was also represented in Christian iconography, as in the Indian parish of Andahuaylillas in Cuzco (Mesa and Gisbert 1982, 1: plate 41). In contrast to the cohabitation suggested by pre-Hispanic ideas, the gap between the dead and the living had widened, making it necessary to conceive of precise spaces to which the dead depart or return,[78] while their material needs, attended to by the living, were gradually replaced by the suffering required for the expiation of sins, a process also needing the help of the living.

The apparently simple program sketched out at the beginning of this chapter actually involved a very long and complex process of change and adaptation. The rites related to death that Christianity brought to the Andes required that a whole series of conditions be met before they could become established. To understand the scope of this process, we need to look beyond what was stipulated in the doctrine and the regulations of the Councils of Lima.[79] A series of organizational measures was essential to the wider colonial project. The transfer of graves from their customary sites to the churches made it necessary to reorganize the space occupied both by the dead and the living. This significant measure went hand in hand with the organization of the population at various levels: villages and towns, parishes and confraternities. The introduction of new ideas about the body and the soul required the creation of institutions such as hospitals as well as the dissemination of devotional practices and associations that helped to spread and domesticate these principles. In short, places, methods, and institutions needed to be established to ensure that a significant portion of the native population would be instructed in the Christian doctrine and way of death. The colonial cities were the spaces from which these changes spread. We will now focus our attention on them.

| **Spaces and Institutions
for the Missionary Project**

Enacting policies to implement the missionary project required defining the spaces, institutions, and methods of reaching the native Andeans. Following age-old European and Spanish precedents, colonial
and ecclesiastical authorities exhorted the Indians to live "politically"
in the belief that cities provided the ideal space in which human
beings could be governed adequately and live in order and harmony.[1]
Hence, the Spanish colonial project was conspicuously characterized
by the development of urban life (Farriss 1984, 160).

The concentration of often-scattered native populations into urban
settlements was intended to make the teaching of the Christian doctrine easier, separate the Indians from their sacred places, and disrupt
the continuity of their religious practices. The spatial reorganization
brought about by the founding of towns and villages was accompanied by the creation of territorial districts and institutions that had
manifold objectives and effects. The new urban centers were divided,
in their turn, into parishes, whose work of spiritual administration was
complemented by the creation of hospitals. The purpose of these establishments was not only to provide health care and practice charity
but also to generate and preserve the social order. Both in the most
important cities of the Peruvian viceroyalty and in the lower-ranking
towns and villages, the parishes and the Indian hospitals were usually
a single institution from which the conversion of the native population was promoted. Finally, the confraternities—associations devoted
to the worship of a particular devotion (that is, saint, relic, or religious

image) in the parish and convent churches—were influential in re-organizing the political and ritual activities of the local populations. These institutions were crucial to the teaching and promotion of Christian ideas about death: the parish and convent churches became mandatory places of burial; and the hospitals diffused ideas about the body, health, and the Christian art of dying well, while an essential part of the confraternities' mission was attending the funerals of their members and commemorating the deceased.

The creation of appropriate spaces in which the Indians might learn, as José de Acosta wished, to be "first men and then Christians," entailed the removal of the native populations to settlements known as *reducciones*.[2] These organized most of the existing Spanish-occupied towns and villages throughout the territories according to a checker-board pattern whose symmetrical shape instilled in the minds of their inhabitants the principles of order and control.[3]

The founding of urban centers in the Andes followed the advance of the first conquistadors, with a handful of inhabitants, as in the case of Piura (1532), or indicated the space from which territory threatened by Indian rebellions would be defended, as with the city of San Juan de la Frontera in Huamanga (1539). In contrast to the *reducciones*, set up to relocate the Indian population once a reasonably well-organized colonial apparatus had developed, by the end of the 1560s the first colonial cities primarily housed Spaniards, who owned *encomiendas* and were seeking a location adapted to their economic and communication needs; these cities were for military defense at a time when the conquest was far from being consolidated. Lima (1535) is an example. The politically important city of Cuzco, however, is a different case because its existence preceded the conquest; hence, its "refounding" by Francisco Pizarro in 1534 in an act of symbolic appropriation (Esquivel y Navia 1980, 1:86). Its Spanish residents constituted a small but powerful group in this city inhabited by a mostly Indian population, whose leading members were descended from the Inca rulers. It is clear, then, that the common principle inspiring the creation of the urban centers took shape according to different itineraries, whose characteristics and significance for the project of religious conversion we need to identify and understand.

To study how the policies formulated for Christianizing death in the Andes were put into practice, I will focus on the cities of Lima and Cuzco, the two most important urban centers of the Peruvian viceroyalty. I will show that the distribution and occupation of space entailed by the creation of the parishes expressed the circumstances of the cities' inhabitants, reasserting and modifying the bonds among them. These social bonds, in their turn, gave a particular character to the institutions—hospitals and confraternities—established to teach the Christian ways of confronting disease and death, assisting and accompanying the dead, commemorating their memory, and caring for the salvation of their souls.

Parishes, Occupation of Space, and Control of the Population

In 1572 Viceroy Francisco de Toledo issued in the small locality of Checacupe a series of ordinances for the government of the city of Cuzco.[4] These stressed the importance of the city as the best possible vantage point from which to promote the conversion of the Indians; they also highlighted the role of the parishes in this plan. The latter, especially from the reforms of the Council of Trent onward, made the presence of the Church and the power of the state palpable in people's lives throughout the Catholic world, whatever their condition (Hsia 1998, 55–56). The parish was the territorial and institutional unit that organized the most significant events in the lives of a city's inhabitants: where the main religious ceremonies marking the different stages of life were carried out as well as the public events that, to a great extent, constituted the heartbeat of a city.[5]

In his ordinances, the viceroy recalled that the city's first parishes were organized around the discovery of shrines, religious objects, and the bodies of several Inca rulers (Toledo 1986, 1:201–2). Many of his ambitious reforms had their origin in changes introduced before his arrival in Peru in 1569. In 1559, when the *licenciado* Ondegardo was commissioned by the government to mark out the limits of the first Cuzco parishes, inquiries made into the organization of existing sacred spaces turned up considerable information about the system of shrines and their respective resources, centered on the temple of the sun, known as the Coricancha. Knowledge of this *ceques* system[6] must have influenced the way in which the new urban districts of the Inca capital were conceived. Though one of the objectives pursued with the creation of the new parishes was to remove the Andean inhabitants from their sacred places, this was not, indeed, achieved. The fact that the Inca shrines coincided with the sites chosen by the then *corregidor* of Cuzco for the new parishes follows a logic that links them (Bauer 2000; Julien 1998).[7] Since, however, this reorganization of the sacred space had, in its turn, to adjust to unequal processes of territorial occupation and distribution of resources, population, and power that had been underway since the Spanish occupation of Cuzco, the correspondence between the old temples and the parish churches could not be exact. The project also depended on other actors and circumstances.[8]

As in other areas of the New World, from the very beginning of the Spanish presence in Peru the religious orders took charge of the teaching of Christianity to the native population.[9] Julien (1998, 82) shows how the population of Cuzco was shared out among the friars, whose custom was to assemble the native inhabitants of the city at the doors of their convents in order to expound the doctrine to them. From a very early date, the religious orders had taken possession of places that had great religious and political significance for the Indians: the friars of Santo Domingo, in 1534, occupied the Coricancha, the city's main temple, while the Franciscans took up temporary residence in Cassana, one of the most impressive palaces of the Inca capital, which also contained two *guacas*.[10] During this long period, it is likely that bonds and even alliances formed between the native population of Cuzco and the religious orders, in which the Indian nobles and notables would have played a decisive role.[11] Since it was not enough that the friars should preach to those already willing to listen, they had to conceive and implement strategies for persuading their audience. The wide scope of their proselytizing and educational activities and their use of existing sacred spaces were crucial in this endeavor and set up patterns that are detectable many years later.

The organization of the parishes, which Ondegardo undertook in 1559 at the command of the viceroy, disrupted not only the preconquest system but also the precarious order established over the approximately twenty-five years of war and anarchy, when different factions struggled to achieve hegemony over the city and its precincts (Julien 1998, 84).[12] The decision to organize the Cuzco parishes signals a decisive moment in the reconceptualization of space and power in the city. The instructions issued by Viceroy Hurtado de Mendoza seem to criticize both the religious orders and the powerful *encomenderos* in their teaching of the doctrine.[13] The viceroy states that in Cuzco there was a population of more than twenty thousand Indians, some of them *encomendados* and others "free," whose conversion would only be achieved once parishes were created in their districts (Esquivel y Navia 1980, 1:198).

Ondegardo was commissioned to supervise the building of a church in each neighborhood, where the Christian doctrine was to be preached to the Indians. Thus, five parish churches were founded in Cuzco, all of them, according to Bauer (2000), in the vicinity or actually on the site of some Inca shrine. Santa Ana, on the crest of a hill in the neighborhood called Carmenca, in the north of the city, took the place of a shrine called Marcatampu (Bauer 2000, 73). San Cristóbal was established in Colcampata, a shrine located on another of the hills surrounding the city, where Paullo Inca had founded a hermitage.[14] San Blas was built in the Tococachi or Toctocachi quarter, where there was a temple to the thunder (136–37).[15] San Sebastián, to the south of Cuzco at Cachipampa, was erected on the site of an ancient shrine called Colcapampa.[16] And finally, the parish church consecrated to Nuestra Señora de Belén, known originally as Los Reyes, was established on the site called Cayocachi or Cayaocache, which was associated with eight shrines.[17]

In the following years, the population of the city increased considerably, mainly as a consequence of migrations from the surrounding areas (Wightman 1990). This obliged the Spanish authorities to mark out new districts. In 1572, when Viceroy Toledo carried out his inspection visit of the territory, to promote the Indian *reducciones*,[18] three more parishes were created: one adjoining the native hospital, consecrated to Nuestra Señora de los Remedios; another dedicated to the Apostle James and a third to Saint Jerome.[19] Except for the latter, which remained the responsibility of the Dominicans, all the parishes were put under the control of the secular clergy. It is no surprise that the religious orders should have united in opposition to the decisions that undermined their past accomplishments and threatened their influence for the future. In 1561, representatives of the regular clergy expressed their dissatisfaction with these measures and demanded that they should be put in control of the parishes (Barriga 1933–1954, 2:235–40; Julien 1998; Esquivel y Navia 1980, 1:198). There is evidence that friars took to the pulpit to defend their cause: the following year the *corregidor* summoned the priors of Santo Domingo, San Francisco, and San Agustín to notify them of a provision of the Real Audiencia that ordered preachers to restrict their sermons to matters of doctrine and not mention questions of government.[20] The friars' efforts did not bear fruit, and they were obliged to recognize that henceforward the secular clergy would play the main role in caring for the souls of Cuzco's inhabitants.[21] However, they continued to be active and influential among the local population.

We must now leave the Inca capital behind and turn to Lima. After founding the city of Jauja, in the central sierra, and occupying it for a short time, the conquistadors led by Francisco Pizarro, arguing that the site presented difficulties in communication, supplies, and defense, decided to remove to the coast (Rostworowski 1978, 73–74). They chose the lands of the *cacique* of Lima for the new city. Politically, the Valley of Lima was broken up into separate *cacicazgos*, or chiefdoms, confederated in the province of Ychsma under the leadership of the *cacique* of Pachacamac (Lowry 1991, 59; Rostworowski 1978, 51–52).[22] This must have facilitated the Spanish occupation as well as the early removal of the native population to marginal zones.[23] Documents such as the acts of the city's founding or the minutes of the town council's meetings give the impression that the conquistadors simply ignored the local population and its authorities.[24]

The collaboration of the *cacique* of Lima with the conquistadors in their occupation of his dominions was taken by the Spaniards as a license to appropriate larger and larger parcels of land. This process was made easier by a demographic crisis in the area,[25] and the local population seem to have been especially vulnerable to hunger, violence, disease, and the loss of livelihood caused by contact with the Europeans. When we read the sources describing the founding of Lima and the building of its churches, convents, and parishes, the scarcity of information about its inhabitants and their sacred places is striking: it seems as if the conquistadors were acting upon a space practically devoid of political and religious meanings. Francisco Pizarro's first gesture was to lay the foundations of what would become the cathedral. Later, the plots for the houses of the conquistadors and other Spaniards were assigned, a process that continued, taking land from the local population, in the following years.[26]

The founding of parishes in Lima responded to the gradual increase in population and, in contrast to Cuzco, it was not guided by an integral project for organizing the city. Some were created as a partial response to the need to efficiently administer a fluctuating Indian population and, more generally, to subordinate social groups that were ethnically diverse. The oldest jurisdiction was the parish of the Iglesia Mayor, also known as the parish of the Sagrario. Some years later, in 1554, San Sebastián was founded (Cobo 1935 [1639?], 197) on lands previously known as Chuntay, where the colonial authorities established the residence of Don Gonzalo, the *cacique* of Lima (Rostworowski 1978, 82). In 1571, Viceroy Toledo, as part of his inspection visit, issued an order from the city of Cuzco for the founding of the *reducción* and Indian parish of Santiago de El Cercado, which was put under the control of the Society of Jesus (Cobo 1935 [1639?], 126). This is where the population of the then-marginal quarter of San Lázaro came to settle. El Cercado housed immigrant Indians as well as the villagers around Lima who came to the city periodically to work and meet the obligations of the *mita*[27] and the tribute, to sell their goods, or to appear before the viceregal authorities. The *barrio* (neighborhood) of El Cercado was conceived as the ideal urban development, whose inhabitants would be safe from contact with Spaniards, mestizos, and blacks; the colonial functionaries considered, besides, that the internal organization of the *barrio* should preserve the divisions and hierarchies that structured Indian society. For this purpose, they assigned specific sectors according to the inhabitants' province of origin or ethnic group.[28]

About ten years after El Cercado was founded, the authorities created three more parishes, thus indicating the extent of the migrations to Lima from within and without the viceroyalty as well as the increased presence of the secular clergy in the life of its inhabitants. In 1579, Santa Ana, a church adjoining an Indian hospital of the same name, whose existence dates from the end of the 1540s, was promoted to the rank of parish church (Cobo 1935 [1639?], 199–200).

Rostworowski (1978, 72) states that it was built on the site of Lima's main *guaca*, which might explain why Santa Ana was from the time of its beginnings a center for the promotion of conversion. The population increase in the parishes of Sagrario and San Sebastián led in 1584 to the creation of a new parish, San Marcelo. And finally, even though, when the parish of El Cercado was created, the viceregal authorities attempted to suppress the *barrio* of San Lázaro by the forced removal of those people who had settled there,[29] there was little they could do to prevent new arrivals in Lima from choosing it as their home. The population of this *barrio*, made up not only of Indians but also of blacks, mestizos, and poorer Spaniards, increased considerably: as a result, in 1626, San Lázaro was promoted to the rank of a parish (Cobo 1935 [1639?], 203).

With the creation of Indian villages or *reducciones* in the areas around Lima, small urban centers were established where the former chieftains of the region took up residence.[30] In their respective studies of the Lima valley's Indian population, Charney (1989, 58–66) and Lowry (1991, 62–64) examine in detail the processes of population removal to the new *reducciones* and the successive changes in land ownership that resulted. These transformations in the Lima valley and the city of Cuzco did not take place without conflict between the colonial and ecclesiastical authorities at different levels. The viceroy, the archbishop, the religious orders, the secular clergy, and the city's inhabitants often clashed in attempts to assert their control over the native population. The original inhabitants also protested against the spoliations and forced removals, while the Indians arriving from other places in search of better living conditions did whatever they could to reach their goal. The parishes were of primary importance in determining the Indians' right to reside in one place or another and in recognizing their local authorities: acknowledging, for example, which representatives of the Church were in charge of teaching the doctrine and administering the sacraments. This was not only an issue of how the native population established itself in these new spaces in obedience to the government and to the Church, but also of how it appropriated them. The situation became especially complex in light of the shifting character of the Indian population in the city and its surrounding areas.

A drawn-out lawsuit that in the seventeenth century opposed the priests of the parish of Santa Ana and the Society of Jesus, who were in charge of the parish of El Cercado, illustrates this complex process. The litigating parties debated before the viceroy and the archbishop about the rights of their respective jurisdictions and about whether, considering the mobility of the inhabitants, new spaces should be provided for the teaching of the doctrine, or whether the population should be incorporated into the existing jurisdictions. In their plea, the priests of Santa Ana maintained that they could tend to the spiritual needs of the Indians working on the outskirts of the city, in chapels in the jurisdictions known as Ate, Manchay, and Cieneguilla. The Jesuits argued that teaching the doctrine to the Indians was their prerogative, because many were their parishioners, although they had settled on the outskirts of the city with their wives, families, slaves, and servants, and from this distance did not attend mass or sermons in El Cercado. No doubt exaggerating the grave consequences of these small migrations, the fathers of the Society of Jesus assured their audience that things had come to such a pass that there was no one "to whom to preach in the aforementioned village [El Cercado]," and that the Indians who failed to attend sermons were now fallen into idleness, while others worked the lands that they rented from the Spaniards. In the eyes of the Jesuits, this was an example of the well-known case of Indians who fled the *reducciones* in order to escape the benefits of a "civilized" life under the control of the authorities and a proper administration of their spiritual life.[31]

After several years of litigation, the *corregidor* of El Cercado, Don Diego Mesia de Zúñiga, found it necessary to visit the Indians of the valley. In his report to the viceroy in 1632, he describes Lima's native population: "I have found many who do not know how to pray and others who do not know how to make the sign of the cross, and many of them . . . for years have not been to confession nor to mass because they are under no priest nor know any parish."[32] The passage is not very flattering to the litigating parties; it also bears eloquent witness to the limited control that the authorities exercised over the native population at the very center of viceregal power.

It seems that the bonds that the priests of Santa Ana had established with the local population of the contested zone—including

Indian laborers and landowners—made them a good deal more flexible than the Jesuits.[33] In effect, the priests of Santa Ana proposed to go to wherever the immigrant Indians found themselves, holding masses on the outskirts of the city, in the chapels of landowners with whom they had already come to an agreement. In his report, the *corregidor* recommended that the order originally imposed by Archbishop Loayza and subsequently confirmed by his successor, which designated the floating population of Lima to be parishioners of Santa Ana, should not be disrupted. For the Indians to make the trip to the parish churches in the city in order to hear mass, explained the *corregidor,* meant temporarily abandoning their work in the fields. (It is possible that the landowners who employed the Indians as farm laborers expressed this concern.) The representatives of the Indians maintained that it was not in their interest to acknowledge the parish jurisdiction of El Cercado, because this meant subjecting themselves to the authorities of the parish, who demanded the payment of contributions that were considered unlawful by the Indians of the areas around Lima.[34] They rejected the Jesuits' attempts to force them to settle in the *reducción* of El Cercado, because this was a threat to their livelihoods, and they also insisted that they were parishioners of Santa Ana. With the support of their priests and the *corregidor's* approval, they requested and obtained the right to have their own authorities to represent them.

It is not clear how or when the suit was resolved, or even if it ever was, but the decision to make elastic the boundaries of the *reducción* was a solution that the Jesuits denounced tenaciously throughout most of the seventeenth century. The court case between the secular clergy and the Society of Jesus illustrates the delicate balance on which the structure of the city's parishes rested as well as the high degree of mobility and autonomy that much of the Indian population of Lima enjoyed. Alliances with other actors—landowners and, particularly, priests—and the differences of opinion among ecclesiastical and government sectors proved very useful in achieving this. Given that it combined the functions of parish church and hospital, Santa Ana was especially important for the Indian population of Lima. Moreover, the church enjoyed a particular prestige because of its location on the site of Lima's ancient *guaca,* a fact with which Archbishop Loayza must have been well acquainted. Its importance is further illustrated by the fact that Don Gonzalo, the *cacique* of Lima, though a resident of the parish of San Sebastián, went to mass in Santa Ana.[35]

Contrary to what might be expected, Santa Ana was not an exclusively Indian parish.[36] The demographic transformations of the city soon brought about changes to its founder's original project. In 1619 an account by the archbishop of Lima to the crown indicated that 45 percent of the church-going population of Santa Ana was black and 41 percent Spanish, while the Indians only represented 7 percent (Lissón 1946, 5: no. 25, 250).[37] Nevertheless, the parish's ritual and missionary activity contradicted these figures. Santa Ana employed two priests who were fluent in Quechua; and in the seventeenth century, two Indian confraternities founded in this parish were very active, with the participation both of indigenous authorities from the Lima valley and of artisans and marketwomen who had achieved relative prosperity in the city. Thus, the priests of Santa Ana maintained contact with the different strata of the native population, while at the same time establishing links with the new arrivals and the temporary inhabitants of the city and its surrounding areas. These priests also formed connections with those settlers who rose in social standing in the viceregal capital, which explains their willingness to accommodate the different living conditions of their parishioners.

Indian Hospitals

The spatial organization involved in the creation of the parishes was complemented by the founding of hospitals which, in the case of those devoted to the care of the Indians (as at Santa Ana), usually adjoined the parish churches. The Indian hospitals were intended not only to treat the native population's illnesses but also to reform their lives and convert them to Christianity. This is very similar to the role assigned to hospitals in Spain during the same period and reinforced during the reign of Philip II and the Counter-Reformation (Arrizabalaga 1999; Grell et al. 1999; Martz 1983; Pullan 1999). While in Spain the purpose of the hospitals was to tend to the poor, the vagabonds, and the beggars whose existence, or so it was believed, threatened

Lima circa 1630

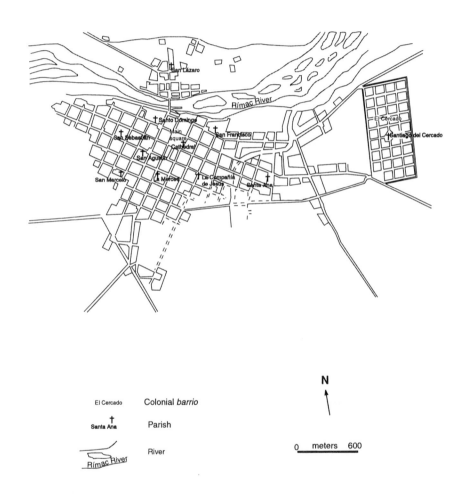

El Cercado   Colonial *barrio*

† Santa Ana   Parish

Rímac River   River

N

0   meters   600

G. Ramos and E. Mesclier 2001

Source: Günther and Lohmann 1992: 124.

Cuzco circa 1600

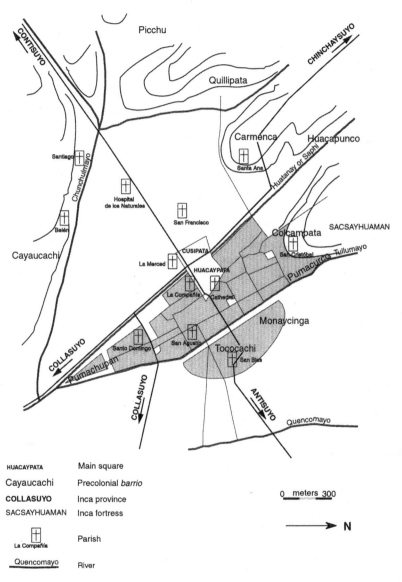

HUACAYPATA	Main square
Cayaucachi	Precolonial *barrio*
COLLASUYO	Inca province
SACSAYHUAMAN	Inca fortress
La Compañía (parish symbol)	Parish
Quencomayo	River

0   meters 300

→ N

G. Ramos and E. Mesclier 2001

Source: Azevedo 1982: 35.

the physical and spiritual security of the cities, in the Andes the persona of the poor was identified with that of the Indian.[38] Examining both the concepts that supported the creation of the hospitals and the effects of their application will help us to understand how the ecclesiastical and civil powers interacted in the slippery spheres of charity, social control, and religious conversion.

The Indian hospitals developed differently in Lima and Cuzco, something that highlights the contrasts in the makeup and strategies of the local elites. In 1548, Archbishop Jerónimo de Loayza founded the hospital of Santa Ana in the city of Lima, thus defeating the attempts of the city's *vecinos* (town councilors), who had from an early date tried to take the initiative.[39] In Cuzco, on the other hand, the town council took charge of founding the Indian hospital in 1556.[40] This illustrates the forceful presence of the Dominican prelate of the Lima diocese, who forged a lasting bond between the Church and the native population. In Cuzco, where most of the *encomenderos* of the Peruvian viceroyalty lived,[41] the town council made the Indian hospital into one of the instruments of their opposition both to ecclesiastical interference and to that of Lima's Real Audiencia (González Pujana 1982, 37). This was made easier by the fact that the see remained vacant for several years, leaving the Cuzco diocese without any leadership comparable to that exercised by Archbishop Loayza and his successor in Lima.

The aims of assistance, conversion, and indoctrination appear very clearly in the first accounts of the hospital of Santa Ana in Lima. The vulnerability of the Indian population to disease and poverty, intensified by the fact that the social networks that might have protected them were weakened or entirely nonexistent for the large migrant population, posed the problem tackled by Archbishop Loayza and his fellow Dominicans. In a letter to the king, dated 1550, Fray Domingo de Santo Tomás mentions that the recently founded hospital of Santa Ana received many Indians arriving in Lima from the sierra. Those who were already Christian could make their confession before dying, while the unbelievers did not leave this world without converting and receiving baptism. A work of charity was thus being accomplished, Fray Domingo insists, because the Indians who died were buried properly, and their bodies were not left as food for the dogs, as was the case for those who expired far away from any care (Lissón 1943, 1: no. 4, 205). In this letter, Fray Domingo bears witness to the impact of the violent changes that the native population was undergoing, and that the Church, whose organization was still very rudimentary, was attempting to confront. He also warns of the consequences of this situation, requesting the attention and support of the crown and explaining the many roles of the hospital: political, sanitary, and ethical. The crown was not indifferent; in fact, comparable conditions—food shortages and epidemics—were experienced periodically in Spain.

During the very years in which the Dominican friar was writing from Lima, the most influential theologians of the time, such as Domingo de Soto, were discussing the responsibilities of the lay authorities and of the Church in the face of poverty, disease, and social disorder (Arrizabalaga 1999; Martz 1983, 26–30; Santolaria Sierra 2003b). From a very early date, the crown was alert to the need to establish hospitals in the New World and showed itself disposed to back various initiatives to do so, whether these came from the Church or from the local citizens (Martz 1983, 64; Olmedo Jiménez 1991, 577). The difficult problem of social welfare, associated with what in today's terminology could be described as public security, found in the hospital the solution that many considered the most appropriate. According to the views of the period, the hospital was the place for treating disease and pain not only of the body but also of the soul. It provided care for those who lacked shelter and food, and it was a place of confinement and rehabilitation for those whose marginal situation made people perceive them as a danger to society (Martz 1983, 67, 87, 144; Henderson 2006; Pullan 1999). Given that conversion and spiritual healing were a priority, it was believed that physical recovery was less important than the soul's salvation. This is why, when discussing the advantages of the Indian hospital, Fray Domingo speaks at length about the conversions and confessions that preceded death,[42] and he explains the hospital's work of beneficence by assuring his reader that the graves of converted Indians would be in consecrated ground.

These ideas, however, were not easily accepted by the intended beneficiaries of this work. The Indians looked with fear and distrust on the practice of confining large numbers of the sick together: seeing that many of them did not leave the hospital alive, they started to call it the "house of the dead." Archbishop Loayza, therefore, in the ordinances that he issued for the administration of the hospital in 1552, gave orders that those patients who had some chance of recovery should be separated from those for whom there was no hope. This measure seemed to respond to the need to make a more favorable impression on the new Christians, rather than to any ideas about contagion or even decency (Lissón 1943, 2: no. 8, 409). The Indians' refusal to go to the hospitals was widespread, and was a cause for concern among the authorities. Years later, when issuing regulations for the Potosí hospital, Viceroy Francisco de Toledo insisted on the need for prompt admittance of the Indians. A better diet, spiritual care, and speedy attention to their illnesses would show them that these institutions were not merely places where one went to die (Toledo 1989, 2:12, 18).

The Indian hospital of Santa Ana was conceived as a center for controlling the behavior of the native population and promoting the teaching of the doctrine, reading and writing, and the education of the *caciques'* children (Olmedo Jiménez 1991, 579). In 1564 the teaching went on in a large room that had been set up in the hospital (584). The adjoining chapel, where mass was said, did not equal the rank of parish church until thirty years after the founding of the hospital, but, as we have seen, it was extremely active long before attaining its new status. The priest of the chapel was in charge of preaching to the Indians in their own language and visiting their homes in the city and the surrounding hamlets, not only to inquire for their health and to carry the sick to the hospital but also to ascertain whether anyone was indulging in "drinking bouts and other public sins" and, if so, to inform the authorities (Lissón 1943, 2: no. 8, 384–85).

Besides the doctrine taught in the hospital, the teaching of the Christian way of dying included instructing the *caciques* and estate owners about the necessity of making a will, in order to name their heirs, draw up an inventory of their property, and give directions for masses to be said for their souls. The priests in charge of assisting the dying were expected to call a scrivener, or, in his absence, to write up the document themselves and later carry it to the archbishop or *provisor*, who was to oversee its execution (Lissón 1943, 2: no. 8, 407).

It is easy to understand how the priests of Santa Ana gained considerable influence over the Indian population of the city and its vicinity, and they firmly believed that the care of the souls of migrant and rootless Indians should also be their prerogative.

Archbishop Loayza did his utmost to ensure that the Church should oversee the work of the hospital. The minutes of the Lima town council indicate, for example, that in the beginning, the hospitals for Spaniards and for Indians were to constitute a single unit. The project was in harmony with the ideas prevailing at the time in Spain concerning the reform of social welfare and the centralization of the hospitals. Nevertheless, when faced with the prospect of having to share the direction of the Indian hospitals with the notables of the city, and of seeing the establishment for Spaniards benefiting from the funds collected for Santa Ana via restitution, Loayza did everything he could to maintain the separation of the two (*Libros de Cabildos de Lima* 1935, 4:343, 465; 5:101, 161, 167). Thus, he personally took over the sponsorship of the hospital, endowed it with goods and decorations,[43] and took up residence there (Cobo 1935 [1639?], 288–91; Olmedo Jiménez 1991, 585). Besides the significant share of influence that Loayza's decision ensured, his actions must also be understood as characteristic of those who, in the context of the Counter-Reformation, had ideological reasons for distrusting the secular administration of charity institutions, which, in the eyes of the clergy, were entirely the responsibility of the Church.[44]

In contrast to Lima, the Cuzco town council, in founding and sponsoring the hospital, ensured a key role for itself in the public exercise of charity (Contreras y Valverde 1983 [1649], 185; Vargas Ugarte 1953, 1:299).[45] Its minutes indicate, moreover, that it added the condition that the ecclesiastical judge would have no right to intervene in its affairs (Esquivel y Navia 1980, 1:180). This was a lasting characteristic of the local elite's strategy in relation to the Cuzco Church and the Lima archbishopric. On the strength of their trusteeship of the hospital, the citizens of Cuzco resisted the authority of the Lima Audiencia. When, in 1637, the *oidor* Andrés de Villela arrived in the city on an inspection tour, the city's attorney general and town council, arguing their rights as founders and trustees, refused him permission to visit the native hospital (Esquivel y Navia 1980, 2:69). In the same vein, and in contrast to what had happened in Lima, the founding of a parish church adjoining the hospital took several years and was the result of a complex process of negotiations between the secular and ecclesiastical authorities. Before the establishment of this church, in response to "the vices and disturbances caused by the Negroes, mulattoes and Indians in the neighborhood of the native hospital" (1:220), it was resolved that the town council would designate a chaplain, to whom the ecclesiastical council would grant a license to administer the sacraments in the hospital's chapel. This transitional solution did not, in fact, happen until 1573.

Although the trusteeship of the Cuzco hospital was not in the hands of the Church, its purpose was not very different from the one in Lima. It was hoped that it would function as a center from which to promote the conversion of the Indians, the practice of charity, and the salvation of the souls of those who were already Christian. For this reason, the town council commissioned two of its members to negotiate the granting of bulls, pardons, and indulgences like those enjoyed by the native hospital in Lima, and to which, in those days, every institution of the same sort aspired (González Pujana 1982, 57–58; Olmedo Jiménez 1991, 585). These promised, to those who paid the appropriate fees, the salvation of the souls of those who died in the hospital. Their distribution became widespread among users of the hospital's services; some members of the local elites even asked to be admitted, so that they could die there and thus become entitled to these favors (Garcilaso de la Vega 1945 [1609], 2: Book 7, chap. 12, 116–17; Toledo 1989, 2:13). In the following years, several highly respected preachers and experts in the Quechua language and culture, such as Fray Luis Jerónimo de Oré (Córdova y Salinas 1957 [1651], chap. 9, 345) and Cristóbal de Molina, were the priests of this parish.

Outside of the more important cities, the creation of hospitals seems to have encountered difficulties and is scantily documented. Whereas the hospitals founded in Lima, Cuzco, La Plata, and Potosí were deemed worthy of the government's attention (Toledo 1986, 1:453–60),[46] those in the Indian parishes struggled for lack of sufficient funding because of the Indians' refusal to use them, and very probably also because the potential staff—local specialists or "healers" and "witch doctors"—were the same people whom the sick would have visited anyway. The money collected for creating and administering these hospitals often ended up in the hands of the *corregidores,* who, the parish priests complained, refused to spend it for its intended purposes.[47] Though part of the tithes as well as of the tribute paid by the Indians (called the *tomín de hospital*) were assigned to founding and maintaining hospitals, very little is known about how this money was directed. In 1585, the priests of the Huaylas region, which belonged to the diocese of Lima, stated that the Indians "died like beasts in the fields" for lack of hospitals where they might be cured.[48] As we know, the theorists of the missionary project had emphasized that to lack all spiritual help in one's last hours meant not dying well. Nevertheless, the priests refused to carry this spiritual help to the homes of the sick. In the same year the vicar of Huaylas, Gutierre de Cárdenas, requested of the Lima archbishop, Toribio Alfonso de Mogrovejo, that so long as there were no decent hospitals, the priests should not be forced to comply with the command to take the viaticum to the sick Indians (Lissón 1943, 3: no. 14, 359).

Practically nothing is known about the functioning, administration, and effectiveness of the hospitals in the Indian parishes. We can deduce from certain ecclesiastical sources that at the local level, cooperative efforts were negotiated for tending to the sick, the poor, and the needy, and that this often involved the participation of the confraternities. The register of diocesan visits (Benito 2006) indicates that the concept of "hospital" and possibly also a building called by this name existed in various localities of the Lima diocese, mostly in the *cabezas de doctrina* (principal seats), although also in less important urban centers and in several other more remote ones. The image emerging from these visits by the archbishop and his retinue is not always—in fact, almost never—that of a miniature version of the Indian hospital of Santa Ana in Lima. The comments about the hospital in village after village mention herds of livestock, occasionally some land, exceptionally some real estate, and often alms, but we hardly ever find any reference to a building, however modest, that shelters the sick or other people in need of care.[49] However, this does not seem to alarm Mogrovejo or preoccupy the parish priests. It is possible that in the rural parishes, the funds for assisting the sick and needy and for covering the costs of their spiritual care were collected under a category labeled "hospital," in which the main force was the local population and not an institution under the exclusive control of the Church. If these were indeed the conditions in which these "hospitals" existed, then the sick, instead of being isolated, would have been tended to in their homes, with nursing care supplied by the local residents. Was this compromise contrary to the "decency" demanded by those priests who refused to carry the last rites to the sick and dying?

These informal establishments posed a problem for those who thought that hospitals should have the clear profile that they had acquired during the Counter-Reformation. In 1619 a report on the Lima diocese, drawn up on the orders of Archbishop Bartolomé Lobo Guerrero, was discouraging: whether near Lima or in the more remote areas, the hospitals did not offer any kind of services or sometimes simply did not exist. Of the village of Magdalena, in the immediate vicinity of Lima, the report stated: "this parish has no hospital, nor does the *corregidor* give anything to the Indians for their sicknesses, they heal themselves in their homes when they are sick" (Lissón 1947, 5: no. 25, 268). The remote parish of Pallasca, in the province of Huaylas, is described in similar terms. One concise yet eloquent sentence sums up the gloomy situation: "this parish has an empty house which they call a hospital" (303). The Indian parish of Huarochirí seems to have been fairly typical: "It has a hospital consecrated to Saint Sebastian where the Indians do not want to go; the sick are assisted in their homes with the income from the 200 sheep that the hospital owns, and sometimes the *corregidor* makes them some presents, such as wine, oil, and sugar" (283).

Although the report commissioned by Archbishop Lobo Guerrero does not indicate who was responsible for those patients who were cared for in the hospitals, it is likely that Indian specialists as well as native medical knowledge were regularly consulted (Calancha 1974 [1638], 3: Book 2, chap. 14, 879–80). According to circumstances, the Indian doctors who lived both in the cities and in more remote areas were sometimes called upon to lend their services and were sometimes prosecuted and punished. An agreement of the Second Council of Lima had permitted some of these specialists to hold licenses, issued by the diocese, to exercise their profession, while others joined the staffs of the hospitals in the big cities.[50] In the smaller districts, they may have taken charge of the sick in collaboration with groups of local residents, possibly organized in confraternities. This form of organization, concrete but not always visible, could be one reason why the inspectors sent by Lobo Guerrero only reported empty or nonexistent hospitals.

The situation in the Indian parishes demonstrates that—beyond the program linking surveillance, charity, and conversion that the city hospitals offered—there was an area of dispute and negotiation between the Church and the Indians' knowledge and beliefs about health, sickness, and death.[51] In contrast to what would happen three centuries later in this and other regions of the colonial world, with the development and dissemination of scientific medicine, the European medical knowledge of the time could neither compete with the Indian methods nor discredit them. Thus, practically the only means of undermining them was by appealing to the spheres of ritual and faith.[52]

Confraternities

The notion of brotherhood suggested by the religious association known as a confraternity actually entailed a hierarchical structure whose purpose was the practice of charity, mutual assistance, and the worship of a devotion (a particular saint, image, or relic).[53] These sodalities commonly offered their members the resources necessary for ensuring an appropriate burial place and funeral as well as the commitment to pray for the salvation of their souls by periodically celebrating masses. Their number, especially those devoted to the cult of the Virgin Mary, the Blessed Sacrament, and the Souls in Purgatory, increased considerably after the Counter-Reformation.[54] Members paid their admission fees and regular contributions in money, wax, and candles; they also gave alms and voluntary donations of various kinds. The confraternities usually elected their own officers, who were responsible for collecting and administering funds; acquiring spaces inside churches for the erection of chapels in honor of the devotion to which the order was consecrated, and for the burial of its members; and organizing regular charitable activities and religious celebrations.

The initiative to found confraternities came from the religious orders, the secular clergy, and even the government. In the great cities of the viceroyalty the main force behind the organization of confraternities that celebrated any Marian devotion was the religious orders, while the secular clergy were especially active in those devoted to the Blessed Sacrament and the Souls in Purgatory. Whereas in Spain the existence of confraternities devoted to assisting the poor in the hospitals was widespread (Martz 1983, 165–66), in the Peruvian viceroyalty this task was often only one among several others: in at least one case, the viceroy decreed the creation of a *hermandad de la caridad* (brotherhood of charity) when the hospital of Spaniards and Indians was founded in the city of La Plata, while the purpose of several confraternities was to visit the sick in the hospitals (Toledo 1986, 1:455; Garland 1994, 201). Most of the Peruvian confraternities about which we have information focused their attention on mutual assistance, occasionally offering charitable help outside of the sphere of the hospitals, and often visiting the sick; but their most consistent activity was to offer support and company to their members in their last moments.

The confraternities were based in the convent and parish churches. In some cases, their remit was confined to the parish, while in others it was broader, with men and women from other districts, parishes, or even provinces, motivated by their devotion to a particular religious cult, to which was sometimes added the members of a professional association. In the colonial context, along with divisions according to parish jurisdiction, profession, and, to a lesser extent, socioeconomic level, the confraternities were also organized according to ethnic origin. The religious orders were the first to set up confraternities for Indians, congregating them under the influence of the Church during the period preceding the creation of the parishes. These associations offered Andean men and women who converted to Christianity opportunities for social integration and leadership, cultural adaptation, and group expression in a variety of contexts. Some researchers have suggested that the Indian confraternities were fundamental in restoring the family and community bonds damaged as a result of the conquest (Celestino and Meyers 1981; Charney 1989). On the basis of the property that some confraternities succeeded in amassing, and their methods of administration, some students of colonial society in the Andes have also argued that the indigenous authorities used these associations for their own economic and political profit (Celestino and Meyers 1981; Varón 1982).[55] A more flexible approach, which provides a good description of Andean groups, considers the colonial confraternities as entities that created manifold social relations, embracing a sphere that was considerably broader than that of the association itself (Garland 1994, 223).

The Indian confraternities in the cities were composed of individuals whose circumstances were diverse and shifting. A considerable proportion of the native population of Lima was of immigrant origin and had lost both their family connections and their bonds to extended kinship groups because of their removal to the viceregal capital.[56] At the head of the confraternities we find individuals who, because of the trade they practiced and their economic position, represented the new community of Indians that came into being in the cities of the viceroyalty. The religious orders and the secular clergy also contributed to this sense of community with their missionary and welfare work and the promise of assistance, their demonstration of the virtues and power of a given religious devotion, the opportunity they offered for participating in public celebrations, and, more important, the fact that certain convent and parish churches stood on sites previously dedicated to pre-Hispanic cults. Local circumstances affected the way in which confraternities connected with the new conditions of the colonial regime. For example, in the city of Cuzco and its surrounding area, in contrast to patterns typical in Lima, the families descended from Inca rulers became the founders and sponsors of these associations. These groups thus redefined for themselves a position of leadership in local society and, by connecting themselves to a given devotion, church, or convent, sought to raise their profile as a prestigious kinship group and thus to distinguish themselves from their peers.[57] In spite of the predominance of traditional Indian families, in the Inca city these brotherhoods also gave leadership opportunities to people of modest origins, who were thus able to rise within the hierarchy of colonial society.

The administration of the symbols of the confraternities was enormously effective. Marian devotions, especially, were enthusiastically embraced in the Andes and in the New World in general, as much so as in Spain and in other areas of the Catholic world, because of the protective and healing role they were believed to play (Nalle 1992, 177–78). All the religious orders promoted, generally with a good deal of success, at least one devotion to the Virgin Mary, which enabled them to gain influence among members with devotions representing them. The Dominicans, for example, founded confraternities consecrated to Our Lady of the Rosary, both in Lima and in Cuzco, while the Franciscans promoted the cult of Our Lady of the Candelaria and of the Immaculate Conception. Other religious orders, such as the Augustinians, besides organizing confraternities devoted to Our Lady of Grace, appealed to saints of their own order whose history and powers were connected with the salvation of the souls in purgatory, such as San Nicolás Tolentino (Schenone 1992, 2:598–601, 605), or the Archangel Michael, in charge of meting out divine justice on the day of the Last Judgment (de la Voragine 1987, 2:621). Inside the churches, chapels consecrated to these devotions continually received alms from the members, which were used for their ornamentation and maintenance, and in return these chapels would house the remains of those persons who had committed their souls to the care of the devotions.

The diaries and chronicles of the period describe how the confraternities vied with each other in lavishing funds on public celebrations and on the decoration of their chapels (Meléndez 1681, 1:63–64). A chapel's prestige, derived from its location, the social standing of its founders and members, and the reputation of the devotion to which it was dedicated, attracted more adepts, donations, and alms. Although, as we have seen, when the parishes were organized, the religious orders were obliged to give way to the secular clergy in the area of the urban populations' spiritual life, and the confraternities represented a very effective way to exert considerable influence over these populations. This is why the friars competed as much among themselves as with the secular clergy for the loyalty of churchgoers who, if they were sufficiently convinced of the superior benefits of a specific devotion, could go so far as to identify more with the church that housed their confraternity than with their own parish. Treating membership as a kind of social capital, wealthier citizens often belonged to several confraternities, which gave them access to more than one burial place. At the end of their life they would, of course, require only one of these; but the fact that several confraternities would accompany the body at the funeral, with the appropriate ceremony and paraphernalia, and that masses and prayers would be offered in several different churches, was a source of security for individuals who had learned to fear for the fate of their souls. As for the poor, their souls also had a price, although a more modest one. Many were convinced of the usefulness of joining a confraternity. It is possible that the visits of group members to the sick in the hospitals led to many last-minute enrolments, in exchange for a modest donation. For the friars and priests, the number of people who could be added to the membership lists of the confraternities was a sure indicator of the effectiveness of their work.

However much these practices may have resembled a commercial transaction, what was at stake—the bodies' rest and the souls' salvation—was too important for them to be reduced to such terms. The preparation for an appropriate death involved elaborate steps that are the subject of the next chapter.

CHAPTER FIVE | # Wills, Graves, and Funeral Rites

The final sacraments, although essential, were not sufficient preparation for death and its aftermath. The will, a document that brought together the two fundamental aspects of life—the spiritual and the material—was also a requirement for leaving this world secure in the knowledge that one's soul was on the right path, and that one's relationship with God and one's fellow man was well tended. For this reason, writing a will took on a religious character (Ariès 1977, 190; Chiffoleau 1980, 108–9; Cline 1998, 16–17; Eire 1995, 21). In this chapter, besides exploring how the will was introduced and adapted to the conversion to Christianity of the Andean populations, I will study two related topics: choice of gravesite, and funeral rites. People's initial resistance to the abandonment of their former burial sites gave way to Christian funerals becoming voluntary and increasingly widespread. To explain this unprecedented change, the spatial transformation involved in the creation of cities, towns, and parishes must be taken into account. I maintain that the choice of gravesites can be seen as an appropriation of sacred space that facilitated the process of Christianizing death in the Andes. The gravesite represents a cluster of social bonds and of moments both in the life of the individual and in the colonial and evangelizing process, whose meaning I will attempt to elaborate. A similar observation may be made about funeral rites, whose dramatic nature—in the sense of performance—despite following models by then well established in the Catholic world, acquires a special dimension upon being appropriated and adapted to the lives and deaths of the new Andean Christians.

Wills

Those who have studied wills from other parts of the Catholic world have underscored the role that their widespread use played in the creation of an individual conscience, as it led those charged with drafting or authoring them to contemplate their own death (Ariès 1977; Chiffoleau 1980). The people of the Andes were no exception to this rule, although it cannot be said that before the conquest, they did not think about questions of personhood. Their tombs, as we have seen, tell us that they thought in great depth about such matters, but not necessarily in the same terms.

Wills have a long history in Western Europe, and they evolved along with changes in religious mentality, the teaching of Christian doctrine, the growing complexity of the political order, and the centralization of the state (Ariès 1977; Burns 2001; Chiffoleau 1980; Cohn 2000; Eire 1995). The Hispanic legal tradition governing wills, inheritance, and succession that was introduced to the New World was a product of Castilian law. Its regulations are meticulously laid out in the *Siete Partidas* (Burns 2001, 5:ix–xviii). At the beginning of the sixteenth century, and as part of the growing centralization of power in Castile, the diverse legal repertoire was assembled in various collections including the Leyes de Toro, issued in 1505. They addressed especially the sphere of civil law, in particular matters concerning family and succession law (Lalinde Abadía 1978, 195; Tomás y Valiente 1966), resulting in an overlap of their content with that of the *Siete Partidas*. Consequently, any historian who studies the sources related to private life in the colonial world will find allusions to both legal codes as well as to other, earlier ones stemming from Roman law. It is striking in these legal codes to see how closely what we understand today as the civil realm is bound up with the religious.

In the Spanish New World possessions, the Laws of the Indies regulated public law, whereas in private law Castilian legislation obtained (Lalinde Abadía 1978, 212; Ots Capdequí 1921; 1943; Tomás y

Valiente 1997, 340; Mirow 2004). We lack the case studies that would provide us with an adequate framework for understanding this complementary relationship.[1] Although scholars maintain that New World law and Castilian law differ in several respects, Castilian law referred to private matters concerning both the Spanish and the indigenous population (Lalinde Abadía 1978; Tomás y Valiente 1997). While there are some studies on law and the private sphere among the indigenous populations of colonial Mexico (Kellogg 1995), this issue has not been sufficiently scrutinized for the Andes.[2]

As a rule, local indigenous authorities were supposed to be instructed in the correct procedure when someone was ill or close to death, and to inform the priest so that he could make the necessary arrangements. The latter had to call a notary or, in the absence of one, to write the will himself.[3] In Lima, the indigenous *alguacil* (law-enforcement officer) was obliged to notify the *corregidor* (royal magistrate) when he became aware that someone ran the risk of dying. In Cuzco, the regulation was similar, although in practice, authorities of higher rank than *alguacil*—the indigenous parish mayors and *caciques*—usually took responsibility for informing the authorities.[4]

Although the Church required that to have a right to a grave in consecrated ground every Christian must author a will, this stipulation seems not to have been within the reach of many people. However, this did not necessarily exclude them from burial in their church. Authoring a will depended principally, though not exclusively, on owning property, on holding a position of some responsibility, on membership in a confraternity or guild, or on being under the effective influence of the authorities involved in will-making. The latter included those who, alone in their final days, were convinced by a priest of the need to drawing one up. This means that wills authored by Indians are not limited to the most powerful, fortunate, or orthodox. Some show us distinct ways of understanding the concept of material value or of the bonds of friendship and blood. Although it may seem that for the overwhelming majority, who had very few possessions and could not read or write, the will would have been less important, it is possible that writing wills was more prevalent among the poor than the archives suggest. Bishop Alonso de la Peña y Montenegro (1995 [1668], 1:346) notes that in general the only option for impoverished Indians was to entrust the recording and disposition of their meager possessions "to the hand of anyone who could write." The jurist Juan de Solórzano y Pereyra states, moreover, that the wills of Indians tended to be made without a notary (Solórzano y Pereyra 1972 [1648], 1: Book 2, chap. 28, n. 55, 429; Peña y Montenegro 1995 [1668], 1:350). This informality, about which the civil and ecclesiastical officials were nonetheless informed, could explain the very small number of these documents to be found in notary records and judicial registers. It also gives us an idea of the ever greater importance of written documents in the life of the indigenous population.

The veracity of wills authored by indigenous peoples was sometimes doubtful, given the irregular circumstances in which many were written. Indeed, through the composition of inauthentic wills and the forgery of donations, alms, and inheritances, priests and others tried to strip the elderly and infirm of their possessions.[5] These abuses were committed frequently and easily among an often illiterate population with little command of Spanish. Despite this, the potential of the will as a valuable source of information must not be dismissed because, in many cases, it constitutes the only written testimony of a person's life (Cline 1998, 14). It is unlikely that all of the information in a will is false, and, considered as part of a larger whole, each of these documents provides details that would be difficult to draw from other sources. Because the will is the expression of a network of social relationships, it allows us to understand the environment in which a person lived; it also offers us a glimpse into the religious beliefs that he or she shared with others, and it gives us a more precise idea of his or her material circumstances. These are essential to understanding, on the one hand, the extent to which the colonial order was imposed upon the lives of indigenous inhabitants and, on the other, the way in which the latter also contributed to forging it.

Much of the appeal of the wills of colonial Indians lies in the way they were adapted to the circumstances of the Andes. Of primary importance are the cultural and linguistic differences. Given that in the Andes there was no tradition of written or pictorial representation (in contrast to Mexico), the transition to the written document was fairly abrupt. Because the evidence indicates that these documents were generally written in Spanish, it can be assumed that their composition came under tighter supervision in Peru than in New Spain.[6]

A crucial feature of the writing of the indigenous will was its public character.[7] If the document was drafted when the author was very close to death, then the act was incorporated into the administration of the last rites and extreme unction. After hearing confession and conferring the absolution and indulgences set forth in the Bull of the Holy Crusade,[8] the priest had to verify that the dying person had made a will (Pérez Bocanegra 1631, 485–86). The *caciques* and nobles of Incan background authored their wills before an audience that tended to include their peers, neighbors, and many subordinates. This was encouraged for its pedagogical benefits, and those who showed up to witness the last rites were rewarded with indulgences.[9] For example, in October 1577, moments before expiring, Don Domingo Chupica, *cacique* of Checras, a town in the highlands of Lima, wrote his will in the presence of a Lima notary, his parish priest, and an undetermined number of Indian witnesses.[10]

When ordinary people made their wills, the presence of the priest who was there to administer the last rites ensured that the act became a public event: "many people," observed Pedro Caillagua, a hatmaker, and his wife, Ana Visacarua, wrote a joint will when they contracted smallpox during an epidemic that hit the town of Paucartambo in the Cuzco diocese in 1589. The *licenciado* Juan Pérez Bocanegra describes how the ringing of the town bell summoned everyone to the procession, presided over by the priest carrying the Blessed Sacrament to the sick person's house (Pérez Bocanegra 1631, 486). The public nature of these declarations of loyalty to the Catholic faith, reinforced by the moments of extreme emotion at which they occurred, surely strengthened the Church. It has been shown, for example, in the case of the residents of the Mixteca in New Spain (Terraciano 1998, 120), that the presence of an audience during the authoring of wills was bound up with ancient Indian rhetorical traditions. Such events made perfect sense in a culture in which use of rituals and oratory was widespread. During the colonial period it was usual for documents considered important to be read out loud before large gatherings not only as a means of divulging their contents but also as a way of making them valid.

Research on the origins, education, social standing, and output of Spanish notaries in Peru is beginning to tell us about those responsible for writing wills (Burns 2005). Due to the size of the viceregal capital and its role as a political and commercial center, there was a greater demand for notaries in Lima than in any other Andean city; Cuzco was much smaller, as was its demand for scribes. From early on, a degree of specialization is evident among the notaries of both cities. A majority served affluent Spanish clients and recorded their numerous commercial operations (Suárez 2001), while a handful, a great deal of whom were of non-European origin, offered their services to the poor.

Although the range of clientele among the notaries of both cities was similar, there is an important distinction in their linguistic abilities, the role of interpreters, and the power relations that surface in the writing and use of legal documents. In Lima's notary registers,[11] the presence of interpreters was variable and became ever more sketchy over the course of the seventeenth century. It is difficult to establish if this was the result of deliberate policy or if the imposition of the Spanish language on the indigenous population in Lima was a spontaneous reaction to the problem of linguistic diversity. In the final decades of the sixteenth century and early part of the seventeenth, several indigenous interpreters appeared on the scene to assist those Lima notaries who were charged with writing wills; in their absence, this function was exercised by some indigenous authority or civil servant, or by a priest who spoke the native language. It seems likely that at least the scribe of the indigenous *reducción* of El Cercado would be bilingual, but information about the smallest localities of Lima is practically nonexistent, and it appears that El Cercado's notary registers have not been preserved. In the small indigenous settlements that ringed the city, too, there remain very few traces of bilingual notaries.

For part of the sixteenth century, Lima's city council occasionally employed interpreters, although the importance accorded them appears to have been minimal (*Libros de Cabildos de Lima* 1935, 5:405; 7:18, 519). During his visit to the highlands of the viceroyalty, Francisco de Toledo created the salaried position of general language interpreter, and despite the widespread opinion that it was not advantageous to employ Indians as interpreters because they were untrustworthy "by nature,"[12] the first interpreter hired by the viceroy as an official of the Real Audiencia de Lima was an Indian, as was his successor (Toledo 1989, 2:97). Until the beginning of the seventeenth century, although not consistently, interpreters appear in records of transactions between Spaniards and Indians as well as in wills authored by the latter. However, as the century progresses, they disappear almost completely, Indian testators becoming regularly described as "*ladinos* (competent) in the Spanish language." Despite the prestige it enjoyed in its early years, the position of general language interpreter in the city of Lima became a less and less attractive office: in 1636, Francisco de León, the interpreter of the natives in the city council, described himself as poor,[13] while in 1650, Alonso de Ávila asked permission from Viceroy Conde de Salvatierra to step down from the position, maintaining that he had to leave Lima because he had more important issues awaiting him in Chuquisaca, Upper Peru.[14] The matter of linguistic diversity in Lima was not limited to the Quechua–Spanish dichotomy. Those who have studied the history of Quechua have described Peru as a "linguistic mosaic" (Mannheim 1991). The capital of the viceroyalty attracted immigrants from all corners of the territory, which meant that its indigenous population spoke a range of Quechua dialects as well as other indigenous languages. Missionaries considered this linguistic diversity to be one of the greatest obstacles to spreading Christianity, particularly among women and ordinary people.[15] Thus, the very idea of a general language interpreter was problematic, given the many languages actually encountered.[16]

The circumstances in Cuzco varied in several important respects from those in Lima. Here, some of the earliest wills used in this study were composed by Indian scribes, and several show that these officials, who on occasion also participated in local government (Covarrubias Pozo 1963), quickly learned the routine formulas of legal documents as well as a good knowledge of Spanish. Some stumbled over the wording of certain requisite phrases, which indicates that they worked from memory rather than from access to a manual from which to copy. Although they wrote in Spanish, they applied the phonetics and syntax of Quechua, again suggesting oral repetition, resulting in distortions of meaning. In the will of Francisca Colloc, written in Cuzco in 1586, for example, the indigenous scribe wrote: "Additionally, I instruct the company with the high cross to pay the offering as customary."[17] The text should have read: "Additionally, I instruct that my parish priest accompany my body with the high cross and that the customary offering be paid."

In seventeenth-century Cuzco, an interpreter was involved in practically every notarial act in which Indians participated, even when the author spoke Spanish. This reveals the complexity of the power relations that were forming in that era. Matters such as personal appearance, perhaps an imperfect command of Spanish, and the conviction that the Indians always needed some intermediary to establish efficient contact with the administrative system and, in general, with anyone who was not indigenous, reinforced the position of the mediators. Soon, mestizo notaries made their appearance, displacing the Indian scribes and acting in many cases as interpreters.[18] Whether in the role of interpreters or of notaries who served an indigenous clientele, mestizos in the city of Cuzco came to exercise almost total control over these written transactions, and they even formed family alliances to ensure that these positions stayed in the hands of their kin (Ramos n.d.). Their power was so great, in many cases, because they were linked to notable indigenous families and also because they often maintained close contacts with provincial indigenous authorities and with ordinary people. Their influence on the writing of documents by indigenous residents was crucial. This predominance of mestizo notaries who took advantage of the use of Spanish as the language of power could explain why, in contrast to the Nahuas, Mixtecas, Mayas, and Zapotecos of New Spain, wills were not written in Quechua, although some researchers assert that this was not always the case.[19]

In both Lima and Cuzco the conventions for structuring wills were the same as those in Spain. The opening phrase introduced the sacramental character of the will: "In the name of God," "In the name of the Blessed Trinity," or even the by-then antiquated "In Dei Nomine, Amen."[20] Next, the identity of the author was established, a more complex issue than one might think: the new Christian names were given, and names in the vernacular became surnames; a colonial identity was also assigned according to the recently created province, town, or parish of origin; inquiries were made into personal history, including, in the earliest cases, the *encomienda* of origin and whether it belonged to an *encomendero*—whose name must then be included— or to the crown. The author's identity was completed by adding his or her provenance and whether his or her address was temporary or permanent. It was thus clearly recorded that there was somebody who exercised effective control over the will's author. Besides the *encomenderos,* the testators were also asked the names of their parents, and, especially in the earliest cases, they were to indicate if they had been baptized and if they were or had been married. Married women were to give the name of their husband, while tax-paying Indians were to give the name of their *cacique.*

Valuable biographical information appears as a result of these questions, and it can be better understood how Andean identities were formed in this changing environment. On occasion, will-authors tell how they arrived in the city; they also explain some of their family background, making it possible to determine if they were the first of their line to convert to Christianity. Some testators describe the circumstances of their non-Christian parents without passing judgment on the absence of Christian laws and customs prior to the conquest: in Cuzco in 1590, Don Gonzalo Guanuco Quispe declared that he was the son of "Lliuyacguaman and of Pamo Yllacsa, his wife, who were married according to their law."[21] Others tell of having no memories of their parents because death or forced migration had separated them at an early age. In 1593, Leonor Chao, a woman originally from Trujillo then living in Lima, explained that she had never known her parents because her *encomendero* brought her to the capital of the viceroyalty when she was still very young.[22]

The fact that a major portion of the Spanish elite had doubts about the sincerity of the Indians' conversion and their adequate preparation beyond rudimentary doctrine rarely appears in these documents. When it does, we find it only in wills authored in Lima. The notary Marcos Franco de Esquivel, for example, saw fit to add to the information on some of his clients an observation about whether they were sufficiently instructed in Christian doctrine. In the will of Alonso Caxa, dated in 1570, Esquivel, in a brief departure from the usual formula, noted: "he said that he is Christian and baptized and knows doctrine and has received the sacrament of confirmation."[23] Between 1610 and 1630, when the climate of religious repression began to worsen for the Indians of the Lima diocese, other Lima notaries—at the request of their clients?—began to add a few lines to reinforce the testators' declarations of faith.[24]

Notaries in sixteenth-century Spain relied on manuals containing ready-made preambles and formulas (Nalle 1992, 183). It is therefore very possible that notaries in Peru also used these sources, which, after identifying the testator and proclaiming the declaration of faith, go on to request divine intervention from Jesus Christ and his "glorious mother," the Virgin Mary, as well as the whole "celestial court."[25] The devotional trends that gained particular strength in Spain (Nalle 1992, 162, 178, 274) had their counterparts in America, with the Immaculate Conception often mentioned in these invocations from the seventeenth century onward, especially in Lima. Other mediating saints are also named, sometimes as if it were simply routine, while in some examples a note of personal interest can be discerned. In 1620, Baltazar de los Reyes invoked Saint Peter and Saint Paul, who, despite their prominence in the Church, are rarely mentioned in Indian wills. Don Martín Chaucaguaman, *cacique* of Sisicaya in the highlands of Lima, in his will authored in 1619, invoked, as well as Peter and Paul, Saint James and Saint William (two famed slayers of infidels) (Schenone 1992, 2:434–35), Saint Gabriel (either the archangel or a Franciscan saint) (424–25), and Saint Valentine the Martyr (Schenone 1992, 2:770; de la Voragine 1990, 1:173). Although these invocations abound in repetition, they should not be disregarded because they can be linked to other manifestations of the authors' religious beliefs, thus leading us to a better understanding of the role of the devotion to saints in the colonial mentality.

The next section of the will also reflects a formula: the meditation on death (Eire 1995, 73). It complements the process of the confession of faith because here, the testator recognizes the inevitability of death as inherent to human nature and subject to God's will. The convention could vary occasionally when the author or notary slipped in a phrase that channeled some devotional trend or the influence of a certain religious order, such as the ideas professed by the followers of Saint Francis. Possibly signaling it as part of the process of her own death, in her will written in Cuzco in 1597, Luisa Tari declared that she was authoring it "in imitation of the Passion of Our Lord Jesus Christ." In writing the will of Doña Juana Mama Guaco Ñusta, notary Juan Flores de Bastidas, perhaps inspired by his readings in Calderón de la Barca, and without diverging from doctrinal conventions of the period, decided to break with the monotony of the formula: "considering that we are born in order to die, which is the most certain thing we have, and that we know not the how or the when of the final hour, and that the brevity of life is a dream subjected to miseries and travails."[26] One may object that these ideas are the notary's rather than the testator's, but inasmuch as the document was reread by the authors themselves—if they had had it prepared sufficiently in advance of their death—or by those who survived them, passages such as these could provoke reflection and teaching among those who knew their content.

The lengthiest part of the will comprised, on the one hand, instructions pertaining to the grave and the funeral ceremonies and, on the other, the payment of debts and restitutions, the division of property, and the bequests that would best position the soul for salvation.

Fulfillment of a will's instructions lay with the executor, whose appointment varied according to the personal circumstances of the author and, in some cases, the degree of neighborhood organization, as with the parish of the native hospital in Cuzco, whose indigenous authorities were often chosen to exercise this duty. Although the authors of the most famous treatises on dying well, such as Alexo Venegas, recommended that at least one of the will's executors be a priest, it is noteworthy that this advice was rarely followed in Lima or Cuzco.[27] Although some Indian testators chose priests as executors—in general, their parish priest or confessor—they were in the minority. The identity of those chosen instead to see that the wishes of the deceased were followed is revealing.[28]

Witnesses were then required to make a will valid. The rules on this varied, and in the colonial context the situation is murky and has not been well researched. It is likely that the criteria established by Castilian civil law, especially the Leyes de Toro (1505), and the recommendations of the Church were applied in alternating or complementary fashion. The former recommended the presence of between five and seven witnesses, although in exceptional circumstances fewer were acceptable (Llamas y Molina 1827, 1:65), while the bishop of Quito, Alonso de la Peña y Montenegro (1995 [1668], 1:349), maintained that in the case of a will made before a scribe, three witnesses should be present. Experts recommended that the witnesses be as neutral as possible. In theory, they could not be neighbors or relatives of the testator, but in practice, the first, especially, must have been virtually impossible. A study of wills authored by Indians in central Mexico shows that, on the contrary, a range of persons close to the will's author attended its writing (Cline 1998, 19–20).

In Lima and Cuzco there are issues worth noting, which concern not so much the degree of closeness between the witnesses and the testator as their ethnic background, their degree of authority, and their gender. In sixteenth-century Lima, and into the seventeenth, the presence of Spaniards as witnesses is consistent in all the cases I have recorded. Apparently, this was a requirement: when Francisco de Guasquanquiche issued his will in 1583, the notary Rodrigo Gómez de Baeza wrote, in an apologetic tone, that all the witnesses were Indians because "no Spaniards could be found."[29] There does not appear to have been such a requirement in Cuzco, although Spaniards appear in many wills. In contrast to Lima, in the sixteenth century the indigenous authorities in the parishes of Cuzco, such as *caciques* and mayors, were always present, which may have reassured the ecclesiastical and colonial authorities that this important act was under sufficient supervision. These indigenous authorities, even if they did not know how to read and write, validated through their presence the writing and recording of the wills, and they must have been well aware of the content and implications. Occasionally, their intervention is recognized in the formulation of the document.[30] In Castile, the Leyes de Toro did not disqualify illiterate witnesses. In Cuzco, the *caciques* and other indigenous authorities were treated in the same way as those who met the conditions of Castilian law for being a town resident (Llamas y Molina 1827), something that did not happen in Lima.

This situation did not last for long. In the seventeenth century an important change occurred, and indigenous authorities no longer appear as frequently. Those *caciques* and mayors who do appear generally know how to read and write or at least have learned to sign their name, which reflects the greater acculturation of indigenous authorities and possibly the affirmation of hierarchies according to the level of familiarity achieved with respect to Spanish culture (Alaperrine-Bouyer 2007). The protector of the natives, whose presence is frequent in other notary documents issued by Indians, such as labor contracts, is practically absent as a witness in wills. Finally, an interesting contrast with Mexico concerns the presence of women. Whereas in central Mexico the appearance of women to certify a document was not unusual (Cline 1998, 20), in the two Peruvian cities we are studying, they appear only in exceptional cases, which could be due to a more effective application of Spanish law, given that both the Leyes de Toro and their commentators ruled out women as acceptable witnesses (Llamas y Molina 1827, 1:71).

To clarify the conditions underlying the examples I use in this chapter and the next, it is necessary to explain the profile of the authors of the wills I am studying. As I have stated, each city had a particular demographic makeup that made for notable contrasts between the two. In Lima we find a local population seriously reduced by the impact of the conquest. The consequence was not, nonetheless, the disappearance of the native population because the city became a magnet for immigrants. The capital of the viceroyalty required a constant labor supply, which generated a movement of workers from the nearby highlands and from locations along the coast. This population influx from the provinces continued during the colonial period, which turned Lima into a city of immigrants (Charney 1989; Cook 1981; Lowry 1991). These conditions are apparent in the examples I have compiled. Eighty percent of the authors of a total of 54 wills, collected for the period from 1570 to 1599, were born outside of Lima. (Throughout this discussion, percentages are rounded off rather than precise.) Although a majority of them lived in the city or even claimed to be under the jurisdiction of one of its parishes, there are within this group those who could be considered nonpermanent residents or occasional visitors: the majority were indigenous authorities and muledrivers who had died unexpectedly on their way through the city. In the period from 1600 to 1670, a greater percentage of Lima-born people is apparent, despite the fact that men and women from other regions and locations continued to be the majority: 67% of a total of 180 authors came from somewhere outside of the city, while 30% were born in Lima or the surrounding area.[31]

Regarding division by gender, 40% of the sixteenth-century group, and 47% of the seventeenth-century one, were men. If we compare these figures with those of the 1613 census, which Cook and Lowry cite in their respective works on Lima's population, we note an interesting difference because the overwhelming majority of men registered by the census is not reflected in my sample.[32] The majority of the women included in the sixteenth-century group were not born in Lima and came from places as far away as Quito, Cuzco, and Arequipa.

Although the immigration influx bolstered the community of native peoples in the city of Lima, it remained a population threatened by instability and faced with enormous difficulties in perpetuating itself biologically and culturally. The poor, especially, were affected by low fertility rates combined with high mortality levels characteristic of the demographics of the Old Regime.[33] These conditions are apparent in the documents analyzed here: in the sixteenth-century group, 53% (divided equally between genders) of the testators were married; 20% were widowed (36% men and 64% women); 19% were single; and 7% did not respond to this item. Of the 40 who were married or widowed, 58% were childless at the moment of authoring their wills. Among the unmarried, two women had one child each. These trends correspond to those recorded by Cook in his analysis of the 1613 census (Cook 1976, 44–47), in which 150 of a total of 249 families were childless and less than one half of the total had only one child at the time of the census. These precarious living conditions, suffered by a significant proportion of the indigenous population of Lima, appear to have continued throughout the seventeenth century.

In the city of Cuzco we find a community much more stable in several respects. The proportion of immigrants is smaller, especially in the seventeenth century, and it is a much more culturally homogeneous population. Of the 62 cases studied for the period from 1559 to 1597, 44% are men and 56% women. Twenty-nine percent of them were born in the city of Cuzco, while 50% came from elsewhere (21% did not state their origins). This greater proportion of people from outside Cuzco could be due in part to the fact that men and women born in other provinces in the sixteenth century arrived with the conquistadors, and, because of their closeness to the Spaniards, they could have been among the first to convert to Christianity, thus leaving traces of this process in the notary records of Cuzco.[34] For the period from 1600 to 1670, we have at our disposal 163 wills authored in the city of Cuzco. In terms of the distribution between men and women, the proportions remain similar to those of the sixteenth century: 39% men and 61% women. Regarding place of origin, while 65% of the total were born in the city of Cuzco, of whom women were the clear majority (67%), the remaining 35% came from other provinces. Practically all of them (87%) were from places within the Cuzco diocese.[35] Cultural homogeneity during this period is reinforced by the community sharing the same language in a city in which the indigenous population is the overwhelming majority. Although other studies show that information on the population of Cuzco is scarce or unclear, there is no doubt about the significance of this factor. While the 1613 census indicates a total of 2,000 indigenous inhabitants in the city of Lima, the most authoritative estimates maintain that in Cuzco there was a population above 10,000 (Cook 1981, 216–17).[36] These demographic differences were crucial for the cultural history of each of these two cities.

The robustness of the indigenous population of Cuzco leads to a greater stability and more favorable conditions for its survival as a community. Of the 1559 to 1597 group, 58% of the total of 62 wills were by married people, of whom 64% were men. The widowed represented 21%, the majority being women, while 18%, of whom only one was a man, were single. Seventy-five percent of the married and one half of the widowed had children, which means that 64% of the total of this adult group had children when writing their wills.

For the 1600–1670 period, 48% of a total of 163 people stated that they were married. Fifty-eight percent of this group were men. The widowed represented 33%, 80% of whom were women. Finally, 13% of the total were single, of whom women also represented the overwhelming majority: 87%. A small number did not indicate their status. Among the married, widowed, and singles altogether, 72% had children at the moment of authoring their will.

These figures give us an idea of the differences that we must take into account in order to interpret the various testamentary provisions. Despite the difficulties in establishing precisely the context in which they are rooted—I concede that these are agglomerated examples and not samples for each city—the overarching narratives that accompany them match up well with the impression derived from the numbers. As a result, these general observations based on the census figures serve as background to explain the character of the social bonds that were forged in each city. More specifically, they allow us to understand how the indigenous inhabitants of each place related to sacred Christian space, a matter that we shall turn to next, in considering the topic of graves.

Graves

The author of every will had to indicate where he or she wanted to be buried and how the funeral ceremony would proceed. The choice was an act of special significance, not only in the cases of elaborate graves or those located in prestigious places but also for those who opted—either by choice or compelled by circumstances—for modest burials. Graves express a network of bonds with a range of individuals and institutions, crystallized in a single place.

To contextualize adequately the circumstances in which the testators expressed their wishes about where they were to be buried, it is necessary to return briefly to the matter of the parishes. As I explained in the previous chapter, the parishes, in their dual role as Church sanctuary and territorial jurisdiction, became the new sacred spaces, sometimes superimposing themselves over the previous ones, sometimes displacing them. As territorial jurisdictions, they put their residents under the control of ecclesiastical and civil authorities and offered a community that could share various holidays, liturgical celebrations, and rites of passage. Ideally, people were buried in their parish: they could identify with it and feel that they belonged. I shall consider, first, the declarations in which the testators indicated the parishes to which they belonged; and, second, in more detail, the correspondence between this and the places selected for their graves.

One must, in doing this, take into account the influence of the institutions already discussed: religious orders, confraternities, and hospitals. Whether cooperatively or in opposition, all these institutions, to one extent or another, played a role in the religious training and ideas about death of the Andean men and women who lived in Cuzco and Lima.

The Slow Process of Identification with Parishes

The measures taken by colonial and ecclesiastical authorities to distribute the indigenous population in the cities in a way that facilitated their governance were effective in the long term but encountered various stumbling blocks. In the city of Lima between 1570 and 1599, the majority of the authors of wills that I have recorded did not clearly identify the parish to which they belonged, thus indicating that the authorities did not have complete control. This may be explained by the precarious conditions in the city into which a significant portion of the population had settled and, additionally, by the fact that the definition of the parish jurisdictions was not a simple matter, giving rise, as we have seen, to prolonged ambiguities and disputes.

An examination of testators' statements allows us to see how the identification with their parishes developed. Only 9% of the 54 people included in the sixteenth-century group mentioned Santa Ana as their parish. It is difficult to know, nonetheless, whether they lived in the parish jurisdiction or if this presumed identification is due to their being residents of the hospital next to the church. Another five people (16%) said that their parish was San Sebastián, a jurisdiction in which indigenous inhabitants were a minority among Spaniards and people of African descent (Mazet 1976). In the seventeenth century there becomes apparent a subtle change that shows a gradual assimilation of the inhabitants of Lima into the system of parish jurisdictions: 19% of 180 people declared Santa Ana as their parish, while 12% claimed to be members of San Lázaro, a parish in which many immigrants of all backgrounds congregated. One quarter of the testators came from somewhere outside the city of Lima and gave the names of their respective towns as their parishes of origin.[37] Only 7% gave their parish as Santiago del Cercado, while 8% identified

Sagrario as their parish, which belonged, as we know, to the cathedral. In contrast to these groups, the 26% who indicated no parish is striking.[38] If we consider the other 26%, from jurisdictions outside Lima, we can confirm both the influence that the immigrant population continued to have in the formation of the city's indigenous community and the resulting instability of their assignment to the parishes.

In the city of Cuzco, although changes brought about by the Spanish conquest and occupation were drastic, the footprint of ancient structures is evident. The establishment of the parish regime was not exactly simple, but the reasons are different from those in Lima. During the 1559–1597 period, 76% of the 62 will-authors gave their parish name. This figure does not necessarily mean that adapting to and recognizing the system was quick or widespread across the population. As I have noted, the wills from earlier dates are composed by people not native to Cuzco. Their link to the city developed on the basis of the conquest and colonial organization of the city. Such is the case of certain parishioners of Santa Ana, where the authorities installed the Cañari and Chachapoya Indians, allies of the Spaniards. Because the Cuzco parishes were not created until the end of the 1550s, the point of reference for identifying sectors of the city was the neighborhood, which reflected pre-Hispanic localities and where people continued to dwell years after the parishes were founded. Both identifications could overlap and, depending on the point of view of those involved in writing the will, the identification of the locality could vary: for the older inhabitants of the city, the neighborhood could eclipse the parish, while the latter had more relevance for those people who had established themselves more recently in Cuzco. The will of Francisca Auatanta, dated in 1566, indicates that this native of Jauja lived "behind the convent of San Francisco." The witnesses identified themselves as indigenous authorities of Santa Ana, while the scribe who recorded the will noted that it was authored in "the neighborhood of Sumanchata" and omitted the name of the parish.[39] The scarcity of information on parish membership in the 1560s is possibly due to this being when the Inca war of resistance in Vilcabamba reached one of its most critical moments, thus affecting the behavior of the inhabitants native to the city. This began

to change in the mid-1580s, when the greatest number of people identify clearly with the parish, and more than one half declare themselves members of the parish of the hospital for Indians.

During the seventeenth century in Cuzco, signs of stability are
much stronger than in Lima. One hundred forty-nine of the 163 people
I have recorded (91%) gave the name of their parish. Thirty-one percent of these said they were parishioners of the Iglesia Mayor, while
24% lived under the jurisdiction of the hospital for natives. The smallest groups are spread among San Blas (10%), San Cristóbal (9%),
and the three parishes of Belén, Santiago, and San Sebastián (10%).
Seven percent indicated that they came from towns outside Cuzco.

The fact that the parishes were established in Cuzco on top of
pre-Hispanic neighborhoods and places of worship could explain this
adaptation to the parish system, particularly in the seventeenth century. But the process was not easy and is not sufficiently known. Between the founding of the city and the creation of the parishes, there
was an interval during which the conquistadors, fearful of uprisings
by the local population, distributed themselves throughout the heart
of the Incan city with great care (Julien 1998; Rivera Serna 1965, 25,
37). To understand how the effective displacement of the major Incan
families of the city center was achieved, or in what way the local population was reorganized into parishes, would require study not only
of the massive violence that certainly must have occurred but also of
the flood of property transactions recorded in the notary records,
which show a series of interactions between Spaniards and Indians
that brought about multiple modifications in the city's use of space.

Social Bonds and the Reappropriation of Consecrated Space

The relationship between urban Andean people and their parishes
constituted, as we have seen, a process of occupying space and forging social bonds that developed out of personal choice, necessity, force,
or persuasion. These bonds and this settling represent relationships
between groups with different degrees of power and different ethnici-
ties; they are evidence of a stage in the connection between a religious movement and its followers. The occupying of the consecrated
space of the grave also symbolizes these bonds, but with a significant

addition, because in the grave the network of ties woven across a lifetime as well as the dying person's hopes in the face of death become permanently fixed. The choice of grave may be explained by a heterogeneous mix of actors and circumstances: missionary policies, which gradually adapted Indian burial regulations to new circumstances; the proselytizing activities of the religious orders, which persisted in their rivalry with the lay clergy over gaining the devotion of the native population; the relationships between people of different social positions and ethnic backgrounds; and the criteria of what constituted prestige and power.

The following two sections deal with the burials of Indians in consecrated ground in Lima and Cuzco, respectively. Within each, I first examine the cases in which the testators opted to be buried in their parishes. Next, I review the distribution of graves in convent churches and then compare this with the parishes of origin of those who chose such burials. I have organized the data in this way to examine the relationship between the indigenous population and the parish system, the lay clergy, and the religious orders. Because of the irregularity of the information, it is not possible to order it chronologically. As well as the secular and regular clergy, the data point to the role of confraternities, which leads us to a clearer appreciation of the part played by the laity in the realization of funeral rites. Moreover, the intersection between parish membership and gravesites, whether the latter were in parishes or convents, offers a view of the trajectory of the Andean population's conversion and its interaction with local regimes. In this respect, the situation of the *caciques* takes on a special interest. Finally, the information offered in the wills confirms the crucial role of hospitals as centers for the promotion of religious conversion.

Indian Burials in Lima

In the 1540s, Fray Domingo de Santo Tomás wrote to the king to condemn the fact that Lima's Indians were dying without appropriate burials. Not everyone, however, seemed to share the Dominican's concern (Lissón 1943, 1: no. 4, 205). There had not been many conversions since the arrival of the Spaniards and the founding of the city, and the benefits of burial in consecrated ground were reserved only for those who had been baptized. In 1539 an ordinance issued by the Lima city council instructed *encomenderos* and other Spaniards who had Indians and black slaves in their service to bury those who were Christian in churches and those who were not, outside the city. It also warned them not to throw the bodies into the street, for which there was a fine of twenty pesos (Torres Saldamando et al. 1888, 1:40).[40] Hospitals, parishes, and confraternities were organized to confront the problem, but the early years of these institutions and their provision of burial spaces and funeral rituals to the newly converted are practically unknown. The available data on Indian burials that I use here begin one quarter-century after Fray Domingo complained to the king.

Indian wills from the city of Lima in the late sixteenth century (Table 5.1) show that in the domain controlled by the secular clergy—in which we include the altar dedicated to Nuestra Señora de Copacabana, then located in the Iglesia Mayor—57% (31) of the 54 cases opted for burial in the parish in which they resided. (See Appendix A for Tables 5.1–5.16.) Twenty-nine percent of these 31 were buried in Santa Ana, while the other groups chose the cathedral (16%) and San Sebastián (16%). To these may be added the very few who opted for El Cercado (6%), San Lázaro (3%), and San Marcelo (3%). Sixteen percent requested that their remains be transferred to churches in their hometowns. The preference for Santa Ana may reflect the dedication shown by the ecclesiastical authorities in using this hospital to reach the resident population, above all those who had no permanent home. Among those who requested a grave in Santa Ana, some offered no information on their parish of origin. These may have been people who had recently arrived in the city or were in Lima only temporarily. Those who chose burial in the cathedral, by contrast, were permanent residents or had been born in Lima. Evidence of their roots appears in their wills' instructions. For example, one of the authors in this group, composed totally of women, explained her choice by noting that her parents were buried in the same place.[41] Another woman wanted to be put in the same tomb as her spouse.[42] The influence of the parish priest, present as a witness, is evident in the case of those who opted for burial in San Sebastián.[43] The momentum gained by the cult of the Virgin of Copacabana as a result of the miracle manifested in her image led to the founding of a confraternity dedicated to her following, under the auspices of Archbishop Mogrovejo. In 1592, requests begin to be made for burial at its altar, in the Iglesia Mayor. As we shall see, burials here would be suspended ten years later by a decision of the ecclesiastical council.[44]

In the same time period, burial in a convent church meant spending approximately one-third more in fees than for a parish grave. The added cost generated controversy and was the subject of manifestos, or written arguments, both for and against, by the religious orders and the secular clergy (Peña y Montenegro (1996 [1668], 2:533–36). Despite the greater cost, those who chose graves in convent churches represent 43% of the total (Table 5.2). The majority of them (61%) chose San Francisco, which suggests that the friars of this order assiduously sought influence over the Indian immigrants who had no greater connections to the city's parishes or confraternities. This supposition is based on the fact that very few in this group stated an affiliation with the confraternity organized by the Franciscans, which was dedicated to Nuestra Señora de la Candelaria. The other religious orders attracted much smaller numbers: the Dominicans received 26%, while the rest are shared between the Augustinians and the Jesuits—religious orders that, it should be noted, had fewer years to their credit in Peru. The impulse to support secular clergy and diocesan authority, especially after the Third Lima Council, may explain the clear predominance of parishes over convents as burial sites.

In the 1600–1670 period (Tables 5.3 and 5.4), the tendencies observed in the late sixteenth century continue, with parishes (52%) still surpassing convents (48%), although the difference in importance between the two types of burial sites narrowed. Santa Ana maintained its predominance with 34% of burials in parishes. The second most important group is those who requested burial in their hometown parish churches outside Lima (30%). The presence in Lima of natives from places not very distant from the city is recorded with greater frequency or perhaps with greater care: the majority of those people were indigenous authorities or male members of the elite who held some post in their locality. The prominence of the Copacabana church (13%) reflects the superior organization of this institution and the spread of the cult, but it is also related to the clear decrease in burials in the cathedral (3%) and in San Lázaro (3%). The parish of El Cercado, under control of the Jesuits, gained in importance but did not achieve a monopoly. As I outlined in the previous chapter, the Jesuits had to compete for parishioners with the priests of Santa Ana both within and without the confines of their jurisdiction. Although parish membership increased in the neighborhood of San Lázaro, its residents preferred as their gravesite the neighboring church dedicated to Nuestra Señora de Copacabana.

The influence of the religious orders rose somewhat, though not significantly, in the seventeenth century. The Franciscans continued to be the most influential among the regular clergy, although they engaged in a competition of sorts with the Dominicans in offering burial places to the indigenous residents of Lima. Notwithstanding their apparent disadvantage vis-à-vis the secular clergy, the convent churches played host to the most renowned confraternities in the city, which may have contributed to the continued popularity of their funeral spaces. The regular clergy held sway especially among the indigenous authorities living in Lima and its surroundings. *Caciques* and their families in several cases assumed leadership of the confraternities. During the seventeenth century, the number of these associations increased considerably, as did the number of affiliates (Table 5.6). Seventy-nine percent of the total number of testators who appear in my records belonged to at least one confraternity, which represents an increase in comparison to the late sixteenth century (Table 5.5).

Between the sixteenth and seventeenth centuries there were significant changes in the use made by the Lima Indians of consecrated space. This process was not exempt from severe prejudice against, and exclusion of, this sector of the city's population. The death of Archbishop Mogrovejo in 1606 signaled a key moment. Until then, the cathedral was home to the chapel dedicated to Nuestra Señora de Copacabana, whose confraternity, made up exclusively of Indians, was founded on the initiative of Mogrovejo. When the archbishop died, the cathedral's council decided to start construction of a new building and denied the confraternity's petition to keep the chapel therein, with its corresponding ritual and funerary functions. Instead, the council authorized the confraternity to build a chapel in the San Lázaro neighborhood (García Irigoyen 1906, 1:208–12). The construction took more than twenty-five years, and the building was not opened until 1633. It is at this point that burials at the altar dedicated to Nuestra Señora de Copacabana recommenced. In contrast to other burial sites in the city, requests for graves here were related to the popularity of the cult rather than to that of a particular space or church. The displacements and lack of a stable location for the worshippers' graves explain why, despite the cult's great appeal, the number of people who sought burial near the image was not very large, although alms offered by the faithful continued unabated. The removal from the cathedral of the cult's altar excluded the city's only confraternity composed exclusively of Indians (García Irigoyen 1906, 1:207). The ecclesiastical council's refusal to allow the image to stay in the cathedral, thus putting a stop to the burial of its worshippers in the principal sacred enclosure of the city, anticipated the position that the Church hierarchy would establish as a rule in the following years. The synod over which Archbishop Bartolomé Lobo Guerrero presided in 1613 prohibited blacks, mulattoes, and Indians from being buried in the cathedral (Lobo Guerrero and Arias de Ugarte 1987 [1613], 135).

Indian Burials in Cuzco

In 1541, when the *provisor* Luis de Morales wrote to the king from Cuzco, he centered his concerns about graves on the rituals and offerings that the Indians continued to give in honor of their ancestors. As the man responsible for the Cuzco diocese, he saw in the custom a serious impediment to the conversion of the Indians; yet, in contrast to the unease expressed by Fray Domingo de Santo Tomás, he does not refer directly to the disposal of bodies. Other sections of Morales's report suggest, as before, that this matter was of concern to very few. There are continual allusions to "the meager sympathy" in which the Spaniards held the natives and to the multiple abuses that were being committed, in the belief that it was not a sin to assault them physically because the Indians were not Christians (Lissón 1943, 1: no. 3, 49–50, 54). The authorities of the Cuzco diocese had warned the Spaniards in their jurisdiction that they would be excommunicated if they did not take on the responsibility for burying the Indians (Torres Saldamando 1888, 1:365). It may be supposed that the measure did not have the hoped-for impact.[45]

Not much information is available for the years between Morales's work and the writing of the earliest wills that I examine here. As noted by Julien (1998), the proselytizing activity of the religious orders during this time was crucial. From 1559 to 1595, the majority of will-authors I have recorded chose to be buried in convent churches, especially in the church of the monastery of La Merced. The friars of this order, who claimed to be the first to establish a house and convent in the Incan capital, had significant influence over the native inhabitants of all social hierarchies.[46] This began to change in the 1580s, when the number of people who chose graves in the parish of the hospital for natives rose considerably; indeed, parishes greatly surpassed convents as the preferred burial sites at the end of the sixteenth century (Tables 5.7 and 5.8). Sixty-one percent of the 62 people in this group chose the parish of the hospital for Indians. The second biggest group requested that their burials take place in their hometown churches (14%). For the cathedral, Santa Ana, and San Cristóbal, the figures are very small. In my records very little information appears on the parishioners of Belén and San Blas, but it is unlikely that this reflects reality, for other indications point to their continued religious and political activity (Covarrubias Pozo 1963).

The initial impetus of the Mercedarians is reflected in the figures corresponding to the late sixteenth century (Table 5.8), when their numbers surpassed the other religious orders, but this momentum gave way in the following century to the ever greater activism of the Franciscans and Dominicans, who persuaded greater numbers of people to choose their convent churches as burial places (Table 5.10). During the seventeenth century, headed by the church of the hospital for natives, the parishes maintained their predominance (Table 5.9). The cathedral grew in importance, becoming the second site most chosen for burial. This marks an important contrast to the city of Lima, where we observed exactly the opposite tendency. In Cuzco, conflicts over jurisdiction also emerged, which meant that the services offered to parishioners became a matter of contention. It is known, for example, that the cathedral brought the parish of San Cristóbal to trial in ecclesiastical court because, when more houses were built in what is today the area surrounding the central square, their jurisdictions overlapped. In contrast to Lima, control over indigenous parishioners was not the only issue; the parish had authority over a diverse population that included criollos and Spanish residents in a prestigious area of the city. During this trial, criollo parishioners sought to distance themselves from the San Cristóbal parish, citing difficulty in the rainy season of climbing the hill on which the church sat, whereas the parish's indigenous authorities threw their support behind their priests.[47] But the ethnic segregation that is apparent in Lima is not repeated in Cuzco. A social framework including more complex and successful missionary strategies explains the differences.

The religious orders, which, from the creation of the parishes were obliged to accept the secular clergy's hegemony, demonstrated their skill at holding onto and even increasing their influence over Cuzco's indigenous population. The fruits of their labor may be seen in the burials in their churches and in the participation of the confraternities that they backed (Tables 5.11 and 5.12). The Franciscans, Dominicans, and Jesuits maintained strict ties with the families of Cuzco's indigenous elite, especially with descendants of the Incas, at the same time that they sought, through religious and educational efforts, to gain the loyalty of ordinary people.

Burials Outside the Cities

The Church made provisions for the transfer of bodies from one place to another, responding to the fact that the deceased must "return" to his or her parish of origin to be buried or that churches themselves could relocate: "When any church moves from one place to another, the bones of the deceased buried in them will be moved to the new site and buried there, being brought in procession with the high cross, as if they were being newly buried, and the same will be done in any case in which the bones of anyone deceased are moved from one church to another" (Lobo Guerrero and Arias de Ugarte 1987 [1613], 139).[48]

In the bishopric of Cuzco, among the decrees of the diocesan synod that met in 1591, there is a similar pronouncement, but with details that situate it in the context of the organization of indigenous *reducciones.* It includes instructions on how to proceed with cadavers of the deceased in the former towns and burial places, and it orders priests not to charge fees for a new funeral:

> And because we have received word that there are many bodies of the faithful buried in the countryside and former towns, we hereby grant license to the priests of the Indians to move said bones to the new churches, without charging anything at all for it and without forcing the Indians to hold wakes or masses for the deceased, under penalty of having to return twice the amount of anything earned in this way; but this does not prohibit them from making any offerings that they wish to of their own free will. (Lassègue 1987, 49)

It may be assumed that these relocations took place regularly for some time. Without doubt, they contributed to the consecration of the new churches, and they must have been crucial in convincing the people to settle in the *reducciones.* Nevertheless, the age of the dead played an important role, and moving the remains of a person recently deceased raised other problems. The *caciques* knew that it was possible to arrange for their remains to be moved if they died outside their jurisdiction. In 1577, Don Domingo Chupica, *cacique* of Checras,[49] requested in his will, authored in Lima, that his body be provisionally buried in the main church and that his bones be taken later to his hometown. Don Domingo's *encomendero* and hometown priest were named as his executors.[50] Wishes concerning the moving of remains continued to be an issue years later: Don Cristóbal Guayana, *cacique* of Huamantanga,[51] decreed in his will in 1606 that his body be taken to his hometown and buried in its church. Once there, the decision as to the exact location of his grave was left to his priest and *encomendero,* again named as his executors.[52]

Clerics and even civil authorities must have been encouraged by these requests that remains be moved to the churches of will-writers' hometowns. When made by *caciques,* they provided an occasion to reaffirm their identity as Christians and community leaders. Such requests had the additional advantage of validating the importance of the *reducciones* in the organization of colonial space. Both for the

Church and for indigenous authorities, as opposed to a probably anonymous tomb in the city, burial in a privileged place in the town church, with the corresponding funeral procession and eulogy, was greatly preferable, and family members and subordinates would be encouraged to follow the example.

The carrying out of these wishes could, however, raise considerable problems. How could one be sure that the transfer of remains from the city would not encourage people to revert to pagan practices? Overseeing the funeral procession en route would have required the presence of a priest; and, although the synods that met in Lima (Lobo Guerrero and Arias de Ugart 1987 [1613], 136) ruled that his should be either the priest from the hospital in which the death occurred or from the deceased's home parish, this was practically impossible. Responses to these requests varied from place to place depending on how the Church judged the advantages and disadvantages of accepting them. There were, for example, practical aspects, such as the distance to be traveled, and the deference owed to the petitioner's social rank was an important factor. While some funerals of gentleman of the rank of Don Domingo and Don Cristóbal could be carried out in the course of a day because their hometowns lay on the outskirts of the city of Lima, moving remains long distances presented great difficulties: even today, journeying to these places is not easy. We have no record of the body of a *cacique* being moved, but for an idea of the care exercised by the Church in these situations, we may study the example of the relocation of Archbishop Toribio Alfonso de Mogrovejo's body.

The archbishop died in 1606, as he was visiting Saña, on the northern coast of Peru. At the time, this town was a twenty-five-day journey from Lima. A canon from the cathedral was appointed to travel to Saña in the company of six priests to ensure the requisite dignity for Mogrovejo's body. The cathedral's council members were uneasy about the impression that the funeral procession might give to the Indians. It was a highly important opportunity to educate them about the meaning of Christian death and the holiness of the body of a man of Mogrovejo's rank and reputation:

> and in fulfillment of this [the canons] have decreed that the Magister Scholae of the Holy Church be accompanied by four or six

priests to deliver his holy body, which shall be brought forth with the form and veneration owed his saintly life and dignity, in such a manner that, since this land is young and its natives have not observed transport of similar prelates, they will understand his holiness and dignity, based on the deference with which they see his remains treated, and so that we, too, may fulfill our obligation, showing him obedience in death and gratitude for the saintly example he always gave us and for the good works he always did on our behalf. (García Irigoyen 1906, 2:297)

By contrast, honoring an indigenous chief could raise support for his office, and, although his example could undoubtedly produce a similar beneficial impression, for some Churchmen there were troubling doubts about the figure of the *cacique,* such as the sincerity of his Christian identity. There are indications that worries about the integrity of these relocations were greater in the Lima diocese. As suspicions about the indigenous population, and especially the authenticity of their Christianity, rose, the return of the remains of prominent Indians to their hometowns seems to have become more difficult. The data we have are for funerals held on the outskirts of Lima, in towns such as Magdalena, Surco, and Lurigancho. Requests for burial in more distant towns practically disappear from Lima's notary registers from the second decade of the seventeenth century. Around 1636, when Lima's diocesan synod met, condemnations of the Indians' supposed "idolatry" were greater than previously. At the same time that synodal guidelines reiterated instructions to priests or, in their absence, to sacristans, to bury in their parishes Indians who died outside their boundaries, complaints of *caciques* being laid in their ancestral tombs appear in the decrees, a violation demanding greater vigilance and punishment of the guilty (Lobo Guerrero and Arias de Ugarte 1987 [1613], 274).

In Cuzco, however, requests appearing in wills suggest that relocation of bodies from the city to towns throughout the diocese, and vice versa, continued until well into the seventeenth century. In 1634, Don Juan Poma Yalli, governor of the town of Oropesa, requested that upon his death his body be transferred from the hospital for natives to the town of Huayllabamba, and he named a landowner as one of his executors; while in 1670, Don Joan Gómez Galán de Solís Ynga decreed in his will that if he were to die in the town of Yaurisque, his body should be transferred to Cuzco for burial in the monastery of Nuestra Señora de la Merced.[53] Although we have no details regarding the carrying out of requests such as these, there are no indications that there were any qualms about the transfer of human remains. It is possible that the priests did not follow the most grueling routes that the funeral processions were supposed to take, but they were authorized to meet them upon their arrival in the towns or to be present in the chapels or sanctuaries that were being built at the entrances to the city (Lassègue 1987, 45).

How many were able to benefit from this attention depended once again on effective social networks. Returning to our examples, we note that one of Poma Yalli's executors was a landowner, either a Spaniard or a descendant of Spaniards, who lived in his town, while Solís Ynga enjoyed the privileges accorded to his status as a noble descendant of the Incas; he even claimed to have command over several *encomiendas*. The obstacle encountered by some *caciques* who had to settle for a grave in the city was a lack of sufficient resources to cover the cost of the funeral procession or of close friends or family to whom they could entrust the details. The poor were suspected of not burying their relatives properly, although the priest did not escape responsibility, as suggested by the *licenciado* Juan Pérez Bocanegra in his *Ritual formulario:*

> As a result of the priest not being notified of the children who are born and of people who are ill in the town, or in the *punas* (high plateaus), or in the ranches, has any child died without baptism, or anyone sick or wounded without confession, and without communion, and without the extreme unction that so many have died without? Where did they die, where did they bury those children who died without baptism? Or those Indians without confession? What did they give you to keep silent? Why did you keep silent? Was it oversight on your part, or was it malice? (Pérez Bocanegra 1631, 359–60)

Throughout this period the old family structures and social ranks characteristic of indigenous society in Cuzco experienced crises and serious breakdowns. But the adaptation to the new conditions that is reflected in the use of funeral plots, whether through relations with the religious orders or participation in the parishes, helped to reinforce the Incas' defining attribute: the social hierarchies over which they presided.

A comparison between the distribution of indigenous burials in Lima and Cuzco (Table 5.13) shows the conditions in which the Andean population gradually adapted to the organization of sacred space in the cities and across the *reducciones*. This adaptation was carried out both by means of the Andean people's identification with colonial jurisdictions and through the appropriation of various defining features, including, in addition to certain religious observances, the graves themselves. Furthermore, the parishes and the secular clergy gained much ground—and many adherents—through their control of hospitals and their proselytizing work among the roving population of the cities. Some followings that were under control of the diocese, such as Nuestra Señora de Copacabana or Nuestra Señora de la Purificación, made possible the success of the confraternities in this realm. The confraternities had the potential to adapt to diverse circumstances. But much more important, for both poor and powerful alike, and regardless of the specific ideas about the afterlife that they professed at one moment or another, the confraternities represented the community of the living, whose help in accompanying and assisting the dead in their rituals, offerings, and prayers made death more tolerable.

Funeral Rites

The interest generated by Christian rituals among the people of the Andes provoked a wide range of colonial responses and commentaries. In convent chronicles and letters, the religious described with satisfaction how their pupils participated enthusiastically in the ceremonies, performances, prayers, and chants in which—for both didactic and propagandistic purposes—matters of doctrine and divine praise were rehearsed.[54] Others, by contrast, judged this attachment to ceremony as a sign of the superficiality of the natives' conversion and their incapacity to understand and interiorize the complexities of faith.[55] Figures such as Viceroy Francisco de Toledo thought that without adequate guidance, the Indians might conclude that the lavishness of Catholic observances and festive occasions were a result of the necessity to address multiple gods.[56]

Funeral rituals, of course, hold great importance as public demonstrations of faith, the affirmation of social hierarchies and respect for authority, and the expression of people's loyalties and commitments among themselves and toward the realm of the sacred.[57] When we attempt to understand them as part of the process of converting the Andean population to Catholicism, given the central place in religious and political life that they occupied in the period prior to the European conquest, funeral rituals take on particular subtleties. Some scholars, basing their work mainly or exclusively on the repressive chapters of the colonial era, have concluded that post-conquest Andean funerals had only a thin veneer of Christianity. It has perhaps not been sufficiently observed that what colonial officials and ecclesiastics considered to be "excesses" and "errors" in indigenous manifestations of grief and, consequently, sure signs of the persistence of idolatry among the Andean people, consistently parallel similar attitudes in Spain. The continued calls to restrain death rituals are signs both of the slim success of these corrective measures and of the tensions resulting from religious anxiety in the majority of the population, the eagerness for social recognition among diverse sectors of the Spanish population, and the political ambitions and exigencies of the crown (Eire 1995).

Considering the matter in broad perspective, we are faced not with a simple opposition between idolatry and Christianity, even if the Andean sources describe the situation in these terms. I maintain that, when seen as part of an institutional and spatial complex related to the formation of social bonds, funeral ceremonies permitted the effective and authentic adaptation and incorporation of ideas, beliefs, necessities, and preoccupations about death held by the people of the Andes in the Christian sphere. The examination of local circumstances and individual experiences permits an appreciation of how this process was fraught with complexities. These adaptations explain the success with which the changes penetrated peoples' lives.

Apparel

Let us consider first the preparation of the body and funeral attire. The conventions followed in this regard in Peru prior to the conquest varied, as we have seen, according to region and the social status of the deceased. With the European invasion and missionary intervention, a noteworthy change for many Andeans was undoubtedly the substitution—in place of the numerous layers and offerings with which the body was wrapped before being deposited in the tomb—of a simple, single-color outfit, a shroud, or a religious habit. For the local populations, continuing to prepare funeral items, which on the coast consisted of great quantities of cotton cloth in addition to functional objects and offerings of various types, must have soon met with serious obstacles that cannot be attributed simply to religious repression. The conquest and its aftermath seriously disrupted the degree of social organization and the availability of resources that made possible the production of textiles in sufficient quantities for this purpose, which surely contributed to the reduction and even the disappearance of this practice.

Local customs varied depending on the balance between what people judged necessary and what the Indian parish priests or other ecclesiastical and government authorities were willing to accept. Council decrees stipulated that no more clothing than was necessary to cover the corpse be allowed and that the body of the deceased not be totally enshrouded (Vargas Ugarte 1951, 1:20). It seems that there were no specific instructions about the characteristics of the clothes themselves or their arrangement: whether the funeral outfit could be the same as that worn while alive, whether it could reflect the ethnic identity of the deceased, or whether, by contrast, it should aim for "neutrality" or reflect a Christian attitude that would place the deceased in better standing before his or her judges in the afterlife. The ecclesiastical authorities reserved the right to interpret this ultimate question, and their attitude changed considerably with time. In 1572, Elvira, a woman native to Jauja who earned her living as a vendor in the city of Lima, was buried in the cathedral dressed in an *anaco* (indigenous woman's outfit) that served as her funeral shroud.[58] But the times were very different in 1660, when the *licenciado* Juan Sarmiento de Vivero visited the region of Huarochirí in the Lima diocese on behalf of the archbishop. Sarmiento de Vivero came across the funeral procession of a woman. To his surprise, he found that the body was completely enshrouded in veils of black, dressed in an *anaco,* and adorned with a *vincha* (headdress) and *tupus* (brooches) of silver and brass. Sarmiento de Vivero immediately issued a decree—recalling the one mandated by the First Council of Lima—that from that point forward, the dead must be buried with their head, hands, and chest uncovered and that anyone disobeying this order should be severely punished.[59] Taking into account the date of this episode, it is unlikely that the local priests were not aware that their parishioners were dressing their dead in this manner. What for Sarmiento de Vivero was clothing "smacking of her paganism," for others was acceptable.

This incident shows the gap between the attitude of an orthodox Lima cleric and that of provincial priests, who saw no reason to oppose a custom that had become ingrained in Andean Catholic practice. Between Elvira's funeral in Lima's cathedral and the procession in Huarochirí, almost a century went by, during which the ecclesiastical hierarchy's attitude toward the indigenous peoples had hardened, demonizing their customs and their past almost indiscriminately (Estenssoro 2003). Apart from artifacts that the clerics called "idols," objects of local origin such as tools, musical instruments, textiles, and vestments were confiscated and destroyed during campaigns of religious repression that took place in the Lima diocese, in the belief that they were reminders of the pagan era that buttressed idolatrous practices (Duviols 1971; 2003). But because several such objects were in common use, even the proponents of eradication, such as the Jesuit Arriaga, left to the *visitadores* (inspectors) and parish priests the difficult task of differentiating between those that served as instruments of idolatrous cult worship and those that had no such connotation (Arriaga 1968 [1621]).

Textiles and clothing occupied an ambiguous place. Although the male garments known as *uncus, cusmas,* or shirts appear among the items that, because of their supposed dangerous nature, should be destroyed, they were not completely eradicated because they also symbolized the power of the *caciques.* I have found no evidence that female outfits were an object of suspicion, although there are records of episodes in which the eradicators found objects of cult worship and representations of the sacred, such as ceramic vases, that were dressed in women's clothing (Duviols 2003). Moreover, at the time of Sarmiento de Vivero, the garments and objects that adorned the body of the unnamed woman of Huarochirí were by no means strange in Lima. Sarmiento de Vivero's reaction appears disproportionate but not at all incoherent: it denotes a prevalent Spanish ambivalence that accepted certain indigenous practices provided that they were free of anything raising suspicions, that welcomed and deemed necessary those objects and behaviors that emphasized the differences that made the Indians distinguishable, in order simultaneously to cast doubt on their legality, validity, and correctness.[60]

In the cities a certain polarization is evident in attitudes on funeral attire in different regions: an overcompensatory urge is sensed in some persons, who claimed that a simple sheet or canvas blanket would serve as their shroud.[61] In Cuzco there were those who, despite listing among their possessions various showy and well-made indigenous garments, requested that their bodies be dressed in simple cotton blankets.[62] The influence of the religious orders—especially the Franciscans, with their promises of preferential treatment and a quicker path to salvation for those who were buried in a habit of their order—became noteworthy in the course of the seventeenth century.[63] Bernardino de Anaya, who in 1617 took charge of the funeral of his wife, Cuzco resident Doña Mariana Quispi Asarpay, chose a Franciscan garment that seemed most appropriate to him for a woman: the habit of Saint Clare.[64] In many cases the choice was most likely based on belief in the extraordinary intercessory powers attributed to Saint Francis and not necessarily on any special link between the petitioners and the Franciscans, for many of those who requested this habit were buried in their parishes or in the churches of other religious orders. Exceptions to wearing this habit are very few and are, as a result, a sign of the special bond that someone established with a particular religious order, perhaps because doctrine had been received from its friars. Doña Magdalena Chimazo was cacica of Chincha, a jurisdiction that belonged directly to the crown and had been under control of the Dominicans since the arrival of the Spaniards. She stated in her will of 1618 that, to gain the promised indulgences, she wanted to die dressed in the habit of Saint Dominic and that her body should be buried in the Dominican convent of Lima or Chincha.[65] The intercession of the saints could inspire the testator, through garments that represented them, to seek the best that each could offer: one woman from the Cuzco elite requested that she be dressed for burial in a habit of Saint Dominic with the sash of Saint Francis.[66]

The monastic habit was within reach of the most well-to-do, who, to qualify, resorted to alms payments or charged their executors and confessors with acquiring it. Understandably, the character of the transaction is not clearly defined: frequently, no distinction is made between the alms and what is being purchased. The price of the habit was substantial: one paid ten or twelve pesos, approximately the value of a horse in 1630. Twenty years later, when the use of the habit was more extensive, its cost rose considerably: some paid twice as much for this garment.[67] In a third strategy, some will-authors requested old Franciscan habits and offered new ones in exchange.[68] Such transactions had ramifications for both this life and the next. Not only did the rich help the poor religious (by providing new clothing), in the hope that the latter would reciprocate with prayers and masses, but it could be believed that a garment previously worn by someone devoted to convent life would have some special attribute that would favor its user. Despite the costs, it is not extraordinary to find examples of men and women of modest means who were willing to pay for an outfit that would more quickly ensure their souls' salvation.

Rituals

Given the codification of Christian funerary ritual in the Hispanic world of the second half of the sixteenth century (Eire 1995), it might be thought that individual expression in wills in the colonial context would be reduced, if not altogether suppressed. A skeptical attitude toward the content of indigenous wills would, moreover, lead one to expect them to be mere copies of imposed traditions that do not reflect the true intent of the authors. Analysis of funerary ritual as described in the wills must, however, be seen in the context of the changes in population and occupation of space, and in the growing institutionalization of doctrine that laid the foundation for a series of transformations and adaptations.

Royal funerals provided the ideal opportunity to spread Christian funerary ritual among the indigenous population. Celebration of the king's funeral rites was an obligation not only in the viceregal capital but also throughout the territory: once the news of his death arrived, the court arranged for all cities to participate in the occasion. The bishops summoned parish priests under their jurisdiction to take part in the funeral rites in the main city of their diocese, in major urban centers as well as in smaller and more remote localities, where local authorities and parish priests, in charge of organizing them, solicited assistance from as many people as possible regardless of their status: all sectors of society were required to be present. The civil and ecclesiastical authorities, dressed in mourning, presided over the ceremonies. For example, in 1621, upon the death of Philip III, both in the city of Huamanga and in the rural communities of the bishopric, burial mounds and funeral chapels were erected, funeral processions were organized, and masses were celebrated in which the priests preached sermons on the meaning of the occasion. The breadth of organization required to replicate royal funerals in the most remote regions of the viceroyalty is still surprising and calls into question the idea that indigenous people in the interior lived in isolation from what was occurring in the main centers of power.[69]

At the same time that royal funeral rites constituted the example par excellence of funerary ritual, the forms available to the general population were carefully regulated. Decrees issued by councils and synods mandated that transfer of the body from the place of death to the grave follow a certain pattern: the parish priest, sacristan, and acolytes went at the head of the funeral procession, bearing the parish cross and holy water, and were followed by other participants indicated by the deceased or his executors: members of confraternities, friars, poor people or orphaned children, and relatives. With the intention of dispelling any doubt as to whether Christian Indians deserved a treatment similar to the Spaniards', the First Council of Lima (1551) ruled that Indians who had been baptized were entitled to the same funerary services, without the priests taking any special fees. The point was to prevent the indigenous population, when they lacked resources for a Christian funeral, from continuing to practice their former, traditional rituals (Vargas Ugarte 1951, 1:20).

Despite the council's insistence on equality in funeral services, there immediately were exceptions. Part and parcel of funeral ceremony was the underscoring of the differences separating people (Eire

1995, 114), especially when these differences involved, in addition to rank and wealth, cultural and religious issues. Clerics and friars, as officiants, demanded the fees that they believed they deserved for their services. Among the complaints that the Cuzco city council brought against its bishop, Sebastián de Lartaún, in 1583, during the Third Council of Lima, was the high cost of graves and funerary services, whose payment priests and sacristans were demanding in advance (Lissón 1944, 3: no. 11, 65–66). The proposed remedy contravened the principle of equality. Faced with the need to put a stop to excessive charges, and following guidelines dictated by the crown and the councils (Recopilación, 1, 89v), provincial synods agreed to regulate the rates charged for the administration of sacraments and religious services. In Cuzco, the successors of Lartaún tried to reform the price system for services offered during burials. The schedules, known as funeral tariffs, set the amounts to be paid in alms, which varied by social standing, ethnic background, and age of the deceased. In the tariffs published by the diocesan synod of Cuzco in 1591, for example, it is indicated that the funeral of an *encomendero* cost forty pesos, while the burial of an adult Spaniard required twenty.

Burials of Indians carried a significantly lower price: for a "cacique or wealthy Indian woman" preceded by the high cross, the price was twelve pesos, whereas *yanacona* Indians (those in the service of a sponsor) and *hatunrunas* (ordinary Indians), who died in the city of Cuzco, had the right to a free burial (Lassègue 1987, 70–71). In Lima, the tariffs approved by the synod headed by Archbishop Bartolomé Lobo Guerrero in 1613 consider social hierarchies somewhat differently: for Spaniards, for example, only one type of full burial is considered, which cost sixteen pesos, and provisions are also made for the burials of mestizos and mulattos, in consideration of their financial means (Lobo Guerrero and Arias de Ugarte 1987 [1613], 223–24). Regarding Indians, new categories appear for those who had climbed the social ladder: unlike in Cuzco, the Lima tariffs make no special provisions for *caciques,* but they do for those better off who could aspire to a full burial, whose basic price was six pesos, as well as for artisans and small agricultural landowners, for eight pesos. If the burial took place in a church or convent, all fees rose by approximately one third (226), a difference that provoked some protests and that, in a large number of cases, was likely covered by confraternities.[70]

The price schedules for funeral services were also inconsistent: on the one hand, they established higher prices for the so-called full burials, meaning those led with the high cross, and, on the other, they ruled that in the case of the "poor of any state or condition, whether full-blooded Spaniards, half-Spaniards, mestizos, mulattos, blacks, and Indians," priests were obliged to bury them at no cost with the high cross and the requisite solemnities (Lobo Guerrero and Arias de Ugarte 1987 [1613], 228). Funerary ritual adapted to local conditions and to the changes that resulted as a consequence of the growth of cities and the diversity of their inhabitants.[71] Thus, funeral tariffs take into account the positions of the *encomenderos* and *caciques* in Cuzco, both a weighty presence in that city and its region, whereas in Lima the discriminatory practices that we have already noted coexist with a greater fluidity among the diverse strata of the population.[72] In this case—Lima being a city with a majority population from beyond its borders—new categories are accepted that do not always depend on titles, privileges, or hereditary positions.[73]

The tariffs issued by the diocesan synods of cities such as Cuzco, Lima, and Quito were very clear about funerals of the poor: they would be buried without being charged for the services or the grave, whether they were Indians or Spaniards.[74] In his *Itinerario para párrocos de indios*, Bishop Alonso de la Peña y Montenegro explained how some priests construed free burials to mean, in place of any ceremony, the recital of a brief prayer for the dead at the foot of the grave (Peña y Montenegro 1996 [1668], 2:531). Some argued that this attitude not only jeopardized the conscience of those who refused poor Indians the right to any ceremony but also that burial could not take place independently from it.

Luis Jerónimo de Oré (see Peña y Montenegro 1996 [1668], 2:531) and especially Juan Pérez Bocanegra (1631, 571)—the latter through his initiative to place the Roman Ritual (1614) at the disposal of the Indians' priests—explained the steps that must be followed. The priest, wearing his vestments and accompanied by clerics carrying the cross, censer, and holy water, would go to the deceased's house to collect the body. The tolling of the parish church bells would summon everyone to pray for the departed soul as the procession began its course. On arrival at the house of the deceased, the priest would say a prayer and sprinkle the body with holy water. The procession then would return to the church, with the participants carrying candles and intoning psalms and litanies in order to proceed with the mass once there.[75] The defense of funerary ritual for people of all stations ensured the fulfillment of a fundamental pillar of reformed Catholicism. In accordance with its vision of the afterlife, the soul's march toward salvation was firmly anchored in the belief in purgatory and in the granting of bulls and indulgences that mitigated the consequences of sin, so that help from the living, through ritual and prayer, was essential (Eire 1995, 119). Social distinctions would not be affirmed through the suppression of ritual for the most humble but rather by making funeral rites for the privileged more complex and grandiose.

The details that added splendor to the funeral included: the height at which the cross leading the procession was borne; the quantity and quality of the participants and even their attire; the tolling of the bells; the number and type of masses to be celebrated on the day of the burial; the paraphernalia considered indispensable for guiding the deceased's soul toward salvation, such as candles or other lights that were to be carried by members of the procession; and the precise location of the grave. Each one of these steps was, apart from being codified, paid for through an alms offering that in theory stayed within the limits of the tariffs published by the diocesan synods, but it was also subject to agreements made by the deceased's relatives and executors with the priests and friars of the convents and confraternities that would participate in the funeral ceremony. It was taken for granted in Spain and other parts of the Catholic world that the very luster of the ritual, expressed in the greatest possible number of masses, participants, and lights, among other things, ensured a safe passage to salvation (Eire 1995; Flynn 1999; Nalle 1992; Strocchia 1992). Indian will-authors were no exception to this rule, although the distance separating the typically ostentatious funerals of well-to-do Spaniards in the principal Andean cities from the burials of the most noteworthy indigenous people was significant. Despite the difference, it is important to emphasize that Catholic funerary ritual took root as a model to be imitated, that this model spread through an ever-greater sector of the indigenous population, and that, despite its obligatory nature, a perceptible process of learning and appropriation occurred that cannot be explained simply by manipulation by notaries, confessors, or other figures who exercised authority.

During the sixteenth century, Indian wills in Cuzco regularly indicate, from the earliest examples in the 1560s, the requirement that parish priests lead the funeral processions, while in Lima the stipulation is not consistent before 1580 but becomes practically continuous from that point on. This could be related to the identification of indigenous residents with their parishes, which, as I have pointed out, happened rather late in Lima. The change is also the result of the spread of the Tridentine Decrees and, shortly afterward, of those issued by the Third Council of Lima. As a sign of the consolidation of this custom among the indigenous inhabitants of the city in the seventeenth century, the priest's presence is not requested in the manner of an act of kindness but rather as an inescapable obligation on his part toward his parishioners.

Some decrees set forth in the funerary tariffs suggest that, because of its greater cost, a person's rank was indicated by the position of the cross—high or low—that led his or her funeral procession. However, this was not always the case. Although the rich and politically powerful tended to request that their funeral procession be headed by the priest carrying the parish high cross, many will-authors of modest means gave similar instructions. The cross symbolized society's concerns with social rank and ethnic identity as well as with the spiritual expectations of those who asked for it. We can better explain the issue by comparing information from the cities we are studying.

The majority of will-authors in Cuzco and Lima chose the high cross, a preference more pronounced in the capital of the viceroyalty, especially in the seventeenth century (Table 5.14). The difference between the two cities in the number of requests for the low cross, clearly greater in Cuzco, is noteworthy. Could this difference suggest that the indigenous population of Lima was not only more homogeneous but also more prosperous? Were there more poor people in Cuzco than in Lima?

The population of Lima had at its disposal diverse channels of social mobility. The greater fluidity of living conditions among Lima's indigenous inhabitants may explain why they were more willing to take on obligations and acquire customs peculiar to their urban environment. As we have seen, the funeral tariff devised for Lima did not make provisions for *caciques,* but it did for prosperous Indians. It bears repeating that these conditions occurred in a context very different from those of the Incan capital: the indigenous population of Lima was in the minority with respect to other ethnic groups, and there was no fully recognized ancient indigenous nobility linked to other sectors of society, whose presence could introduce major instabilities into the heart of the indigenous population.

Regarding the city of Cuzco, close observation of the personal circumstances of will-authors allows us to discern fine shades of meaning in the understanding of the term "poor," which did not depend exclusively on material circumstances but also on ethnic criteria, religious ideas, and perceptions of social rank. The equation between "Indian" and "poor" gave rise to some low-cross burial requests based on the Indian identity of the testator, especially in the sixteenth century. Additionally, there were those persons who, despite comfortable incomes, requested burials with the low cross, from which one might conclude that this was their way of affirming their Indian identity or that, confident in the spiritual benefits implied in such an attitude, they opted to make a public gesture of humility.[76] Finally, the proliferation of burial requests from the poor in specific periods—around the 1640s, for example—would be an indication of the material crisis and loss of power or prestige among once-privileged figures of the indigenous elite.

On its way to the church, the funeral procession paused for a few moments, during which the priest recited a prayer for the dead. Known as *posas,* these stations were made at street corners, and according to the tariffs of the Lima diocesan synod that met in 1613, each one was worth two pesos (Lobo Guerrero and Arias de Ugarte 1987 [1613], 224), whereas wills from Cuzco indicate a one-peso fee. There is no doubt that these recitations increased the prestige of the deceased, at the same time that additional prayers placed his or her soul in better standing. Though coveted, *posas* were not obligatory. The testator or executors could specify their number or, in the absence of sufficient resources, instruct that there be none. *Posas* were also common in Madrid in the sixteenth century (Eire 1995, 125), and our information suggests that they spread throughout Lima and Cuzco in the seventeenth. In comparing requests for *posas* in the two Andean cities, we observe another noteworthy contrast in the economy of funeral ritual.

As Table 5.15 shows, the number of requests for *posas* in Cuzco was practically triple that in Lima. It should be pointed out that five of the eleven requests for the viceregal capital correspond to *caciques* or major figures who expected their funerals to take place in their respective hometowns, located on the outskirts of the city, such as Surco (1), Magdalena (2), and others farther away (Sisicaya and Chinchaycocha). In Cuzco, except for two will-authors who expected their funerals to take place in the towns in which they were *caciques* (Caycay and Paruro), all anticipated that their funerals would be in the city.[77] The requests for *posas* imply the use of public space consistent with the tendencies we observed in examining the distribution of graves among the parishes and monasteries of both cities. If we attempt to map the path of the funeral processions that included *posas*, we note that at least one third of these processions in Cuzco passed through the city's main square, whereas the data on Lima suggest that their routes went outside the city center, which may be due to the fact that, as we have seen, burials of Indians in the cathedral were suspended at the beginning of the seventeenth century.[78] The fact that the number of requests for *posas* in Cuzco is much greater than in Lima is even more noteworthy if we remember that there were a greater number of people in the Incan capital who claimed to be poor or who requested burial with the low cross.

How are we to understand this imbalance? Preoccupation with social prestige would explain this decision in various testators: six stated themselves to be descendants of the Incas, two were *caciques* of towns in the region, one was related to a family of *caciques*, and four were artisans, who were among the most significant figures of the local indigenous population in the seventeenth century.[79] One sign that these moves reinforced existing inequalities among the Indians of colonial Cuzco is that the greatest number of requests for *posas* more or less coincides with the years in which declarations of poverty proliferated. The wills suggest that preoccupation with social rank grew in Cuzco in the 1640s and 1650s.

It is worth asking what, exactly, claimed the attention of the participants during these brief *posas*. The language of the wills suggests a certain ambiguity. Some indicate that the objective was the deceased's soul, while others call attention to the body: *"x* number of *posas* shall be recited over my body," or "the *posas* shall be performed with my body." These instructions reinforce the idea that, besides aiding the deceased's soul in its passage to the afterlife, this pause in the procession was also meant to pay homage to the person of the deceased, in both body and soul, and to his or her social standing. Although applicable to various cases, the social-prestige argument is not sufficient to explain all of them. The remaining examples from the city of Cuzco, like all those who were not *caciques* in Lima, pertain to people who, besides having the means necessary to pay for the additional details of their funerals, harbored an intense religious sentiment, if one is to judge from their membership in several confraternities, from their possession of religious images, and from their bequests.

The journey culminated at the church, where the rites of the dead and the funeral mass were said. In his work on the liturgy, Pérez Bocanegra (1631, 565) emphasized their importance: "Inasmuch as possible, that which was instituted in ancient times should be retained and preserved, such as celebrating mass in the presence of the deceased's body before burying it." If the funeral procession marked a transitional moment in which the deceased continued, to some extent, to be a person and retained the unity of body and soul, then the funeral mass signals an even more critical step, in which those two components grow further apart, at the same time that the deceased begins his or her definitive separation from the community of the living. The soul is exposed to numerous dangers by having recently left the body, and the body without the soul is simply corrupt matter. The ritual in the church is therefore one of transit, separation, and purification. The body was placed in the center of the church, depending on the standing of the deceased: if a layman, the feet were to face the altar. In all cases, the body would be flanked by candles. After the mass and additional prayers, the priest was to approach the deceased and, walking around the body, sprinkle it with holy water and then perfume it with incense. The grave was also blessed with water and incense (Pérez Bocanegra 1631, 573–76).

A reading of the wills indicates that in both Lima and Cuzco during the sixteenth and seventeenth centuries, the majority of will-authors provided for a funeral mass on the day of their burial (Table 5.16). The data not only represent the majority of people but also are fairly uniform in both cities, indicating the practically obligatory character of this mass, as Pérez Bocanegra described. But behind the data's simplicity lies a more complex reality. For example, the sustained and uniform nature of the instructions regarding this mass means that we are unable to tell whether there were changes in it over time. The decrease observed in Cuzco during the seventeenth century should not be interpreted as a falloff in the number of requests but rather as a sign that testators took it for granted that the mass would be sung, so that explicit instructions were not necessary.[80] Nor is it completely clear if an alms payment was required, or what form and amount it would have taken. In many wills the instruction is simply stated without, it would seem, much concern about the cost. Nevertheless, some refer to the payment of the "customary alms," the "customary offering," or the "offering as determined by the executors." Pedro Aculi, a man sentenced to death in Lima in 1624, instructed that on the day of his burial a funeral mass be sung with offerings of bread, wine, and candles,[81] while Don Cristóbal Guayana, cacique of Huamantanga, arranged for his funeral mass in 1606 to be paid for with a Castilian sheep.[82] Some testators, such as Juan Gómez, an Indian sacristan from the St. Francis Monastery, requested that their masses be sung "through alms" on account of their poverty and many years of service to the order,[83] while others, citing their great poverty, requested nothing more than a mass.[84] This wide range indicates that the conventions governing what constituted an alms offering sufficient to pay for the funeral mass were not clearly defined, so that the value of these exchanges could be very fluid. The determining factors must have included personal agreements, adaptations to local situations, and varied perceptions about the value of the items exchanged as well as what each party believed that he or she deserved, or thought that he or she was obliged to give: we must recall that some priests maintained that a graveside prayer for the dead was sufficient for poor Indians. In his study on death in the south of France at the end of the Middle Ages, Chiffoleau (1980, 130–31) observed the importance of the funeral mass for the process of Christianizing death. Centuries later in the Andes, the effectiveness of this strategy was proved once more.

| # Ancestors, Successors, and Memory

On Palm Sunday in 1606, an elderly woman called Luisa Quina wrote her last will before a notary and an Indian interpreter in the town of Santa Cruz de Lati, east of the city of Lima. Luisa recounted that she had had five children and that the eldest, Constanza, had been married to Don Rodrigo, one of the village *caciques*. Both were already dead as well as her other children. The marriage of Constanza and Don Rodrigo had produced one child, Don Cristóbal Ycuri, who left for the mining town of Huancavelica when he was very young, and Luisa had never heard from him again. For years, she tried to find her grandson, without success. Luisa wanted to bequeath to him a portion of her land and some money that she had earned. Hence, she arranged for both land and cash to remain untouched until Don Cristóbal returned. She had family ties with the group that still controlled the chiefdom of Lati not only through her daughter's marriage but also because she, herself, was the daughter of Chinaluiri and Pomaticlla, unbaptized Indians and old *caciques*. Nevertheless, her social standing is unclear, since Luisa did not use, nor was she attributed, the title of *doña*, which was typical of women of her status. Neither did she petition for her rank to be recognized or for her to be assigned any title. Given that she had lost her closest relatives and that it is likely that she had seen many others die during her lifetime, her task of searching for her lost grandson seemed hopeless. This preoccupation of hers points to issues that transcend material concerns. Her attitude reflects the general anxiety among will-authors to incorporate themselves into a chain of ancestors, objects, histories and descendants that, I suspect, would make sense of their past, present, and whatever awaited them upon death.[1]

This chapter explores what Andean men and women did with their ancestors, how they thought about their own death, and what place or role their successors would have. To analyze these changes I will consider relationships between the living and the dead in three spheres: the bequest of material and symbolic inheritance, the use of sacred space, and the creation and preservation of memory.

Succession and Inheritance

Let us briefly recall the ideas about ancestors in the pre-Hispanic Andes: they were as much specific characters as undifferentiated collective entities who protected and looked after their descendants, but they could also be a source of misery, especially when the obligations that tied them to the living were not properly honored. Ancestors also constituted a historical referent that validated or explained the existence of the group identified with them, reinforced the authority of the group's leaders, and guaranteed the control that they exercised over their territory. Ancestors were simultaneously abstract, diffuse, and tangible; the bond that united them with their descendants depended on complex and constant ritual activity founded on the conviction that there existed both continuity and reciprocity between the two. The descendants, as guardians of their ancestors, were, on their part, responsible for ensuring that those who succeeded them maintained and renewed these bonds. Faced with conquest and colonization, they found, on the one hand, the demand to submit to Spanish law and Christian doctrine and, on the other, the need to overcome the aftermath of the demographic crisis, the dispersion and weakening of related groups and of the bonds that united them.

A study of their wills facilitates an understanding of the strategies devised by the indigenous inhabitants of the Andes to confront these problems. The analysis presents some difficulties, for knowledge about pre-Hispanic forms of kinship, with the exception of the works of María Rostworowski (1983), tends to be concentrated in the

162 DEATH AND CONVERSION IN THE ANDES

Incas of Cuzco, and, even within this sphere, certain topics, such as the building of alliances and the creation of fictitious kinships, are poorly understood.[2] A second difficulty, closely related to the first, arises from the problems posed by the sources, which require a close reading to distinguish between the colonial footprint left in the documents and the pre-Hispanic customs to which they seem to be referring.[3] And third, systematic studies of the application of Castilian law in the private sphere to the native Andeans are necessary to discern the criteria employed to impose the law, and to recognize the importance of custom in fostering adaptation processes or even, as we shall see, to admit the coexistence of both law and custom with an eye toward reaching an intricate balance.[4]

Very broadly speaking, three strata are evident in the indigenous population of Lima and Cuzco: the ethnic authorities and "nobles," the intermediate groups, and the poor people and commoners. The classification is arbitrary given that, for example, the concept of poverty is a changing one,[5] as are some occupations and statuses such as servant or *señor*. For this reason it is necessary to underline how mobile these groups are. Although the role of the elites is essential, the attention given to them is not sufficient. This is especially so because, on the one hand, the emerging groups contributed to deepening the process of assimilation in the colonial environment, and, on the other, lack of position or fortune fostered their adherence to Catholicism, which influenced their view of life and death. This granted them, moreover, a place in society and a group with which to establish bonds cemented by religion and ritual.

Dilemmas and Practices

For the *caciques* or indigenous authorities, ensuring succession in the period following the conquest involved several difficulties. In addition to the profound impact on them of the conquest, there was the demand for them to convert to Christianity in order not to run the risk of losing their social position. The adoption of Catholicism brought with it the acceptance of Christian views on matrimony, but this entailed the prohibition of the polygyny that was common practice prior to the European invasion, which had been an effective means of establishing political alliances and strengthening the standing of those who held political positions and headed kinship groups (Pärssinen 2003; Rostworowski 1983). To this prohibition was added a restriction on marriages among close relatives. The introduction of criteria of legitimacy to establish rank and the right of descendants to inheritance and succession significantly limited the number of possible successors. Neither the Church nor the state imposed these demands harshly, indiscriminately, or inflexibly, nor did the affected parties accept them immediately and fully.

Political concerns account for a certain flexibility regarding lineage, marital strategies, and norms of succession in the early colonial period. This explains, for example, the fact that while the Second Council of Lima (1567) decreed that *caciques* must marry and live with only one wife,[6] its highest authorities interceded before the king to have the *caciques* granted the necessary exceptions to marriage impediments of any degree of consanguinity, as Archbishop Mogrovejo did in 1599.[7] Castilian law provided for the legitimization of offspring, and the crown also responded favorably to petitions of legitimacy submitted by some descendants of the Incas.[8] Rostworowski (1983, 154–57) has shown that in the early decades of the Spanish presence, some colonial authorities admitted as valid the prevailing criteria in the Andes, which provided for the bequest of the position of *cacique* to collaterals (brothers) over direct descendants (sons). This measure held advantages for both sides especially when, as we shall see, the *cacicazgos* ran the risk of disappearing in the face of the demographic crisis, thus deepening the political disorder.

Because wills contain dispositions regarding material and symbolic inheritances, their study permits an understanding of the impact that the measures described here had on the indigenous authorities in particular and on the native population in general, as well as on the ways in which their application was negotiated. A close reading of the sources allows us to discern the differences between the criteria that governed the bequest of material property—what we strictly understand as inheritance—and those used to bequeath positions, rights, and privileges, in other words, issues concerning succession. Although at first glance lineage, succession, and inheritance should be easily distinguishable,[9] especially in regard to the indigenous authorities, the cession of certain material possessions of symbolic significance such as land and other real estate, or objects such as emblems and clothing, complemented and corroborated the act of succession, despite the fact that the act could be presented as an inheritance in the strict sense, without repercussions at the official level. These bequests could signify either a statement about the position held by the recipient in the line of succession or an eloquent way of evoking one's ancestors and of thinking about the past and the place held there by the legatee.[10]

The situation of the *caciques* in the outskirts of Lima followed the same course as that of the majority of the indigenous population of the area (see chapter 4). The European invasion and the early years of colonization were especially hard on them, in terms of both physical survival and political authority. Some opted to abandon their positions and places of origin, as recorded by the *visitador* Rodrigo Cantos de Andrade, who, during his tour of the Pachacamac valley, noted that a chief and his entourage had fled to Trujillo at the beginning of the 1560s to escape taxation demands (Rostworowski 1999, 65). Many coastal *caciques* lost their lands, saw their resources diminished, and faced taxes based on census figures that soon ceased to have any connection to reality. Even when fewer and fewer people were fit to work, the authorities and *encomenderos* expected to reap the same amount of goods and money. The continuous pressure on an increasingly impoverished population contributed to weakening it even further.

As well as these threats to their own position, the likelihood of *caciques* leaving their jobs to their descendants was ever smaller because of the slim chances of survival among the next generation. In 1578, Don Hernando Anchiguaman, *cacique* of Lurigancho, declared in his will that his legitimate son, Juan Ayculi, was to succeed him. Nevertheless, because the son was nine years old, Don Hernando named his brother as successor until Juan reached maturity.[11] Two years later, Don Cristóbal Xuto Chumbe, head *cacique* of the neighboring village of Lati, made clear that his son Marcos, the product of a legitimate marriage, would be his successor. Given that Marcos was only one year old and Don Cristóbal apparently had no other relative who could replace him, doubt remained about who would take charge of the *cacicazgo*.[12] Other *caciques*, lacking male children, were unable to name a successor. Diego Fiño, heir of the *cacicazgo* of Lunahuaná, who in 1579 was a prisoner in the Lima city jail on debt-related charges, had a daughter who was still a child. Not only because of her age but also because of her gender, she had little or no possibility of succeeding her father.[13] In 1606, Don Fernando Nacara, *cacique* of Carabayllo, enjoyed a comparatively comfortable lifestyle, but, although he had illegitimate daughters,[14] he did not have a legitimate male heir to whom he could leave his possessions or his post.[15]

In other cases, *caciques* managed to live a long life, but their successions were truncated for lack of descendants who had survived to adulthood. Don Francisco Tantachumbi, primary *cacique* and governor of the town of Santiago de Surco, declared in his will in 1602 that after thirty years of marriage he had no children to whom he could leave his possessions and transfer his position.[16] This situation became the norm for the *caciques* of the central coast. In 1662 the *cacique* of the port of Callao, Don Pedro Manchipula, had witnessed the death of his son as well as his grandson. His only daughter, although she assumed several of his ritual responsibilities, apparently was unable to succeed him in his post.[17] An even more dramatic situation, which reveals the extent of the crisis that afflicted the population of the Lima valley, is that of *caciques* who had no one over whom to exercise their authority: the residents of their towns had disappeared. Don Pedro de la Cruz, head *cacique* and governor of Guanchoguaylas, to the east of the city of Lima, related in 1619 that the only survivor of the Indians of his territory who had been resettled in the town of Lati was a now very aged woman. Although Don Pedro had two sons, after his death the question of who would succeed him was irrelevant.[18]

The case of the indigenous authorities and Indians of the Cuzco elite, as well as of other highland regions, clearly contrasts with the situation of the *caciques* of the Lima valley. In comparison to the devastation suffered on the coast, the inhabitants of the highlands were affected to a lesser degree (Cook 1981, 247). There are sufficient indications that the *caciques* of the Cuzco region and other parts of the highlands had descendants who managed not only to reach adulthood but also to take possession of the father's post. This situation made it possible for the indigenous authorities to make provisions for the political future of the communities over which they presided, and, unlike their coastal peers, they were able to name their successor and even to negotiate the position of their descendants in the line of succession. Don Diego Condorguacho, *cacique* of Andahuaylas, one of the richest territories of Cuzco, stated in his will, authored in 1568, that he had ten children born prior to his Christian marriage. It is clear that they had different mothers and that special care was taken in designating the first and last names of each child in the will, thus putting them in a better position to claim their due. When he became Christian and was married, Don Diego's "official" family was considerably reduced in size: in two successive marriages, he had only three children who, in the eyes of the colonial administration, were legitimate. The oldest of these, Don Juan Condorguacho, appears to have been called to succeed his father as *cacique,* although the document does not indicate a definitive decision.[19]

The political negotiations that occurred between the colonial and indigenous authorities is evident in the case of Don Gonzalo Guanuco Quispe. When he authored his will in the city of Cuzco in 1590, Don Gonzalo must have been very old, given that he states that he had arrived in the Incan capital from Cajamarca in the company of the armies of Francisco and Hernando Pizarro and that he had especially served the latter. In the years following the conquest, Don Gonzalo became *cacique* of the *yanaconas,* or people in the service of Hernando Pizarro, and, some decades later, when the parish of the hospital for natives was organized, he was given the title of *cacique* of one hundred Indians in compensation for his service.[20] We do not know exactly his social standing or political office when he arrived in Cuzco, but his position of authority in the Incan capital was clearly due to the colonial situation.[21] Don Gonzalo states that he had two male children and one female, all *naturales* (illegitimate), that is, born while he was unmarried and of women who were also unmarried.[22] Apparently, he had no children by the woman to whom he was married at the time he wrote his will. Of the three mentioned in the will, he had his son, Don Rodrigo, and his daughter, Catalina, with a Christian woman, while his other male child, Don Diego, was the result of a relationship with an unbaptized woman named Mallau. Don Gonzalo stipulated that his successor to the *cacicazgo* be Don Rodrigo "because he was a man of the right age and ability for the task," and he instructed his executors to give him the titles that accredited him.

The aplomb with which Don Gonzalo resolved his succession despite having no legitimate children is noteworthy given that, at that moment, the strictest of political reforms had been implemented in the Andes, headed by Viceroy Toledo, as well as the guidelines for missionary policy, promoted by the Third Council of Lima. Don Gonzalo's attitude reflects the most important of the "Andean" criteria governing the inheritance of power: the ability to serve in the post (Rostworowksi 1983, 154). We must also emphasize, however, that Castilian legislation regulating the private sphere allowed control of succession in this manner because, in being recognized as illegitimate, not only could Don Gonzalo's children claim their portion of their father's possessions (Burns 2001, 4: xxi), but Don Rodrigo also had the right to the same honors that he would have had as a legitimate son (Álvarez Posadilla 1826, 112).[23]

As I observed above, the passing on of emblems of power was an act that reinforced the meaning of succession for a diverse audience. Examples from Cuzco and other highland areas will serve to illustrate their implications. Don Juan Gualpa Sucso Ynga, a man of Incan lineage, was the head *cacique* of the parish of the hospital for natives of Cuzco when he wrote his will in January 1590. Don Juan belonged to the lineage of Viracocha Inca; his ancestors had been governors of Antisuyo, a province located to the east of Cuzco that includes lands with a warm, temperate climate and also wide tracts of Amazon rainforest.[24] Because of these family precedents, Don Juan was made *cacique* of his parish and given authority over one hundred Indians by Viceroys Count Villar and Francisco de Toledo, respectively. Don Juan states that he had two children, Don Hernando Gualpatito, whom he describes in the first half of his will as his "illegitimate son," and another who was not yet born, conceived with the woman to whom he was married. He names Don Hernando as his successor in a clause that refers to him as his "legitimate son." The father reinforced the act of succession by leaving to Don Hernando a pair of *queros,* wooden goblets used for ceremonial purposes (Cummins 2002), and a pair of *duhos* or *tianas,* wooden stools that were emblems par excellence of the power of the *caciques* (Cummins 2002, 303; Martínez Cereceda 1995, 131–50).[25]

Don Domingo Chupica, *cacique* of the town of Checras, in the highlands north of Lima, wrote his will shortly before dying in Lima in 1577 in the presence of his *encomendero,* his village priest, and several other people.[26] Describing his family, he mentions first of all Ana Chumbe, to whom he refers as "my wife." Don Domingo declares that he was the father of various illegitimate children with her, but names only Don García, who was possibly the oldest. He then goes on to state that he was married to Ana Llapa, with whom he had "several children," although he names only two, Don Antonio Llaca and Doña Ana Astu. The disposition of his possessions shows his intention to reconcile the rights of both families as much as possible. The position of the "bastard" son is particularly important. Don Domingo declares Don Antonio and Doña Ana, as his legitimate children, to be his inheritors, with rights to their share of his farmlands as well as the rest of his possessions, whereas he leaves Don García several llamas, a small sum of money, and a pair of silver goblets or *aquillas,* which had monetary as well as symbolic value (Cummins 2002, 30). Furthermore, Don Domingo directs his executors to divide up some of his lands among his "bastard" children. The *cacique* of Checras did not indicate who was to succeed him in his post.

Don Domingo Chupica's will permits us to see how, by making use of what was prescribed by Castilian law, the highland *caciques* maintained a space for negotiating decisive aspects of kinship and succession. It is evident that the Indian parish priest and the *encomendero,* both present when he wrote his will, were well informed of his family situation. Despite the Church's prohibitions on *caciques* having more than one wife, Ana Chumbe and her children are not hidden.[27] Strictly within the field of "official" or Spanish legality, this recognition could be seen as crucial for ensuring the welfare of the "illegitimate" family, which explains the reference to their inheritance of lands and even livestock. But why the mention of the silver goblets left to the "bastard" son?[28] On the one hand, the mention of valuable ritual objects is a sign of the way in which the will was incorporated into the lives of the people of the Andes; on the other, Domingo, by this bequest, could mark the right of his oldest son to be his successor, something that, as we have seen with Don Gonzalo, was recognized under Castilian law.

Even when there was no post to be inherited, what was being transferred was the prestige of the lineage, the condition of nobility, which conferred on its beneficiaries not only public recognition and authority but also exemption from such burdens as taxation. In his will written in Cuzco in December 1600, Don Luis Chalco Yupanqui Ynga, who at that time held no public post whatsoever, left his only son several Incan emblems, chief among them three *mascapaychas,* insignias that symbolized Incan power. He directed the son to give one of the emblems to his daughter and asked his children to not quarrel among themselves and to "look out for their nobility."[29] With time, the majority of these noble Incas, although adapted to the Castilian laws and customs that regulated succession and inheritance, continued to stamp their own impression on the decisions made in their wills.

The procedure thus became significantly more complex than in the earlier examples. In 1646, Don Fernando Ynga had been serving for thirty years as mayor of the eight parishes of Cuzco, a post that was owed him, he claimed, as a descendant of the Inca Huayna Cápac. The job, the most important that an "Indian" could hold in the ancient Incan capital, entailed the collection of taxes owed by the city's indigenous inhabitants. In a clause in his will, Don Fernando recommended that the colonial authorities confer upon his illegitimate son, Don Juan Carlos, the provisions and dispensations necessary to take over the post. However, he named his brother, Don Martín Quispi Topa, as his heir. He also left Don Martín his emblems of Incan authority and all the property—mainly land—that formed part of his inheritance from his ancestors. Don Fernando also asked his son to make a donation of oil for the lamp that lit the Holy Sacrament in San Cristóbal Parish, a pious request that he likely thought would help his soul attain salvation, but he left in the hands of his brother other ritual responsibilities, such as the maintenance of a chantry established in the chapel in which the family tomb was located.[30]

The care taken with their symbolic legacy by all those in Cuzco who claimed Incan lineage understandably persisted throughout the years, although the means of expression were modified to make them more Christian and European.[31] Traditional emblems gave way to objects of clearly colonial manufacture, but the idea persisted of the passing down of objects that recalled pre-Hispanic ancestors, who sometimes retained their own names and were sometimes conceived of as an undifferentiated group of "Incan kings." The insignias passed on to future generations verified that they were descendants of the sovereign Incas and thus deserved their protection, such as those that Don Esteban Challco Viracocha Ynga asked his wife to recover for their children in his 1651 will so that they would have a way to escape from their misery.[32] Portraits of the Incas were also passed down, such as those that Don Lázaro Quispe Topa Ynga left his children in 1655: canvases that were hung in San Cristóbal Parish, possibly as part of the decoration of the family tomb.[33]

An important factor in the process of succession, as we have seen, was the gender of the descendants. At an early stage, during the sixteenth century, fathers were succeeded in their *cacicazgos* predominantly, and perhaps exclusively, by sons. In the following century, the preeminence of males persisted in Cuzco. In his will of 1617, Don Jerónimo Quipquin, head *cacique* of the territory of Chinchaypuquio, west of Cuzco, states that he had a legitimate daughter. Although she inherited significant portions of her father's possessions, it is evident that she could not succeed him in the post of *cacique* because Don Jerónimo orders that "the provision" held in his possession—possibly the document that confirmed his post—be handed over to the nearest relative to whom succession rightfully fell.[34] Don Jerónimo's case is not an isolated one. Although during the majority of the seventeenth century, women played a key role in the control of political structures, they were not allowed to take over the post of *cacicas*. Until 1670, the end date of this study, no examples of women heading *cacicazgos* in Cuzco are to be found.

Conditions along the central coast are more complex. In Lima, allusions to women *cacicas* are not unusual, although they did not necessarily occupy the position in the same way as did men.[35] While sometimes, for example, women inherited their fathers' posts, there also existed a custom of attributing the husband's job to the wife as a purely symbolic honor. An example of the former is Doña Magdalena Chimazo, who stated that she was the head *cacica* of the Chincha valley in 1618, though all indications are that she no longer held actual power, for the ravages of the conquest had irreversibly decimated the area's native population. Her personal fortune had dwindled at the same time and, apart from Dominican friars, she had no one to assist her, not even relatives.[36] Regarding the latter, in her will in 1607, for example, Doña María Llavin asserted that she was head *cacica* of the town of Magdalena, although her husband was, in fact, head *cacique;* Doña María had been born in Pachamacac, which fact confirms that she had acquired her title through marriage.[37] The case of Doña Ana Quipan is more difficult to interpret. She states in 1636 that she was a *cacica segunda persona* (second-in-charge) in the town of Magdalena; her father had had a similar position, meaning that she may have inherited his title, although her husband was also a second-in-charge *cacique* in the town. Although we do not know if she enjoyed any official titles or prerogatives, she did have social status. Doña Ana left no descendants.[38]

In another example, Doña Francisca Ignacia de Carvajal was the only surviving daughter of the *cacique* of Callao, Don Pedro Manchipula; her mother had been *cacica* of the town of Maranga. Doña Francisca inherited her parents' properties but not the *cacicazgo* of either of those towns. When her father died in 1662, she took charge of various pious works on his behalf; she thus kept her father's memory alive by attending to his political and ritualistic obligations. Eight years later, in her will, she states that she had no descendants.[39] Although we cannot determine with any certainty the origin of these female *cacicazgos*, their public image and the contrast they pose to highland customs are of interest. In a city inhabited by people from all over the Andes, the presence of these *cacicas* may have considerably modified the perception that many people had of the indigenous authorities, thus transforming the image of ancestors.

If we consider sectors of the indigenous population for whom political office and nobility were unattainable, then the matter of succession might seem irrelevant. However, the changes introduced by missionary policies as well as new settlement patterns, migrations, and unprecedented economic activities made possible the emergence of individuals of modest origin who managed to forge ever more important positions for themselves. This new social mobility is particularly evident in Lima, whereas among the indigenous population of Cuzco it is much more rare.

Confraternities, artisans' guilds, and, later, the military provided opportunities for these emerging groups as well as for those who already had power and influence. The degree to which it was possible to manipulate succession to these positions was not large, and it varied by institution and place. Given that hierarchy in an artisans' guild depended on seniority, social status, and economic means in addition to skill at one's trade, leadership could come under the control of successive generations, although demographic dynamics acted as a serious impediment to attempts at continuity.[40] The military ranks offered access to positions of authority and prestige to those who progressed materially in the cities, often the same artisans who were becoming leaders in the guilds. There are indications that with the title of *alférez* (second lieutenant) or captain and the opportunity of appearing in public ceremonies in charge of indigenous squadrons showing off their loyalty to the king,[41] some provincial noblemen managed to shore up their positions, particularly in the city of Lima.[42] It appears that these military titles could not be passed on to descendants, although attempts to do so cannot be ruled out.[43] Finally, the confraternities, because of their hierarchical organization and the ties and obligations implied in their activities, could raise the idea of succession among their leaders. Certain examples demonstrate how the political strategies of the indigenous elite were bound up with the religious practices of a growing number of Andean inhabitants.

When the religious orders organized confraternities to promote conversion to Christianity and active participation in devotional worship and care for the souls of the deceased, they tried to place the indigenous authorities at the forefront, and they offered them privileged burial spaces in their chapels. In this way they tied together the representation of the *caciques'* families, the care for the memory of their ancestors and of all those who were members of the brotherhood, and worship of the holy figure to whom the confraternity was dedicated. The *caciques* and other leaders became part of these associations in the role of "patrons" of their chapels, that is to say, both as organizers and as "founders" of the confraternities. This meant that—like the beneficiaries of a title—they were required to participate in the formation of these brotherhoods and oversee them, but not to manage their assets. The latter task was undertaken by the *mayordomo*, also generally chosen from among a select few,[44] who served in this role for a limited time. The position also carried social prestige, although on occasion it could prove onerous, and the integrity of the *mayordomo* could often be the subject of controversy.[45]

The *veinticuatro* was also more of a title than a position in the leadership of the confraternity. The *veinticuatros* were members who, rather like council directors, made decisions regarding the activities, leadership, and assets of the brotherhood, generally under the guidance of the priest who fulfilled the duties of chaplain. (The title *veinticuatro* arose from the fact that, ideally, there were twenty-four of these leading members.) When a *veinticuatro* had participated in the creation of a confraternity, he was known by the title of "founder," indicating that he was at the forefront of the activities that had made the very process of religious conversion possible.

The objective of the confraternities with respect to all their members could be reinforced and concentrated on an individual and his family if he had sufficient resources. A person could establish a chantry to have a certain number of masses said on behalf of his soul and the souls of other people with whom he was linked through kinship, whether real or fictitious. The chantries remained under the charge of a patron, who was responsible for seeing that the commemorative masses arranged by the founder were indeed said and that the funds set aside for compensating the priest who said them did not run out. Although intimately related to the confraternities, forming part of a ritual continuum, their activity was distinct, and the chantry patrons were independent of the confraternities.

The position of chantry patron as well as that of confraternity *veinticuatro* could be passed down to subsequent generations. However, this succession depended on the survival of members of the next or same generation, an area in which, as we have seen, the inhabitants of Lima were particularly vulnerable. This vulnerability could be remedied with the ties of fictitious kinship offered by the confraternity. While offering hope for those who lacked relatives, this remedy was more problematic for those who, like the *caciques* and other prominent families, wanted to ensure the continuity of their family line; hence, their interest in the chantries. The fact that the chantries were independent of the confraternities gave leeway to their founders to decide who would take charge, choosing from among relatives or people who enjoyed authority, economic solvency, or other related attributes. The idea of family succession became entangled here with the forging of alliances that would affirm the position of the family or individual who headed the chantry. Thus, for example, Doña Ana Quispe Asarpay Coya, a descendant of Atahualpa, arranged for her brother, Don Francisco Hilaquita, to be the patron of the chantry she had established in Cuzco in 1611;[46] and in 1630, Don Juan de Castro, a weaver native to Zurite, west of Cuzco, left his daughter in charge of the patronage, indicating that upon her death she was to be succeeded by the "closest relative with perpetual preference to men over women."[47] Doña Magdalena Quispe Sisa Ñusta, on the other hand, named a cathedral canon in her will of 1636 written in Cuzco,[48] while Don Juan de Espino y Torres, an Indian native to Pachacamac, designated Father Juan Vásquez, a Jesuit priest in charge of the parish of El Cercado, in his will of 1637 written in Lima.[49]

Apart from demographic factors, local sociopolitical conditions came to bear on whether the holders of positions in confraternities could or could not choose the people who would replace them. Significantly, only in Cuzco do we find people who left their office to a family member or other person of their choosing. In 1586, for example, Alonso Hanco, who was officially a resident in the parish of the hospital for natives of Cuzco and apparently had matters to attend to in various towns of the region, left his position as *veinticuatro* in the confraternity of the Espíritu Santo to Martín Utumaca, whom he describes simply as an "Indian from the town of Paruro," located to the south of Cuzco. Hanco also specifies in his will that his brother-in-law was to take over as *veinticuatro* in another confraternity, dedicated to the worship of Nuestra Señora de la Asunción.[50] The fact that people of low social standing were interested in ensuring their succession in the confraternities reveals the influence that these associations held as vehicles for reproducing and prolonging the memory of their members and that of their ancestors. Through these actions, we also see how Andean men and women of different origins and generations constructed the socioreligious space of the city. The scope revealed by this example permits us to move beyond the commonly accepted idea that the confraternities contributed to the reproduction of "the community" on its own terms and, preferably, within its own borders. Utumaca was neither Hanco's fellow citizen nor his relative, nor was he a native of Cuzco.[51] His integration into the confraternity might offer clues to the relationships established by people of the provinces with the indigenous parishes and confraternities of the Incan city thanks to the mediation of people who, like Alonso Hanco, moved about the region, established ties in the provincial towns, and spread abroad their ideas and beliefs.[52]

In the city of Cuzco we find indications that the hierarchies of society at large were reproduced in the confraternities; it is likely that only members of the Incan nobility could gain admission into the *veinticuatro* councils, although in other cases it was done through the mediation of a patron. Men and women of the indigenous elite in the Incan capital who did not preside over *cacicazgo*s could apply succession criteria to the confraternities to strengthen their circles of family members and close ties. The dispositions in the will authored by Doña Juana Quispe Sisa Ñusta in 1635 provide a good illustration of the strategies of succession and kinship employed by the descendants of the Incas in these religious brotherhoods. Doña Juana was a member of several confraternities in the city, including one dedicated to the Blessed Sacrament in the church of the convent of San Francisco, where the family tomb was located. She designates her nephew, Don Fernando Ynga, mayor of the city's eight parishes, as her successor in the position of *veinticuatro;* and she names Doña Juana Carrasco, possibly a mestiza and certainly a relative,[53] as her successor in the confraternity of Nuestra Señora de Copacabana, which Doña Juana had founded in the parish of San Cristóbal.[54] Finally, she designates two women whose names indicate their youth as well as their socially inferior status as her replacements in the confraternities of Nuestra Señora de la Asunción and San Miguel, in San Sebastián Parish, justifying her decision with the explanation that both were "orphans and my servants."[55] Noteworthy in these arrangements is the use of family members and close ties in various confraternities according to their proximity in kinship and in accordance with each person's standing; this ordering followed, moreover, what begins to look like a hierarchy of religious followings and sacred places.

What we have seen up to this point takes us back to the nexus between sacred places and burial spaces to which I referred in treating the organization of the parishes and the establishment of the convent churches, but before examining this point in greater detail, it is necessary to mention two others. First, we will see how the testators chose their heirs and executors. This analysis will shed light on where the substantial portion of the material inheritance of will-authors ended up, how the matter of succession was treated, and, consequently, what tendencies developed in each of the cities we are investigating. And second, a survey of the executors offers an additional perspective from which to evaluate the problem of social and cultural reproduction and to try to establish a profile of those who were responsible for ensuring that the living complied with the wishes of the deceased.

Inheritance and Heirs

Will dispositions have an importance for society that goes far beyond the redistribution of material property. Referring to inheritance, a commentator on the Leyes de Toro writes: "Inheritance is a representation of the deceased's person, whether or not he has possessions, and the right to name one who will represent and inherit from him after death is given to all free men who are not expressly prohibited by law from leaving wills" (Álvarez Posadilla 1826, 46). This invites us to consider the interaction between the idea of personhood in pre-Hispanic customs and the one that came about subsequently through conquest and evangelization. Distribution of the deceased's possessions in accordance with the instructions in a will shares an affinity for linking objects and people with other funerary contexts, including that of the pre-Hispanic Andean world (see chapter 1). The division of possessions evokes the idea of the person's disintegration and reintegration into the regenerative process of society (Barraud 1994; Mauss 1985), and exploring where and how that reintegration comes about sheds light on the process of the Christianization of death in the Andes.

From a strictly material point of view, inheritance consisted of, on the one hand, the portion of the testator's possessions due to his or her descendants or obligatory successors and, on the other, the portion that he or she could freely distribute. In the Iberian peninsula, the way that possessions were to be distributed has a long history marked by the intervention of state and Church.[56] Studying the problem of inheritance in cases where there was no will, Tomás y Valiente (1966, 227–29) explains how the monarchy imposed restrictions on the degree of kinship that could legitimate inheritance claims, which facilitated the crown's appropriation of those possessions, whereas ecclesiastical institutions claimed for themselves the portion of the inheritance that was considered freely available.

A detailed study of how Castilian legislation was applied to inheritance among the Andean population, and its consequences, is not possible here. It is sufficient to emphasize that decisions on wills and inheritance affirm central aspects of the evangelization discourse, with important social consequences. I will refer in this section to the figure of the universal heir, that is to say, the person who was in charge of the rights and obligations of the testator and took his or her place (Burns 2001, 5:xii). In the last section of this chapter, devoted to the memory of the deceased, I will study other bequests made by the testators with the expectation of receiving from the living the help they would need in the afterlife.

In the *Siete Partidas,* it was established that the most important part of the will was the naming of the universal heir; without this, the document lost validity (Burns 2001, 5:xiii).[57] Although they allow for a fictitious person or an association as universal heir (5:xii), the subsequent law compilations make no reference to this matter. For the purposes of this analysis, I will concentrate on identifying the universal heir and on the consequences of the appointment without elaborating on the juridical implications, a matter beyond the scope of the present study.

The appointment of a universal heir depended primarily, though not exclusively, on the testator's having descendants. As we know, legitimate children had priority over illegitimate ones, who could receive one-fifth of their father's possessions. Illegitimate children had the right to be the universal heirs of their mothers (Álvarez Posadilla 1826, 109). For many persons who had no children or other relatives at the end of their lives, the choice of universal heir and successor raised important questions. Who would take control of their possessions and of everything that represented them? Who would be in charge of looking after their memory? For those already converted to Catholicism, who would help them achieve their soul's salvation?

Intervention by the Church was important here. The Christian idea of personhood was crucial: a creature "composed of a body that dies and a soul that shall never die." This notion is based on the premise that every human being is also a person: a unique entity composed of body and soul. By contrast, as suggested in both pre-Hispanic funerary settings and chronicle descriptions, becoming a person was not within everyone's reach in the Andes: it depended on the degree of one's authority and possibly on one's gender, age, relationship with one's ancestors, and whether one had any descendants. As has been affirmed for other societies that base their organization on these distinctions, personhood represented a network of social relationships (La Fontaine 1985, 137).[58] Moreover, the dual image of personhood advocated by Christianity gave rise to the concept that the soul could inherit: the testator could be donor and heir at the same time. Some testators declared their soul to be their universal heir or left possessions and offerings for its benefit. Such bequests went for masses, various pious causes, commemorations, and charitable work, all of which were intended to ensure the soul's salvation. Although spread out among different groups and institutions, the Church, in effect, became the universal heir by entering the testator's kinship group or even replacing it.

Although subject to prescriptions imposed by law and doctrine, the designation of universal heir reveals a wide range of decisions that varied according to local conditions, personal circumstances, and, often, the way in which certain authorities, especially priests, brought their influence to bear. For those who had legitimate descendants, the decision need not have been complicated. But if a child was very young, it was not certain that he or she would reach adulthood, in which case some will-authors preferred to name an alternate. This was the case, for example, for Tomás Palta, who found it necessary to write his will in Lima in 1572 when he fell sick. Tomás's wife was expecting a child, whom his father named as his universal heir. Since the child might not even be born, much less survive, Tomás declared that should the child die before receiving baptism, his universal heirs would be his soul and his wife.[59]

In some cases these alternates were people from the family's inner circle even though, according to Castilian law, they had no inheritance rights. They were named with the condition that they take charge of commemorating the deceased and his or her ancestors. Don Juan Guaman, who said he was a prominent Indian native to Chicama and who resided in the town of Lurigancho, arranged his will while he lay sick in the Indian hospital of Santa Ana in Lima in 1616.[60] Guaman, who owned houses and farmlands, was a widower and had a legitimate son whom he named his universal heir. Because the latter was only four years old, Guaman stipulated that if the child died before reaching an appropriate age, his universal heiresses would be his godmother and his sister, who would be obligated to ensure that masses were said perpetually for the souls of Don Juan, his son, his parents, and his ancestors.[61]

Illegitimate children were dealt with inconsistently. Some cases suggest an attitude toward illegitimate children even harsher than what the law required, not just limiting but denying their right to inherit, as seen in the will of María Guacacha, a woman native to Arequipa who resided in Lima. María had an illegitimate mestizo son and a legitimate daughter from her marriage to an Indian. In dividing up her possessions, she left the former a sum of money and declared the latter her universal heiress.[62] Other examples suggest that the choice of universal heir could be arbitrary: Inés Pérez, also a native of Arequipa, states that she had had no children during her marriage, but she had given birth to a mestiza daughter who was still a child. Despite the fact that the daughter had a right to be her universal heiress, Inés named her mother instead. The reasons for this decision cannot be explained, unless Inés was advised to exclude her daughter because she was mestiza as well as illegitimate.[63] Some stories reveal very complex situations that contributed even more to destabilizing traditional forms of kinship, chains of property transferal, and the destiny of subsequent generations. In the city of Cuzco in 1600, Juana Cusi Chimbo explained in her will that she had three children, two of whom were daughters of the cleric Gerónimo de Mesa, whom Juana had served for twenty-two years, while the father of her third child, a son, was a merchant of possibly Spanish origin. The law gave children of priests and nuns an even lower status than that conferred on other illegitimate children; they had no right of inheritance from either the father or the mother.[64] Juana left almost all of her estate to only one of her daughters, also declaring her to be her universal heiress.[65]

In some cases, following patterns well established in Europe, appointments of children or subsequent generations as universal heirs were tied to demands that the beneficiaries follow a Christian code of conduct or fulfill obligations toward their relatives under penalty of being disinherited. Isabel Tocto wrote in her will in Cuzco in 1600 that she was making her three granddaughters her universal heiresses, with the condition that they not sell their house and lots in the neighborhood of the hospital for natives; and she warned them that if they led an "evil life," committing "offenses against God," they would be stripped of the property. Isabel's executors were required in this case to establish a chantry for masses on her soul's behalf.[66] Addressing his only male child in 1588, Juan Enríquez Chuircho stated: "my son shall live in this city and not live in the Andes province and shall make a life with his wife in this city and shall live in a Christian fashion."[67] In commenting on similar examples in his study of the Italian city of Siena, Cohn (1988) concludes that these demands show how testators tried to control their successors from beyond the grave. While this interpretation may be correct, it should be added that statements of this type in the Castilian context were also supported by the *Siete Partidas,* which had long ago established the cases in which the right to inherit was annulled—for example, for physically attacking one's parents, failing to tend to their needs, and, in the case of women, leading an "evil life" (Burns 2001, 5:xiv). Isabel Tocto hoped for more virtuous women among her descendants: her daughter—whom she named as one of her executors—was a nun in the convent of Santa Clara. Enríquez Chuircho, for his part, wanted to be sure that his son would remain in the city of Cuzco to look after the properties left him by his father.

Both in Lima and in Cuzco, spouses were the second option as universal heirs. A testator could name his wife as his universal heir only if he had no heir apparent, such as children or parents, in which case she had a right to one-fifth or one-third of the estate. Jointly held property (*bienes gananciales*), that is, possessions acquired by the couple during the marriage, was excluded from the inheritance.[68] In both cities the majority of these appointments came with no conditions attached. A fairly common example is Doña Magdalena Sulcamo, a native of the Nazca valley, south of Lima, who named her husband as her universal heir with the condition that he have fifty pesos' worth of masses said every year on behalf of her soul and those of her parents and her grandparents.[69] Even more frequent are cases such as that of Diego Tantaquileche, a tailor native to Cajamarca, in the highlands north of Lima, who states in his will of 1589 that because his parents had died years ago and he had no children, he was naming his wife as his universal heir "for the many good works she has done me and the great love I have for her."[70] Leonor Pagua, who wrote her will in Lima in 1605, justified her decision to name her husband as her universal heir by offering a brief review of her family fortunes: when she married, her father did not give her a dowry or her share of her mother's possessions; everything that Leonor owned, she had acquired during her marriage.[71]

After relatives, bequests left to the soul, confraternities, and religious devotions are the most representative during the sixteenth and seventeenth centuries. Made with the intention of benefiting not only the testator but also his family and ancestors, bequests of this type represented an alternative in the case of an absence of descendants and relatives in general. Frequently, in accordance with legal proscriptions on inheritances left to spouses, siblings, and collateral relatives, a number of testators opted to name their soul as universal heir rather than any surviving relatives. For those Indians who had moved to Lima from the provinces, decisions of this type confirmed the breakup of the family line. Doña Ana de Carvajal, daughter of the head *cacique* of Otuzco, a highland province north of Lima, and a resident of the viceroyalty's capital, named her soul as her universal heir even though her brother was a *cacique* in her home province. Doña Ana was a widow and stated that she had no heir apparent among either her ancestors or her descendants.[72] Inés Jutuy, who owned a house and lands in the Lima neighborhood of San Lázaro, left to her husband, "because of my love for him and his kind treatment of me," a small sum of money and the "odds and ends" in her household, but she named her soul as her universal heir.[73]

The influence of confessors and priests promoted a practice that, besides being common in Castile (Eire 1995, 236–47), was part of the

missionary strategy in the Andes. Juana, a woman native to Huarochirí, in the Lima highlands, stipulated in her will written in 1579
that her universal heir would be her soul, for which purpose half of
her possessions were to be spent for masses while the other half
were to be donated to the Santa Ana hospital.[74] In various wills the
salvation of the soul is directly linked to charitable work. In 1573, María
Curi, in naming her soul as universal heir, did not request masses
but instead stipulated that her estate was to be divided among "poor
Indians for the love of God," whereas Catalina Payco ordered that her
possessions go toward "masses and offerings to poor people, half to
Indian men and women and half to Spanish men and women."[75]

Although in the following century offerings to the poor continued to appear in wills, from that point onward, naming one's soul as
universal heir meant that inheritances would go toward masses, while
charitable works appeared in other sections of the document.[76] It is
impossible to tell whether bequests to confraternities or religious
groups interfered with the rights of close relatives. Those who left all
their possessions to these organizations tended to be widows, who
stated that they had no surviving relatives. Such was the case of María
Quito, *veinticuatro* of the confraternity of Nuestra Señora del Rosario
in Lima, who left her possessions to this brotherhood in 1612.[77] In
Cuzco, Doña Angelina Pilco Sisa Ñusta, who claimed to be the daughter of Don Cristóbal Paullo Inca and the granddaughter of Inca Huayna
Capac, named the chapel of Nuestra Señora de la Consolación in the
Jesuit church as her universal heir in 1623. Doña Angelina gave as-
surances that she had no heirs, which seems odd because various
people living in Cuzco claimed to be descended from similar ancestors. This may be one example of the Society of Jesus's effectiveness
in claiming a relationship to an Incan descendant and thus gaining
access to her possessions.[78]

To give a quantitative view of the appointments of universal heirs,
Tables 6.1–6.4 identify them first within the family line, including
ancestors and descendants. (See Appendix B for Tables 6.1–6.12.) All
the children belong to the single category of descendants. To avoid
excessively complicating the presentation, I do not distinguish between legitimate and illegitimate children, but I do show whether the
inheritance was divided among only children, if they were men or

women, and if the testators had several children. Disaggregated figures and percentages are shown as well as the overall percentage for the full set of descendants. Regarding the ancestors, who could inherit if the testator had no children, I have also opted to make distinctions, primarily to show the importance that mothers acquired as universal heiresses in Lima in comparison to Cuzco. Finally, the cases in which the testator named his or her soul, a religious following, or a confraternity as universal heir are indicated individually but with a collective percentage since the three pertain to the sphere of the Church.

Analyses of the wills allow us to see some significant parallels and contrasts between the cities of Lima and Cuzco. The consequences of the demographic crisis and migratory patterns that created each city's unique profile are reflected in the identity of the universal heir. In Lima, where many testators lacked descendants, competition between them and ecclesiastical institutions was particularly acute in the late sixteenth century (Table 6.1), when population decline was gravest. Inheritances are divided into roughly equal proportions: 33% of testators in Lima appoint their children as universal heirs, while the Church assumes that role in 30% of cases, with a majority naming their soul as beneficiary. In Cuzco in the late sixteenth century (Table 6.3), the situation is very different: 64% of testators named their children as universal heirs, whereas Church-related institutions represent only 8%. The indigenous population of Lima recovered in the seventeenth century (Table 6.2), resulting in a greater number of direct descendants inheriting, with a decrease in estates left to the soul. In contrast, in Cuzco in the seventeenth century there is a decrease in bequests to children, offset by a higher rate of bequests to the Church (Table 6.4).

Explaining this change as the result of a population contraction would require additional information on the city's population in the period. Testators with no heir apparent may well have been ever greater in number. Certainly, and in contrast to the early decades, when we note what appears to be a stricter observance of the Castilian laws of succession, some persons opted to leave their possessions to family members not fully recognized by the law: siblings, nieces and nephews, aunts and uncles, and adopted children; these appear in the column titled "Others."[79] This group also includes those who, in lesser numbers, decided or were convinced—even forced—by different people to declare them their universal heirs.[80] As can be seen, the proportion of these inheritances remained stable in Lima in the sixteenth and seventeenth centuries, but it increased notably from one century to the next in Cuzco. This is a sign of the increasing impoverishment of the indigenous population during this period, resulting from the plundering of their possessions and the disintegration of their family fortunes.

Role of the Executors

Although the number varied between one and five, each testator generally named two executors. There are several significant features of these appointments. First, literacy was not always a requirement. In Lima during the late sixteenth (Table 6.5) and especially the seventeenth (Table 6.6) centuries, a large group of primary executors were the testators' spouses, whereas in Cuzco in the late sixteenth century (Table 6.7), *caciques* were the most frequently solicited for this task, and they remained significant in the seventeenth century (Table 6.8). In both cases we are dealing with largely illiterate people. This raises questions about the ways in which records were kept and their contents communicated. Wills contain inventories not only of objects that were within view at the time of writing but also of others that were not. They also include accounts of people, debts, lands, and events from the past narrated by the testator. How did one keep track of it all? How did the executors meet their obligations if not all of them could read? It is likely that one of the executors was in charge of looking after the deceased's possessions, and this may generally have been the role of the spouse, while the second executor carried out the tasks that required dividing up the property in a specific way through offerings, paying and collecting debts, and ordering masses.

We cannot know with certainty how the stipulations were recorded and fulfilled or even how information was circulated about the document's contents.[81] The assumption that unfamiliarity with writing was exploited by priests or other people in positions of authority is not without foundation, but the documents themselves also suggest that there were more complex mechanisms in play than the simple alienation of the indigenous population from the written word, and that families, individuals, and ethnic authorities maintained records about their ancestors. In Lima in the late sixteenth century, the second executor was sometimes, in addition to a Spaniard or a priest, the father or brother of the testator or a *cacique* or *mayordomo* (Table 6.9).[82] In the seventeenth century, 22% of the total of 45 people who accompanied the testator's spouse as executors were brothers of the deceased, and 27% were his or her friends, also Indians (Table 6.10). In Cuzco in the late sixteenth century, the testator's spouse was assisted by *caciques* (12%), Indian friends or *compadres* (45%), and, in only one case, a priest (Table 6.11). In the seventeenth century, in close to half the cases (46%) the spouse was named as sole executor. Those who accompanied the spouse in the other cases were primarily people, also indigenous, who were close to the deceased (Table 6.12).

Second, local forms of authority varied from one city to another. In Lima some testators chose the *alcalde* (mayor) of Indians as their executor, but the confraternity *mayordomos* most frequently filled the role. In the sixteenth century there are frequent cases in which confraternity *mayordomos* were named as sole executors (29%) or together with another person close to the testator, identified as indigenous (43%). In the following century, the second person was a confraternity *mayordomo* (55%). These figures show the influence achieved by religious brotherhoods as institutions that steered the religious life of the indigenous population, taking charge of the burial and commemoration of its members. A comparison with Cuzco raises important contrasts. *Mayordomos* do not explicitly appear as an option in the Incan city, possibly because these positions tended to be associated with the indigenous authorities or prominent residents, for which reason the latter are alluded to more frequently. Although it might be said that the position of parish *cacique* was a colonial creation, the person filling it evoked traditional authority at the same time that his leadership was reaffirmed once it became a model of Christianity and of obedience to the established order. In the seventeenth century, the position of the *caciques* appeared to decline considerably, from 21% to only 7%. The more frequent presence of priests, Spaniards, and mestizo intermediaries as executors eclipsed *caciques* in the Incan city, although the parallel development and consolidation of the elite group recognizable by the title of *don* probably filled leadership roles in ritual and civic activities.

Third, an important group emerged in both Lima and Cuzco in the sixteenth and seventeenth centuries: a group of individuals who were not family members of the testators. Their identity and relationship to the will's author are not always possible to determine: often we know only their names. In Lima, some testators leaned toward friends, colleagues, and godparents,[83] but the tendency in both cities was to appeal to people in a responsible and trustworthy position: master artisans, bosses, and general language interpreters, who would act independently in cooperation with the testator's family.[84] As well as administering inheritances, collecting debts, and arranging commemorative masses with confraternities and priests, in some cases, the guardianship of minor children was added to that of executor.[85]

Finally, it remains to evaluate the role of priests and Spaniards as executors of Indian wills in the two cities. In Lima, the former went from a prominent position in the sixteenth century to a rather more subdued one in the next. But it is not plausible to suggest that the clergy's influence declined. The fact that some of the sixteenth-century wills were made in the Santa Ana hospital, which does not happen in the following century, may partially explain this imbalance. The cases in which testators named priests and men of the cloth as their executors speak of the esteem in which confraternity chaplains,[86] confessors,[87] and men with a reputation for holiness[88] were held. The growing influence of clerics in Cuzco was probably due to intense activity by the religious orders, the vigor of the confraternities, and the fact that the convents opened their doors to indigenous men and women despite the subordinate role assigned to them. The use by indigenous will-authors of Spanish executors was characterized in both cities by guardianship and cronyism, as in the cases of *caciques* interested in negotiating optimal conditions for their own relatives. Some appointments can be explained by paternalistic bonds, as with Alonso Pacomanta, who named the Spanish woman who hosted him in her house as his executor; or Joana Bello, who chose her godfather so that he could take charge of her affairs and raise her daughter.[89] A similar type of relationship appears to explain why women of different standings chose *regidores* (city councilmen) as their executors.[90] Probably in the expectation that their interests would be adequately safeguarded, some chose as their executors civil servants, collectors of tithes and other taxes,[91] and merchants.[92] Some of these arrangements, rather than expressing votes of confidence, appear to disguise the plundering of some Indians by their creditors.[93]

Executors, over time, became increasingly diverse both ethnically and socially, to the point of forming clientship networks of relatives, indigenous and religious authorities, tradesmen, and civil servants. The diverse nature of the group and the tightness of the bonds that united its members suggest that the notion that Indian testators were often victims of manipulation by the Spaniards needs to be replaced with a more complex portrait. Material and symbolic exchanges as well as links of dependency forged over time were primary in the decisions taken by will-authors when choosing who was to take charge of carrying out their last wishes.

From *Guacas* to Chapels

One of the most important changes to Christianity occurred when bodies of the faithful were allowed to be buried in churches (Ligou 1975). The impact on the process of Christianizing death was enormous, in the Andes and elsewhere. The move from the multiple forms and varied placements of graves that were characteristic of the pre-Hispanic era to the uniform setting of burials in churches represents one of the most significant cultural and political transformations in the history of this region. Nevertheless, historiography has paid more attention to those who disinterred family members buried in churches in order to take them back to their old burial grounds.[94] A study of documents from campaigns of religious repression carried out in the Lima diocese during the colonial period has resulted in practically no research into how and why the people of the Andes finally agreed to church burials.[95] Descriptions of sinister judicial processes in which men and women were forced to display the cadavers of their relatives, in order then to watch them be reduced to ashes, give weight to the hypothesis that repression was the means employed to lead the people of the Andes to abandon the custom of burying their dead in *guacas* and *machayes*.[96] A policy of repression, no matter its scope, intensity, and duration, is not only insufficient to explain the extraordinary change brought about in the colonial Andes, but it also gives undue credit to another argument, untenable but widespread, that the Andean population's conversion to Catholicism was only pretense, and that ancient rituals continued to be practiced in secret. Both history and the current reality of the Andes contradict these claims. Churches became spaces that guarded and reified the memory of groups linked through blood or fictitious kinship, and they were also the places in which these ties were manifested.

Graves of the Caciques

We noted earlier that the arrangement of burial places is directly linked to the formation of cities and their sociopolitical dynamics. Crucial to this was the role of the indigenous authorities and the place they occupied in the cities' spaces. While each Cuzco parish had its *caciques,* in Lima the indigenous authorities were officially housed in towns where the *reducciones* were established.

Although the place where *caciques* should fix their residence was not a matter of controversy, the place and form of their graves did provoke some debate.[97] Council resolutions made clear that new Christians must be buried in churches, but the way in which *caciques* were to be treated was left to the discretion of priests and *doctrineros* (Indian parish priests). The idea of assigning to the *caciques* privileged spots in churches had to spread very quickly if it was to persuade them to convert to Christianity and cooperate with the government. Not all colonial authorities, however, were in favor of this initiative. After traveling across wide areas of the viceroyalty on inspection trips, the *oidor* Gregorio González de Cuenca, in a letter addressed to the provincial council that was meeting in Lima in 1567, urged the bishops not to allow *caciques* to build burial vaults in churches because their relatives performed "many spells and superstitions from their rites" on top of them. He recommended instead that *caciques* be buried with complete simplicity, just as other Indians were (Lissón 1944, 2: no. 7, 354–55). Although we do not know if the council issued any answer or comment, practice shows that this was one recommendation that the Church rejected categorically.

In the Indian towns surrounding Lima, burial spaces assigned to *caciques* must have practically paralleled the *reducciones*. It is likely that they were part of the means employed to convince *caciques* of the convenience of moving to the new towns. Don Alonso Anchiguaman, head *cacique* of Lurigancho, arranged in his will of 1578 for his body to be buried in the town church and in the "part and place where caciques are buried."[98] Don Bartolomé Guamac Chumbi, head *cacique* of the town of Guanchallay or Guanchohuaylas, ten miles from Lima, ordered in 1577 that his burial take place in the town church of whatever *reducción* his *encomienda* was ultimately resettled in, "in the Gospel area," which suggests that even before the *reducciones* were completely finished, some *caciques* anticipated where their graves would be.[99]

After several decades of Spanish presence, funeral vaults for *caciques* were common in the main town churches. Burial arrangements in wills show a determination to occupy important spaces inside the churches and to be reunited in those spaces with parents and ancestors as much as possible. In 1628, Don Cristóbal Guacay, then fifteen years old, indicated that he wanted to be buried in the town of Magdalena in "the grave left . . . by my father, which is beneath the high altar."[100] In his will written ten years earlier, Don Esteban, Don Cristóbal's father, had asked to be buried "at the foot of the high altar above the steps," or, if that proved impossible, in "the grave that my mother, Doña Ana Cuyte, has in the same church, there where she is buried which is beneath the high altar of said church."[101] There are many indications that in subsequent years other members of the family chose this spot for their graves. This custom was also pronounced in other towns of the Lima diocese.[102] As we saw earlier, some *caciques* who wrote their wills in Lima arranged for their remains to be transferred to their hometowns and buried in graves already held in those churches. There can be no doubt that burials in such prominent places were the marker of a leadership status that was perpetuated after death.

We find a similar state of affairs in various towns of the Cuzco diocese. Graves of the indigenous authorities there also tended to be in privileged places in churches. In 1583, Don Francisco Orco Supa, *cacique* of Anta, ordered his body to be transferred from Cuzco to his hometown to be buried in the main church, in the grave where his father's remains lay.[103] In Cuzco, the first *caciques* of the parish of the hospital for natives were promised by the priests that their burials would take place with as much ceremony as possible. Don Juan Gualpa Sucso Ynga, one of these first *caciques*, alludes in his will to a written agreement made with his priest.[104] According to the *fe de muerte* issued by the local notary, Don Gonzalo Guanuco Quispe, who was also a *cacique* of the parish of the hospital for natives, he was buried beneath the high altar of his church.[105]

In one city after another of the Peruvian viceroyalty we find exceptions that raise questions about the political standing of *caciques* and their religiosity. For example, some ethnic authorities in the town of Pachacamac did not have graves in their hometown church but rather in the parish of Santa Ana in the city of Lima. A possible explanation is the political crisis that affected them due to the dispersion of governing families and the sharp decline in the local population (Rostworowski 1999, 12–18; 2002, 108–9).[106] The standing of towns such as Pachacamac in the context of ecclesiastical jurisdiction is still being explored,[107] and the importance of certain religious followings might also explain the different location of the indigenous authorities' tombs.

In Cuzco there may have been other reasons for *caciques* and other ethnic authorities to chose tombs in the city rather than in their hometowns. When Doña Leonor Coca Pinto wrote her will in 1619, she left careful instructions about the resting place of her remains and those of her husband, Don Pedro Agustín Callapiña, who had died some time ago. Both were native to the town of Pacaritambo, where Don Pedro had been head *cacique*.[108] Doña Leonor ordered that, at her death, her body be buried in the church of the Santo Domingo convent; if she should die in the town of Pacaritambo or some other place, her and her husband's remains were to be transferred to Cuzco to be buried in Santo Domingo. They were not the only *caciques* from towns outside Cuzco whose graves were in the convent. Doña Ana Quispe Asarpay, a descendant of the Inca Atahualpa, stated in her will of 1611 that she wanted to be buried at the altar of the chapel of Nuestra Señora del Rosario in Santo Domingo, in the same grave as her husband, Don Jerónimo Paucaruinche, *cacique* of the town of Papres. In both cases two elements stand out: first, the strategy followed by the religious orders, the Dominicans in this case, for earning the loyalty of the ethnic authorities was very successful. Because education of the *caciques* was often in the charge of the friars, the relationship that some Indians established with the religious orders was very intense. Perhaps to show the closeness of these ties, some chose to have their graves in the order's main convent. This would explain the case of the *caciques* of Papres, located south of Cuzco, whose Indian parish was in the hands of the Dominicans (Meléndez 1681, 605). Second, the clergy had an additional argument with which to entice *caciques* and noble Indians onto their property: the church of Santo Domingo in Cuzco was built over the Coricancha, the primary Incan temple.

It is likely that indigenous authorities in Lima played a rather more discreet role and that, with the exception of cases such as those of the Pachacamac *caciques,* their graves were not in the viceregal capital's churches. Provincial families or their representatives, at least for a period, had a certain notoriety in the capital and consequently aspired to occupy a corresponding spot in its sacred space. Like the majority of immigrants, the prospect of economic betterment probably drew them to the city, in addition to political ambitions that drove them to make contact with the powers of government. Here, too, the religious orders were an important factor in the introduction of these men and women into the city's public life, in permitting them to assume a role in the religious sphere. The most important example is undoubtedly Doña Constanza Caxachumbi, a woman from a family of *caciques* in Chinchaycocha, a central highlands province, who lived in Lima between the end of the sixteenth century and beginning of the seventeenth. In the summer of 1605, Doña Constanza found it necessary to draw up her will because she was planning a trip to her hometown. She arranged for a vault to be built in the chapel of the confraternity of Nuestra Señora de la Candelaria, in the convent of San Francisco, where her remains were to be placed alongside those of her first husband, Don Pedro Mayz, and the body of her second husband, Don Diego Solsol, upon his death. Doña Constanza's siblings and their descendants would also be entitled to be buried there.

What did Doña Constanza's funeral vault represent? We do not know when she was born or when she arrived in Lima. We do know for certain that she was crucial to her family's privileged position at the heart of the viceregal administration, where she was known as the *cacica* of Chinchaycocha. Her father, Don Cristóbal Luna Atoc, was a powerful and prosperous *cacique* who maintained ties with several neighboring regions and with the city of Lima owing to his dealings in agricultural products, textiles, and livestock.[109] Don Pedro Mayz, Doña Constanza's first husband, was the Real Audiencia de Lima's general language interpreter, and it is safe to say that in his day he was the most powerful indigenous official in the viceregal capital. His origins are unknown, and it is possible that he did not come from the indigenous nobility. His primary cachet was due to his position, thanks to which he served as the law's intermediary with the indigenous population. In addition, he was the patron and founder of the confraternity of Nuestra Señora de la Candelaria in the convent of San Francisco, a title that Doña Constanza would later bear as well.[110] Don Pedro's performance as an efficient collaborator with the colonial government was generously rewarded: when Viceroy Francisco de Toledo allocated *mitayos* (Indian workers) to the farmers and *encomenderos* of the Lima valley, Don Pedro was the only Indian who received this benefit.[111] Before marrying Doña Constanza, probably in the 1580s, he was married to Doña María Pasña, a woman from Quito.[112] Don Pedro owned several properties in the city of Lima that Doña Constanza inherited upon his death in 1597 and that of their son a couple of years later. Shortly afterward, Doña Constanza married Don Diego Solsol, *cacique* of Chasmal, a small territory in the province of Chachapoyas.[113]

Don Diego's position as an indigenous authority was insignificant, but his situation in Lima was not because, like Doña Constanza's previous husband, he also occupied the position of general language interpreter in the Real Audiencia. The couple resided in the Santa Ana parish neighborhood and had no children. In her will, Doña Constanza left her mother as universal heiress and established an entailed estate for her properties, ensuring that upon her death they would pass into the hands of family members in Chinchaycocha: her brother, the *cacique* Don Cristóbal Ticsi Luna Atoc, and his children. Meanwhile, Don Diego was authorized to possess the houses in Lima and collect their rent as long as he did not remarry, an additional means by which Doña Constanza ensured that her bequest of real estate would not leave the family. Additionally, Don Diego was obliged to have one of his properties available for his brother-in-law when Don Cristóbal and his entourage came to Lima.[114] Years later, when Doña Constanza and Don Diego were both dead, Don Cristóbal became patron of the chapel under the protection of Nuestra Señora de la Candelaria in Lima and, as such, was responsible for seeing to it that masses were said for the souls of those buried in his sister's vault.[115] The tomb was the material representation of the ties that Doña Constanza had woven in the viceregal capital and of the role that she played as a link between Lima and her native land, not only favoring her relatives' political interests but also spreading among her own family members several practices of the Spanish *hidalgos,* such as the use of religious foundations and entailed estates as inheritance strategies. The funeral vault and the bodies buried in it prolonged her presence and that of her provincial kinship group in the city, and they affirmed her personal prestige and that of her family.

Despite the elaborate and consistent efforts by men and women such as Mayz, Solsol, Caxachumbi, and Ticsi Luna Atoc in establishing themselves as an indigenous nobility at the heart of the viceroyalty, various adverse conditions undermined this attempt, such as the small and unstable indigenous population and the difficulty of leaving successors. Moreover, what symbolism and historical memory could they fall back on? Of what ancestors could they avail themselves to legitimize their own position?[116] A whole well-articulated set of institutions and people was necessary to produce and maintain the histories, names, and emblems that could perpetuate ancestors through a variety of means and over a sufficiently vast domain. In this respect the Cuzco Incas held an undeniable advantage over the provincial nobles.

Graves of Incan Nobles

The descendants of the Incas represented an exceptional group in the Peruvian viceroyalty, and the location of their graves in the churches of Cuzco is of utmost importance in better understanding how the city's sacred space was reconfigured. The religious orders and the ancient sacred places heavily influenced the way in which death and the historical memory of the Incan nobles were Christianized in the colonial period.

The Incan kinship group that appears most frequently in the Cuzco sources, and that eventually became the most prestigious, numerous, and active, is that of the descendants of the Inca Huayna Capac and one of his sons, Don Cristóbal Paullo Inca, the latter an ambivalent figure who effectively helped the Spanish conquistadors.

One of the most startling testimonies regarding Don Cristóbal's Christian indoctrination is that of the *provisor* Luis de Morales, who asked him, as proof of his conversion, for the body of his father. Morales recounts that Don Cristóbal turned over to him his father's mummified remains as well as those of his relatives, despite the grief it caused his family (Lissón 1943, 1: no. 3, 80–81).[117] The episode did not dissuade Don Cristóbal's family members and intimates from according him, years later, a burial and funeral rites in the custom of the Incas. Chroniclers such as Cieza de León (1986, Second Part, chap. 32, 98–99, 178) and Juan de Betanzos (2004 [1551], 183) report that the ceremonies a year after his death took place in Cuzco's central square and that both Indians and Spaniards witnessed them. Although the location of Don Cristóbal's tomb is unknown, his descendants felt sure that his grave was in the San Francisco convent church, in a chapel that was dedicated to Nuestra Señora de Guadalupe at the beginning of the seventeenth century.[118] All indications are that the Franciscans played a crucial role in Christianizing the memory of Don Cristóbal and of his descendants by allowing the latter to have their family tomb in this chapel. For several decades, men and women descended from Huayna Capac and Don Cristóbal arranged for their remains to be buried on that spot. In 1636, Doña Magdalena Quispe Sisa Ñusta asked to be buried there because it was the place "where my parents and ancestors are buried chapels [sic] of the yngas"; and ten years later, Don Fernando Ynga, mayor of the eight Cuzco parishes, cited similar reasons for having his grave in this chapel.[119]

The missionary strategy of establishing a special relationship with one group of Incan descendants was followed with varying success by Dominican friars,[120] Mercedarians,[121] and Jesuits.[122] Burials and rituals for the dead in these places made possible the regeneration and

Christianization of their ancestors' memories. In this way, some of Cuzco's primary sacred sites were redefined and promoted as they were simultaneously saturated with Incan and Christian resonances.

Sacred Spaces, Ties, and Alliances

I explained earlier how clerics in charge of the parishes and friars in charge of the religious orders competed to attract the indigenous population to their churches. Although the interest of Indian parish priests and confessors in influencing the choices of will-authors is evident, the decisions should not be seen solely as the result of their interaction with the Indian inhabitants of the colonial cities. Family and other close ties, such as alliances or membership in confraternities, went into the choice of graves. Thus is revealed the complex texture of colonial society, the characteristics shared by the cities we are studying, and each one's peculiarities.

During the 1590s, the rivalries between the secular clergy and the religious orders over control of Lima's indigenous population were staged in the neighborhoods of San Lázaro and El Cercado, with the archbishop and his immediate collaborators from the diocesan clergy pitted against the Jesuits, and with the following of Nuestra Señora de Copacabana as a powerful symbol that the different actors attempted to have on their side.[123] Pedro de Lesana, a native of a central highlands province and a resident of the El Cercado neighborhood, arranged in his will written in 1592 for his burial to take place in the chapel of Nuestra Señora de Copacabana in the Iglesia Mayor, "over the steps of the high altar." Lesana explained that he was due a grave in that prime location because the archbishop had granted that chapel to the Indians and because he, Lesana, had offered many services to the confraternity since its foundation. Despite these shows of loyalty, we find that in a second will authored ten years later, Lesana requested burial "in the best spot" in the town church of El Cercado or, if he was in Santa Ana parish, in its church.[124] What had led Lesana to change his mind? Ten years after his first will, his loyalty to the Copacabana cult continued: in the customary review of his affiliations, he stated that he was a founding member of the confraternity, he left it donations, and he chose one of its *mayordomos* as his executor.

It is not difficult to imagine that the ongoing rivalries influenced his decision and that the Jesuits might have had a decisive role in it, expecting that residents of the parish in their charge be buried in their church and nowhere else. It is evident that for a religious following and a confraternity to take root and for a sacred space to deserve the name, it was necessary to have the bodies of their adherents buried in their church. As had been preached and practiced for years, the church itself was supposed to become a relative of its parishioners (P. Brown 1981, 31). In 1598, María de Jesús, a childless widow native to the province of Huamachuco and a resident of the San Lázaro neighborhood, requested in her will that the provincial of the Society of Jesus allow her to be buried in the chapel for natives in the church of San Pablo, given that both she and her husband had been its founders and were among the first confraternity members to receive the doctrine.[125] Although the sincerity of her will is beyond doubt, it must be pointed out that when María de Jesús—whose name indicates her close ties to the Society of Jesus—wrote it, two Jesuits were present as witnesses. From this woman's point of view, her decision had a solid justification: she had no other family, and she did not know her parents or even know their names. In some respects, the priests of the Society of Jesus were her closest relatives. In the eyes of the Jesuits, it may be that the initiative of allowing Indians graves in their church was strengthened by a petition preceded by the story of how María de Jesús had learned the basics of Christian doctrine thanks to the order.

Aspiring to a grave with one's relatives, whether blood-related or fictitious, was not unique to the nobility and indigenous authorities. In the majority of cases, petitions needed no further justification: it was accepted as natural that family members could be reunited in their graves. There are many examples of widows such as Francisca Chimbo Urma, who resided in the Cuzco parish of San Cristóbal, who hoped to be buried on the same spot as their husbands.[126] The common burial site was the confraternity's chapel,[127] and inside these vaults some Indians made efforts to create spaces for the greatest possible number of family members. In 1624, Elena de Barrionuevo, a widow residing in Lima who had been born in the town of Lati, an indigenous *reducción* east of the city, indicated her burial site in the convent church of San Francisco with great precision: it was to be at the altar pedestal of the chapel dedicated to Nuestra Señora de la Candelaria, "where all my relatives are buried."[128]

There were also those who cited their right to compensation for some donation made to a particular chapel, for a privilege granted for some merit or task performed, or for the payment of some sufficiently significant "moral" debt. Domingo Benegas, a farmer residing in the El Cercado neighborhood, arranged his burial in the chapel of the Santo Crucifijo in the convent church of San Francisco in Lima, explaining that he was not only a founding member but had also donated the confraternity's tabernacle.[129] Lucía Cusi invoked the promise made to her husband by the *mayordomos* of the confraternity of Nuestra Señora de la Consolación in the convent church of La Merced in Lima: that because he himself had been *mayordomo*, she could be buried there.[130] In 1638, Inés Chumbe, an old woman living in the Cuzco parish of San Sebastián, indicated that her burial was to be in the parish church "at the foot of the high altar steps," where a Spanish officer had assigned a grave to her husband and family in compensation for his services.[131] Francisco Rimasca, an Indian sacristan, pleaded to be buried in the Cuzco cathedral on account of being very poor and having served there for many years; and Don Pedro Gualpa, a master carpenter who had fallen sick while working on repairs to the Santa Clara convent in Cuzco, requested to be buried there in the chapel dedicated to Nuestra Señora de la Candelaria.[132]

A very significant feature that seems to have been unique to Cuzco was the existence of funerary vaults for kinship groups known as *ayllus*, although it is very likely that not all *ayllus* represented in the city were buried there and that they were not necessarily closed groups. In 1640, Miguel Quito, a man originally from Cajamarca and a resident in the hospital for natives, left instructions for his body to be placed in the grave of the Sañoc *ayllu* in the chapel dedicated to the Limpia Concepción in the church of the San Francisco convent.[133] Half a century earlier, in 1586, Joan Guamani, from the parish of the hospital for natives, chose to be buried in its church "by the seat of the Indians under the authority of cacique Don Francisco Morocho and where they tend to preach the doctrine every Sunday." In this way, Guamani not only would continue to be near the people of his *ayllu*, but he also hoped to continue, even after his death, his religious education and to reap the benefits of his companions' prayers.[134]

Graves also represented political alliances and complicated ties formed in life. The city of Cuzco, because of its intricate social fabric, offers examples. In 1582, Doña María Chimbo Ocllo, widow of the *cacique* of Parinacochas, a rich province west of Cuzco, and owner of an estate consisting primarily of livestock, arranged for her burial in the convent of San Francisco, in the chapel belonging to Don Alonso de Hinojosa, where her husband's remains were also buried. As we have seen, it was common for a widow to request a grave next to her husband's. What is noteworthy is that Don Alonso was the *encomendero* of Parinacochas.[135] We do not know how unusual it was for a *cacique* to share a grave with his *encomendero*, but this may be one of the most eloquent examples of a paternalistic relationship between Spaniards and *caciques*.[136] We find further examples of this type of relationship in which women prolong the bond of servitude with their *encomenderos*, as a way of remaining under their protection. Doña Leonor Chimbo Ocllo requested in her will written in Cuzco in 1588 that her burial take place in the cathedral, in a grave adjacent to that of Don Pedro Arias de Ávila, an *encomendero*, and she left the latter's son in charge of bringing up her children and administering the fund for masses that she established to ensure her soul's salvation.[137]

Ethnic identities, at the same time that they followed the patterns by which society was formally organized (chapels for Indians, for Spaniards, for blacks), could be as malleable for the dead as they were for the living. Mariana Urbina, a mestiza and a native of the town of San Damián in Huarochirí, arranged for her burial in the chapel for Indians in the church of the Society of Jesus in Lima, whereas Doña Isabel Chimbo Quipe, a woman possibly from Cuzco's indigenous elite, was buried in the Veracruz chapel for Spaniards in the convent church of Santo Domingo, as a founder and *veinticuatro* of the confraternity.[138] In Lima in 1637, Miguel Mesquirán, a *ladino* Indian from the neighborhood of Malambo, where a large number of people of African descent resided, despite being a member of the confraternity of Nuestra Señora de Copacabana, asked to be buried in the chapel of Nuestra Señora del Rosario for criollos *morenos* (dark-skinned).[139]

The burial places of the poor were clearly defined in Lima but not in Cuzco. In the viceregal capital, similar to the custom in Spain, the poor werc buried in cemeteries beyond churchyards (Martínez Gil 1993, 436). The most common was in the parish of the Santa Ana hospital, known as Monte Calvario or simply Calvario.[140] No such custom was followed in Cuzco. The word *cementerio* (cemetery) does not appear in any of the wills from Cuzco that I have reviewed. When the issue was limiting funeral costs, testators who cited their poverty asked for the funeral procession to be simplified and charged their executors with choosing their grave, but there was apparently no specific site in the Incan capital intended for burial of the poor.[141] To explain this contrast, it would be necessary to explore in detail the different concepts of poverty and the poor as well as the ways in which the latter lived in colonial cities. While in Lima, funerary rituals were less showy, burial places assigned to the poor were more visible. In Cuzco the standing of the poor was reflected above all in ritual, whereas there was apparently no separate site assigned for their burial.

Despite the cultural, political, and social differences that separated the cities of Lima and Cuzco, it is evident that burials in churches were the common denominator that gave rise to the formation of a solid, understandable, and even desirable link between Andean men and women and with the Church. This was the overwhelming force that compelled the people of the Andes to enter the churches and convert to Catholicism.

Rituals and Memory

Display of the deceased's public image was an important aspect of the funeral. The will-author generally planned the form that this would take, although executors and relatives were frequently left in charge of interpreting and carrying out the deceased's desires, while members of the clergy played a crucial role in prescribing, guiding, and often controlling the process. Some of the rituals, offerings, and donations involved could be very private, even secret, whereas others might include, for example, a large public ceremony or far-reaching charitable work. This display, the objective of which was to make a statement about a person's character and relationships as well as to establish the basis on which to perpetuate his or her memory, might involve a large funeral; or it could consist of a specific or unlimited number of masses; or it could be of ephemeral value and duration, such as certain modest alms and offerings; or it could aim for perpetuity through donations of large sums, real estate, religious images or jewels, or charitable foundations.

My purpose in this section is, first, to discuss several specific cases in order to examine how practice differed from the inherently opposed ideals of uniformity in funerary rituals and preservation of ethnic divisions, without destabilizing the social order but rather contributing to its consolidation. Second, I will analyze the means by which will-authors sought to perpetuate memory of themselves, maintain their relationship with the living, and, at the same time, make possible their passage to the afterlife, where their own pagan background or that of their ancestors as well as the failings in their life as Christians could be swept away to achieve eternal salvation. Finally, I will offer an explanation of the material and symbolic exchanges—masses, offerings, and bequests—that testators arranged to achieve these ends.

It would be desirable to trace the history of the growing incorporation of Christian rituals and motifs into Andean funerals, with a point of departure in, for example, the funeral rites of Don Cristóbal Paullo Inca in Cuzco in the 1540s, to arrive at the will arrangements of both *caciques* and commoners. It appears impossible to discern any difference between their funerals and those arranged by Spaniards. How and when did Andean funerary rituals disappear from the public view? Parallel to the codification of ritual and the growing homogenization of exchanges between the living and the dead by way of offerings and bequests, practices that we might recognize as "Andean" did not completely disappear, nor were they all clandestine. Notwithstanding the differences between the two, similarities are traceable in Andean and Christian practices: funeral processions, wakes, offerings, and bequests left to family members and close acquaintances in hopes of maintaining reciprocal relationships. This made it possible to incorporate cultural elements unique to the Andes into the framework of the Catholic vision of death and the bonds that human beings—both living and dead—establish among themselves.

Funeral Processions

Any hypothesis suggesting a rapid suppression of Andean funerary customs followed by a quick retreat of the indigenous population into clandestine ritual life is not plausible. To prove it would require overlooking the crucial role played by the indigenous nobility and ethnic authorities in the formation and consolidation of colonial Andean society and in the process of religious conversion. The nobles and *caciques* were among the first to favor the incorporation not only of European cultural elements into their religious practices and beliefs but also the persistence and reformulation of Andean customs and ideas. To assert the authority necessary to achieve this, their public visibility was crucial. Doña María Cusi Rimay, for example, a member of the Cuzco elite who died in the Incan capital toward the end of the 1560s, hoped that on the day of her burial the majority of the city's residents, regardless of their class or ethnicity, would share in the events recognizing her standing as an indigenous noblewoman and a devout Christian. To that end, she arranged for masses to be said for her soul in all of the city's monasteries and in several of its parishes. Given her special relationship with the Dominican order, in whose church she arranged to be buried, she instructed that fifteen vigil masses be said to facilitate her passage to the afterlife. Her funeral procession was to be presided over by priests from the main church and two sacristans carrying the high cross, and accompanied by brothers from the confraternity housed in the Santo Domingo church and by an unspecified number of Dominican friars. It is likely that a funeral such as this, at a moment when Cuzco was still reeling from the confrontations taking place in the rebel stronghold of Vilcabamba, would be seen as a positive sign of adherence to the political order and the Church by the Incan elite. In the city of Lima at the beginning of the seventeenth century, Doña Constanza Caxachumbi contemplated a funeral comparable to or even more ambitious than Cusi Rimay's. The procession was to be led by the priests and sacristans of Santa Ana, her parish, who would carry the high cross. Four clerics would accompany the procession in addition to the number of friars that her husband considered appropriate from each of the city's religious orders. All confraternities, both Spanish and

Indian, would also take part. The scope of this ceremony was quite possibly exceptional. Throughout the seventeenth century other ethnic authorities followed, on a more modest scale, the model of Spanish funerals staged in all Spanish-American cities (Eire 1995; Varela 1990).[142]

In the viceregal capital, there were restrictions by ethnic criteria on the use of public space, especially following the death of Archbishop Mogrovejo in 1606, at the same time that social mobility was more fluid than in Cuzco. In 1589, María Sánchez, an Indian woman residing in Lima who did not claim descent from a line of *caciques* or nobles, was able to request burial in the main church, with a tolling of bells, and her funeral procession was to be accompanied by the priest and sacristan from the cathedral as well as by four clerics.[143] Years later, in 1618, Don Esteban Guacay, the *cacique* of Magdalena, stated that if he died in the city of Lima, members of all the confraternities of his hometown were to come to the city to collect his body and take it away for burial in Magdalena.[144] Although we cannot know how such moves were made, we can deduce from the will's instructions that the most eloquent displays of homage were reserved for the moment when the body of the *cacique* arrived in his hometown. The instructions that Don Diego Machumbi left for his burial in 1663 would seem to indicate that, as the seventeenth century progressed, a clear contrast arose between the formalities that could be shown in the burial of an Indian in the viceregal capital and what was permissible in his birthplace. Don Diego, who was native to Lurigancho, arranged that if he died in his hometown, his burial was to take place with as much ceremony as possible, but if he died in Lima and was buried in that city, the funeral details would be left to the discretion of his executor.[145]

Instructions in the wills reveal a special concern in Cuzco with the vestments worn by the priest who would preside over the procession,[146] whereas, in Lima, testators paid more attention to who would accompany the cortege. The majority of will-authors stipulated that those accompanying the procession be clergymen,[147] and some arranged for additional groups of the poor or of orphaned children, who were fed and given clothes or alms, to take part. A clause in the will of Catalina Payco, written in Lima in 1577, ordered her executors on the day of her burial to give out one cotton blanket apiece to five Indians so that they could take part in her funeral procession.[148] Ynés Quispe, a native of the central highlands who earned her living selling goods in the market, directed in her will in 1623 that twenty pesos be distributed among poor persons, who were to attend her burial bearing torches or large candles.[149] In 1635, Catalina Carua, a native of the province of Cajatambo, in addition to requesting that her burial be attended by a group of Dominican friars, who were to carry her body, arranged for "the city's orphaned children" to walk in the procession and be given a small offering.[150]

These funeral arrangements, when considered in isolation, give the impression of being faithful copies of Christian ritual, possibly leading us to conclude that the testators held on to little or nothing of their old beliefs and traditions. Nevertheless, the principals of such public ceremonies cannot be viewed in isolation from their family, friends, and political ties. In the matter of bequests and offerings we can detect the linking of objects and people that occurred in preconquest funerals.

Offerings, Bequests, and Memory

Once the testator had distributed what was due to his heirs apparent, he was free to allocate a portion of his estate, usually set at one fifth, as he wished. The testator's concern with preserving the survivors' memory of him or her and attaining salvation is revealed in the offerings, alms, and bequests specified in the wills. The instructions show various types of ties that the will-authors maintained or hoped to establish with people and entities both real and fictitious as well as the desire to be remembered by and through them. The image of the testator formed by this memory consisted of true aspects such as his or her life story or social rank; but it also involved the creation of an ideal image suffused with generosity, fairness and respectability of customs, and religious piety. In the course of this process of creating and maintaining the memory of the dead, Andean elements were superimposed onto a Christian framework.

Will arrangements resulted from the instructions dictated by Indian parish priests and confessors as well as the influence of notaries.

But to be viable they had to be acceptable to all parties involved. For this reason, the wills' instructions had to evoke values common to the group. Men and women of the indigenous elite, who generally had to address a wide and varied set of relationships, carefully managed the criteria of authority and generosity in their last act. Doña María Cusi Rimay, for example, left bequests that were not intended to significantly change the fortunes of the recipient but rather were to leave behind a good memory of her and to reaffirm the sentimental and political ties that bound her and her husband to a large entourage of relatives and servants. Consequently, Doña María granted to her closest servants the right to retain control over the houses in which they lived and to the usufruct of various plots of land. She also doled out some of her own clothes as well as heads of cattle, spools of wool, and food among the men and women who lived in her house and worked on her lands and estate. These gifts undoubtedly had a practical purpose, but of greater importance was the symbolic value of the items themselves and the very act of passing them on. The beneficiaries were named one by one, together with the modest gifts: "I leave to the Indian woman Ynes Guanai a blanket and a spool of wool from the land." The will includes sentimental phrases about some of the recipients: "I leave to Ynes Ocllo a large ram from the land and two loads of potatoes, and I charge my above-mentioned husband with keeping track of and favoring the above-said Ynes Ocllo." While this will singled out relatives, a subsequent one refers to them as a group, uniting them around the figure of the deceased: Doña María anticipated the banquet that would follow her funeral, and to that end she left her relatives a llama and a certain amount of *chuño* (freeze-dried potato) with the request that they eat "all together." Her image as a generous person who was conscious of her obligations to a wider social network was consolidated in the task she left her husband, Don Francisco Chalco Yupangui, of distributing alms to everyone who habitually visited her house.[151]

This series of gestures could be read as "Andean," and it is quite possible that those who benefited from them saw them in that way, but it would be incorrect to consider them only as such. Although the majority of the items passed on were characteristically Andean, the gestures were not. The parallels with customs practiced in other parts of the world are evident, and this is what made assimilation and mutual influence possible. Certainly, interpretation and approval of these gestures was not unanimous or immediate. For example, funeral banquets could raise the suspicion of clerics. In Spain the Church had tried to control or even suppress them (Martínez Gil 1993), and in the Andes some priests believed that they fostered idolatrous practices (Ramos 2005a), but it is clear that they continued to take place, especially among the indigenous authorities.[152]

Doña María Cusi Rimay's will arrangements, perhaps because of the document's relatively early date or because it was taken for granted, do not explain what she anticipated in return from the beneficiaries of her bequests. Over time, promises made in wills became more homogeneous and acquired more clearly Christian overtones, and they explicitly stated that the beneficiaries were expected to respond with prayers for the deceased's soul. Works of charity and, above all, requests for masses took hold in wills at the end of sixteenth century and established themselves definitively in the course of the seventeenth, with instructions that indicated the growing importance of religious followings and the souls of the deceased.

Both in arrangements that were kept secret—which we know about because the wills state that only the confessor would see to carrying them out—and in those designed to reach as many people as possible, testators expressed ever more frequently their concern with easing their consciences and saving their souls. Confessors acted as mentors to men and women of all stations, though we have more evidence of their importance for those who belonged to the indigenous elite. Confidential arrangements must have originated in the confessional, where the testator would be advised to give back what had been unfairly acquired and to make amends.[153] In the cases in which reparations are spoken of openly, it is possible that the confessor intervened to convince the testator, but the intention of making them was also the sign of a custom that began to take root. Formalities unique to the will imposed it, and also, because of the power of preaching and the likelihood of social pressure, subordinates and the weakest members of society generally demanded just conduct from the authorities. This is how we may read a clause from the will of Lucía Ruiz, daughter of the *cacique* of Cañete, who in 1613 directed

her executors to give ten pesos to her husband "so that he may distribute them among people to whom I am a burden"; or this passage
from the will of Cuzco noblewoman Doña Ana Quispe Asarpay Coya:
"I declare that my oxen caused damage in the town of Asumpcion
de los Papres and order that my executors confirm and pay for the
damage."[154] The mediation of priests and confessors became indispensable when the offended parties or people to whom the testator
owed some unpaid debt were dead or gone. Easing such guilt was
possible because the debts, both large and petty, could be settled
through the saying of masses. Domingo de Cárdenas, a native of the
town of Pachacamac, instructed in his will of 1601 that five masses
be said for the soul of a woman named Juana Baraganga "on account
of some pots and an old crate I owe her, and let [the masses] be said
in the order that my executors deem fit."[155]

Anxiety over relations with the living was accompanied by interest in the fate of ancestors and of the dead in general, and all those
with whom the testator would be reunited after death. This included
people whom he or she knew in addition to many others of undifferentiated and anonymous identity, whose well-being depended to a
great extent on what the living could do for them. Belief in the effi-
cacy of masses, then widespread throughout the Christian world, took
hold strongly in the Andes.[156] Requests for masses, for various purposes, appear in almost all Indian wills, and there is hardly any difference between these and requests made in Spain (Eire 1995) except
that the number requested by the indigenous people, even in the
most generous cases, was comparatively modest. Confessors surely
explained to their proselytes that the benefit of masses could be enjoyed only by those who had been baptized. This may help to explain
the clause we find in the will of the *cacique* of Guanchoguaylas, Don
Bartolomé Guamac Chumbi, issued in Lima in 1577. Don Bartolomé
instructed that twenty masses be said, half for his "parents and relatives who died Christians," and the other half "for the conversion of
the natives and souls in purgatory."[157]

On the one hand, the growing interest in purgatory was based on
testators' concern with what would happen to them after their death,
which, in Christian terms, would translate into concern for their souls.
On the other hand, it sprang from the mystery of the vast universe

of anonymous souls—the dead in general—who counted on the assistance of the living to alleviate their sorrows, and who would generously repay those who helped them. Of course, helping souls in purgatory also meant helping oneself. The ever higher number of requests in wills for masses on behalf of the souls in purgatory shows the effectiveness of preaching about its importance and the centrality that purgatory came to occupy in the minds of Andean men and women. In the cities of Lima and Cuzco as well as in the smaller settlements, confraternities devoted to the souls in purgatory were organized, and practically every church had an altar dedicated to facilitating the soul's passage from purgatory to heaven.[158] Despite this proliferation of altars, there were those who, like Doña María Cissa, who wrote her will in Cuzco in 1633, requested that masses be said at all of them.[159] The faithful could, if they so desired, identify a group or an individual soul with whom to form a special bond, such as blood or fictitious relatives, friends, or neighbors. They could then invest that relationship with sentiments and concerns that saw the convergence of memory, loyalty, gratitude, hope for forgiveness, or the practice of acts of charity beyond the grave. In 1629, Pedro Guaman, a native of the city of Ica who resided in the town of Lurigancho, ordered in his will "twenty masses said for the souls of my above-mentioned parents and ancestors and for souls in purgatory and people to whom I may be a burden for something I don't remember."[160]

Perhaps in the belief that souls in purgatory could offer assistance to those near their own end, Pedro Aculi, a man condemned to death for murder in Lima in 1624, made an offering for two masses to be said for souls in purgatory in the chapel of the jail where he was awaiting his execution.[161] Testators often linked their last requests with their personal circumstances in this way. Juana Chumbi, a woman living in Lima who authored her will shortly before checking into the Santa Ana hospital, requested that if she died, she be buried in the Monte Calvario. Additionally, she arranged for "four masses on behalf of the souls in purgatory of all the Indians both men and women who are buried in the Monte Calvario of said hospital of Santa Ana in this city."[162] The Church also taught that there were souls in purgatory who, like the poor on earth, had no friends or relatives and suffered the consequences of their isolation. This notion led people such as

Lucía Matías, a resident of Lima in 1613, to leave alms for masses to be said on behalf of the "most needy soul among those in the torments of purgatory."[163] Referred to years later as the "lonely soul," this concept acquired, as in other parts of the Christian world, an individual character that fostered its transformation into an object of devotion. Around the middle of the seventeenth century this "person" was so clearly delineated that indigenous testators could make references to it similar to those made to the memory or souls of relatives and friends and to religious followings.[164]

If we are to take the last wishes in wills not as mere notarial formulas imposed by missionaries and colonial authorities but as signs of the assimilation of new attitudes toward death in the inhabitants of the Andes, we must pay attention to the practices that were becoming more and more common. The idea of exchange and its material dimension is essential for explaining this process. To this end, we will consider two closely related matters. The first concerns the principles spread among the populations seeking conversion to Christianity through inheritance law and the Church. The second deals with what was offered in material terms in exchange for the coveted favor.

As we have seen, debates in the Andes over the treasures placed in tombs and offerings dedicated to the dead were a central focus of missionaries and colonial authorities. This was an old topic, for the question of the proper fate of deceased people's property recurred in different religious conversion contexts. The principles applied originated, on the one hand, in the evangelization strategies deployed centuries earlier on the European continent, and, on the other, in defining what would happen to the property of those lacking successors and to the share that relatives reserved for offerings to commemorate them. Missionaries sought to have part of the deceased's possessions reserved for donations to the Church, which benefited the testator in spiritual terms; additionally, as Saint Augustine advised, they preached that Christ be considered an additional relative and thus receive a share of the inheritance, a decision that would also have favorable repercussions for the soul (Maldonado y Fernández del Torco 1944, 28–29). With time, these practices took root to such an extent that they were incorporated into law, as noted in Spanish legal codes (fueros) from the era of the Reconquista (32–36).[165]

The process briefly described here helps us to understand the strategy followed by missionaries in Christianizing death in the Andes. There is evidence that offerings of clothing became an explicit means for improving one's well-being in the afterlife, primarily through masses. In 1586 in the will of Martín Orcoguaranca, a parishioner of the hospital for natives in Cuzco, for example, we find the following stipulation from Pedro Quispe, the parish's Indian notary: "the day of my burial a mass shall be said for me with a black shirt which is in the possession of Rodrigo, the main law-enforcement officer [*alguacil*]."[166] The missionaries had to explain to their proselytes the direct relationship that existed between offerings of items that represented the person of the deceased and works that would have favorable consequences for him or her, as well as the way in which this relationship was understood. Later in the same year, Magdalena Caruayaco, a resident of the same parish, included the following stipulation, among others, in her will: "I have three pairs of gourds for drinking and four pairs for eating to go toward the masses for my soul."[167] The will of Diego Payco, also written in this parish, states, among other things: "I declare in my possession a grayish-brown blanket called a *chumbe* made out of *avasca* which I'm leaving for my soul."[168] These personal items, especially the garments and textiles, suggest that these arrangements have an "Andean" flavor.[169] The universal significance behind offerings of objects that carry something of the person with them explains how effectively meanings could be bridged through Christian preaching and practice. In this way it became possible to inscribe Andean ideas and practices within a Catholic framework. This does not necessarily imply an understanding of the Christian idea of the soul or the topic of salvation. Although involved in material exchanges, these concepts were incorporated at a slower pace, informed by orthodox elements and always susceptible to multiple interpretations.

In various will arrangements, especially in Lima, the confessors' influence is detected in instructions about offerings, alms, and bequests. In a city in which the majority of residents came from other provinces, the ties that formed between indigenous inhabitants followed, for the most part, the models set by missionaries and colonial authorities. The conditions—material instability, a high mortality rate, permanent migration—explain why the bequests tended to be modest, and it is very possible that even those that were intended to be perpetual tended to be shortlived. In the early seventeenth century, Luis Pérez, a prosperous man native to Trujillo and residing in Lima, whom the scribe characterizes as a "*ladino* [Spanish speaking] Indian," left alms to, among others, the Blessed Sacrament of his parish of Santa Ana, which he justified "by the honor of the sacraments I have received and expect to receive," and to "all the poor blind Indians in this city," whom he asked to pray for his soul.[170] In 1670 a woman native to Cuzco, Doña Juana Ñusta, became a modest benefactor of the infirmary of the San Francisco convent, left some small offerings to different confraternities in the city, and contributed to the campaign then underway for the canonization of Lima's Santa Rosa.[171] Perhaps the most important bequest made by a notable figure from Lima's indigenous population was the one left by Doña Francisca Ignacia de Carvajal, daughter of the *cacique* of Callao, Don Pedro Manchipula; toward the end of the seventeenth century, she was likely one of the primary benefactors of a *beaterio* (beguinage) for daughters of *caciques* in the San Lázaro neighborhood, dedicated to the following of Nuestra Señora de Copacabana. The bequest was intended to help laywomen such as Doña Francisca herself, by giving them a place where they could withdraw and lead a virtuous life, away from the dangers that threatened their honor, whether as single women or as widows. The initiative was guided by goals similar to those that inspired many other women in the Christian world at that point.[172]

In contrast to the examples from Lima, in Cuzco various bequests were probably inspired at least partially by the forms of generosity practiced in the Andes, employing the preexisting social bonds and networks at the same time that they incorporated new conditions unique to the colonial situation. The arrangements in the will of Doña Magdalena Quispe Sisa Ñusta, a descendant of Don Cristóbal Paullo Inca, indicate that she was considerably more prosperous than her contemporaries from any region of the Peruvian viceroyalty. They also point to a fairly solid and complex social standing owing to her rank and to her family history: relationships she wove and maintained in Cuzco itself, and bonds of subordination and patronage she maintained in Huanoquite, where her husband was the principal *cacique*.

In bequests in wills such as Doña Magdalena's, the practices, objects, and ideas assimilated in the cities by members of the indigenous elite were spread among the towns and peoples of the interior. Doña Magdalena stipulated that her executors hand over to the three Inca *ayllus* of the town of Huanoquite several plots of land so that poor Indians could plant them and reap the harvest to pay their taxes. This act of generosity toward the *ayllus*, to whom her husband may have been linked through kinship bonds, was reinforced with other gestures that brought forth a definitively Christian concern: Doña Magdalena donated lands to the town's confraternities dedicated to the Blessed Sacrament and the Souls in Purgatory at the same time that she left a painting of the Holy Trinity and various silver ornaments to the same *ayllus* to whom she had given land. In the city of Cuzco she also distributed houses, lands, alms, clothing, and furniture among a large number of individuals and groups of diverse social standing including relatives, servants, confraternities, a convent of nuns, Indian women who organized themselves into a religious community of the third Franciscan order, and the "poor in prison."[173]

Gestures of generosity that were also intended to memorialize the benefactor became over time more and more imbued with traces of Catholicism at the same time that they were adopted by people who did not necessarily belong to the Cuzco nobility. To a great extent, the networks and connections built among people of different social standings were validated because they shared in the religious sentiment that infused society overall with meaning. In contemplating the end of their lives, many testators were captivated by the possibility of instilling that spirit in those left behind. Don Fernando Ynga, the mayor of the eight parishes of Cuzco to whom we referred earlier, made a bequest to the confraternity of Nuestra Señora de Copacabana and asked his executors to make him a member of the brotherhood in the tradition of his mother and grandfather.[174] Others, inspired by their confessors, preferred to leave traces of themselves in some religious image worshipped by their contemporaries. In 1646 the most generous bequest left by Doña Inés Chuqui Ñusta in her will was for finishing the altarpiece dedicated to Nuestra Señora de Gracia in the convent church of San Agustín.[175] There were those who, like Don Lorenzo Paucar, parishioner of San Blas, found in religious images an eloquent means for reinforcing their family ties. In 1650, Don Lorenzo left houses and lands to each of his children as well as religious images: "I leave a portrait of San Lorenzo to Angelina Cusirimay and another portrait of San Juan to Juana Cusirimay and a large bust of Christ that I loved to Lucia Cusirimay and the statue of the Soledad to Don Felipe Uaypatopa plus an engraving of Ecce Homo to Juana and an engraving of the Birunica [*sic* for Veronica] to Angelina Cusirimay and a small Baby Jesus to Lucia Cusirimay and a large Baby Jesus to Juan Uaupar to have and enjoy."[176]

The Church was especially effective in cases in which the absence of offspring fed the fear of not having any possible continuity or memory of oneself. In a will of 1651 a resident of Cuzco named María Panti left alms to various confraternities in the city, ordered masses to be said for her soul with profits from the sale of some of her lands, and left a generous donation for the construction of a chapel dedicated to Nuestra Señora de Copacabana in her hometown of Yaurisque. But this apparently did not seem sufficient; she also instructed that her five female slaves be freed on the condition that three of them become beguines (*beatas*) of the order of San Agustín or San Francisco, whereas the other two, upon reaching the appropriate age, would enter the convent of Santa Catalina as servants (*donadas*). All of them were to pray for her soul. Fifteen years later, when María authored another will, her plan to turn her slaves into servants of the Church as secular and religious convent members and sacristans survived despite a few variations, still inspired by the idea that, since she had no descendants, she could turn her domestic staff into a small group of relatives who would dedicate the rest of their lives to keeping her memory alive.[177] The idea that servants, lacking the social standing that would grant them full personhood, could be turned into support and company for the dead master or mistress undoubtedly has resonances with the pre-Christian past, although I am not postulating that Christian funerary customs and beliefs were mechanically superimposed over pre-Hispanic ones. What I wish to emphasize is that, from the conquest onward, human concerns such as uncertainty about what happens after death or the need for company in the afterlife fostered the formation or adaptation of rituals and practices that would offer some consolation in the face of death. Isolation, an increasing problem for the colonial Andeans, led to the fear that memory of the dead would vanish. To be forgotten by the living suggested the intolerable prospect of a permanent death.

The evangelization project proposed to bring about radical changes through the use of methods that, to be effective, had to adapt to local circumstances; to this end, their means needed to be perceived as much as possible as familiar, legible, and concrete. Certainly, neither the Church nor the colonial authorities viewed their strategy in those terms and as a one-time approach, nor was the mood to annihilate "paganism" and impose doctrine at all costs, as some clerics and colonial authorities wished. From the perspective of the Andean people, submission and resistance were not the only alternatives. In analyzing a wide array of individual experiences, we find that on both sides there were arguments, negotiations, and exploitations of loopholes in the law, in doctrine, or in disputed criteria, and that opportunities were seized to forge new niches, maintain or recreate privileges, and establish legitimacies. The key in this process was the necessity to resolve the practical problems involved in the possibility and imminence of death, such as determining succession and inheritance, deciding who would be in charge of administering the estate and bringing up minor children, or defining the relationship with one's ancestors, superiors, friends and acquaintances, and subordinates. Consequently, in our analysis we have identified the axes along which interactions, disputes, and negotiations took place: social relations, space, and objects. Without these concrete, material, and tangible factors, doctrine could have little effect, especially because it was thought of as universal and fixed. It was in the domain of interaction—that is to say, the domain of practice—that the changes and adaptations at the heart of the Christianization of death in the Andes were generated.

Conclusion

This book has sought to show how the Christianization of death was crucial in the conversion of the Andean peoples. Compared to similar processes in other parts of the world, the transformation of practices and ideas regarding death in the Andes came about in a surprisingly brief period and on a very large scale. This monumental change brought about after the Spanish conquest was made possible by a series of factors that I have grouped into three major areas: places and spaces, bodies and selves, and ritual.

Places and Spaces

A visitor to the Andes just a century after the Spanish conquest would find a number of funerary monuments in disuse: the clay pyramids built up and down the coast, the stone towers and houses, and the caves that proliferated among the peaks of the mountainous region. It is true that, as with many apparently abandoned sites, several of these continued to be visited or even used. Some Andean men and women made offerings to ancestors who had lived before the European invasion, occasionally placed belongings of the dead in the tombs, and, with less and less frequency, transferred to these sites the bodies of their relatives who had been baptized in the churches (Duviols 1971; 2003; Gose 2003; Taylor 1987; 1999). Others came looking for relics to use in rituals intended to remedy some sorrow or sickness (Estenssoro 2003), or, encouraged or forced by Spanish adventurers, plundered the tombs hoping to find some treasure

(Ramírez 1997; Zevallos Quiñones 1994). Many of these funerary monuments, although significant and impossible to dismiss, no longer constituted on their own the center of the religious and political life of the Andean peoples.

Without doubt, the ancient burial sites continued to signal a vital relationship with the past; many symbolized some group's presence in or even control over a territory. But the reconfiguration of space resulting from the measures taken by colonial authorities to facilitate governance and doctrine, from the reorientation of the economy, and from the crises and displacements of the population had a decisive impact on the redefinition of the ancient sacred spaces and their connections to the ancestors. The creation of urban centers and the establishment of churches there had a defining influence on the ritual life of Andean populations. Although a set of uniform guidelines regulating the organization of space was applied throughout the Andes, its form and pace varied with local conditions. Parish and convent churches in the city of Cuzco, and in the surrounding region, were erected on top of ancient temples and sites of worship. In Lima this superimposition may not have occurred so regularly, although the Santa Ana church, which was the base for a significant amount of missionary activity, was built on top of one of the most important pre-Hispanic sacred sites. Whether local settlers agreed with or rejected the location of churches and cemeteries likely depended on either the rupture or continuity with the past represented by these sites or on the possibility of establishing at least some temporal link between the new and the old.

Considering burial sites as crystallizations of social bonds allows us to understand how the changes that Andean societies underwent affected people's relationships with each other as well as with their ancestors. When we look into the conditions and strategies of the different sectors of the indigenous population, we find that the ethnic authorities' role in reconfiguring sacred spaces was crucial: as *caciques* and their families claimed privileged spots in churches in which to build funerary vaults and deposit their remains, they contributed to the spread and acceptance among other sectors of the Andean population of the custom of having burial sites on consecrated ground. There is sufficient evidence to show that a growing number of families of the indigenous elite opted for these burials as a result of their negotiations with friars and priests. At stake in these negotiations were not only the use of sites considered at the time as sacred and prominent but also the chance to cultivate a position of honor and political standing.

These general conditions adapted to the specific situations of the ethnic authorities in Cuzco and Lima. In the Incan capital, families descended from the ancient leaders sought to affirm their new position by both evoking and reformulating the past, which was incarnated mainly in people and places. In the viceregal capital, because of migrations, discontinuity between generations, and social mobility, funerary vaults in churches could not give the full picture of the history of families who emerged into public life with a thoroughly Christian stamp. In one variation after another, as they accepted the graves of *caciques,* their families, and representatives of the indigenous elite, churches became places where the members of a family line could be united once again, and they developed into ever more attractive centers of ritual activity. Confraternities—the religious brotherhoods devoted to a particular religious following and charged with providing funeral services and keeping alive the memory of their deceased members—played a crucial role in shoring up the position of the indigenous elites and in redefining their ties to their subordinates.

In the context of ritual life related to death, the so-called common people copied their ethnic leaders or, in their absence, established ties with religious orders, with local leaders, and with their peers through the confraternities. Besides these forms of social organization, which extended widely and quickly throughout the Andes, for people of all stations social existence depended on being part of the activities and rituals that marked the cycle of life. Although they retained a great many of their pre-conquest rituals, by means of constant interaction with the Christian sphere they absorbed more and more of its features. Changes in the organization of space accelerated that process. Consequently, a burial outside the church quickly came to mean a severance from society with undesirable consequences for both the deceased and the living. Complaints from communities about priests not coming to the dying to offer the last rites or to bury the dead with proper respect or in the right place cannot be taken simply as people's attempts to free themselves from abusive clerics.[1]

The fact that churches became burial sites also led residents of the new jurisdictions to think of them as their own property. Tombs before the conquest had also attached a group to the territory it controlled, but the change brought about by the appropriation of new sacred spaces was no doubt very significant. Despite the fears of some colonial authorities that church grounds and their funeral vaults would become centers of idolatry, the Church permitted and even encouraged the development of this sense of belonging among the Andean populations. Among other elements such as altars and images, made with the help of parishioners and the faithful, tombs and the funeral vaults situated at their feet and within the perimeter of Christian churches were perhaps a better representation, more personal and intimate, of the bonds that Andean settlers forged with their churches. For *caciques,* members of distinguished families, or men or women of the common people, to know that upon their death they were ensured a grave in a church—often next to the bodies of their ancestors and relatives or others from the same neighborhood, profession, parish, or religious following—meant that there was a more concrete connection with the place they inhabited, with their intimates, and with their past. The right to choose a burial place was subject to consensus building and conflicts, conditioned by the way in which different ethnic groups related to one another. In the viceregal capital, the ecclesiastical council limited Indians' access to burial spaces in the cathedral, whereas in the parish churches, sites for the poor were clearly demarcated. Religious orders invited the indigenous artisans' guilds to build their vaults in their churches.

In contrast to Lima, in Cuzco there is no evidence of spaces intended exclusively for the Indians or the poor; religious orders competed in offering places to families descended from the Incas; and while there were no burials intended exclusively for guild members in the period studied, there were burials for *ayllus* or kinship groups. The ties that the Spanish elite forged with the indigenous elite, in particular, and with the broader indigenous population, in general— to the extent that some *caciques* and their families were buried in the tombs of their *encomenderos*—explain what appears to have been an integration made effective through the maintenance of subordinate relationships. This integration was facilitated by the fact that kinship ties prevailed in all groups, which was characteristic of the region's population.

Whereas in the big cities, ecclesiastical authorities and local elites controlled the sacred sites, in more remote settings the idea gradually spread that churches and their funeral spaces belonged to the native population, as represented by their leaders. In 1643 the Indian mayors and *caciques* of San Pedro de Andahuaylillas, south of Cuzco, met with a notary to declare that they were donating a grave in the town church to the niece of the famed *licenciado* Juan Pérez Bocanegra.[2] The latter, who had been the town priest for close to a quarter century, was named in the same deed as the beneficiary of the tomb he held at the foot of the altar dedicated to Nuestra Señora de Monserrate. Although Pérez Bocanegra had had the funeral vault built at his own expense, it is significant that the town's indigenous authorities found it necessary to hand over the space by means of a notarial document. Besides the circumstantial evidence that would explain why the act took place precisely at that moment, it is important to emphasize that the mayors and *caciques* considered themselves owners of the holy site and as such were donating the graves, even to the very priest who had taught them their faith.[3] Across the Andean territory, the population had sufficient reason to identify churches as their own: they had built them with their own hands, they were in charge of their maintenance, they paid for their decorations and images with their donations, and they were responsible for keeping the priest's kitchen well stocked. If all that was not enough, they had a powerful reason to feel a close tie to these buildings because the remains of their dead were buried therein.

Bodies and Selves

In contrast to the diverse forms of handling the dead that were practiced before the conquest, with multiple burials and differing categories of individuals, complementarity of human remains and objects, and various approaches to the idea of self—represented, at one extreme, by the preservation of bodies and, at the other, by varying states of decomposition of human remains—Christianity introduced the idea that each person was made up of a body and a soul. As a consequence, each death implied the disappearance of a person, and, in principle, it was taken for granted that each grave represented an individual.[4] The consequences of these assertions were many. They had a direct relationship with the reconfiguration of sacred space and with the spread and assimilation of ideas and practices regarding such fundamental matters as the origin and fate of human beings. In concrete terms, the quality and quantity of resources allocated to the preparation of burials varied. The manner of preparing the body was gradually standardized as the number of church burials increased. Burial spaces in the churches admitted almost no variation in how the bodies were to be treated: the representation of death as sleep had arrived in the Andes to stay. The fact that priests were always required to preside over the funerals helped to standardize the practice, and, although there were varying interpretations of whether the dead could or could not be dressed in the local fashion for burial, in comparison to the concern over dress in pre-Hispanic times there was a notable decrease in the importance of funeral attire.

To what extent, how quickly, or even whether the Christian concept of the soul penetrated the consciences of Andean men and women is difficult to determine precisely. It certainly did not happen rapidly or simply. It is true that Christianity taught that only humans had souls and that, as a result, missionaries reproached the people of the Andes for believing in a common force animating people, animals, and objects alike, but this did not negate the possibility of establishing some points in common. Observations and explanations about what happened during death to the soul, or to the force that had animated the body, generated similar concerns. The most significant of these was the nature of the link maintained by the living with the dead, and vice versa. Christian ideas about what constituted a human being and the links that bound him to his or her ancestors and to subsequent generations influenced forms of succession, introduced new hierarchies within kinship groups, and favored the creation of nuclear families. The fate of the deceased's possessions varied with the introduction of criteria such as legitimacy of offspring and was considerably modified in the context of the high mortality and intense migration that characterized the early colonial period. At this point, lacking successors and increasingly concerned over their own fate after death, people began to establish inheritances on behalf of their souls and were encouraged to leave bequests intended for religious purposes, which ultimately resulted in a significant increase in the Church's wealth.

In the winter of 1653 a Lima scribe noted in his record book at the end of his visit to a house in the Indian neighborhood of El Cercado: "I Joan Castañeda scribe of the King Our Lord give my word and true testimony that today around one in the afternoon I witnessed the natural death and passing from this present life as far as I could tell of Captain Domingo Francisco whom I knew in life and saw placed in a casket and shrouded with the habit of St. Francis . . . in her living room and at the request of Joana Dabalos his wife I offer this testimony."[5] Domingo Francisco's wife—who was also his executor—and relatives were to proceed to the burial of the body and then to the reading and execution of the will. The main characters' behavior in this episode was routine, and the document they requested explained that Domingo Francisco's death had occurred under natural circumstances and that his body had been prepared correctly. Nevertheless, just a century earlier, even in the viceregal capital where they resided, this behavior of the relatives would have been unthinkable. The introduction of documents and wills and of witnesses who annotated the details of a person's death constituted a significant innovation that confirmed the religious and juridical criteria underlying the idea of self that was imposed in the Andes.

Ritual

Even in its most brutal context—the violence that came with the European invasion—the death ritual made up the primordial language in which Andeans and Europeans communicated and exchanged their visions of power and the sacred. Death rituals were also the first factor that organized both parties by ethnic and social distinctions. In the subsequent decades, with the advance of evangelization and colonization, the role of funerary ritual deepened, widened, and diversified. This did not mean, however, that missionaries and colonial officials always had control over it, for the context was one in which there was resistance in addition to adaptation and assimilation. Ritual provides an effective way for a group to take control of the dead. We can recall the uncertain fate of Atahualpa's body and his controversial funeral, or the funeral rites of Paullo Inca, baptized Don Cristóbal Paullo, which took place in the Cuzco town square according to Incan ceremonial ritual over a decade after the conquest.[6] The power of Christian funerary ritual lay in the strict detail with which it regulated all the steps from the death throes up to the moment in which the separation of body and soul was symbolically consecrated, and in which everyone's participation was crucial in order for the process to be meaningful and effective both in the present and in the afterlife. A solitary death was feared and could only harbor bad omens.

The inclusion of the greatest number of people possible in funerary ritual necessarily implied a complex set of factors. First, at the same time that participation and inclusion were encouraged, it was essential to maintain the distinctions that separated people according to their origin, social standing, or level of doctrinal training. The guidelines issued by synods in Lima and Cuzco adjusted to local conditions, recognizing, for example, the central presence of ethnic authorities in Cuzco, whereas in the viceregal capital the importance of social mobility and of the aspirations of a visible group of prosperous Indians was accepted. In this way, the organizing tendency of funerary ritual, manifested from the first moments of the European invasion, continued to operate and increase in complexity throughout the period we have studied.

Second, the way in which the steps of the ritual and the guidelines that regulated it were communicated implied using example, repetition, and vigilance in such a way that the ritual would come to be seen as not only an obligation but also a necessity. From the staging of the Spanish king's funeral, replayed in the most remote Indian parishes, to routine inquiries made during pastoral visits about community life and priestly behavior, there was an insistence on ritual correctly conducted in order to honor the dead and console the living. After a few years, not only did priests and other colonial authorities observe whether the people of the Andes were carrying out appropriate rituals for the dead, but indigenous inhabitants of cities and smaller settlements also reported their priests if they were not fulfilling their obligation to administer the last rites.

These factors do not imply that Andean funerary beliefs and practices were completely suppressed and supplanted by Hispano-Christian models. If such a thing had occurred, the overall process would not have been successful. To be effective, each of the steps of the funerary ritual had to be meaningful for the participants, who also had to witness them. Reporting to the beds of the dying, observing or walking in funeral processions, burying the dead, leaving offerings in tombs, giving or receiving bequests, and attending commemorations for the deceased all imply an intense process of exchange: each individual and each group put forth something of its own and at the same time borrowed something from each tradition. Each of these factors involved, moreover, the need to resolve practical problems, and these answers demanded a constant interaction between what was desirable and what was possible. It was at those sites of exchange where the transformations we have studied were brought about. Can anyone possibly experience another's death up close and remain unchanged?

APPENDIX A.

BURIAL SITES, CONFRATERNITY MEMBERSHIP,

AND FUNERAL RITES

Table 5.1 Burial Sites of Lima Indians, 1571–1591 (54 people: 22 men and 32 women), in Parishes and Copacabana (31 cases, 57%)

Burial/ Parish	F/M	N.D.	Cathedral	Santa Ana	San Sebastián	San Lázaro	San Marcelo	El Cercado	Home-town	Copaca-bana	Total
N.D.	F	0	0	2	0	0	0	0	0	1	3
	M	0	0	2	0	0	0	0	0	1	3
Cathedral	F	0	5	0	0	0	0	0	0	0	5
	M	0	0	0	0	0	0	0	0	0	0
Santa Ana	F	0	0	3	0	0	0	0	0	0	3
	M	0	0	2	0	0	0	0	0	0	2
San Sebastián	F	0	0	0	5	0	0	0	0	0	5
	M	0	0	0	0	0	0	0	0	0	0
San Lázaro	F	0	0	0	0	1	0	0	0	0	1
	M	0	0	0	0	0	0	0	0	0	0
San Marcelo	F	0	0	0	0	0	0	0	0	0	0
	M	0	0	0	0	0	1	0	0	0	1
El Cercado	F	0	0	0	0	0	0	0	0	0	0
	M	0	0	0	0	0	0	1	0	0	1
Hometown	F	0	0	0	0	0	0	0	1	1	2
	M	0	0	0	0	0	0	1	4	0	5
Total		0	5	9	5	1	1	2	5	3	31
%		0	16	29	16	3	3	6	16	10	99

Source: Archivo General de la Nación (AGN), Protocolos Notariales (PN), sixteenth century

Note: Percentages in the tables in Appendix A are rounded. Percentage totals may be more or less than 100 as a result.

Table 5.2   Burial Sites of Lima Indians, 1571–1591, in Convents
(23 cases, 43%)

Burial/ Parish	F/M	San Francisco	Santo Domingo	San Agustín	La Merced	Jesuits	Total
N.D.	F	7	0	1	0	0	8
	M	4	1	1	0	0	6
Cathedral	F	1	1	0	0	1	3
	M	1	0	0	0	0	1
Santa Ana	F	0	0	0	0	0	0
	M	0	0	0	0	0	0
San Sebastián	F	0	1	0	0	0	1
	M	0	0	0	0	0	0
San Lázaro	F	0	0	0	0	0	0
	M	0	0	0	0	0	0
San Marcelo	F	0	0	0	0	0	0
	M	0	0	0	0	0	0
El Cercado	F	0	0	0	0	0	0
	M	0	0	0	0	0	0
Hometown	F	0	1	0	0	0	1
	M	1	2	0	0	0	3
Total		14	6	2	0	1	23
%		61	26	9	0	4	100

Source: AGN, PN, sixteenth century

Table 5.3 Burial Sites of Lima Indians, 1600–1670 (180 people: 95 men and 85 women), in Parishes and Copacabana (93 cases, 52%)

Burial/Parish	F/M	N.D.	Cathedral	Santa Ana	San Sebastián	San Lázaro	San Marcelo	El Cercado	Hometown	Copacabana	Total
N.D.	F	2	0	1	0	0	0	1	0	0	4
	M	0	1	2	0	0	0	0	0	2	5
Cathedral	F	0	1	0	0	0	0	0	0	0	1
	M	0	1	1	0	0	0	0	0	2	4
Santa Ana	F	0	0	11	0	0	0	0	0	0	11
	M	0	0	12	0	0	0	1	0	0	13
San Sebastián	F	0	0	0	2	0	0	0	0	0	2
	M	0	0	0	0	0	0	0	0	0	0
San Lázaro	F	0	0	0	0	3	0	0	0	1	4
	M	0	0	0	0	0	0	0	0	4	4
San Marcelo	F	0	0	0	0	0	1	0	0	0	1
	M	0	0	0	0	0	0	0	0	0	0
El Cercado	F	0	0	0	0	0	0	1	0	0	1
	M	0	0	1	0	0	0	6	0	0	7
Hometown	F	0	0	1	0	0	0	0	8	1	10
	M	0	0	3	0	0	0	1	20	2	26
Total		2	3	32	2	3	1	10	28	12	93
%		2	3	34	2	3	1	11	30	13	99

Source: AGN, PN, seventeenth century

Table 5.4 Burial Sites of Lima Indians, 1600–1670, in Convents (87 cases, 48%)

Burial/ Parish	F/M	San Francisco	Santo Domingo	San Agustín	Jesuits	La Merced	Other	Total
N.D.	F	11	3	4	1	3	2	24
	M	5	3	1	1	3	1	14
Cathedral	F	1	2	1	0	1	0	5
	M	3	0	0	0	0	1	4
Santa Ana	F	4	2	0	1	1	0	8
	M	1	0	1	0	1	0	3
San Sebastián	F	0	0	0	0	0	0	0
	M	0	0	0	0	0	0	0
San Lázaro	F	2	6	0	0	0	0	8
	M	4	1	1	0	0	0	6
San Marcelo	F	0	0	0	0	0	0	0
	M	0	0	0	0	0	0	0
El Cercado	F	2	0	1	0	1	0	4
	M	1	0	0	0	0	0	1
Hometown	F	2	1	0	0	0	0	3
	M	1	5	0	0	1	0	7
Total		37	23	9	3	11	4	87
%		43	26	10	3	13	5	100

Source: AGN, PN, seventeenth century

Table 5.5   Membership in Confraternities in Lima, 1571–1591
(54 people: 22 men and 32 women)

	Men	Women	Total
Candelaria	2	2	4
Rosario	5	6	11
San Miguel	1	1	2
Consolación	0	0	0
Loreto	0	0	0
Nombre de Jesús	0	0	0
San Joaquín	0	0	0
Ssmo. Sacramento	2	1	3
Ánimas Purgatorio	0	1	1
Copacabana	2	0	2
Niño Jesús	0	1	1
Concepción	1	1	2
San Antonio de Padua	0	0	0
Other	4	7	11
Belongs to at least one	13	14	27
%	59	44	50
Belongs to none	9	18	27
%	41	56	50
Total	22	32	54

Source: AGN, PN, sixteenth century

Table 5.6   Membership in Confraternities in Lima, 1600–1670
(180 people: 95 men and 85 women)

	Men	Women	Total
Candelaria	17	23	40
Rosario	20	20	40
San Miguel	9	16	25
Consolación	8	11	19
Loreto	10	7	17
Nombre de Jesús	3	1	4
San Joaquín	4	2	6
Ssmo. Sacramento	9	8	17
Ánimas Purgatorio	18	21	39
Copacabana	16	12	28
Niño Jesús	2	5	7
Concepción	9	3	12
San Antonio de Padua	1	2	3
Other	32	21	53
Belongs to at least one	72	70	142
%	76	82	79
Belongs to none	23	15	38
%	24	18	21
Total	95	85	180

Source: AGN, PN, seventeenth century

Table 5.7 Burial Sites of Cuzco Indians, 1559–1595
(62 people: 27 men and 35 women), in Parishes (36 cases, 58%)

Burial/ Parish	F/M	N.D.	Hospital	Cathedral	Santa Ana	Home- town	San Cristóbal	Belén	Total
Hospital	F	0	12	0	0	0	0	0	12
	M	0	9	1	0	0	0	0	10
Cathedral	F	0	0	0	0	0	0	0	0
	M	0	0	0	0	0	0	0	0
Santa Ana	F	0	0	0	0	0	0	0	0
	M	0	0	0	2	0	0	0	2
Hometown	F	0	0	0	0	2	0	0	2
	M	0	0	0	0	3	0	0	3
San Cristóbal	F	0	0	0	0	0	1	0	1
	M	0	0	0	0	0	1	0	1
Belén	F	0	0	0	0	0	0	0	0
	M	0	0	0	0	0	0	1	1
San Blas	F	0	0	0	0	0	0	0	0
	M	0	0	0	0	0	0	0	0
San Sebastián	F	0	0	0	0	0	0	0	0
	M	0	0	0	0	0	0	0	0
Santiago	F	0	0	0	0	0	0	0	0
	M	0	0	0	0	0	0	0	0
N.D.	F	0	0	1	0	0	0	0	1
	M	1	1	1	0	0	0	0	3
Total		1	22	3	2	5	2	1	36
%		3	61	8	6	14	6	3	101

Source: Archivo Departamental de Cuzco (ADC), PN, sixteenth century

Table 5.8 Burial Sites of Cuzco Indians, 1559–1595, in Convents
(26 cases, 42%)

Burial/Parish	F/M	San Francisco	Santo Domingo	La Merced	San Agustín	Total
Hospital	F	1	1	1	1	4
	M	1	0	2	0	3
Cathedral	F	0	1	2	0	3
	M	0	0	0	0	0
Santa Ana	F	1	0	0	0	1
	M	0	0	0	0	0
Hometown	F	0	0	0	0	0
	M	0	0	0	0	0
San Cristóbal	F	2	0	0	0	2
	M	0	0	1	0	1
Belén	F	0	0	0	0	0
	M	0	0	0	0	0
San Blas	F	0	0	0	0	0
	M	0	0	0	0	0
San Sebastián	F	0	0	0	0	0
	M	0	0	0	0	0
Santiago	F	1	0	0	0	1
	M	0	0	0	0	0
N.D.	F	1	3	3	1	8
	M	1	1	1	0	3
Total		8	6	10	2	26
%		31	23	38	8	100

Source: ADC, PN, sixteenth century

Table 5.9 Burial Sites of Cuzco Indians, 1600–1670 (163 people: 62 men and 101 women), in Parishes (86 cases, 53%)

Burial/Parish	F/M	N.D.	Hospital	Santa Ana	Belén	San Blas	San Cristóbal	San Sebastián	Santiago	Cathedral	Hometown	Total
N.D.	F	2	0	0	0	0	0	0	0	0	0	2
	M	1	0	0	0	0	0	0	0	0	0	1
Hospital	F	0	17	0	0	0	0	0	0	0	0	17
	M	0	9	0	0	0	0	0	0	0	0	9
Santa Ana	F	0	0	0	0	0	0	0	0	0	0	0
	M	0	0	0	0	0	0	0	0	0	0	0
Belén	F	0	0	0	1	0	0	0	0	0	0	1
	M	1	0	0	2	0	0	0	0	0	0	3
San Blas	F	0	1	0	0	5	0	0	0	0	0	6
	M	0	0	0	0	2	0	0	0	0	0	2
San Cristóbal	F	0	0	0	0	0	7	0	0	1	0	8
	M	0	0	0	0	0	3	0	0	0	0	3
San Sebastián	F	0	0	0	0	0	0	1	0	0	0	1
	M	0	0	0	0	0	0	1	0	1	0	2
Santiago	F	0	0	0	0	0	0	0	3	0	0	3
	M	0	0	0	0	0	0	0	2	0	0	2
Cathedral	F	0	0	0	0	0	0	0	0	11	0	11
	M	0	0	0	0	0	0	0	0	7	0	7
Hometown	F	0	0	0	0	0	0	0	0	0	1	1
	M	0	0	1	0	0	0	0	0	0	6	7
Total		4	27	1	3	7	10	2	5	20	7	86
%		5	31	1	3	8	12	2	6	23	8	99

Source: ADC, PN, seventeenth century

Table 5.10 Burial Sites of Cuzco Indians, 1600–1670, in Convents (77 cases, 47%)

Burial/ Parish	F/M	San Francisco	Santo Domingo	La Merced	San Agustín	Jesuits	Santa Clara	Santa Catalina	Other	Total
N.D.	F	1	1	4	0	0	0	0	0	6
	M	1	1	0	0	0	0	0	3	5
Hospital	F	2	1	2	0	0	0	0	0	5
	M	2	0	1	0	4	1	0	0	8
Santa Ana	F	1	0	0	0	0	0	0	0	1
	M	0	0	0	0	0	0	0	0	0
Belén	F	0	1	0	0	1	0	0	0	2
	M	0	0	0	0	0	0	0	0	0
San Blas	F	0	1	0	3	2	0	0	0	7
	M	1	0	0	0	0	1	0	0	1
San Cristóbal	F	1	0	1	0	0	0	0	0	2
	M	1	0	1	0	0	0	0	0	2
San Sebastián	F	0	0	0	0	0	0	0	0	0
	M	0	0	0	0	0	0	1	0	1
Santiago	F	0	0	0	0	0	1	0	0	1
	M	0	0	0	0	0	0	0	0	0
Cathedral	F	7	9	1	3	2	0	2	1	25
	M	1	4	1	0	2	0	0	0	8
Hometown	F	1	1	0	0	0	0	0	0	2
	M	0	0	1	0	0	0	0	0	1
Total		19	19	12	6	11	3	3	4	77
%		25	25	16	8	14	4	4	4	100

Source: ADC, PN, seventeenth century

Table 5.11   Membership in Confraternities in Cuzco, 1559–1595
(62 people: 27 men and 35 women)

	Men	Women	Total
Concepción	0	0	0
Rosario	0	3	3
San Agustín	1	0	1
Ánimas Purgatorio	0	4	4
Guadalupe	1	2	3
Soledad	0	3	3
Espíritu Santo	4	2	6
Ssmo. Sacramento	4	2	6
Nicolás Tolentino	1	2	3
Copacabana	0	0	0
Nombre de Jesús	0	1	1
Loreto	0	0	0
Other	10	13	23
Belongs to at least one	13	18	31
%	48	51	50
Belongs to none	14	17	31
%	52	49	50
Total	27	35	62

Source: ADC, PN, sixteenth century

Table 5.12 Membership in Confraternities in Cuzco, 1600–1670
(163 people: 62 men and 101 women)

	Men	Women	Total
Concepción	6	12	18
Rosario	7	21	28
San Agustín	4	11	15
Ánimas Purgatorio	11	17	28
Guadalupe	6	6	12
Soledad	7	12	19
Espíritu Santo	0	1	1
Ssmo. Sacramento	5	9	14
Nicolás Tolentino	1	4	5
Copacabana	4	10	14
Nombre de Jesús	2	5	7
Loreto	5	7	12
Other	31	51	82
Belongs to at least one	45	78	123
%	73	77	75
Belongs to none	17	23	40
%	27	23	25
Total	62	101	163

Source: ADC, PN, seventeenth century

Table 5.13 Distribution of Burial Sites in Lima and Cuzco, Sixteenth and Seventeenth Centuries

	Lima 1571–1591		Lima 1600–1670		Cuzco 1559–1595		Cuzco 1600–1670	
	Value	%	Value	%	Value	%	Value	%
Convents	23	43	87	49	26	43	77	48
Parishes	14	26	19	11	8	13	48	30
Hometown	5	9	28	16	5	8	7	4
Hospitals	9	17	32	18	22	36	27	17
Copacabana	3	6	12	7	0	0	0	0
Total with Known Burial Site	54	-	178	-	61	-	159	-

Source: AGN and ADC, PN, sixteenth and seventeenth centuries

Table 5.14 Requests for Funeral Procession Crosses in Lima and Cuzco, Sixteenth and Seventeenth Centuries

	Lima[a]	*Cuzco*[b]
Sixteenth Century		
High Cross	17	29
%	89	76
Low Cross	2	9
%	11	24
Total	19	38
Seventeenth Century		
High Cross	110	89
%	98	79
Low Cross	2	24
%	2	21
Total	112	113

Source: AGN and ADC, PN, sixteenth and seventeenth centuries

[a] Thirty-five wills from the sixteenth century and sixty-eight from the seventeenth do not explicitly indicate what type of cross would head the funeral procession.

[b] Twenty-four wills from the sixteenth century and fifty from the seventeenth do not explicitly indicate what type of cross would head the funeral procession.

Table 5.15 Requests for *Posas* in Lima and Cuzco, 1600–1670

	Lima	Cuzco
Cases	180	163
1600–1609	3	2
1610–19	4 (2)	4
1620–29	–	3
1630–39	3 (3)	3 (1)
1640–49	1	7
1650–59	–	9
1660–69	–	4 (1)
Total	11 (6)	32 (30)
% of Total	6% (4%)	20% (18%)

Source: AGN and ADC, PN, seventeenth century

Note: The figures in parentheses specify the number of *caciques* who planned the funeral in their hometown.

Table 5.16 Requests for Funeral Masses in Lima and Cuzco, Sixteenth and Seventeenth Centuries

	Lima	Cuzco
Sixteenth Century	76%	91%
Seventeenth Century	79%	79%

Source: AGN and ADC, PN, sixteenth and seventeenth centuries

APPENDIX B.

HEIRS AND EXECUTORS

Table 6.1 Universal Heir, Lima, 1571–1599

Years	Son	Daughter	Children	Father	Mother	Parents	Spouse	Soul	Confrat.	Devotion	Other	N.D.	Total
1571–79	3	6	3	0	2	0	1	9	1	0	3	0	28
1580–89	1	0	0	0	1	0	6	1	1	0	1	0	11
1591–99	3	0	2	0	1	1	1	4	0	0	3	0	15
Total	7	6	5	0	4	1	8	14	2	0	7	0	54
%	13	11	9	0	7	2	15	26	4	0	13	0	100

Source: Archivo General de la Nación (AGN), Protocolos Notariales (PN), sixteenth century

Note: Percentages in the tables in Appendix B are rounded. Percentage totals may be more or less than 100 as a result.

Table 6.2 Universal Heir, Lima, 1600–1670

Years	Son	Daughter	Children	Father	Mother	Parents	Spouse	Soul	Confrat.	Devotion	Other	N.D.	Total
1600–1609	6	7	0	0	5	2	7	6	0	0	0	0	33
1611–19	2	2	9	0	3	0	3	7	3	0	2	0	31
1621–28	3	1	2	0	1	0	1	7	1	0	4	0	20
1630–39	3	10	10	0	6	0	4	9	0	0	8	3	53
1640–48	0	2	1	0	1	0	1	2	0	0	2	0	9
1650–57	4	1	2	0	1	0	4	2	0	0	1	1	16
1660–70	2	1	4	0	1	0	1	2	0	0	7	0	18
Total	20	24	28	0	18	2	21	35	4	0	24	4	180
%	11	13	16	0	10	1	12	19	2	0	13	2	99

Source: AGN, PN, seventeenth century

Table 6.3   Universal Heir, Cuzco, 1559–1595

Years	Son	Daughter	Children	Father	Mother	Parents	Spouse	Soul	Confrat.	Devotion	Other	N.D.	Total
1559–69	4	1	4	0	0	0	4	1	0	0	2	0	16
1571–72	1	2	1	0	0	0	0	0	0	0	0	0	4
1583–89	6	4	11	0	2	0	4	4	0	0	2	2	35
1590–95	1	1	4	0	0	0	1	0	0	0	0	0	7
Total	12	8	20	0	2	0	9	5	0	0	4	2	62
%	19	13	32	0	3	0	15	8	0	0	6	3	99

Source: Archivo Departamental de Cuzco (ADC), PN, sixteenth century

Table 6.4 Universal Heir, Cuzco, 1600–1670

Years	Son	Daughter	Children	Father	Mother	Parents	Spouse	Soul	Confrat.	Devotion	Other	N.D.	Total
1600–1606	1	1	5	0	2	1	1	3	0	0	2	0	16
1610–19	0	5	6	0	0	0	0	2	0	0	3	1	17
1620–29	3	3	7	1	0	0	2	4	1	0	1	1	23
1630–39	1	4	17	0	1	0	1	1	1	0	1	1	28
1640–49	0	3	7	0	0	1	3	5	1	1	6	1	28
1650–59	1	2	12	0	1	0	4	7	0	0	4	1	32
1660–70	0	4	7	0	1	0	2	2	0	0	3	0	19
Total	6	22	61	1	5	2	13	24	3	1	20	5	163
%	4	13	37	1	3	1	8	15	2	1	12	3	100

Source: ADC, PN, seventeenth century

Table 6.5 Main Executors, Lima, 1572–1599

	Total	%
Father	3	3
Brother	6	6
Spouse	15	14
Child	1	1
Brother-in-law	0	0
Son-in-law	0	0
Cacique	8	7
Priest	16	15
Mayordomo	0	0
Confraternity	8	7
Spaniard	15	14
Other	22	20
N.D.	14	13
Total	108	100

Source: AGN, PN, sixteenth century

Table 6.6 Main Executors, Lima, 1600–1670

	Total	%
Father	11	3
Brother	30	8
Spouse	59	16
Son	11	3
Brother-in-law	3	1
Son-in-law	8	2
Cacique	25	7
Priest	18	5
Mayordomo	0	0
Confraternity	39	11
Spaniard	34	9
Other	75	21
N.D.	47	13
Total	360	99

Source: AGN, PN, seventeenth century

Table 6.7   Main Executors, Cuzco, 1559–1595

	Total	%
Father	1	1
Brother	6	5
Spouse	9	7
Son	9	7
Brother-in-law	1	1
Son-in-law	4	3
Cacique	21	17
Priest	5	4
Mayordomo	0	0
Confraternity	0	0
Spaniard	13	10
Other	48	39
N.D. ·	7	6
Total	124	100

Source: ADC, PN, sixteenth century

Table 6.8   Main Executors, Cuzco, 1600–1670

	Total	%
Father	7	2
Brother	8	2
Spouse	28	9
Son	29	9
Brother-in-law	1	0
Son-in-law	10	3
Cacique	28	9
Priest	39	12
Mayordomo	0	0
Confraternity	0	0
Spaniard	45	14
Other	80	25
N.D.	51	16
Total	326	100

Source: ADC, PN, seventeenth century

Table 6.9 Executors Appointed in Addition to Spouse, Lima, 1572–1599

Main Executor	Additional Executors	Total	%
	Father	1	9
	Brother	1	9
	Son	0	0
Spouse	Brother-in-law	0	0
(11)	Son-in-law	0	0
	Cacique	2	18
	Priest	1	9
	Mayordomo	1	9
	Spaniard	3	27
	Other	1	9
	Former partner	1	9
	Total	11	99

Source: AGN, PN, sixteenth century

Table 6.10 Executors Appointed in Addition to Spouse, Lima, 1600–1670

Main Executor	Additional Executors	Total	%
	Father	2	4
	Brother	10	22
	Son	4	9
Spouse	Brother-in-law	1	2
(38)	Son-in-law	0	0
	Cacique	5	11
	Priest	1	2
	Mayordomo	2	4
	Spaniard	2	4
	Other	12	27
	No add. executors	6	13
	Total	45	98

Source: AGN, PN, seventeenth century

Table 6.11   Executors Appointed in Addition to Spouse, Cuzco,
1559–1595

Main Executor	Additional Executors	Total	%
	Father	0	0
	Brother	1	3
	Son	2	6
Spouse	Brother-in-law	0	0
(26)	Son-in-law	0	0
	Cacique	4	12
	Priest	1	3
	Mayordomo	0	0
	Spaniard	0	0
	Other	15	45
	No add. executors	10	30
Total		33	99

Source: ADC, PN, sixteenth century

Table 6.12   Executors Appointed in Addition to Spouse, Cuzco,
1600–1670

Main Executor	Additional Executors	Total	%
	Father	0	0
	Brother	1	4
	Son	3	13
Spouse	Brother-in-law	0	0
(20)	Son-in-law	1	4
	Cacique	1	4
	Priest	0	0
	Mayordomo	0	0
	Spaniard	1	4
	Other	6	25
	No add. executors	11	46
	Total	24	100

Source: ADC, PN, seventeenth century

NOTES

Introduction

1. See, for example, Horton (1972); Ifeka-Moller (1974); Horton and Peel (1976); Schreuder and Oddie (1989); and Ranger (2003). Some treat the term with suspicion, suggesting that it is insufficient for expressing the diversity of the situations and experiences involved, while others maintain that "conversion" evokes the image of an abrupt change instead of a process (Gose 2003). In her extraordinary study of the transformation undergone by Mayan society in the colonial period, Farriss (1984) uses the term "syncretism" instead. However, the concept of syncretism also has its critics (Cummins 2002). For specialists today, "conversion" evokes ideas of diversity (Hefner 1993), adaptation, and, especially, social process (McLynn 2003). In studying Andean societies in the colonial period, MacCormack (1991), Griffiths (1996), Mills (1997), and Estenssoro (2003), all with different emphases and perspectives, conceptualize religious conversion as a complex process of adaptation and change. In the introduction to a recent collection of studies on religious conversion edited by Mills and Grafton (2003b), the authors emphasize adaptation as the central feature as well as diverse characteristics and rhythms, concluding that it is impossible for a religious conversion to be "total." For a refreshing approach to conversion emphasizing cultural accommodation and acknowledging indigenous agency, see Reff (2005). This author offers a brief and useful discussion of conversion theories (2005, 29–31).

2. These aspects and their consequences are not unique. The history of conversion to Christianity in Europe is laced with similar processes, the most notable of which is the expansion of the Carolingian empire (Duggan 1997; Muldoon 1997, 5).

3. A more detailed investigation of this point may be found in Estenssoro (2003). For a general review of the reforms introduced by the Council of Trent, see Hsia (1998).

4. On Mexico see, for example, Burkhart (1989; 1996); Gruzinski (1988); and Brading (1991).

5. The problems discussed include the formation of evangelizing strategies (Armas 1953; Borges 1960; Vargas Ugarte 1953–1962), or, as others have opted to call it, the struggle against autochthonous religions (Duviols 1971; Huertas 1981; Griffiths 1996; Mills 1997). Other studies cover ideological and doctrinal matters of Andean religion and Catholicism in the sixteenth century (MacCormack 1991). One innovative and ambitious study of the Andean religious and cultural process between the conquest and the eighteenth century is that of Estenssoro (2003).

6. See Ariès (1977); Chiffoleau (1980); and Vovelle (1983).

7. Verdery's book (1999) is especially important for these topics.

8. A recent collection of studies, edited by Gordon and Marshall (2000), pays special attention to the different forms taken by the ties between the living and the dead.

9. Because of its abundance and diversity, I believe that the body of documents is reasonably representative, since it is complemented with an ample array of other sources to ensure a reliable interpretation. Given its magnitude, the notary archive of Lima imposes a particularly arduous task on the researcher. The notary section (Escribanías) of the Archivo General de la Nación del Perú in Lima contains 164 files for the sixteenth century and 2,062 files for the seventeenth century. Identifying the notaries who catered to indigenous men and women has been very laborious, given that, at first sight, it is impossible to recognize them. Very few of these files contain indices, and these are of little or no use, since they do not list the participants in the testaments and other deeds alphabetically by family name, but instead by first name. Hence, these indices, often incomplete, contain long lists of Juan, Pedro, and María!

10. In the Andes, chiefs were known as *curacas,* thus the institution should be *curacazgo.* The Spaniards imported the word *cacique* from the Caribbean. For clarity, I will use the words *caciques* and *cacicazgo* throughout the book.

O N E. **Death in Pre-Hispanic Peru**

1. The use of the concept is extensive nowadays, especially in the field of archaeology. In the most recent literature the term "ancestors" is habitually employed to refer to an important but indefinite number that at times would appear to comprise the totality of human remains found in Andean funerary contexts.

2. Dulanto (2002, 37) points out that one reason for the difficulty in studying the cult of the ancestors via archaeology is that it "has been thought of as the equivalent of beliefs and practices concerning death." He adds that despite their importance, they are but one among many other practices and beliefs regarding the ancestors. However, the author does not offer an explanation of how one might separate death from other spheres of human life.

3. These authors offer an excellent synthesis of the meaning and expression of the cult of the ancestors in the Andes.

4. See in this regard Isbell's (1997) important study.

5. Frank Salomon (1995) classifies the ethnohistorical sources that report on Andean funerary practices, which he interprets by applying anthropological theory to the cult of the ancestors, particularly the contributions of Hertz (1960), Fortes (1965; 1976), and Bloch and Parry (1982). Through this, he analyzes the different phases of funerary ritual and mourning among the Incas and in the Lima highlands. He also uses colonial sources, especially those concerning the extirpation of idolatry, to illumine little-known aspects of pre-Hispanic funerary practice. Mary E. Doyle (1988) also studies the characteristics of the regional cults, examining their connection to pre-Hispanic practices and establishing the extent of continuity and change during the colonial period. William Isbell (1997) undertook his study of the Andean funerary monuments known as *chullpas* with the intention of reporting on their presence as an indicator of the rise of the kin group known as the *ayllu*. Isbell concludes that the institution of the *ayllu* has not existed always and everywhere in the Andes, as the majority of scholars assert, but rather that it arose in much more recent times as an expression of resistance to the appearance of the state in the Andes. Peter Kaulicke (2000) has also carried out an examination of Inca funerary rituals based on written sources. His main lines of inquiry involve concepts and practices in the maintenance of historical memory. Kaulicke devotes particular attention to funerary practices of the Moche society, which flourished on the north coast of Peru between AD 200 and 800, in order to arrive at some conclusions about the antiquity and extent of the practice of the cult of the ancestors in ancient Peru. The volume edited by Tom Dillehay (1995) marks an important milestone in the study of death in the pre-Hispanic Andes in drawing together a series of archaeological, anthropological, and historical studies on the theme. Other studies cited throughout this chapter address the problem from the perspective of particular regions.

6. Both types of sources offer certain challenges for the researcher. On the one hand, the data quite often appear in the written sources in a very general, imprecise way, while in the archaeological register they often seem fragmented and incomplete. The criteria for interpretation are the subject of debate.

7. Sabine MacCormack (1991, 89) points out that the chronicler's interest originated in concerns very distant from the Andean reality. On the one

hand, the matter is a recurring theme in the works of the Greek and Roman historians that Cieza had read, and on the other, it had preoccupied the missionaries committed to the Christian conversion of the Muslims of Granada.

8. Such as objects from looted burials or that could not be properly excavated. More than a few cases exist for which we lack sufficient data about the contexts or dating. In this regard, see, for example, the observations of Kaulicke (1997).

9. In his study of the burials and funerary chambers in the northern Andes, in territory belonging to present-day Ecuador and Colombia, Leon Doyon (2002, 81) agrees that "the physiographic context, and not social competition alone, was a determining factor."

10. Observing this type of construction led the American traveler and scholar G. E. Squier (1877, 74) to believe that the tombs he had excavated in Pachacamac had been dwellings.

11. This indicates that he is referring to the impact generated by El Niño, the climatic disturbances that must have occasioned the drastic diminution of the resources needed to ensure subsistence. It is quite possible that, in consequence, social conflicts were exacerbated. Archaeological research, particularly in the north of Peru but also on its central coast, confirms some of these processes and their serious, long-lasting, consequences (Moseley and Deeds 1982, 47–49; Conlee et al. 2004, 213).

12. Dorothy Menzel (1976, 227) has observed that in Ica, in a period before the arrival of the Incas, the stakes that served as grave markers had been cut off and buried. She interprets this as the way in which kin sought to protect the tombs from potential looters, not of treasure but of human remains. The absence or presence of tomb markers in Moche has been interpreted in different ways; whether they were signs indicating the position of the burial or whether they performed a communicative or symbolic function has not been established (Donnan 1995, 145).

13. This practice is difficult to determine in some coastal sites, as Eeckhout (1999) has noted. Concerning Ancón, see Ravines (1977; 1981); and Kaulicke (1997). Uhle (1988 [1913]) reported that he had difficulty locating tombs in Chancay.

14. The sacred character of Pachacamac preceded the Incas. The sanctuary, dedicated to a deity known as Ychsma, was the most important on the central coast. Its history is tied to a long mythic cycle and to successive occupations that articulate the cultural processes of the peoples of the coast as well as those of the highlands. The powers with which it is identified include, among others, the forces that animate and create the world, and the capacity of the divinity who dwells there to act as an oracle. Researchers have identified distinct phases of occupation and construction of the site, and they agree that Pachacamac was a ceremonial center of prime importance, a pilgrimage destination,

or the seat of the zone's most prominent ethnic lords and their retinues. Shimada (2005) has called attention to the importance of understanding the dynamic, changing character of this site. The bibliography on Pachacamac is very extensive, and perspectives on its meaning have been reevaluated in the most recent studies. See, for example, Max Uhle (1991 [1903]); Rostworowski (1992b; 2005); Shimada (1991; 2005); and Eeckhout 2004. An up-to-date literature review of the research can be found in Shimada (1991; 2005). On Chinchaycamac, see Cieza (1984b [1553], First Part, chap. 74, 220). In this passage the chronicler relates that the cult of Chinchaycamac continued after the conquest of Chincha by the Incas. On Chincha, see Uhle (1924); Rostworowski (2004 [1970]); and Sandweiss (1992).

15. Undoubtedly this place was for centuries an important supply center for fishermen, and drew in populations devoted to fishing over the course of successive occupations. Some burials suggest that during the tenure of the Wari and Inca, high-ranking individuals lived there (Ravines 1981, 164–65). There exist other examples of isolated cemeteries, such as those discussed in Parsons et al. (2000, 172–75) for the central highlands.

16. Menzel states that the site could have been under the control of Pachacamac (Kaulicke 1997, 71). Ravines (1981, 165) concurs with this hypothesis but argues that the site was not, as Menzel suggests, a necropolis, because enough traces have been found to indicate that the site was inhabited without interruption until the European conquest. Ancón is not the only site that raises questions of this sort. Paracas, where in the 1920s the archaeologist J. C. Tello excavated a large cemetery, has some similarities. In Paracas the origin of the resources that were used to produce the magnificent funerary offerings cannot be clearly determined. Neither are there any vestiges that would indicate the location of workshops that, for example, produced the extraordinarily fine textiles that wrapped the bodies of the dead (Frame 2001).

17. This is the case in Chan Chan, where different types of entombments are combined, organized in cemeteries of different sizes, with buildings found both within the city and on its periphery (Conrad 1982, 87).

18. This practice had taken root on the coast from very early times. See, for example, the analysis of Dwyer and Dwyer (1975, 147–49) on Paracas (AD 600).

19. Another significant recent find is that of a bundle dating from the Inca period in the Rinconada Alta site, in a sector bordering the canal of Ate (Frame et al. 2004).

20. Salazar (2007) suggests a similar case in Machu Picchu.

21. The cemetery excavated by Cock (2002) can be found today beneath a zone of recent urban occupation.

22. Hyslop states that a cemetery in an Inca site was unusual. He assumed that once the soldiers finished their service to the state, they were obliged to

return to their homes. Inca strategies of occupation have since become better understood. As we see here, other examples showed the existence of Inca tombs in the provinces. Hyslop did not conduct excavations in the zone and determined the placement of the cemetery by surface indicators, which he verified by comparing the surface study to aerial photography. The site where Incahuasi was found belonged to the *señorío*, or chiefdom, of Lunaguaná. On the history of this *señorío*, see Rostworowski (1978, 80).

23. DeLeonardis and Lau (2004, 82) have explained these "intentional acts of appropriation" by means of the occupation of cemeteries.

24. He remarks: "There is another kind of temple, that was the sepulcher of the dead, made in the fields; that so then as nowadays a Christian marked for himself and for his kin some sepulcher, and so adorns it each one according to his caudal, so also did the Peruvians in ancient times, marking and building sepulchers in the fields or in the desert. The tomb of the kings and great lords was like a house that was lived in, with its main room, chamber and *recámara*, with all the rest of the areas needed for the pantry, kitchen, patios, hallways, etc."

25. Known also as Chimor. It is considered by some to be a kingdom (Rowe 1948), while others describe it as an empire. It developed between AD 1000 and 1470, when it was conquered by the Incas. Its center was the city of Chan Chan, situated in the Moche valley, in the environs of present-day Trujillo, and extended in a wide area on the north coast of Peru, exerting its influence from the south all the way to an area north of present-day Lima (Conrad 1982, 106; Conlee et al. 2004, 214–15).

26. In their analysis of the politico-religious dynamic in Chan Chan, Conlee et al. (2004, 215) suggest that rather than the unifying religious principles of the society, what is being observed is the reaffirmation of hierarchy and of the rights of the elite. Although this is an interesting hypothesis, it is problematic to disassociate political from religious power. See also Isbell (1997, 146) for an analysis of the meaning of Moche tombs on the north coast.

27. Parsons et al. (2000, 172–75) has also studied some isolated cemeteries in Junín, dating from the Late Intermediate and Late Horizon (AD 1450–1532) periods, which comprise different types of tombs. They propose that these cemeteries could have been spaces of religious integration for the different groups that had access to them.

28. The Lupaqa were a powerful and prosperous Aymara-speaking ethnic group that settled the altiplano zone. They became subject to the Incas (Conlee et al. 2004, 230–32).

29. The authors do not consider this possibility, but the description of the place conforms to these conditions: the cave where at least 133 bodies were found is located in one of the hills of the mountain chain that dominates this part of the altiplano (De la Vega et al. 2002, 121–22).

30. Determining the rank of the occupants of these graves is practically impossible because of the state in which the remains were found, due to previous interventions (Llanos 1941; Isbell 1997). It has been reported that early archaeological explorations carried out in the Andes also ended up destroying the evidence (Arriaza et al. 1998, 208). The chronology of these caves is, in general, not well understood. In this regard, see Salomon (1995, 333).

31. Although Isbell (1997) asserts that the term *chullpa* must be incorrect, because it derives from a nineteenth-century source, we use it here because it is the best known. For a sixteenth-century usage of the term within a discussion of funerary monuments, see Matienzo (1967 [1567], chap. 39, 128–29).

32. Janusek (2004, 176), for example, proposes that their appearance in the Titicaca basin coincided with the collapse of Tiwanaku, which had developed in the south central Andes between ca. AD 400 and 1000.

33. Its cultural development and political formation preceded the Inca empire. It had its political center in the region corresponding to the present-day department of Ayacucho, and it exerted great influence in the central Andes.

34. In his research at the Pampa de las Flores site, Eeckhout (1999, 280) found traces of domestic occupation in sections of the common cemetery. However, this would appear to correspond to very brief periods, from which Eeckhout concludes that this must have occurred strictly for ritual purposes.

35. It is also quite possible that the custom of burying the dead in dwellings was not necessarily for defensive reasons but primarily religious and political ones. Gillespie (2002) maintains that the Maya, who customarily placed the graves of their kin in their houses, thus ensured the care of their intangible parts: the soul and the memory.

36. See the extraordinary passage in which Inca Garcilaso de la Vega (1945 [1609], 1: Book 5, chap. 29, 286–88) describes his visit to the home of the *corregidor* (royal magistrate) Polo de Ondegardo to see the mummies of the Incas. See also Acosta (2002 [1590], Book 5, chap. 6, 310–11).

37. This compact description is based on one of the most vivid and complete reports of the Inca mummies, written by Pedro Pizarro, who was a member of the first group of conquistadors to arrive in Cuzco (1978 [1571], 52–54). See also Araníbar (1969); Alonso Sagaseta (1989); Guillén (1983); MacCormack (1991, 118–38); Salomon (1995); and Vreeland (1998, 171–74).

38. The world's oldest examples of artificial mummification (Guillén 2005, 142), dating from approximately 7000 BC (Arriaza et al. 1998, 190; Rivera 1995, 63–65), are from Chinchorro, a settlement of fishermen who lived in an area that comprised southern Peru and the north of present-day Chile.

39. See also Guillén (2005). Sillar's interpretation (1996) proposes a different route: he maintains that the *chullpas* where the corpses were dried provided a model for the techniques of warehousing foodstuffs in the repositories known as *qollcas* or *colcas*.

40. An examination of Acosta's thought on this subject can be found in MacCormack (1991, 265–66).

41. In 1929 the Peruvian archaeologist J.C. Tello maintained that the mummies that he found in the Paracas site to the south of Lima had been specially treated by means of drying with fire and extraction of the viscera. Three years later, in 1932, Eugenio Yacovleff and Jorge Muelle, based on research on bodies taken from this same site, rejected Tello's theory. On this controversy, see Daggett 1991.

42. It is interesting to note, for example, that in approximately 1863 when G.E. Squier (1877, 72) extracted and examined some funerary bundles at the Pachacamac site, he observed that although they were called mummies, they were, in fact, desiccated corpses. Squier does not explain how he came to this conclusion.

43. Vreeland (1998, 180) has suggested that Andeans could have assimilated the preservation techniques employed by people of other regions, such as the Amazonian slopes. The techniques that Cieza de León describes (1984b [1553], chap. 32, 108–9; chap. 28, 89) for northern South America could also have been assimilated by the Incas.

44. But see Eeckhout (1999, 365), who describes the body of a woman found in the Pampa de las Flores site whose entrails had been removed. De la Vega et al. (2002) suggest that the bodies found at Molino-Chilacachi underwent a similar treatment. The authors support this last case with documentary references only.

45. Dwyer and Dwyer (1975, 152) cite much earlier cases such as Paracas (AD 500), in which drying by fire and the application of resins could have been employed.

46. Eeckhout (1999, 353) observed at Pampa de las Flores that the children's bodies were laid out in an extended position and a dark liquid had been poured over them. Only some of the bodies were dressed and held objects arranged in the manner of offerings.

47. In contrast, referring to the burials at Chincha, Cieza de León (1984b [1553], First Part, chap. 63, 197) affirms that in this province the inhabitants placed the bodies of the deceased in an extended position on litters (*camillas*) made of reeds. When Max Uhle (1924, 88) carried out excavations at this site, he claimed to have found "mummies lying down on their backs" that he attributed to the period immediately before or after the Spanish conquest. There is, however, no detailed description in this text of the finding of these remains.

48. See, for example, the description of a tomb excavated by Uhle in Ica corresponding to the Late Horizon period (1450–1532) in Menzel (1976, 223–24). Uhle found three funerary bundles and the remains of youths whose bodies seem never to have been wrapped. For examples of social hierarchy

represented in highland funerary contexts, see Eaton (1916) and Andrushko (2007).

49. Frame et al. (2004) offer a very interesting description of a bundle, found in the Rinconada site in Lima, belonging to a person of a certain rank who, to judge by the alternating layers of clothing in his funeral ensemble, appears to have been caught between loyalty to his coastal identity and his bond to the Inca conquerors of his region. The offerings had been arranged to maintain a symmetry between various types of objects and parts of the body.

50. For the case of Paracas, Dwyer and Dwyer (1975, 152) suggest that the larger bundles, which possibly corresponded to the elites who held political power, appeared sporadically, possibly one per generation. Vreeland (1978, 213) proposes that the production of textiles for funerary purposes was augmented during the Late Intermediate period (AD 1000–1450). Some of the most surprising examples contain huge quantities of plain cotton cloth. A bundle from the central coast that contained the body of a young woman consisted of twenty-four layers of cotton cloth and weighed 150 kilos. Vreeland (1978, 213) calculates that to produce the fiber that wrapped her body would have required harvesting between 3,000 and 5,000 square meters of cotton plants. See also Murra (1975, 152).

51. Regarding the funeral customs of the inhabitants of Jauja, Cieza de León (1984b [1553], First Part, chap. 63, 196) writes that the bodies were kept in sheepskins that "form[ed] for them on the outside the face, nostrils, mouth and the rest." He states that this custom still existed at the time in which he was writing, possibly toward the mid-1540s, and that Archbishop Jerónimo de Loayza ordered that the Jauja rituals be suppressed, stipulating instead that the bodies be buried. See Bishop Loayza's 1545 *Instrucción* in Lissón (1943, 1: no. 4, 143) (Loayza became archbishop in 1548).

52. Compare the examples illustrated in Ancón and Pachacamac (Reiss and Stübel 1880–1887; Kaulicke 1997; Fleming 1986) to the mummies with faceless false heads found in Puruchuco (Tabío 1965; Cock 2002), Cajamarquilla (Segura et al. 2002), and Pachacamac (Squier 1877; Eeckhout 1999).

53. A bundle found by Tabío (1965) and Jiménez Borja in Puruchuco contained the bodies of four people. One of Cock's finds (2002) in an area nearby held the remains of an adult and a child.

54. A bundle from the excavations at Paracas that was opened by J.C. Tello in 1929 during a public function held in Lima, to the surprise of both the scientist and those in attendance, contained not a body but some bean seeds (Daggett 1991, 47–48).

55. In this regard see Betanzos (2004 [1551], First part, chaps. 30–32, 179–88).

56. This synthesis is based on the descriptions offered by Cieza de León (1984b [1553], First Part, chap. 63, 197–98); Cobo (1956 [1653], Book 14, chap. 19, 273–75); and Guaman Poma (1989 [1615], 289–97).

57. Salomon (1995, 331) states that women had an important role in funerary rituals while the process of decomposition was taking place, while men took control "once the body assumes its rigid, permanent form."

58. This type of homage was possibly reserved for the ethnic lords, as observed by, for example, Cieza de León (1984b [1553], First Part, chap. 63, 197–98) and Garcilaso de la Vega (1945 [1609], 2: Book 6, chap. 5, 17–18). For a description of this ceremony at the highest state level, see Betanzos (2004 [1551], First Part, chap. 31, 182–85).

59. These procedures can be better verified because of the preservation of the remains. They are described more fully in the section concerning the treatment of bodies on the coast.

60. Garcilaso de la Vega (1945 [1609], 1: Book 1, chap. 12, 35–36) offers a very similar description, although in this passage ethnic group, province, and time are unclear.

61. On the Inca presence in the eastern territories and other Amazonian groups, see Pärsinnen (2003, 102–12).

62. Also known as Machiguenga, an Arawak-speaking ethnic group that lives in the Amazonian forest area of the departments of Cuzco and Madre de Dios, in southeastern Peru.

63. It is thought that the bodies of shamans do not decompose. Their corpses departed for an unknown destination, and it was known only that they continued to live (Shepard 2002, 210).

64. Cannibalism occurred in other Amazonian groups until relatively recent times, as in the case of the Wari, who inhabit the Amazonian forest within the present-day territory of Brazil (Conklin 1993; 2001). Shepard (2002, 222) maintains that this practice, along with other demonstrations of mourning that accompany it, helps to ease the pain caused by the loss of a near one more effectively.

65. In her ethnographic study of the Laymi, inhabitants of the highlands of Bolivia, Harris (1982, 67) reports that the dead are held to be demons and thus are feared.

66. Molina (1989 [1575?], 76–79) offers a detailed description of the living interacting with the bodies of the dead in Inca Cuzco during the Citua festival.

67. In the elaborate burials of the elites of the north coast, painstaking procedures to prepare and preserve the corpse must have preceded its placement in the tomb. The construction of this last implies a considerable amount of work, and offerings of objects and human beings were not placed in the grave all at once, indicating that the secondary funeral rituals went on for an extended period (Shimada et al. 2004, 386–87).

68. He refers to the opening as *ttoco*, Quechua for "window."

69. "Las exequias que les hazen sus parientes son que por encima de su sepultura les echan de aquel su brevaje que llaman chicha, que por unas cañas o arcaduzes van a dar en la boca del muerto."

70. The custom of applying red colorant to the body is very old and widespread in the Andes. The bodies found by Quilter (1989) in the pre-ceramic site of La Paloma, Chilca, show traces of this paint. The practice is also documented on the north coast, although it appears that here the paint is applied over the entire body in the primary interment (Shimada et al. 2004, 375). In other cases it is applied only to the face (Donnan 1995, 123). Painting the body is also followed on the central coast (Segura et al. 2002; Ravines 1981, 150). The colorant must be the substance called *llimpi* or *ichma,* described by the *licenciado* Polo de Ondegardo, a royal officer investigating Andean religion in the sixteenth century, in his treatise on superstitions (1982 [1585], 453).

71. Menzel (1976) has inferred that these removals of body parts took place before the Spanish conquest because, although there were signs of intrusion, only the bones had been taken, leaving gold and silver objects intact. Indications of similar practices, in which skulls were apparently used to watch over a tomb, can be found in, for example, Ancón (Ravines 1981, 132; Shimada et al. 2004, 386).

72. See also Kroeber and Strong (1924, 83).

73. Usually the disarticulation of skeletons would be interpreted solely as the result of looting (Llanos 1941; Parsons et al. 2000; Salomon 1995). It has also been suggested that religious repression during the colonial period explains the existence of the ossuaries. In his commentary on those that Llanos explored in Cuzco, Rowe (1995, 35) writes that the case has long intrigued him, since these deposits of disarticulated bodies do not correspond to any funerary pattern that existed in the pre-Hispanic Andes. Rowe attributed the formation of these ossuaries to Viceroy Francisco de Toledo's order commanding that the *chullpas* be destroyed and the remains of the dead be dispersed. Owen and Norconk (1987) describe funerary contexts with disarticulated or incomplete skeletons among the Wanka in the Mantaro valley.

74. The funerary bundle studied by Frame et al. (2004, 824) contained a human rib among the layers of clothing in which it was wrapped. Incomplete bodies were found in most of the burials that Owen and Norconk (1987, 121–22) studied in the Mantaro valley. Verano (2001, 171) has shown that the use of body parts such as skulls, bones of the extremities, and teeth either for rituals or for personal adornment was common in the Andes. The acquisition of these objects could have occurred in the context of war, but it also appears to have taken place within the same Andean group. For a discussion of the possible meaning and increased value of human remains in the Pacific, see Weiner (1985, 218–19).

75. See also Joyce (2005, 150).

TWO. **Death during the Conquest**

1. The original French edition of *Violence and the Sacred* was published in 1972. Here I quote the English edition, published in 2005.

2. Girard maintains that religion is "that obscurity that surrounds man's efforts to defend himself by curative or preventive means against his own violence. It is that enigmatic quality that pervades the judicial system when that system replaces sacrifice. This obscurity coincides with the transcendental effectiveness of a violence that is holy, legal, and legitimate successfully opposed to a violence that is unjust, illegal, and illegitimate" (2005, 24).

3. See the volume edited by Pierce and Rao (2006a) as well as their introductory study, in which the focus is on Dutch and British colonialism (2006b). In this 356-page book only six lines refer to the Spanish conquest, which is described simply as "genocide" (Pierce and Rao 2006b, 8).

4. Girard (2005, 25) makes an observation that is very relevant here, concerning the resemblance between revenge, sacrifice, and judicial punishment, all widespread during this period: "While acknowledging the differences, both functional and mythical, between vengeance, sacrifice, and legal punishment, it is important to recognize their fundamental identity. Precisely because these institutions are essentially the same they tend to adopt the same types of violent response in times of crisis."

5. Burga (1988, 85) also sees violence as an ordering principle of colonial society. However, while my focus is on death, punishment, and attitudes toward the body, Burga refers to "structural violence": the Spanish violation of the principles of reciprocity and redistribution, the racial and cultural differences that separated Spaniards and Andeans, religious conversion, the end of the *ayllu*'s autonomy, and the establishment of a market economy in the Andes.

6. Burga (1988, 69–84) has also studied the death of Atahualpa, from another perspective and with a different aim: to understand the significance of utopian views about the resurrection of the Inca.

7. Sancho replaced Francisco de Xerez as Pizarro's secretary in Cajamarca (Pease 1995, 20–21). Xerez, as we shall see, included the episode of Atahualpa's execution in his chronicle.

8. None of the other sources that recount Atahualpa's trial alludes to this legal expert. Sancho's reference to his presence certainly means to imply that the Inca's summary trial and execution had a legal foundation.

9. "The governor ordered that he should not be burned, but tied to a stake in the town square and strangled, and it was done as he commanded" (Xerez 1985 [1534], 155–56).

10. Mena claims that he witnessed the events he is recounting. However, Pease (1995, 17–18) states that this would have been impossible, since only a few days after Atahualpa's death, Mena was in Panama.

11. See also the Letter of the *licenciado* Espinosa to Charles V, August 1, 1533, in Levillier (1921, 2:18).

12. Pizarro's decision was considered a mistake by a number of people, including the crown. Bartolomé de las Casas (Pease 1984, xvii; 1995, 215–16) discussed the problem at length, condemning the fact that a legitimate sovereign should have been put to death. Counterarguments were soon formulated, and a few decades later the thesis prevailed that Atahualpa had been justly executed: his power was illegitimate because the Incas had been tyrants (MacCormack 1985, 430).

13. On these occasions, the condemned person usually addressed the audience before dying, in order to express his or her repentance, beg for the authorities' mercy, or ask for the onlookers' prayers (Merback 1999, 147–48). Besides the political and stylistic reasons for Cieza to include this piece, we may suppose that from a ritual and moralistic point of view, a message to the spectators at the scene was required (Foucault 1991, 65).

14. The previous chapter described the importance attached by the Incas and other Andean peoples to the bodies of their rulers and forebears. Among the Incas, the role of these bodies in legitimizing the heir was crucial. For a detailed explanation of their significance in Inca rites of succession, see MacCormack (1991, 118–37). See also the accounts of the honors that Atahualpa commanded should be rendered to the mummy of his father, Huayna Cápac (Betanzos 2004 [1551], Second Part, chap. 2, 246); and of those that Huáscar showed to his father in Cuzco (Murúa 2001 [1613], chap. 39, 131–32; Guaman Poma 1989 [1615], 377–78).

15. The story of the exhumation of Atahualpa's body appears later in other sources. See Murúa (2001 [1613], chap. 63, 212), and Bernabé Cobo (1956 [1653], Book 12, chap. 19, 99–100).

16. Betanzos, in mentioning this episode and the role played in it by Cuxi Yupangue, confirms statements that he makes earlier in his account, when he discusses Inca rituals. The Inca Huayna Cápac had granted Cuxi Yupangue the privilege of bearing what the chronicler calls the "idol of battles," an effigy that must have been one of the various representations of the Inca's body (Betanzos 2004 [1551], Second Part, chap. 3, 249–50).

17. According to Pease (1995, 143), the chronicles of Cieza de León, Betanzos, and Zárate together provide a more complete picture of the events in Cajamarca.

18. As we saw in the previous chapter, beheading was common for executing or sacrificing victims in pre-Hispanic Peru. The chronicles mention the existence of trophy heads among the Incas, and archaeological finds support these statements (Verano 1995).

19. The murder of Huáscar's family in Cuzco at the hands of Atahualpa's messengers is told in Betanzos (2004 [1551], chap. 19, 296–300); Murúa (2001 [1613], chap. 57, 190–93); and Cobo (1956 [1653], Book 12, chap. 19, 98).

20. The dispute between Huáscar and Atahualpa, in its turn, had its origin in the failure of the succession ritual following the death of Huayna Capac (MacCormack 1991, 129–30).

21. The title of the drawing is: "Conquista. Cortanle la cavesa a Atagualpa Inga *umanta cuchun*" (they have cut off the Inca's head). I owe the translation of this last segment, in Quechua, to César Itier. This is not the way in which criminals were beheaded in Europe. Tomás y Valiente (1969, 384), for example, quotes a text written by a high official of Charles V in the middle of the sixteenth century, which states that in Spain, people sentenced to death "are made to lie down on the ground, with their heads on a block, and the head is cut off with an axe." The peaceful demeanor of the Inca, who has his eyes closed, suggests that he is dead or fainting—in which case, the three men holding him would be unnecessary. However, the custom of strangling the prisoner before beheading him had begun to be adopted in Spain after the end of the fifteenth century (Guillaume-Alonso 1990, 181).

22. This is how Girard (2005, 54) describes the sacrificial crisis: "In this situation, no one and nothing is spared; coherent thinking collapses and rational activities are abandoned. All associative forms are dissolved or become antagonistic; all values, spiritual or material, perish."

23. Burga (1988, 80–81) maintains that Guaman Poma's version is, in fact, an Andean interpretation of the events. He further argues that this account "completes a cycle of Andean alterations of the story of Atahualpa's death leading to the birth of a new cycle of messianic expectations."

24. Martyrdom, a form of sacrifice, has a high expiatory value in Christian thought (Gorringe 1996). Merback (1999, 152–57) explains how the spectacle of suffering served as expiation not only for the sins of the condemned person but also for those of the spectators attending the execution (see also Martínez Gil 1993, 161). Reff (2005, 20) discusses the significance of the stories of martyrs in the rise of Christianity and in colonial religious culture.

25. Passive endurance in the face of pain was the revolutionary ideal of the martyr (Straw 2000). This endurance was described as a "virile" quality (Cohen 2000, 41).

26. See Adorno's suggestive analysis (1989, 148) of the various perspectives that Guaman Poma uses in his work to underpin the authority of his words.

27. Spierenburg (1984, 12) gives a convincing description of how the state appropriated acts of private violence, usually in the form of physical punishment, as it began to establish itself in the early modern period. Even though he focuses on the historical process taking place in northern Europe, his analysis is very useful for an overall understanding of this period. Tomás y Valiente's study of the penal law of absolute monarchy (1969) is indispensable for an understanding of the Spanish case.

28. In the sixteenth century in the rural areas of Castile, the Santa Hermandad—a kind of rural police force—was in charge of maintaining order

and punishing various kinds of transgressions, especially those committed by highwaymen. The sentences passed were carried out without delay, with executions preceded by torture; and punishments including flogging, amputation of limbs, and capital punishment, in which the condemned person was shot dead with arrows. Not until 1532 did changes begin to be introduced, with the aim of making the sentences less cruel, as, for example, when the empress, Doña Juana, issued a decree proclaiming that the prisoners sentenced to death by shooting should first be strangled. Charles V subsequently enacted a writ commuting physical punishment to the galleys (Guillaume-Alonso 1997). This was reaffirmed by Philip II in 1566 (Redondo 1990b, 199). In other parts of Europe, penal law called for similar physical punishments (Spierenburg 1984; Cohen 2000, 51).

29. The cultural and legal justifications for this punishment are complex. It is possible that the use of fire was grounded in a literal interpretation of the Bible, which documents the destruction by fire of those who rebelled against authority (Numbers 16:35). The Old Testament presents God as "a consuming fire, even a jealous God" (Deuteronomy 4:24). Another passage explains the proceedings to be used against pagans: "When the Lord thy God shall bring thee into the land whither thou goest to possess it, and hath cast out many nations before thee, . . . and when the Lord thy God shall deliver them before thee; thou shalt smite them, and utterly destroy them; thou shalt make no covenant with them, nor shew mercy unto them . . . ye shall destroy their altars, and break down their images, and cut down their groves, and burn their graven images with fire" (Deuteronomy 7:1–5). The force of this message fills the acts of invasion, conquest, and subjugation that, with both divine and earthly pretexts, have occurred for centuries. On the significance of fire and its purifying effect in medieval Christian Europe, see Le Goff (1984) and P. Brown (2000).

30. To debate the meaning of "treason" as a crime in the context we are discussing would raise the question of the legitimacy of the conquest. Moreover, Tomás y Valiente maintains that in Castilian penal law, even though treason headed the list of the most serious crimes—since it implied an offense against the king's person—no actual definition existed (Tomás y Valiente 1969, 205–6).

31. Other accounts of Chalcochima's execution agree on this point as well as stating that Pizarro thus hoped to take advantage of the opposition between Chalcochima's lineage and that of the Cuzco Incas (Yupanqui 1992 [1570], 13; Murúa 2001 [1613], chap. 64, 216).

32. Luis de Morales was the most important ecclesiastical functionary in the city of Cuzco at the time. On the death of the friar Valverde, who had been appointed bishop of Cuzco but never arrived to occupy his post, the *provisor* was in charge of the ecclesiastical seat.

33. Similar actions were carried out by the troops commanded by Alonso de Alvarado in 1545 (see Assadourian 1995, 29–30) and by Gonzalo Pizarro during the civil war (see Levillier 1921, 2:285–86).

34. In Germany, the stake was the common punishment for arson, heresy, witchcraft, and sodomy (Merback 1999, 140). In Spain, the bodies of suicides were burned (Martínez Gil 1993, 150; Tomás y Valiente 1969).

35. See, for example, the *oidor* Gregorio González de Cuenca's letter to the king, dated February 1567 (Lissón 1943, 2: no. 7, 350), in which he mentions the investigation of acts committed by the *encomendero* Melchor Verdugo in Cajamarca.

36. There are very few studies of this topic. See, for instance, Pease (1965).

37. He presents a scale of punishments in which respect for the moral order and correct behavior are particularly important. Whatever the accuracy or effectiveness of these precepts, such observations are part of Guaman Poma's critique of the colonial system (Adorno 1989).

38. A similar punishment was decreed by the Inca Pachacutec during the conquest of Chincha. See Garcilaso de la Vega (1945 [1609], 2: Book 6, chap. 19, 45–46).

39. There is archaeological evidence that this punishment was carried out in the Andes; see, for example, Shimada et al. (2004).

40. The news of Manco Inca's murder must have reached Cuzco by various routes. Garcilaso de la Vega claims that his own version came from his maternal relatives, who were in Vilcabamba at the time. Other versions are to be found in Cieza de León (1985, Third Part, chap. 51, 340–41); Murúa (2001 [1613], chap. 73, 248–52); and Cobo (1956 [1653], Book 12, chap. 22, 102–3).

41. This was a common gesture among the rebel Incas. Titu Cusi Yupanqui (1992 [1570], 48) claims that Manco Inca's captains sent him, after some fortunate encounters in Lima and Jauja, "many Spaniards' heads" as well as prisoners, slaves, and horses.

42. "The antagonists caught up in the sacrificial crisis invariably believe themselves separated by insurmountable differences. In reality, however, these differences gradually wear away. Everywhere we now encounter the same desire, the same antagonism, the same strategies, the same illusion of rigid differentiation within a pattern of ever-expanding uniformity. As the crisis grows more acute, the community members are transformed into 'twins,' matching images of violence. I would be tempted to say that they are each doubles of the other" (Girard 2005, 83).

43. See, for example, Verano's thesis about the meaning of the Moche sacrifices, in Arkush and Stanish (2005, 19–20).

44. The account suggests that the Spaniards did not rob the dead. Cieza mentions that after the battle of Quito, in which Gonzalo Pizarro defeated the troops remaining loyal to the crown, led by Viceroy Blasco Núñez Vela, black

and Indian soldiers proceeded to strip the dead and wounded (Cieza de León 1985, Third Part, chap. 182, 500–501).

45. After his defeat in Chupas four years later, Diego de Almagro's mestizo son was also beheaded in the city of Cuzco. Diego de Almagro "the Younger" asked that his body be buried in the same place, La Merced, beneath the bones of his father (Cieza de León 1985, Second Part, chap. 84, 264–65).

46. This has its precedent in the decreees of the Catholic monarchs in order to subdue the nobles in Spain. See Tomás y Valiente (1969, 30).

THREE.   **The Conquest of Death**

1. Concerning the different conversion strategies used in the Andes, see the work of Duviols (1971); Estenssoro (2003); Griffiths (1996); MacCormack (1985; 1991); Marzal (1983); and Mills (1997).

2. Perhaps in order to mitigate the seriousness of the action, the author of this account wrote that the Spaniards did not entirely strip the mummies of their ornaments, in consideration of Atahualpa's having begged them to show respect because one of them was that of his father (Porras Barrenechea 1937, 93). Concerning the early perceptions of the sacred places, in particular the oracles, among the conquistadors, and the effects of these perceptions, see MacCormack (1991, 55–63).

3. The conquistadors reported that they had found a great deal of gold in the tombs that they had profaned in the coastal temple of Pachacamac (Porras Barrenechea 1937, 94). On the collection of treasure in Pachacamac, see Guillén (1974).

4. Duviols (1971, 299) has drawn attention to the early association established by the Spaniards in the Andes between the concept of the sacred and the idea of wealth. See also the *Instrucciones* issued to Governor Vaca de Castro in Hanke and Rodriguez (1978–1980, 1:36).

5. The reader will recall that the Quechua term *guaca* means sacred place.

6. This leads Duviols (1971, 82–83) to call this document "the first ecclesiastical text on extirpation."

7. This topic has other facets, which have been studied at length by Lohmann (1966). See also Brading (1991); Gutiérrez (1992, 502–6); Lopétegui (1945); and MacCormack (1991, 241–44). Though the term "restitution" applies to any Christian, since it is among the obligations derived from confession and penitence, and it requires that any ill-gotten goods be restored to their owners, I am referring here exclusively to the problem of the Indian property taken by the Spaniards during the conquest.

8. MacCormack (1991, 244) affirms that Las Casas's analysis, inspired as it was in classical and medieval authorities and in the Church Fathers, ideal-

izes and simplifies these aspects of Andean religion. To her mind, this does not really help us to understand this aspect of Andean culture on its own terms. I believe that in taking into account both what we learn from archaeology and the anthropological analysis of Andean funeral practices, the ideas of Las Casas allow us to appreciate the significance of Andean religion in universal terms, thus freeing the topic from a certain halo of uniqueness or even exoticism.

9. See also Las Casas (1992b [1565], chap. 37, 181–84, chap. 38, 186). Duviols (1971, 46–47) discusses these ideas in the context of theories about idolatry and just titles, and what he calls the "economic circumstances of extirpation" (1971, 303). As we can see, the implications of Las Casas's reflection go well beyond the purely economic.

10. "Instrucción de la horden que se a de tener en doctrina de los naturales" (Lissón 1943, 1: no. 4, 135). This text also appears in Vargas Ugarte (1951, 2:139–48). Duviols (1971, 83–84) considers it "the first legislative text" and indicates that it was corrected and approved in 1549.

11. First Council of Lima, "Constituciones de los Naturales, 3a" (Vargas Ugarte 1951, 1:8).

12. First Council of Lima, "Constituciones de los Naturales, no 25, De la manera que han de ser enterrados los indios" (Vargas Ugarte 1951, 1:20).

13. Duviols (1971, 86–87) remarks that this clear distinction between believers and unbelievers is a new development that can be attributed to a disregard of the optimistic spirit of the *Instrucción* of 1545.

14. See, for example, his report to the *licenciado* Briviesca de Muñatones (Ondegardo 1906 [1561]). Inquiries concerning taxation during "the time of the Ynga" provided many clues about pre-Hispanic political and religious organization. The best-known examples are Chucuito (Diez de San Miguel 1964 [1567]) and Huánuco (Ortiz de Zúñiga 1967 [1562]). See also Murra (1975, 193–223).

15. The system of *ceques,* or imaginary lines organizing the distribution of the sacred space, started out from the Coricancha, the main temple of Cuzco, and spread to the four corners of the Inca empire. On this point, see Bauer (1998; 2000); Cobo (1956 [1653]); Duviols (1971, 103, 301); MacCormack (1991, 187–95); Rowe (1981); and Zuidema (1964).

16. Ondegardo exhibited the mummies in a room in his house in Cuzco where Garcilaso de la Vega saw them (1945 [1609], 1: Book 5, chap. 29, 286–88). Subsequently, the mummies were sent to the court of the viceroy in Lima. Curiously, the viceroy, Hurtado de Mendoza, ordered them to be buried (rather than burned), which was done in the hospital of San Andrés. The accounts of their number, identity, and fate are diverse and sometimes contradictory. See Acosta (2002 [1590], Book 6, chap. 21, 406); Duviols (1971, 105); Guillén (1983); and Hampe (1982).

17. Acosta (2002 [1590], Book 5, chap. 23, 347) asserts that Ondegardo wrote his report on idolatries for Archbishop Jerónimo de Loayza. The Third

Council of Lima based many of its proposals on his studies in Andean religion, even including fragments of his work in the materials that it produced in 1585 (Duviols 1971, 145, and n.72). Later, others, such as Cristóbal de Molina (1989 [1575?]) and Cristóbal de Albornoz (1989 [1583?]), increased the available knowledge about Andean religion. Rowe (1981) has suggested that several other actors participated in these inquiries in Cuzco between 1550 and 1570.

18. For example, in a letter written to the king from Lima in February 1570, Toledo writes about stoppages due to a shortage of workers and about the difficulties and dangers inherent in both stripping tombs and mining (Levillier 1921, 3:331). See also the letter written by the viceroy from Cuzco on March 25, 1571 (3:484–86).

19. In a letter from Cuzco, dated March 1, 1572 (Levillier 1921, 3:595), Viceroy Toledo describes the proliferation of permits issued by the *corregidores* for exploiting the *guacas*. The search for *guacas* and treasures continued throughout the colonial period and was often associated with religious repression (Albornoz 1988 [1583?]; Duviols 1971, 307–33; 1989, 136–59).

20. Although it could be argued that the Third Council, in declaring that the edicts of the previous councils were to be respected, was including the rules concerning burial places formulated by the bishops in 1567, something that is implicit in Acosta's text. See Vargas Ugarte (1951, 1:322).

21. A detailed presentation of the materials put together by the Third Council of Lima may be found in Durán (1982) and Durston (2004).

22. See, for example, the "Represión para los idólatras y supersticiosos" (Rebuke to idolaters and superstitious people), in the *Confesionario*, f. 24v (Durán 1982, 441); *Instrucción contra las ceremonias* . . . (Instructions against ceremonies), f. 1, chap. 1, "De las idolatrías" (Of idolatries), n. 3 (447); and *Los errores y supersticiones* . . . (Errors and superstitions), f. 7r, chap. 2, "De las ánimas y difuntos" (Of souls and the dead) (460–61). These instructions can already be found in the documents of the Second Council of Lima, and they are undoubtedly based on the recommendations made by Dr. Gregorio González de Cuenca to the bishops in 1567 (Lissón 1944, 2: no. 7, 354).

23. On doctrinal primers and the concern for unifying their contents, see the letter from Viceroy Toledo to the king (Levillier 1921, 3:496). Concerning the primers that predated those produced by the Second Council of Lima, see Durán (1982, 212–15) and Domínguez (1993).

24. MacCormack's (1991) study includes a detailed analysis of the conceptual apparatus used and the methods advocated by missionaries, politicians, functionaries, and travelers in the sixteenth and early seventeenth centuries.

25. The historical and anthropological literature concerning the religion of the colonial Andes and the place occupied by the ancestors is abundant. See, for example, Duviols (1971; 2003); Estenssoro (2003); Griffiths (1996); Huertas (1981); MacCormack (1991); Marzal (1983); Mills (1997); and Salomon (1995).

26. On Andean ideas about death and the role played by the dead in the world of the living, especially in the writings of Cieza de León, see MacCormack (1991, 85–98). On the religious and political significance of the Inca mummies, see also MacCormack (118–37).

27. For a comparison between Christian and Andean conceptions, see MacCormack (1991, 134 and n. 73). A concise and efficient overview of the history of Christian doctrines and ideas about the soul can be found in Crabbe (1999). Des Chene (2000) offers an interesting analysis of the doctrines about the soul in the late sixteenth and early seventeenth centuries.

28. See also Cieza de León: "it was the general belief . . . that the souls of the dead did not die, but lived forever and assembled in the other world: where, as I said before, it is believed that they made merry, and ate and drank, which is their main glory" (1984b, First Part, chap. 62, 194). Garcilaso de la Vega agrees: "They did not understand that the next life was spiritual, but believed it to be material like this one" (1945 [1609], 1: Book 2, chap. 7, 80).

29. Cieza de León (1984b [1553], First Part, chap. 62, 193); Zárate 1995 [1555], chap. 12, 54; Garcilaso de la Vega 1945 [1609], 1: Book 2, chap. 7, 80).

30. This perception is connected with changes in conversion strategies and in general colonial policies, which became very apparent from the end of the 1560s, particularly after the Third Council of Lima (Duviols 1971; Estenssoro 2003; MacCormack 1985; 1991).

31. The objectives and methods for achieving this goal are concisely expressed in the "Preamble concerning the confessionary and instruction of the superstitions and rites of the Indians in which it is declared how the priests are to take advantage of these things," in *Doctrina Christiana* (1585), Durán (1982, 425–27).

32. Estenssoro (2003) has carried out an exhaustive comparison of the methods and texts used for missionary work before the Third Council with those that were fixed upon according to the guidelines of the Council of Trent. Catechisms written to attack the so-called errors of the Indians include: "Catecismo breve para los rudos y ocupados," f. 14r (Short catechism for unpolished and busy persons); "Plática breve en que se contiene la suma de lo que ha de saber el que se hace cristiano," f. 18v (Short speech in which is to be found the whole of what he who becomes a Christian must know); "Catecismo mayor para los que son más capaces," First Part, f. 31r, f. 58–59v (Greater catechism for the more able); "Confesionario para los curas de indios, especialmente lo que concierne al primer mandamiento," ff. 6v–7v (Treatise of confessions for the priests to the Indians, especially with respect to the first commandment); "Preguntas para los caciques y curacas," f. 15v (Questions for *caciques* and *curacas*); "Represión para los idólatras y supersticiosos" (Rebuke to idolaters and superstitious persons), f. 24v (see note 22 above). Taylor (2003) has made a detailed linguistic analysis of some of these texts.

33. Something similar happens with other key concepts, such as God and the negative, malignant, or angry forces that the Christian view sums up under the name of the devil. Concerning the use, translation, and accommodation of Christian terms in Andean languages, especially Quechua, see Durston (2004); Estenssoro (2003); Itier (1991; 1992a; 1992b); and Taylor (2000a; 2000b; 2000c; 2003).

34. On the difficulties surrounding eschatology in the Christian tradition, see Bynum and Freedman (2000).

35. Garcilaso explains that the need to prevent any part of the body from being lost was so great that, in fact, every fragment as well as every drop of human fluid had to be preserved (1945 [1609], 1: Book 2, chap. 7, 80).

36. Zárate (1995 [1555], chap. 10, 50–51) describes the end of the world, but he is referring to a great drought, a truly fearful and devastating event. Moseley (2002) has suggested that the effects of this drought had begun to be suffered in the Andes several centuries before the Spanish invasion. Unlike the Christian view, this picture of the end of the world was unconnected with any idea of a Last Judgment.

37. Garcilaso himself admits that attributing to the Indians a belief in the resurrection could seem an invention of his own, and he expresses his satisfaction that other chroniclers should give a similar version (1945 [1609], 1: Book 2, chap. 7, 81).

38. On this topic, see the important study by Javier Varela (1990).

39. In his widely read *Agonía del tránsito de la muerte* (Agony of the transit to death), Alejo Venegas wrote: "the death of those who die in grace is no more than a departure from prison, an end to exile, a crowning of the body's labors, a haven in storms, a conclusion to the journey, a relinquishing of the heavy burden, an egress from the tottering building, a flight from perils, a banishing of all evils, the payment of our debt to nature, a return to our native land, and finally, a welcoming and entering into glory" (1911 [1537], 121–22).

40. Bynum describes in detail the debates that were renewed in the thirteenth century about the relation between the body and the soul at the moment of the resurrection. She explains that the preservation of the bodies evoked hostile reactions, and she cites the example of Pope Boniface IX, who was accused of heresy in the fourteenth century for ordering that his body should be embalmed (Bynum 1995, 323).

41. Varela (1990, 22–29, 92–98) gives a detailed explanation of these changes, including the attention given to funerary architecture at the time. Later on, when discussing funeral ceremonies in the cities of Lima and Cuzco, we will examine the possible impact of this last point on Andean urban centers.

42. Unlike other European monarchies, such as the French or the English, the Spanish kings reasserted the identity between the physical body and the body politic as represented in the person of the absolute monarch (Varela 1990, 60).

43. See the examples quoted by Varela (1990, 106), including Charles V's body, which, despite not having been embalmed, was found in a state of excellent preservation.

44. See Brading (1991); Duviols (1971); Estensssoro (2003); MacCormack (1991); and Pagden (1982).

45. On questions of ecclesiastical policies and methods of conversion, see Abbott (1996); Duviols (1971); Estensssoro (2003); MacCormack (1985; 1991); and Mills (1997). On the problem of the language and the translation of Christian concepts, especially into Quechua, Taylor (2000a; 2000b; 2003) is particularly important. See also Barnes (1992); Durston (2004); Estensssoro (2003); and Mannheim (1998; 2002).

46. The first question asked in the Greater Catechism is, "What is man?" to which the correct answer was, "a creature composed of a body that dies and a soul that will never die, because God made it in his own image" (*Doctrina Christiana* 1985 [1585], 70).

47. In a letter addressed to the Council of the Indies in 1572, the Jesuit Bartolomé Hernández argued that it was vital to ensure that the Indians lived politically, since otherwise it was impossible to communicate the faith (Lissón 1943, 2: no. 9, 602). Later in this book we will see the impact of the policies derived from Hernández's observations: the establishing of urban centers and villages of converted Indians, or *reducciones*.

48. The methods for teaching the doctrine based on this view include, among others, learning and reciting speeches and verses, viewing theatrical performances, and learning and playing music. See Abbott (1996); Burkhart (1989; 1998); Estensssoro (1992; 2003); and Gruzinski (1988).

49. "Rather than sharpening swords we must threaten them with the lash" (Acosta 1984 [1588], 1:355). This passage from Acosta should not be interpreted as a defense of violence as a method. Elsewhere he condemns the violence that had characterized the conquest and that continued to prevail during the period in which he wrote (1:147, 247, 249, 253, 255, 379). See also chapter 2 for an examination of the significance attributed to physical torture. Studies on the use of corporal punishment in colonial Mexico, such as those of Cañeque (1996) and Pardo (2006), allow us to understand the development of the pedagogy of pain that was applied to the native population.

50. Not all ecclesiastical or civil circles agreed with these proceedings, and there were disagreements about who should administer these punishments and for what motives. For example, in a letter addressed to the king and dated November 25, 1566, Friar Francisco de la Cruz, a lecturer in theology, considered it inappropriate that the same penalty should be inflicted on idolaters, who in his view deserved death, and on those who had committed less serious offenses (Lissón 1943, 2: no. 7, 304–8). Acosta (1984 [1588], 2:153) was of the opinion that priests should avoid administering physical punishments

themselves. Some years earlier, in 1565, Governor Lope García de Castro expressed the opinion that it was inappropriate for the clergy to inflict corporal punishments (Levillier 1921, 3:116–30).

51. Subsequently, with the founding of the hospitals, the parish priests gave similar reasons to do with "lack of decency" as an obstacle to administering the viaticum. On the larger problem of whether communion should be given to the Indians, see Pardo (2004, 131–58).

52. This advice does not spring from the novelty of the colonial situation, since the old confessors' treatises, which predate the discovery of America, also discuss the question of whether priests could absolve foreigners even though they did not understand their language. See, for example, *Tratado de las absoluciones*, Anonymous (1999 [1479?], 143).

53. Paxton describes a similar situation in his study of the Christianizing of death between later Antiquity and the early Middle Ages: in this context, the Nicene Council of 325 ordered that no one should die without receiving the viaticum, whatever their status in the Church (Paxton 1990, 36).

54. The insistence on cleanliness and decency recurs both in the council decrees and in the handbooks written later as guides for the liturgy. The Synod of Cuzco in 1591 repeats this requirement and gives precise instructions that the Blessed Sacrament be carried to the Indian villages with the requisite ceremony and the greatest possible attendance (Lassègue 1987, 43).

55. The number of guides to dying well published in Spain in the sixteenth and seventeenth centuries is considerable; however, I use here the anonymous guide published at the end of the fifteenth century by Pablo Hurus in Zaragoza, and the one by Alejo Venegas. The simplicity and profusion of illustrations in the former suggest that it was addressed to a wide audience, which gives us a clearer idea of the message that it attempted to spread among an uneducated public. I use the latter because the *Agony of the Transit to Death*, by Alejo Venegas, was possibly the most widely read work of its kind during this period. Not only was Venegas's book reprinted several times (Martínez Gil 1993, 54; Morel d'Arleux 1993, 725; Rey Hazas 2003a, 94), but it also appears in the inventories of Peruvian private libraries in the sixteenth century (González Sánchez 1996, 28).

56. The engravings that illustrate the guides usually present at the foot of the dying person's bed not one but several devils, in the company of other malevolent figures (Anonymous 1999 [1479?], 52–73). Idolatry is also represented, in the figure of a monarch who appears to be adoring a human effigy.

57. For a detailed analysis of Acosta's thoughts on the last rites, see Pardo (2004, 145–51).

58. Concerning confession among the Indians, see Acosta (1987 [1588], 2:425–27); Estenssoro (2003); and Ondegardo (1906 [1561], 211–12). Acosta

wrote: "Why, I ask, are we to exclude from the communication and benefit [of the last rites] the new peoples of Indians, when they are baptized like us, profess the same faith and ardently desire the Church to offer them its help at the hour of death? This is a great proof of cruelty to brothers: If any mortals need the aid of the Church, it is most of all these when they find themselves in their last pangs" (1987 [1588], 2:451).

59. The synod instructed the priests "not to confess anyone through an interpreter, except in cases of extreme need, and [to warn] the penitent that he has no obligation to confess under such circumstances, while reminding the interpreter of his own obligation to keep the secrets of the confession" (Lassègue 1987, 42).

60. The Franciscan friar Luis Jerónimo de Oré was the author of some of the most important pastoral works in native languages and participated in the preparation of the documents published by the Third Council of Lima (Cook 1992, 38–40).

61. "Exhortación breve para que los indios que estan ya muy al cabo de la vida para que el sacerdote o algun otro les ayude a bien morir" (Brief exhortation for that the Indians who are at the very end of their existence, for that the priest or some other person may help them to die well). *Doctrina Christiana* (1985 [1585], 285–89).

62. Discussing the distress suffered by the dying, and the indispensable assistance that the priests must give to those at the point of death, Peña y Montenegro writes: "it is a lamentation on account of the sinners who die without the assistance of their priests, who are fathers to them in the place of God" (1995 [1668], 1:219).

63. Venegas (1911 [1537], 137) explains that extreme unction had to be administered once the doctors had decided that no recovery was possible, but care must be taken that the sick person should still show all the signs of life. See also the *licenciado* Juan Pérez Bocanegra's *Ritual formulario* (1631, 505) and Alonso de la Peña y Montenegro's *Itinerario para párrocos de indios* (1995 [1668], 1:224–25). This has not always been a requisite in the history of this sacrament (see Isambert 1975; Paxton 1990).

64. This continues a practice, used in the Church since the end of the thirteenth century, of making available to priests who lacked sufficient training handbooks in the vernacular that might serve as everyday guides (Homza 1999, 38–41). The Roman catechism also responded to the need to educate and guide the clergy, whose preparation for teaching the doctrine, administering the sacraments, and preaching the Word was very poor (Rodríguez and Lanzetti 1982, 125–26).

65. Other New World catechisms describe the purpose of extreme unction in the same terms, although they introduce small changes to the original sentence (see Acosta 1987 [1588], 2:450–51). Certain Mexican examples studied

by Resines (1992), for example, retain the expression "relics of sin," although the catechism of the Third Council of Lima omits it.

66. Paxton (1990, 51) studies the historical evolution of extreme unction from Antiquity to the Middle Ages, especially its change from a ritual for restoring bodily health to an alternative to pagan magical practices, and the vehicle of spiritual health and eternal life.

67. In her study of the European connections of Bartolomé de Alva's Mexican confessionary, Homza (1999, 46) mentions that handbooks of this sort published in Spain did not discuss the problem of inappropriate religious conduct as a generational problem, but conceived of it as a deviation from a fundamentally Christian basis.

68. The caution shown with respect to purgatory in the earlier documents can be explained by the Council of Trent's advice to the clergy, who were encouraged, when addressing the multitudes, to avoid difficult and subtle topics that might foster superstition (*El sacrosanto Concilio de Trento*, session 25, quoted in Martínez Gil 1993, 313).

69. On the problems involved in the formation of coherent eschatologies in the history of Christianity, see Bynum and Freedman (2000).

70. The idea of death as a social leveler is an old topic, but one that became especially popular during this period (Martínez Gil 1993, 333–36). It was also well understood that only an entire life devoted to adequate preparation for death could make it cease to be "unexpected" in this sense (see, for example, Antonio de Guevara [1481–1545], *Reloj de príncipes*, in Rey Hazas 2003a, 204).

71. To describe this process, the sermon uses metaphors that establish analogies between the quality of souls and the value of metals. The image of fire is also applied here to compare the effects of the fire of purgatory to those obtained in refining minerals. These metaphors, which are of ancient date (Le Goff 1984), must have been very effective in the Andes (Estenssoro 1996).

72. Native wills show the existence of Indian confraternities devoted to the service of the souls in purgatory and the celebration of masses for the salvation of souls many years before the Third Council of Lima and the subsequent dissemination of its decrees and pastoral writings. For a different opinion, see Estenssoro (2003, 69, 251–52) and Robin (2004, 158–59).

73. This ban was ineffective. The *Manuscript of Huarochirí* (Taylor 1999, 371) bears witness to the custom of setting offerings of hot food on the graves inside the church as part of the rites celebrated on All Saints' Day.

74. In Spain the Church encountered similar situations and gave similar answers. The synodal constitutions of several dioceses established as regular offerings wine, bread, and wax; where these were not available, substitutes were accepted. This was also intended to regulate the quantity and authenticity of the offerings, distorted by the desire of the rich to flaunt their wealth and by

the difficulties encountered by those who were attempting to appear wealthy (Martínez Gil 1993, 429–32).

75. Starting from an ethnographic inquiry into death in the high provinces of Cuzco, Robin (2004) has studied the domestication of the idea of purgatory in the Andean religious imagination. The author draws attention to how this sermon accepts and even encourages offerings of food to the deceased, thus modifying the role of the receiver (not the dead, but God) and asserting the role of the priest as mediator.

76. Cieza attributed these apparitions to a trick of the devil.

77. The *Manuscript of Huarochirí* also describes the return of the dead to the *guaca* from which they came.

78. Let us remember that Alejo Venegas had defined death, among other things, as "a return to [the soul's] native land."

79. For example, the need to give more detailed explanations concerning the administering of the sacraments, and to resolve the questions that arose in the everyday teaching of the doctrine, led to works such as those written by Juan Pérez Bocanegra in Cuzco (1631), or Alonso de la Peña y Montenegro (1995 [1668]) in Quito.

FOUR. **Spaces and Institutions for the Missionary Project**

1. The Spanish term is *policía,* which evokes ideas of urbanity and courtesy. See Covarrubias (2003 [1611], 875).

2. On *reducciones* in the Andes, see Gade and Escobar (1982); Kubler (1946); Málaga Medina (1974); and Rowe (1957). A transcription of the ordinances regulating *reducciones* can be found in Toledo (1986, 1:33–36).

3. Farriss (1984, 158–63) gives the best explanation of the spatial reconceptualization achieved by the *reducciones.* Her analysis focuses on the Yucatán region, which means that it presents certain culturally specific traits, but its value for understanding the motives, interpretations, and methods that guided this transformation is extraordinary. For a sociological perspective on the cities of Hispanoamerica, see also Hardoy and Schaedel (1969; 1978). Kagan and Marías (2000) propose a cultural and artistic analysis of the urban phenomenon in Hispanoamerica.

4. "Ordenanzas para la ciudad del Cuzco y sus términos," Checacupe, October 18, 1572 (Toledo 1986, 1:153–221).

5. In the villages created as a result of the *reducciones,* the local population was generally grouped in an ecclesiastical jurisdiction, the *doctrina* or Indian parish, organized hierarchically and usually subdivided in smaller sections independent from each other and subordinated to a principal seat, or *cabeza de doctrina.* In his study of the ecclesiastical legislation in the viceroyalty of Peru,

Trujillo Mena asserts that the *doctrinas* were of lower status than the parishes that housed only Spaniards. Given the characteristics of many parishes in the main colonial cities of Peru, I suspect that the application of such a legal criterion must have given rise to several problems of interpretation (Trujillo Mena 1981, 241–44).

6. See chapter 3. Because of discrepancies between various accounts that have reached us, it is unclear who wrote the description of the *ceques* system. Rowe (1981) concludes that Cobo's version (1956 [1653], 167–86) was independent of the one written by Ondegardo, which Bauer (2000, 13–23), after a very detailed analysis, asserts to be the original. See also Duviols (1989, 139–41).

7. Julien (1998, 90) declares that the *ceques* system, "besides communicating in a very impressive way the radial shape of the system . . . does not seem to provide information on any kind of spatial organization." This statement, based on an analysis of Cobo's narrative, would have to be compared to Ondegardo's position: he apparently drew up an outline on the basis of his information about the *ceques*.

8. Julien (1998, 89) proposes a useful chronology of this reorganization, although she mistakenly calls it the "process of parish formation." This leads the author to affirm that the parishes might have been created "at any moment" since the founding of Cuzco (82). In fact, this would have been quite impossible because of the particular territorial and pastoral conditions that were needed to create a parish.

9. Histories of religious orders provide abundant information regarding these first years of the missionary project. See, for example, Córdova y Salinas (1957 [1651]); Calancha (1974 [1638]); and Meléndez (1681). On the role allotted to the religious orders during the early years of the Spanish presence, see Armas (1953); Borges (1960); Tibesar (1991); and Villarejo (1965). For the case of New Spain and especially Guatemala, see Van Oss (2002, 15).

10. The temple of Coricancha was first appropriated by one of the Pizarro brothers, who then ceded it to the Dominicans (Esquivel y Navia 1980, 1:90). For a study of the Coricancha, see Bauer (2004, 139–57). When the Franciscans arrived in Cuzco, they established themselves in the Toctocachi quarter, now known as San Blas (Esquivel y Navia 1980, 1:91); from there they removed to Cassana. Concerning Cassana, and the *guacas* located on the site, see Bauer (2000, 70–71; 2004, 117–21) and Garcilaso de la Vega (1945 [1609], 2: Book 7, chap. 10, 110–11). This Inca building was demolished two years later. In 1549 the Franciscans removed to the place where they now have their convent (Esquivel y Navia 1980, 1:153).

11. See Van Oss (2002, 16) for an interesting analysis of such alliances in Guatemala.

12. On the cultural characteristics and aftermath of this period, see chapter 2. Speaking of these early years, Esquivel y Navia wrote that the profound

instability that the area experienced and the scarceness of agents of the Church hindered the progress of the Christian doctrine. In what seems an excessive display of enthusiasm motivated by the desire to highlight the civilizing role of the Church, the author asserts that as soon as the wars had ended, the number of conversions rose massively (Esquivel y Navia 1980, 1:111).

13. The records of the Cuzco town council for this year show the *encomenderos* refuting the accusation that they were neglecting the teaching of Christianity to the Indians for whom they were responsible (González Pujana 1982, 70).

14. See Bauer (2000, 187), who asserts that Paullo Inca's house was located there.

15. According to Cobo, Tococachi was the site of the *guaca* Michosamaro, whose history is associated with Manco Capac, the first Inca, and the founders of Cuzco (Bauer 2000, 185).

16. Cobo indicates that San Sebastián was built on the "square of the martyrs" and that there was a stone idol (Bauer 2000, 102, 192).

17. See Bauer (2000, 142–43) for a description of these shrines.

18. See the document containing instructions to *visitadores* (Toledo 1986, 1:33–36).

19. See Julien (1998, 85). An architectural study of colonial Cuzco (Chara Zereceda and Caparó Gil 1998) provides abundant information on the parishes and churches of the city, although unfortunately the authors do not identify their sources.

20. Gregorio González de Cuenca, an *oidor* of the Real Audiencia of Lima, who played a prominent role in colonial organization, had arrived in Cuzco as *corregidor* three months before the priors of the convents were summoned (Esquivel y Navia 1980, 1:207). During his career in Peru, González de Cuenca distinguished himself for asserting the authority of the crown over that of the Church.

21. It is worth noting the contrast between this situation and that of the viceroyalty of New Spain, where the religious orders were in charge of organizing not only the parishes but also the villages, taking population counts and estimating the amount of the Indian tribute (Van Oss 2002, 23).

22. The literature about the central coast during the period immediately preceding the conquest and during the early colonial period has increased considerably since María Rostworowski's research was published. An overview of these studies is available in Silverman (2004, 217–22) and also in Eeckhout (2004).

23. Rostworowski (1978, 89) asserts that the population of the Lima valley was numerous, but that by 1549 a considerable percentage had disappeared. Recent bioarchaeological studies of human remains of the period show clear signs of malnutrition. Since this finding contradicts the widely established

opinion that the Incan regime was one of general well-being, this has not yet been sufficiently studied, but it would have made the inhabitants of the central coast even more vulnerable to the crisis triggered by the conquest and colonization. I am grateful to the University of Cambridge physical anthropologist Trisha Biers for explaining her observations on the material collected in funeral contexts found in the important pre-Hispanic site of Puruchuco, in the Lima valley. Eeckhout (1999), through X-rays of human remains found in Pachacamac, arrived at similar conclusions.

24. See Torres Saldamando et al. (1888, 1).

25. Charney (1989, 35–48); Cook (1981); Lowry (1991, 62); Rostworowski (1978, 53). Though we have no figures for the population before the conquest, there is evidence of an acute demographic crisis along the central coast shortly after the Spanish invasion. Cook (1981, 114) maintains that the Indian population of the coast collapsed completely, and that only migration from the sierra prevented its total disappearance.

26. Rostworowski (1978, 76–77) summarizes how the native population of the Lima valley was displaced from its original settlements during the early colonial period. Lowry (1991, 62–64) provides a detailed description of these relocations. She explains how the former *cacicazgos* of the Lima valley were transformed with the creation of the Indian village of Magdalena, where the inhabitants of Lima were removed. Charney (1989, 58–66) describes how the Spaniards took possession of the best lands in the Lima valley.

27. A type of *corvée* labor.

28. Many years earlier, the town council had agreed to assign plots of land to the *caciques* whose Indians served the inhabitants of Lima. There could be a connection between these early assignments, made in 1539, and the location of the district of El Cercado some years later. See Torres Saldamando et al. (1888, 1:271–76).

29. Descriptions of the incidents that followed upon the forced removal of the Indians from San Lázaro are found in Lissón (1945, 3: no. 16).

30. In the immediate vicinity of Lima there was a series of Indian villages that today are districts fully incorporated into the city, such as Magdalena, Lurigancho, Ate, Pachacamac, Surco, and Carabayllo (Varón 1997).

31. "Memorial del padre Juan Vasquez de la Compañía de Jesús," Lima, March 12, 1626, AAL, Curatos, Leg. 12, 1623–1671, Exp. IV, f. 5.

32. "El padre Rector del pueblo del Cercado con los curas de la parrochia de Santa Ana sobre la feligresía de los indios," AAL, Curatos, Leg. 12, 1623–1671, Exp. IV.

33. The diversity of approaches within the Church must have contributed to prolonging the case. It is striking that even an archbishop as energetic and as sympathetic to the Jesuits as Bartolomé Lobo Guerrero, who intervened in support of their suit, did not succeed in making the Indians obey the order to

submit to the priests of El Cercado. The letter written by Lobo Guerrero in 1613 to the Indians and the priests of Cieneguilla and Manchay exhorting them to respect the jurisdiction of the Jesuits may be seen in Ramos (1994, 253–54).

34. While the Indians of these peripheral areas claimed to be "free and without ties to the *reducción*," they also maintained that they paid tribute to their *caciques* and *encomenderos*. See "Representación de los yndios de la Cieneguilla y Manchay," AAL, Curatos, Leg. 12, 1623–1671, Exp. IV, f. 66.

35. Rostworowski (1978, 86–87) remarks with some disappointment that Don Gonzalo became a fervent Catholic, though it is possible that his conversion was easier to live with because he attended mass in Santa Ana (82).

36. Nor was El Cercado. Various accounts show that this parish received churchgoers belonging to other ethnic groups. See, for example, the information collected in connection with the miracle that took place in the church of Nuestra Señora de Copacabana, in which several of the Spaniards who gave affidavits stated that they went to mass regularly in the church of El Cercado (*El Amigo del Clero* 1909).

37. The percentages given here come from the census taken by order of Viceroy Marqués de Montesclaros in 1613–1614 (Varón 1997, 447).

38. Concerning the image of the Indian as a poor wretch, see Cañeque (2004); Castañeda (1971); and Cuena Boy (1998).

39. Letter from Archbishop Jerónimo de Loayza to the king, dated August 2, 1564, in Lissón (1944, 2: no. 7, 276).

40. The hospital was located in what is nowadays the parish of San Pedro.

41. Concerning the number of *encomenderos* in the city of Cuzco, and for a comparison to the other cities of the Peruvian viceroyalty, see Puente Brunke (1992, 141: table 2).

42. In his study of the hospitals of Toledo, Martz (1983, 179) explains that the lists of people cured included the names of those who had died but who had confessed, received the last rites, and been properly buried.

43. An appraisal made in 1564 indicates that there were several paintings on the walls of the Santa Ana hospital. The document does not describe them all, but it mentions "six stories of the works of mercy" that were painted in the cloister (Lissón 1943, 2: no. 8, 422). Doctrine teaches that there are seven bodily works of mercy: feeding the hungry, giving drink to the thirsty, clothing the naked, housing the pilgrim, visiting the sick, redeeming the captive, and burying the dead—although the Gospel according to Matthew, from which these are taken, does not include the last one.

44. The reform of the welfare institutions in Europe during this period was especially vigorous in Protestant areas, with increasing secular participation in the administration of the hospitals, something that aroused criticism and suspicion among the Catholics (Santolaria Sierra 2003b, 17). Discussing

the founding of hospitals in Spain, Martz (1983, 64, 83) indicates that tensions between the civil and ecclesiastical authorities were also common when it came to deciding questions of patronage. Loayza refused to allow the Real Audiencia to take possession of the Santa Ana hospital in the name of the crown, a position to which the latter eventually submitted (Cobo 1935 [1639?], 288–91).

45. Garcilaso de la Vega (1945 [1609], 2: Book 7, chap. 12, 115) asserts that the hospital was founded on the initiative of the Franciscan friars, who convinced the Cuzco town council to build it and assume the trusteeship of the institution.

46. Viceroy Toledo, as the crown's delegate to the provincial councils held in Toledo in 1565–1566 to examine the legislation voted in Trent, was well acquainted with the decrees concerning hospitals that were discussed there (Martz 1983, 50).

47. In other cases, the donations made by *encomenderos* for the founding of hospitals were not used as stipulated. For example, the Augustinian friars designated as trustees of the hospital of Paria (Upper Peru) did not actually build it (Toledo 1989, 2:40).

48. See "Copia de un memorial que en el Perú dieron al arzobispo de Los Reyes acerca de la necesidad que padecen las iglesias y hospitales en aquellas partes," dated April 1585, in Lissón (1943, 3: no. 13, 337).

49. See the "Libro de visitas antiguo," which records the inspections made by Archbishop Toribio Alfonso de Mogrovejo between 1593 and 1605 in Benito (2006). Certain areas, for example, in the region now known as the Callejón de Huaylas (Benito 2006, 19, 22, 23) as well as Lambayeque (42–51) and parts of the sierra in the department of La Libertad (75) were better organized. See note 5 for an explanation of *cabezas de doctrina*.

50. The Second Council of Lima resolved that the Indian specialists were to be examined in order to ascertain whether they confined themselves to healing with plants, or whether their practices were considered superstitious. If the Church was satisfied with the results of the examination, it would issue a license (Vargas Ugarte 1951, 1:255). On the presence of Indian specialists in the native hospital in Cuzco, see Esquivel y Navia (1980, 2:48).

51. In the first years of the Spanish presence, some Franciscan friars, such as Mateo Jumilla, combined the destruction of idols with healing by the laying on of hands (Córdova y Salinas 1957 [1651], 296; Tibesar 1991, 90), while the sanctity of the archbishop of Lima, Toribio Alfonso de Mogrovejo, was made manifest by the miraculous cures that he performed when visiting his diocese between the end of the sixteenth century and the first years of the seventeenth (Montalvo 1683, 297). Despite these miraculous cures, the practices of the Indian medical specialists were often viewed with extreme distrust, and their rituals were seen as superstitition.

52. For a sharp criticism of the custom of consulting the Indian doctors, expressed in a mid-seventeenth-century sermon, see Ávila (1648, 1:127).

53. A historical view of these associations may be found in Bossy (1985, 56–75). On the Spanish confraternities, see Christian (1981, 50–69); Flynn (1989; 1999); Martz (1983, 159–99); and Nalle (1992, 156–66). For the Andes, a study focused on the cultural and political aspects of the confraternities is lacking, but see Celestino and Meyers (1981); Garland (1994); and Varón (1982).

54. The popularity of the Marian devotions in Spain was enormous from the sixteenth century onward (Christian 1989; Nalle 1992, 176–79). The cult of the Holy Sacrament was promoted from the middle of the sixteenth century to the extent that every parish had to have its own confraternity devoted to it. Similarly, the membership of the cult of the Souls in Purgatory increased greatly (Flynn 1999; Nalle 1992, 163, 191–93).

55. In his study of colonial Catholicism in Guatemala, Van Oss (2002, 109–15) focuses on the economic aspects during the eighteenth century. It is interesting to note that by that period, the colonial authorities had changed their view of confraternities, which they now considered detrimental to a proper religious life.

56. The role of the confraternity as a group offering fictitious kinship bonds has been noticed by several other researchers. For some examples, see Bossy (1985); Celestino and Meyers (1981); Chiffoleau (1980); and Redondo (1988).

57. The confraternities created to worship the cult of Nuestra Señora de Copacabana in Cuzco during the seventeenth century are an example. A detailed examination may be found in Ramos (2005c).

FIVE. **Wills, Graves, and Funeral Rites**

1. There are various commentaries on the Leyes de Toro; see, for example, Llamas y Molina (1827). A book has recently been published in Spain on the occasion of the quincentennial of the publication of this legal corpus (González Alonso 2006).

2. But see Díaz Rementería (1977, 166–68) for a discussion on the use of the Leyes de Toro and their application to the succession to *cacicazgo*.

3. In chapter 3, referring to the sacramental aspect of the will, I explain the established procedures in the decrees of the Councils of Lima.

4. Formally, the procedure was similar to that followed in Spanish cities in the sixteenth century (Eire 1995, 29). One example of how the local indigenous authorities proceeded can be seen in the will of Antón Atao, executed in Lima in 1589, found in: Archivo General de la Nación (henceforward AGN),

Protocolos Notariales (PN), sixteenth century, Bartolomé Rodríguez de Torquemada 224, f. 871. In this case, the indigenous *alguacil* also assumed the role of interpreter.

5. The scope and frequency of these abuses were well known by the Church, which repeatedly issued instructions to put a stop to the clergy's rapacity. See, for example, Lobo Guerrero and Arias de Ugarte (1987 [1613], 85).

6. The number of wills written in indigenous languages in Mexico and the existence of a documentary corpus in Mesoamerican vernacular languages are testimony to the stronger footing of writing there, to which the early literary education of the indigenous elites contributed. Various recent studies have made use of these documents (Cline 1986; Cline and Portilla 1984; Kellogg 1995; Lockhart 1992; Pizzigoni 2007; Restall 1997a; 1997b; Terraciano 1998). On the transition to writing in the Andes and on representation in the Western manner in general, the works of Tom Cummins are of special importance (Cummins 1994; 1998; 2002). Boone (1994) provides an essential study on written representation in New World indigenous societies.

7. In her study of Mexican wills, Cline (1986, 29–30) also notes this, although she attributes the presence of various people to eminently practical reasons: witnesses could certify the existence of a will in case the document was misplaced. Cline's conclusion leaves aside the political and spiritual issues of will-writing. For the European context of the late Middle Ages, see Chiffoleau (1980, 84).

8. A fairly complete explanation of the origins of the Bull of the Holy Crusade and its introduction into the New World, particularly Mexico, may be found in Lugo Olín (1998). The study includes a bibliography and documentary appendix that help situate the document in the American context. A sermon written in Quechua explaining the meaning of the bull to the Indians can be found in Itier (1992b).

9. John Bossy (1985, 32) notes this in his study on the formation of Christian conscience in Western Europe. Pérez Bocanegra (1631, 493) advised priests to explain to their Indian parishioners, in their own language, how, in witnessing the Holy Sacrament in the house of a sick person, they had also performed an act of mercy and earned indulgences.

10. Will of Don Domingo Chupica, Lima, October 28, 1577, AGN, PN, sixteenth century, Marcos Franco de Esquivel 33, f. 786.

11. Several loose pages from these registers can be found in the Archivo General de la Nación in Lima under the heading "Testamentos de Indios."

12. An early statement of this view may be seen in the letter from the *licenciado* Martel de Santoyo to the king from Lima in 1542, found in Lissón (1943, 1: no. 3, 112–13). In 1608, Viceroy Montesclaros instructed the royal magistrates of Cuzco not to employ Indians and mestizos as interpreters (Esquivel y Navia 1980, 2:9).

13. A native of the town of Zupián, in the province of Chancay, north of Lima, León requested in his will a very simple funeral because of his poverty. AGN, PN, seventeenth century, Francisco de Bustamante 246, f. 86.

14. The city of Chuquisaca is present-day Sucre, in the Republic of Bolivia. Ávila's petition may be found in "Dejación de oficio de intérprete. Alonso Dávila indio," Lima, July 16, 1650, AGN, PN, seventeenth century, Fernando García 682, f. 404.

15. Father Luis López, director of the Jesuit college of Lima, explains this problem to the head of his order in Rome, Francis Borja, Lima, January 21, 1570 (Egaña 1954, 1: no. 71, 366–67).

16. On the topic of Quechua diversity, see Mannheim (1991); and Torero (1974; 1995). On the relationship between the local languages of the Lima highlands and the general language, see Cerrón Palomino (1991); Itier (2003); and Taylor (1985). On interpreters, see Ramos (n.d.). References to the linguistic diversity in the colonial chronicles are multiple; see, for example, Betanzos (2004 [1551], First Part, chap. 22, 153); Cobo (1956 [1653], Book 11, chap. 9, 27–29); Guaman Poma (1989 [1615], 58–60); Murúa (2001 [1613], Book 3, chap. 3, 457–58); and Zárate (1995 [1555], chap. 4, 39). The descriptions of rural Indian communities collected by Archbishop Mogrovejo and his retinue during inspection visits to the diocese offer one of the richest and most detailed accounts of the distribution of Quechua dialects and other now-extinct Andean languages (Benito 2006).

17. Will of Francisca Colloc, Cuzco, September 11, 1586, in the Archivo Departamental de Cuzco (henceforward ADC), PN, sixteenth century, Pedro de la Carrera Ron 4, f. 1687.

18. Lack of fluency in Spanish undoubtedly played a crucial role in these Indian officials losing their jobs to mestizos.

19. Mannheim (1991) claims that there were notary documents written in Quechua. For studies on Quechua as a written language, see Itier (1992b) and Durston (2004).

20. Examples and analysis of the invocations used in these documents in Madrid in the sixteenth century may be found in Eire (1995, 62–63).

21. Will of Don Gonzalo Guanuco Quispe, ADC, PN, sixteenth century, Pedro de la Carrera Ron 4, f. 880.

22. Will of Leonor Chao, AGN, PN, sixteenth century, Rodríguez de Torquemada 144, f. 10v.

23. Will of Alonso Caxa, AGN, PN, sixteenth century, Marcos Franco de Esquivel 33, f. 75.

24. The will of Don Cristóbal Guacay, an Indian singer for the town of Magdalena, added to his will that he believed in "everything declared and preached by the Holy Mother Church of Rome, in whose faith I proclaim to live and die *and never to venture from*." AGN, PN, sixteenth century, Pedro López de

Mallea 980, f. 221 (my italics). On the religious repression experienced in the Lima diocese in this period, see Duviols (1971).

25. This occurs in a very old formula used to request divine intervention, widespread in Western Europe. Examples with exactly the same wording may be found in Ariès (1977, 189); and Chiffoleau (1980, 356–89).

26. Will of Luisa Tari, ADC, PN, sixteenth century, Antonio de Salas 14, f. 727; will of Doña Juana Mama Guaco Ñusta, ADC, PN, seventeenth century, Juan Flores de Bastidas 100, f. 7.

27. Venegas advises the following: "It appears to me that an honest and scrupulous cleric, together with a good married man neither rich nor poor, about whom nothing vile or defamatory has been said, because both are presumed to be God-fearing, will make good executors" (quoted in Rey Hazas 2003a, 104).

28. This issue, which we will address in the next chapter, is a subject of historiographic debate on which only comparative studies can begin to shed light. In his study on the Christianization of death at the end of the Middle Ages in France, Chiffoleau postulates that wills and Christian death created an individual free from the "snares of obedience, submissiveness, and solidarity" (Chiffoleau 1980, 88). In a recent study based on a comparison between the cities of Douai (Flanders) and Florence, Samuel Cohn (2000, 40) shows convincingly that Chiffoleau's thesis cannot be generalized because the opposite is apparent in Florence: the strengthening of the family unit and the ever-greater importance of ancestors.

29. The notary indicates the presence of the Indians Diego Xanquirmi, Francisco Chulcarue, and Juan Mus. Will of Francisco de Guasquanquiche, AGN, PN, sixteenth century, Rodrigo Gómez de Baeza 43, f. 262.

30. In 1586, Don Felipe Yarise, mayor of the parish of Santiago in the city of Cuzco, assisted Doña Jerónima Tocto when she authored her will. Yarise did not know how to read or write. See the will of Doña Jerónima Tocto, ADC, PN, sixteenth century, Pedro de la Carrera Ron 4, f. 663.

31. Mazet's study (1976) on the population of the Lima parish of San Sebastián during this period gives similar figures.

32. This is a very rough comparison, as the 1613 census reflects distinct circumstances: it was formed from a database of 2,000 entries including both adults and children (Cook 1976, 42; Lowry 1991, 127–28). The wills, by contrast, collect information from a group that in all cases reached adulthood.

33. Using the analysis proposed by Cook (1981), Lowry (1991, 197) maintains that the fertility and longevity rates were far below the minimum necessary to ensure the reproduction of the group as a whole.

34. This possibility is suggested by the provinces of origin of some of these men and women, whose chiefs allied themselves with the conquistadors: among them are natives of Jauja, Tumebamba, Cañaris, and Chachapoyas.

35. The outsiders did not come from too far away: Huamanga, Arequipa, and Chuquisaca. A few had been born in Chachapoyas, Cajamarca, and Huánuco.

36. Cook calculates the population of Cuzco between the end of the sixteenth and beginning of the seventeenth centuries using descriptions by chroniclers and travelers as well as tax rates established in 1572 by order of Viceroy Toledo (Cook 1981, 216: table 49). In her book on indigenous migration in Cuzco, Ann Wightman (1990, 64) sought to compile, with the greatest detail possible, demographic information on the indigenous population for the period between 1570 and 1720, but she could not find sufficiently solid information on the population of the city and its outskirts for the period prior to the census carried out in 1689–1690 by order of Viceroy Duque de la Palata. In fact, her information for the sixteenth century and the first half of the seventeenth, as the author indicates, is taken from Cook (1981).

37. I include in this group people who came from parishes of the indigenous villages around Lima, such as Magdalena, Pachacamac, Lurigancho, Ate, Surco, and the port of Callao.

38. The scarce number of parishioners of El Cercado could also be explained by the fact that this jurisdiction had its own authorities and probably its own scribe. There is no evidence of notary registers from El Cercado. Other sources paint a different picture for some jurisdictions. For example, Cook (1976, 47), in analyzing the ethnic distribution by parish of the population of Lima in 1619, concludes that El Sagrario had many more indigenous parishioners than Santa Ana.

39. Will of Francisca Auatanta, Cuzco, December 19, 1566, ADC, PN, sixteenth century, Antonio Sánchez 16, 1566–1567, f. 357.

40. See the discussion of these regulations in chapter 3. Many Indians, even baptized ones, were not being buried in churches because their bosses refused to pay the fees (Vargas Ugarte 1951, 1:81). On burials for unbaptized Indians, see also Barriga (1933–1954, 4:180).

41. Will of María Cuticunca, AGN, PN, sixteenth century, Marcos Franco de Equivel 33, 1569–1577, f. 285v.

42. AGN, PN, sixteenth century, Juan Gutiérrez 73, f. 764.

43. Note the involvement of the priest Antonio Polanco in AGN, PN, sixteenth century, Juan Gutiérrez 71, f. 517.

44. On the miracle of the Virgin of Copacabana and the development of her cult in Lima, see Angulo (1935, 91–135); García Irigoyen (1906, 2:178–200); Lissón (1946); Lowry (1991, 21, 39–49); and the documents published in *El Amigo del Clero* (1909).

45. There is a record of this move because the Lima city council took note of it in one of its sessions of October 1539.

46. On the early history of the Mercedarians in Cuzco, see "Información hecha en el Cuzco, por fray Francisco de Obregón, Procurador de la Orden de

la Merced, en que consta ser aquella casa el primer monasterio fundado en la ciudad después de poblada, y los servicios hechos por sus religiosos. Junio de 1564," in Barriga (1933–1954, 1:141–59).

47. The trial that set the San Cristóbal priests against those of the cathedral may be seen in "Miguel de Medina en nombre del licenciado Josephe Hurtado de Mendoza, cura de la parroquia de San Cristóbal de la ciudad del Cuzco en la causa que sigue sobre administrar los santos sacramentos a los que biven en las casas que de nuevo se han fabricado en la jurisdicción de dicha parroquia," Archivo Arzobispal de Lima (henceforward AAL), Apelaciones del Cuzco, Leg. 15, 1658–1659. To this dispute may be added the one in which the parish hospital opposed Santa Ana, the case documents for which may be seen in "El maestro Pedro Arias contra el padre Gaspar de Villagra," Cuzco, July 1631, AAL, Apelaciones del Cuzco, Leg. 3, Exp. 1. Rowe (1990) studied and published the map that was given as evidence in this dispute.

48. The pronouncement is found in chapter 15 of the decrees of the diocesan synod that met in Lima in 1613.

49. Checras belonged to the province of Cajatambo, in the highlands northeast of Lima.

50. Will of Don Domingo Chupica (see note 10).

51. Huamantanga is located 12,000 feet above sea level in the present-day province of Canta, northeast of Lima.

52. Will of Don Cristóbal Guayana, Lima, July 11, 1606, AGN, PN, seventeenth century, Alonso Cortés 379, f. 143v.

53. Will of Don Juan Poma Yalli, Cuzco, June 28, 1634, ADC, PN, seventeenth century, Domingo de Oro 264, f. 1010; will of Don Joan Gómez Galán de Solís Ynga, Cuzco, October 22, 1670, ADC, PN, seventeenth century, Lorenzo de Mesa Andueza 208, f. 99. It is true that the latter refers to a person assimilated into Spanish culture, but precisely this fact is an important feature of the conduct of the Inca elite in the city of Cuzco.

54. See, for example, Córdova y Salinas (1957 [1651], 158); Meléndez (1681, 2:104); and Vargas Ugarte (1963, 1:24). An analysis of the contents, thematic and musical adaptations, and methods used may be found in Estenssoro (2003).

55. Letter from Father Bartolomé Hernández, S.J., to Juan de Ovando, Lima, April 19, 1572, *Monumenta Peruana* (Egaña 1954, 1:463–64).

56. Letter from Viceroy Francisco de Toledo to the king, La Plata, March 20, 1574 (Levillier 1921, 5:409).

57. The literature on this topic is extensive. See, among others, Bloch and Parry 1982; Eire 1995; Gordon and Marshall 2000; Hertz 1960; Metcalf and Huntington 1980; Strocchia 1992; and Varela 1990.

58. Will of Elvira, Lima, April 15, 1572, AGN, PN, sixteenth century, Marcos Franco de Esquivel 33, f. 303.

59. "Visita de la doctrina de San Lorenzo de Quinti. Auto para que se entierren descubiertos los difuntos," AAL, Visitas Pastorales, Leg. 9, Exp. XXXIII, 1660, f. 5.

60. Among the positions held by Sarmiento de Vivero during his career is that of extirpator of idolatries (Mills 1997; Sánchez 1991).

61. See, for example, the will of Catalina Payco, Lima, August 1, 1577, AGN, PN, sixteenth century, Marcos Franco de Esquivel 33, f. 509.

62. Will of Leonor Cisa Ocllo Palla, Cuzco, October 30, 1589, ADC, PN, sixteenth century, Pedro de la Carrera Ron 4, f. 855.

63. On the custom of dressing in monastic habits to shorten the passage through purgatory, see Eire (1995, 105–13); and Nalle (1992, 194–96).

64. Will of Doña Mariana Quispi Asarpay, Cuzco, April 4, 1617, ADC, PN, seventeenth century, Cristóbal de Luzero 159, f. 163.

65. On the work of the Dominicans in Chincha, see Meléndez (1681). Will of Doña Magdalena Chimazo, Lima, October 25, 1618, AGN, PN, seventeenth century, Cristóbal de Pineda 1534, f. 264.

66. Will of Doña Ana Quispe Asarpay Coya, Cuzco, September 19, 1611, ADC, PN, seventeenth century, Francisco de la Fuente 107, f. 152. The sash of Saint Francis has three knots that symbolize the vows of poverty, chastity, and obedience (Schenone 1992, 1:64). Some paintings show souls in purgatory grasping for a handhold on the sash in an attempt to save themselves (1:393–94).

67. Will of Antonia Vásquez, Lima, April 6, 1648, AGN, PN, seventeenth century, Fernando García 682, f. 393.

68. In a will authored in Cuzco at the beginning of the seventeenth century, we read: "I decree that my body be wrapped in the habit of Señor Saint Francis, to which end I order that an old habit be requested and a new one donated in its place." Will of Beatriz Nachi, Cuzco, March 13, 1601, ADC, PN, seventeenth century, Antonio de Salas 289, f. 147.

69. "Relación de las obsequias que se hizieron en la yglessia cathedral de la ciudad de Guamanga por el Catholico rey nuestro señor don Philippe Tercero de gloriossa memoria el año 1621," Archivo General de Indias, Lima 308. This *Relación* is followed by brief descriptions from rural priests about the ceremonies carried out in the parishes under their charge. For the description of these royal funeral ceremonies in the city of Cuzco that same year, see Esquivel y Navia (1980, 2:45). For earlier examples, although focused in the city of Lima, see Barriga (1933–1954, 2:208–9; 5:145–46).

70. The Cuzco synod (1591) ruled that fees for burial in a monastery would be double the cost of one in a parish (Lassègue 1987, 71).

71. This point is demonstrated in the tariff we are discussing; it was arrived at using the tariff prepared during the episcopate of Toribio Alfonso de Mogrovejo as a point of reference, and it was subsequently modified in the

synod headed by Lobo Guerrero (1603). The edition cited here includes commentaries and additions from Archbishops Hernando Arias de Ugarte (synod of 1636) and Melchor Liñán y Cisneros (1674).

72. A similar act of adaptation to the local environment is evident in the "Aranzel de los derechos que han de llevar los curas sachristanes y personas ecclesiasticas en los obispados de la Ymperial y Sanctiago del Nuevo Extremo de Chile fecho y ordenado por el sancto concilio provincial legitimamente congregado en la ciudad de Los Reyes del Peru, Los Reyes (Lima), 15 de septiembre de 1583" (Lissón 1945, no. 13, 254–58).

73. This does not mean that the indigenous population of Lima was indifferent to privileges and their corresponding symbols.

74. See, for example, Pérez Bocanegra (1631, 566).

75. Writing at the beginning of the seventeenth century, Pérez Bocanegra (1631, 564) took it for granted that the Indians should know their part in the ritual, which included "the three prayers, so full of consolation and tenderness, that all Indians in the parish are to know by heart to produce the said effect."

76. In his study of death at the end of the Middle Ages in southern France, Chiffoleau (1980) asserts that the attitude of wealthy people who arranged very low-profile funerals should be interpreted as equivalent to the behavior of those who ordered ostentatious ones. This insight may also be applicable to the Andes, although the topic of social rank according to ethnic identity merits careful consideration.

77. Some of those who requested burial outside the city of Cuzco did not instruct their funeral processions to stop for *posas.*

78. We reconstruct the path of the funeral processions using the testator's parish of origin and the burial place as reference points. In the majority of cases we do not know the place of death or residence.

79. It is very difficult to identify the occupation of most will-authors. In colonial cities, Indian artisans came to occupy socially prestigious positions.

80. Eire (1995) suggests a similar analysis for interpreting certain lacunae of information in testamentary instructions regarding funeral rituals in wills from Madrid, a proposal that strikes me as plausible.

81. Will of Pedro Aculi, Lima, November 11, 1624, AGN, PN, seventeenth century, Antonio de Tamayo 1851, f. 485v.

82. Will of Don Cristóbal Guayana, Lima, July 11, 1606, AGN, PN, seventeenth century, Alonso Cortés 379, f. 143v.

83. Will of Juan Gómez, Lima, May 7, 1600, AGN, PN, seventeenth century, Diego Jiménez 103, f. 187.

84. Will of María Caxacarua, Lima, January 27, 1591, AGN, PN, sixteenth century, Juan Rodríguez de Torquemada 143, f. 37.

six. **Ancestors, Successors, and Memory**

1. Will of Luisa Quina, Lati, March 19, 1606, AGN, PN, seventeenth century, Cristóbal de Quesada 1557, f. 199.

2. For example, the relationship between Incas of "royal blood" and those adopted or "privileged" is still to be elucidated. Incas of "royal blood" were those who were part of the core that was initially established in Cuzco, led the expansion of this group, and were its leaders, while "privileged" Incas, inhabitants of the conquered areas around Cuzco, were incorporated by the former as allies, generally through marriage, by which they were granted special concessions. A recent contribution to the topic is Julien (2000). On the issue of Andean kinship, see the works of Rostworowski (1983), Lounsbury (1986), and Zuidema (1980; 1995). Other studies on Incan status include Bauer (2000; 2004); Covey (2006); D'Altroy (2002); and Pärssinen (2003).

3. An example of this difficulty is represented by Zuidema's analysis (1980) on the kinship system of the Cuzco Incas. The author bases his study on the depiction of kinship given by the *licenciado* Juan Pérez Bocanegra (1631) in his work intended for evangelization, without discussing the problems inherent in the use of a patently colonial work to analyze pre-Hispanic Andean kinship. Lounsbury (1986) approaches the same source from a different viewpoint.

4. On the topic of the creation of legislation to address Spanish-American New World population and territories (*derecho indiano*), see the works of Benton (2002); Mirow (2004); Ots Capdequí (1921); and Zavala (1971). A useful discussion of the application of Castilian law in the private sphere in Spanish-American territory may be found in Tomás y Valiente (1997), García Gallo (1972), and Lalinde Abadía (1978).

5. On the historical dimension of the concept of poverty, see, for example, Beaudoin (2007); Geremek (1994); and Iliffe (1987). For a recent example in Spanish-American historiography, see Arrom (2000) and Milton (2007).

6. Constituciones del Segundo Concilio Limense, Constituciones de los naturales, number 16: "Indians shall marry their first wife" (Vargas Ugarte 1951, 1:16).

7. "Carta original del arzobispo de la ciudad de Los Reyes a S.M. pide se solicite a S.S. la renovación de ciertos privilegios para los indios," Lima, April 23, 1599 (Lissón 1946, 4: no. 19, 277–78). Archbishop Mogrovejo was following the Catholic Church's tradition in the conversion of Western Europe, when the introduction of new rules regarding kinship and marriage also had to adopt a flexible attitude toward local customs (Bestard Camps 1992, 113).

8. The concession of legitimacy as a prerogative of the monarch was a fully established practice in Castile and accepted in the *Siete Partidas* (Burns 2001, 4:xxi). In her study on illegitimacy in colonial Lima, Mannarelli (1993, 161–67) explains changes in the notion of illegitimacy in Spanish law and

includes some notes on its application in the colonial sphere. See also Ots Capdequí (1921). On the ways in which some of the first *encomenderos* in colonial Peru legitimized their descendants, see Ares (2005, 127–28). Regarding legitimization of the descendants of the Incas, see, for example, the will of Don Luis Sayre Topa, Cuzco, October 7, 1636, ADC, PN, sixteenth century, Luis de Morales 82, f. 1871.

9. For a concise explanation of the concept of kinship and a useful review of the debates and anthropological literature on the topic, see the article "Kinship" in Barnard and Spencer (2002, 311–17), especially 313.

10. I refer to this issue in examining the use of the symbols and emblems of Incan power in colonial Cuzco (Ramos 2005b). See also the works of Cummins (1998; 2002).

11. Will of Don Hernando Anchiguaman, Lima, July 28, 1578, AGN, PN, sixteenth century, Alonso de la Cueva 28, f. 210.

12. Will of Don Cristóbal Xuto Chumbe, Lima, July 4, 1580, AGN, PN, sixteenth century, Alonso de la Cueva 29, f. 325.

13. Will of Diego Fiño, also known as Diego Allaucan, Lima, July 9, 1579, AGN, PN, sixteenth century, Alonso de la Cueva 29, f. 170. During the early colonial period it appears to have become possible for women to inherit chiefdoms, at least on the northern coast, as Rostworowski has shown. My evidence shows that in the sixteenth and early seventeenth centuries, women were ineligible to take the post of *cacique* or, more appropriately, *cacica* throughout the Andes. I have found a few cases of coastal women who used the title *cacica*, but it is clear that it imposed no effective right to rule. For a different viewpoint, see Garrett (2008), who extends his findings for the eighteenth-century southeastern Andes to the earlier period and to the whole Andean region. See also Díaz Rementería (1977) and Graubart (2007, 160–67).

14. If both Don Fernando and the notary who composed his will are using the term *bastarda* accurately, it would mean that he had these daughters while married. On the classification of illegitimate children according to the *Siete Partidas*, see Burns (2001, 4:xxi).

15. Will of Don Diego Nacara, Lima, May 17, 1606, AGN, PN, seventeenth century, Alonso Cortés 379, f. 86.

16. Will of Don Francisco Tantachumbi, Lima, April 17, 1602, AGN, PN, seventeenth century, Francisco Dávila 416, f. 80v.

17. Will of Don Pedro Manchipula, Lima, November 2, 1662, AGN, PN, seventeenth century, Gaspar de Monzón 1153, Registro 6, f. 1039v.

18. Will of Don Pedro de la Cruz, Lima, January 28, 1619, AGN, PN, seventeenth century, Diego Sánchez Vadillo 1747, f. 3699.

19. Will of Don Diego Condorguacho, Cuzco, May 8, 1568, ADC, PN, sixteenth century, Antonio Sánchez 17, f. 61.

20. This suggests that Hernando Pizarro's *yanaconas* and their descendants formed part of the population who were resettled in the parish of the

hospital for Cuzco natives. On the creation of this parish and the reorganization of sacred space in the city of Cuzco, see chapter 4.

21. Don Gonzalo Guanuco Quispe appears as a witness in various writings authored by Indian inhabitants of the parish of the hospital for natives.

22. See Ley XI in Leyes de Toro (Álvarez Posadilla 1826, 110) and Recopilación (1982, 3:18).

23. Will of Don Gonzalo Guanuco Quispe, Cuzco, June 28, 1590, ADC, PN, sixteenth century, Pedro de la Carrera Ron 4, f. 880.

24. Various sources referring to Incan genealogy indicate that the *ayllo* Sucso Panaca, known in other sources as Çocço Panaca (Julien 2000, 73), was descended from Viracocha Ynga and connected to the Antisuyo (Bauer 2000, 44–45), as Don Juan affirmed in referring to his ancestors. Pärssinen (2003) devotes part of his study on the Tahuantinsuyo to the Incan expansion in this region. See also Rowe (1985, 211–12).

25. Will of Don Juan Gualpa Sucso Ynga, Cuzco, January 28, 1590, ADC, PN, sixteenth century, Pedro de la Carrera Ron 4, f. 874v.

26. I referred to this *cacique* in chapter 5 to illustrate the public nature of the will-authoring process.

27. This tolerance offers a strong contrast to cases in which, only decades later in the same region, indigenous chiefs were accused of "adultery," for which the ecclesiastical authorities put them on trial (Sánchez 1991).

28. In addition to these goblets, which were in the possession of Ana Chumbe, Don Domingo mentions that she also held a *cumbi* shirt, a highly valued garment that constituted an emblem of the power of the ethnic authorities. On the symbolic value of these garments in the colonial period, see Phipps (2004; 2005); and Ramos (2005b).

29. Will of Don Luis Chalco Yupanqui Ynga, December 24, 1600, ADC, PN, seventeenth century, Antonio Salas 289, f. 560. For a succinct definition of the term *mascapaycha,* see González Holguín (1989 [1608], 232). For a study of the indigenous nobility in Cuzco, see Garrett (2005).

30. Chantries (*capellanía*) were foundations usually set up with real estate funds to pay the cost of masses said for the salvation of the founder's soul and those of his family members. A more detailed explanation may be found in von Wobeser (1999) and Schwaller (2001). For the central Andes, see Burga (1988, 197–227). Will of Don Fernando Ynga, Cuzco, July 11, 1646, ADC, PN, seventeenth century, Juan Flores de Bastidas 91, f. 908.

31. Various studies analyze this process, in the context of clothing and textiles (Dean 1999; Iriarte 1993; Phipps 2004; 2005; Ramos 2005b) and visual representation (Buntinx and Wuffarden 1991; Cummins 1991; 1994; 1998; 2002; 2005; Estenssoro 1992; 2003; 2005; Majluf 2005; Rowe 1951; Wuffarden 2005).

32. Will of Don Esteban Challco Viracocha Ynga, Cuzco, March 23, 1651, ADC, PN, seventeenth century, Juan Flores de Bastidas 94, f. 468.

33. Will of Don Lázaro Quispe Topa Ynga, Cuzco, August 4, 1655, ADC, PN, seventeenth century, Lorenzo de Messa Andueza 184, f. 1584.

34. Will of Don Jerónimo Quipquin, Cuzco, July 28, 1617, ADC, PN, seventeenth century, Cristóbal de Luzero 159, f. 197.

35. In his study on the Lima valley's indigenous population during the colonial period, Paul Charney (2001, 83, 85) maintains that it was not unusual to find women in positions of ethnic authority, but he doubts whether their presence spoke to a long tradition both before and after the Spanish conquest. On the topic of a woman's right to succeed her father in the *cacicazgo*, see the comments of Ots Capdequí, who, primarily on the basis of his reading of Solórzano y Pereyra (1972 [1648]), maintains that the practice was adapted to local conditions (Ots Capdequí 1921, 118–19). See also Graubart (2007, 160–85) and Garrett (2008).

36. Will of Doña Magdalena Chimazo, Lima, October 25, 1618, AGN, PN, seventeenth century, Cristóbal de Pineda 1534, f. 264. A similar case is that of Doña Melchora Caruaquilpo, who said in her will, composed in 1636, that she was the "head Indian and cacica of the town of Santa Ana de Pangos," but lived in very precarious conditions in Lima. See AGN, PN, seventeenth century, Francisco de Bustamante 245, f. 1599. See also Doña Francisca Corque, who asserted that she was *cacica* of the town of Santiago de Surco and left no descendants: Lima, April 30, 1612, AGN, PN, seventeenth century, Rodrigo Gómez de Baeza 743, f. 302.

37. Will of Doña María Llavin, Lima, October 29, 1607, AGN, PN, seventeenth century, Augustín Atencia 171, f. 256.

38. Will of Doña Ana Quipan, Lima, November 17, 1636, AGN, PN, seventeenth century, Antonio de Tamayo, 1857, f. 983.

39. Will of Doña Francisca Ignacia de Carvajal, Lima, March 1, 1670, AGN, PN, seventeenth century, Gaspar de Monzón 1156, f. 66v.

40. It is possible that some prestigious trades were controlled by noble families, such as candlemakers in Cuzco, although it is unclear whether they were organized in a guild. See, for example, Don Juan Quispi Tito, Cuzco, October 1639, in ADC, PN, seventeenth century, Alonso Beltrán Luzero 6, f. 820; and Don Lázaro Quispe Topa Ynga (see note 33).

41. See Suardo (1935, 88) for a description of one of these public events presided over by the viceroy, which took place in October 1630 in the town of Magdalena.

42. See, for example, the wills of Captain Diego Ynlot, a native of Chachapoyas, Lima, March 20, 1630, in AGN, PN, seventeenth century, Antonio de Tamayo 1853, f. 185; Second Lieutenant Francisco Barreto, a native of the town of Olmos, in the northern bishopric of Trujillo, Lima, December 9, 1636, in AGN, PN, seventeenth century, Francisco Ordóñez 1309, f. 875v; and Captain Don Juan Ynga Gutiérrez, a native of the city of Huamanga, Lima, January 8, 1660, in AGN, PN, seventeenth century, Bartolomé Maldonado 1053, f. 3v.

43. In litigation for *cacicazgo* that took place in the late seventeenth century in the province of Cajatambo, one of the contenders, Don Alonso Curi Paucar, presented the rank of captain that the viceroy had bestowed upon his ancestor of the same name for having fought with his men against the Dutch, who had pillaged the central Peruvian coast in 1624. Curi Páucar did not seek to use the title of his predecessor, but he did its benefits. AGN, Derecho Indígena, Cuad. 805, f. 27.

44. Eligibility required having a prominent social position, but it was not necessary to be part of the indigenous nobility, especially in the city of Lima.

45. See, for example, "Autos seguidos por la cofradía de Nuestra Señora de la Candelaria sobre que Pedro Cóndor, mayordomo que fue de dicha cofradía, no tenga voto en el cabildo de ella, y que sea expelido . . . por revoltoso y malicioso," Lima, April 1657–February 1659, AAL, Cofradías, Leg. 6A, Exp. III.

46. Will of Doña Ana Quispe Asarpay Coya, Cuzco, September 19, 1611, ADC, PN, seventeenth century, Francisco de la Fuente 107, f. 155.

47. Will of Don Juan de Castro, Cuzco, November 11, 1630, ADC, PN, seventeenth century, Domingo de Oro 260, f. 1801.

48. Will of Doña Magdalena Quispe Sisa Ñusta, Cuzco, November 18, 1636, ADC, PN, seventeenth century, Luis Diez de Morales 82, f. 2266.

49. Will of Don Juan de Espino y Torres, Lima, February 12, 1637, AGN, PN, seventeenth century, Juan Bautista de Herrera 873, f. 1385.

50. Will of Alonso Hanco, Cuzco, February 12, 1586, ADC, PN, sixteenth century, Pedro de la Carrera Ron 4, f. 653.

51. Hanco was a native of Santo Tomás, in Chumbivilcas, southeast of Cuzco.

52. On the reorganization of religious space in the city of Cuzco through the creation of parishes, see chapter 4.

53. Doña Juana Carrasco was probably descended from the conquistador Pedro Alonso Carrasco, who had several children by a woman descended from Don Cristóbal Paullo Inca. I am grateful to Berta Ares for this information.

54. On the origins of San Cristóbal Parish, which is also linked to Don Cristóbal Paullo Inca, the ancestor of Doña Juana, see chapter 4. Regarding the confraternity of Copacabana and its relationship with the indigenous population of Cuzco, see Ramos (2005c).

55. Will of Doña Juana Quispe Sisa Ñusta, Cuzco, October 30, 1635, ADC, PN, seventeenth century, Francisco de la Fuente 109, f. 322.

56. See chapter 5 on the regulations of inheritance law in Castile. A useful historical survey on the division of possessions and the issue of succession is Tomás y Valiente (1966). Although the Church and the state were not the only actors involved, for the purposes of our discussion we will limit ourselves to those two for now.

57. Burns's explanation is based on his reading of the sixth *Partida*. This position derives directly from Roman law. Ley III of the Leyes de Toro (1505),

which deals with wills, does not specifically refer to this issue. The matter is dealt with in those commentaries and interpretations that anticipate in extreme (and justified) detail a series of possibilities that could invalidate the will, assuming that the residuary legatee or the complete set of heirs was not named.

58. Accompaniment of the main figure in certain funerary settings might reflect this idea, as would the wearing of masks, decorations, paint, and clothing on some bodies and not on others, as well as the number, quality, and arrangement of the objects surrounding the body. See chapter 1 for examples.

59. Will of Tomás Palta, Lima, February 20, 1572, AGN, PN, sixteenth century, Marcos Franco de Esquivel 33, f. 311.

60. The town of Chicama lies north of Lima, in the jurisdiction of the Trujillo diocese.

61. Will of Don Juan Guaman, Lima, November 16, 1616, AGN, PN, seventeenth century, Francisco de Bustamante 232, f. 498v.

62. Will of María Guacacha, Lima, April 24, 1573, AGN, PN, sixteenth century, Juan Gutiérrez 71, f. 473.

63. Will of Inés Pérez in AGN, PN, sixteenth century, Juan Gutiérrez 71, f. 517. The Leyes de Toro established that if a father had no legitimate descendants and only illegitimate children, the latter could inherit his possessions even if he had legitimate ancestors. See Ley de Toro X (Álvarez Posadilla 1826, 108).

64. According to the Leyes de Toro, children of "damnable and punishable union," in addition to the children of clerics and friars, could not be heirs apparent to their mothers (Álvarez Posadilla 1826, 109).

65. Will of Juana Cusi Chimbo, Cuzco, April 18, 1600, ADC, PN, seventeenth century, Diego Gaitán 110, f. 316.

66. Will of Isabel Tocto, Cuzco, November 26, 1600, ADC, PN, seventeenth century, Juan de Olave 239, f. 718.

67. Will of Juan Enríquez Chuircho, Cuzco, June 14, 1588, ADC, PN, sixteenth century, Antonio Sánchez 25, f. 693.

68. See Ley de Toro XVI (Álvarez Posadilla 1826, 127–28).

69. Will of Doña Magdalena Sulcamo, Lima, June 12, 1606, AGN, PN, seventeenth century, Diego García 675, f. 29.

70. Will of Diego Tantaquileche, Lima, June 8, 1589, AGN, PN, sixteenth century, Bartolomé Rodríguez de Torquemada 141, f. 864v.

71. Will of Leonor Pagua, Lima, March 6, 1605, AGN, PN, seventeenth century, García López 1046, f. 222.

72. Will of Doña Ana de Carvajal, Lima, October 22, 1610, AGN, PN, seventeenth century, Rodrigo Gómez de Baeza 740, f. 711.

73. Will of Inés Jutuy, Lima, November 25, 1609, AGN, PN, seventeenth century, Aparicio y Urrutia 114, f. 120.

74. Will of Juana, Lima, October 8, 1579, AGN, PN, sixteenth century, Marcos Franco de Esquivel 34, f. 375.

75. Wills of María Curi, Lima, June 6, 1573, AGN, PN, Marcos Franco de Esquvel 33, f. 358; and Catalina Payco, Lima, August 1, 1577, AGN, PN, sixteenth century, Marcos Franco de Esquivel 33, f. 509.

76. This was also typical in other parts of the Catholic world (Cohn 1988; Eire 1995).

77. Will of María Quito, Lima, May 7, 1612, AGN, PN, Aparicio y Urrutia 114, f. 79.

78. Will of Doña Angelina Pilco Sisa Ñusta, Cuzco, September 23, 1623, ADC, Luis Diez de Morales 67, f. 1749.

79. Issues such as prestige and the need to prevent the splintering of the family fortune or family relations formed the basis of these decisions. Doña Juana Quispe Sisa Ñusta named her nephew as her universal heir, and Don Juan Gómez de Solís Ynga named his first cousin, a woman, as his universal heiress in 1670. Wills of Doña Juana Quispe Sisa Ñusta, ADC, PN, seventeenth century, Francisco de la Fuente 109, f. 322; and Don Juan Gómez de Solís Ynga, ADC, PN, seventeenth century, Lorenzo de Mesa Andueza 208, f. 990. In Lima, Pedro González Calambar, a childless widower, named his godmother as his universal heiress in 1611, in appreciation for her having fed and clothed him, while in 1644, Juana de Pays named a young man whom she had raised. Wills of Pedro González Calambar, Lima, December 16, 1611, AGN, PN, seventeenth century, Pedro González de Contreras 794, f. 2115; and Juana de Pays, Lima, April 18, 1644, AGN, PN, Francisco Ordóñez 1310, year 1645 notebook, f. 21.

80. Examples vary from the somewhat suspect to the clearly irregular. Luisa Gallega named the priest of the Lima parish of San Sebastián as her universal heir in 1578; in 1661, Andrés de Velasco, *cacique* of Latacunga (present-day Ecuador) and a resident of Lima, named Sergeant Don Juan Gaytán de Araujo, his landlord. Diego Machumbi, a farmer in the Lima valley, named Don Joseph de Vega, lifetime *regidor* of the city, who rented out his lands. Wills of Luisa Gallega, Lima, July 28, 1578, AGN, PN, sixteenth century, Juan Gutiérrez 73, f. 764; Andrés de Velasco, Lima, June 4, 1661, AGN, PN, seventeenth century, Alvaro Basilio de Ortiz 1322, f. 303; and Diego Machumbi, Los Reyes, April 22, 1663, AGN, PN, seventeenth century, Francisco Holguín 953, f. 179. In Cuzco, Juana Paico named her confessor as her universal heir in 1600, while Francisca Pilco named the son of a lifetime *regidor* of the city in 1643. Juana Paico, Cuzco, March 15, 1600, ADC, PN, seventeenth century, Diego Gaitán 110, f. 241v; and Francisca Pilco, Cuzco, April 29, 1643, ADC, PN, seventeenth century, Juan Flores de Bastidas 88, f. 280.

81. *Quipus* (knotted cords) and other forms of recordkeeping may have been used in conjunction with written documents. In the sixteenth century,

the Mercedarian missionary Fray Diego de Porres recommended that Indians used *quipus* for the writing of wills and inventories (Barriga 1933–1954, 4:179). On the role of objects as records of memory, see the works of Cummins (1998; 2002). On *quipus*, see, for example, Brokaw 2003; Pärssinen and Kiviharju 2004; Salomon (2004); Urton and Quilter (2002); and Urton (2003).

82. Unlike the towns surrounding Lima, there were no *caciques* in the city itself, only mayors of Indians. For ease of comparison with Cuzco, I have grouped them all under the heading "*caciques.*"

83. Pedro, a carpenter native to the central highlands who wrote his will in Lima in 1571, named another artisan as his executor, an Indian swordmaker. Will of Pedro, Lima, February 26, 1571, AGN, PN, sixteenth century, Juan de Salamanca 150, f. 553. In 1583, Francisco de Guascuanquiche, a fisherman in the town of Surco, charged his brother and his "companion Diego Xenquiam, an Indian," with executing his will. Will of Francisco de Guascuanquiche, Lima, June 14, 1583, AGN, PN, sixteenth century, Rodrigo Gómez de Baeza 43, f. 262.

84. In 1597, Juan Alonso, a tailor native to the northern province of Huamachuco and a resident of Lima, arranged for the master for whom he worked to be his executor. Will of Juan Alonso, Lima, January 17, 1597, AGN, PN, sixteenth century, Rodrigo Gómez de Baeza 56, f. 43. In Cuzco in 1642, Catalina Poco named Juan de Aliaga, a master barber, and Juan Alonso, a master tailor. Will of Catalina Poco, Cuzco, July 1, 1571, ADC, PN, sixteenth century, Antonio Sánchez 19, f. 1063. In Lima between the end of the sixteenth and the beginning of the seventeenth centuries, various women named Pedro Mayz and Don Diego Solsol, general language interpreters for the Real Audiencia, as their executors. See, for example, the wills of María Cuticunca, Lima, January 23, 1572, AGN, PN, sixteenth century, Marcos Franco de Esquivel 33, f. 285v; Catalina Yacsamurma, Lima, February 4, 1600, AGN, PN, seventeenth century, Diego Jiménez 103, f. 666v; Isabel Corzo, Lima, December 5, 1606, AGN, PN, seventeenth century, Rodrigo Gómez de Baeza 740, f. 784; and Leonor Pagua (see note 71).

85. Juan Gómez, a tailor native to Guamanga and a resident of Lima, named Cristóbal Sánchez, his godfather, as his executor, and he charged him with looking after the upbringing of his two godchildren. Will of Juan Gómez, Lima, November 11, 1632, AGN, PN, seventeenth century, Francisco Ordóñez 1308, f. 570v. Bartolomé Corimanya, condemned to death in Cuzco in 1630, requested that Antonio Maldonado, his godfather and executor, take charge of his son's upbringing. ADC, PN, seventeenth century, Domingo de Oro 260, f. 1719.

86. See, for example, the will of Francisca Cacsa, who named Fray Félix Ferrán, chaplain of the San Miguel confraternity in the convent church of San Agustín, as her executor. Lima, January 29, 1637, AGN, PN, seventeenth century, Antonio Tamayo 1858, f. 72.

87. We know that Juana Paico, daughter of a "heathen Indian" and a black man and a resident of Cuzco, named her confessor, the *licenciado* Fernán

Martín Olivas, as her executor (see note 80). See also the will of María Cayo, Cuzco, October 15, 1658, ADC, PN, seventeenth century, Lorenzo de Messa Andueza 182, f. 821.

88. In 1636 the barber Alonso Vilca chose the Dominican Fray Martín de Porras, already regarded as a saint in the city of Lima, as his executor. Will of Alonso Vilca, Lima, February 18, 1636, AGN, PN, seventeenth century, Pedro López de Mallea 985, f. 101. This choice may have been due to the fact that Vilca belonged to the same trade as Porras.

89. Pacomanta left slaves to this same woman. Will of Alonso Pacomanta, Lima, January 10, 1611, AGN, PN, seventeenth century, Rodrigo Gómez de Baeza 743, f. 54; and will of Joana Bello, Lima, July 17, 1611, AGN, PN, seventeenth century, Diego Nieto Maldonado 1199, f. 1310.

90. See the wills of Doña Catalina Chapo, Cuzco, October 24, 1612, ADC, PN, seventeenth century, Juan de Olave 244, f. 516; Isabel Rojo, a local storekeeper, Cuzco, August 13, 1617, ADC, PN, seventeenth century, Francisco Hurtado 114, f. 1673; and Francisca Pilco (see note 80).

91. See, for example, the will of Inés Chumbiyauya, "a prominent Indian of Pachacamac," who named a Spaniard who worked as treasurer of the Holy Crusade. Lima, September 28, 1613, AGN, PN, seventeenth century, Pedro Juan de Rivera 1612, f. 659. Cristóbal Yanchichumbi, second-in-charge in the town of Santiago de Surco, south of Lima, named a tithe collector as his executor. Lima, August 10, 1635, AGN, PN, seventeenth century, Antonio de Tamayo 1856, f. 736.

92. See, for example, the will of Doña María Mañari Ñusta, Cuzco, June 10, 1624, ADC, PN, seventeenth century, Francisco Hurtado 119, f. 708; and will of Don Pedro Gualpa, master carpenter, Cuzco, April 30, 1657, ADC, PN, seventeenth century, Martín López de Paredes 140, f. 1054.

93. See, for example, the case of Alonso Cayari, who left a Spaniard who rented out his lands in Santiago de Surco in charge of the chantry that he established and named him executor and universal heir. Lima, July 23, 1623, AGN, PN, seventeenth century, Pedro Juan de Rivera 1620, reg. 1623, f. 688. In Cuzco, Esteban Challco Viracocha Ynga named his primary creditor as his executor (see note 32).

94. A description may be found in "Causa hecha a los curacas, camachicos y mandones de el pueblo de San Francisco de Otuco anejo de la dotrina de San Pedro de Hacas [por] tener una yndia de mas de 35 años sin bautisar dedicada a el culto de la guaca y ydolos y otras quatro pequeñas asimesmo dedicadas al dicho culto y descubrimiento de 205 cuerpos cristianos." In Duviols (2003), 213–60).

95. I have attempted to give an initial answer to this question in studying the funerals of indigenous authorities (Ramos 2005a).

96. Caves in the hills where some Andean groups placed their relatives' remains. For an explanation of funerary caves in the Andes, see chapter 1.

97. On the Church, the colonial state, and the policy followed regarding the old graves, see chapter 3.

98. Will of Don Alonso Anchiguaman, Lima, July 28, 1578, AGN, PN, sixteenth century, Alonso de la Cueva 28, f. 210. Similarly, Don Cristóbal Xuto Chumbe, *cacique* of Lati, ordered in his will of 1580 that his body be buried in the town church (see note 12).

99. Based on other arrangements contained in his will and on the description of his possessions, it can be deduced that Don Bartolomé, like other men of his class, was familiar with Spanish culture and thus knew very well what to expect when he died. Will of Don Bartolomé Guamac Chumbi, Lima, March 20, 1577, AGN, PN, sixteenth century, Marcos Franco de Esquivel 33, f. 730.

100. Will of Don Cristóbal Guacay, Lima, May 6, 1628, AGN, PN, seventeenth century, Pedro López de Mallea 980, f. 221.

101. Will of Don Esteban Guacay, Lima, April 22, 1618, AGN, PN, seventeenth century, Cristóbal de Pineda 1534, f. 102.

102. In 1619, Don Martín Chaucaguaman, *cacique* of Sisicaya, instructed in his will that he was to be buried next to the high altar of his town church, in the spot where the remains of his daughters were interred. Sisicaya, May 17, 1619, AGN, PN, seventeenth century, Gabriel Martínez 1087, n.p. That same year, Don Rodrigo Rupaychagua, *cacique* of Guamantanga, arranged to be buried in the grave he held in Guamantanga's Church of Nuestra Señora de la Natividad. Huamantanga, January 14, 1619, National Library of Peru, Ms. BN784, 1619.

103. Will of Don Francisco Orco Supa, Cuzco, April 25, 1583, ADC, PN, sixteenth century, Antonio Sánchez 25, f. 500. See also the will of Don Juan Poma Yalli, governor of the marquisate of Oropesa and *cacique* of Guayllabamba, Cuzco, June 28, 1634, ADC, PN, seventeenth century, Domingo de Oro 264, f. 1010. In 1618, Doña Leonor Asto, wife of the "captain of the Colca Indians," from the town of the same name in the outskirts of Cuzco, arranged for her body to be buried in the convent of San Francisco and her bones then transferred to her hometown church. Will of Doña Leonor Asto, Cuzco, July 28, 1618, ADC, PN, seventeenth century, Joseph de Solórzano 304, f. 126.

104. Will of Don Juan Gualpa Sucso Ynga (see note 25).

105. The *fe de muerte* was a certificate issued by the parish notary, in which he confirmed the identity of the body before him. This statement comes at the end of Don Gonzalo's will (see note 23).

106. Don Martín Canchomacan, who was *cacique* of Pachacamac, was buried in Santa Ana; then in 1614 his daughter, Doña Catalina Bernarda Pasña, asked to be buried in her parents' grave. Will of Doña Catalina Bernarda Pasña, Lima, July 21, 1614, AGN, PN, seventeenth century, Francisco Hernández 823, f. 1351.

107. *Reducciones* located in the outskirts of Lima fell under the jurisdiction of the *corregimiento* of El Cercado (Lissón 1947, 5: no. 25, 266–69). Some Indian towns, such as Magdalena or Surco, were under the care of Franciscan friars. In Pachacamac, for several decades of the sixteenth century its population's religious indoctrination was in the hands of various people and religious orders who passed through the town or established themselves there temporarily (Rostworowski 1999, 49–59).

108. The name Callapiña is identified with the *caciques* of this town, to which the Incas pointed as their place of origin. One of the *quipucamayos* or persons responsible for recording and safeguarding the memory of the Incas has this name. See Discurso (2004 [1542], 363) and Vega (1974).

109. Chinchaycocha's population was headed by *caciques* of this name since possibly before the Spanish conquest. The document recording the grant of this territory as an *encomienda* mentions the *cacique* Lunato or Runato (Rostworowski 2005 [1975], 5:305, 309). For an assessment of the *encomienda* of Chinchaycocha from a Spanish viewpoint, see Puente Brunke and Janssen (1997).

110. AAL, Cofradías, Leg. 6, Cuad. 1.

111. See "Ordenanzas para los indios yungas repartidos a agricultores y vecinos de Lima" (Toledo 1989, 2: n. 73, 336).

112. See the will of Doña María Pasña, Lima, June 19, 1581, AGN, PN, sixteenth century, Marcos Franco de Esquivel 35, f. 131.

113. In 1602 the *encomiendas* of Cheto and Chasmal had only 184 taxpayers (Puente Brunke 1992, 479).

114. Will of Doña Constanza Caxachumbi, Lima, February 28, 1605, AGN, PN, seventeenth century, Rodrigo Gómez de Baeza 739, f. 266.

115. Don Cristóbal had the assurance of knowing that if one of his descendants died in Lima, he could be buried in this place. However, his own burial was in his town's main church. Will of Don Cristóbal Ticsi Luna Atoc, Los Reyes de Chinchaycocha, April 23, 1617, Archivo Departamental de Ayacucho, Notary Registers, seventeenth century, Bartolomé de Toro 1864, f. 1282.

116. Doña Constanza Caxachumbi understood this matter very well and also directed her efforts at supplementing her symbolic inheritance. When her brother Don Cristóbal Ticsi Luna Atoc made his will, he listed among his possessions a "golden jewel cast from my grandparents' and ancestors' coat of arms" that Doña Constanza had bequeathed him. Studies of the construction and reconstruction of indigenous symbols and emblems that took place during the colonial period may be found in Cummins (1998; 2002; 2005); Dean (1999); Estenssoro (2005); Gisbert (1994); Iriarte (1993); Mesa and Gisbert (1982); Majluf (2005); Phipps (2005); Ramos (2005b); Rowe (1951); Stastny (1993); and Wuffarden (2005).

117. Because there are differing versions of the fate of Huayna Capac's body, it is likely that what Don Cristóbal handed over was not his father's corpse

but rather a representation of it. On the representation of the deceased's body in pre-Hispanic Peru, see chapter 1.

118. Esquivel y Navia (1980, 2:33) affirms that the image of Nuestra Señora de Guadalupe was placed in the church of San Francisco in October 1617, amid solemn celebrations.

119. Will of Doña Magdalena Quispe Sisa Ñusta, Cuzco (see note 48); will of Don Fernando Ynga, Cuzco, July 11, 1646, ADC, PN, seventeenth century, Juan Flores de Bastidas 91, f. 908. In 1586, Doña Gerónima Tocto affirmed that "the legitimate children and grandchildren and wives of Don Cristóbal Paullo" were to be buried in this chapel. The date precedes the site's consecration to Nuestra Señora de Guadalupe, and this following is not mentioned in the document. Cuzco, March 23, 1586, ADC, PN, sixteenth century, Pedro de la Carrera Ron 4, f. 663. Mestizo descendants of the Incas were also buried in this chapel: in 1627, Bernardino de Mesa, descendant of the conquistador Alonso de Mesa and an Incan noblewoman, requested burial there by virtue of being a successor of Paullo. Cuzco, March 3, 1627, ADC, PN, seventeenth century, Luis Diez de Morales 71, f. 579. Doña Juana Soto Carrillo Ynga, also a mestiza, requested a similar burial. Cuzco, November 11, 1635, ADC, PN, seventeenth century, Francisco de la Fuente 109, f. 578. Juan Maldonado Cornejo, a mestizo interpreter, declared that his mother, "as a descendant of Topa Amaro Ynga," was buried in that chapel. Cuzco, May 21, 1657, ADC, PN, seventeenth century, Juan Flores de Bastidas 98, f. 266.

120. Don Francisco Hilaquita Inga and other descendants of Atahualpa were buried in the chapel of Nuestra Señora del Rosario in Santo Domingo. Cuzco, October 27, 1623, ADC, PN, seventeenth century, Francisco de Hurtado 118, f. 1559.

121. Don Joan Pascac Ynga and his in-laws endowed a chapel dedicated to Saint John the Baptist in the church of La Merced, which they established as their burial place. In 1590, Don Joan expected that other "yngas from the city" would form a confraternity on this site. Will of Don Joan Pascac Ynga, Cuzco, August 26, 1590, ADC, PN, sixteenth century, Antonio Sánchez 27, f. 1099.

122. A descendant of Huayna Capac and Paullo, Doña Angelina Pillco Sisa was buried in the chapel of Nuestra Señora de la Consolación in the church of the Society of Jesus. Cuzco, April 29, 1643, ADC, PN, seventeenth century, Juan Flores de Bastidas 88, f. 280.

123. See chapter 4. Lowry (1991) extensively analyzes the conflict. The sources for these episodes may be found in *El Amigo del Clero* (1909) and Lissón (1944, 3: no. 16). I have studied the role of the following of Nuestra Señora de Copacabana as a cultural intermediary (Ramos 2005c).

124. Wills of Pedro de Lesana, Lima, November 3, 1592, AGN, PN, sixteenth century, Rodríguez Gómez de Baeza 52, f. 1073; and Lima, December 8, 1603, AGN, PN, seventeenth century, Cristóbal de Pineda 1534, f. 347.

125. Will of María de Jesús, Lima, August 4, 1598, AGN, PN, sixteenth century, Diego Jiménez 102, f. 836v.

126. Will of Francisca Chimbo Urma, Cuzco, September 26, 1651, ADC, PN, seventeenth century, Lorenzo de Messa Andueza 177, f. 1672.

127. For an explanation of how the confraternities built these funeral vaults inside the convent church of San Francisco de Lima, famous today for its catacombs, see San Cristóbal (1988, 132–34). An illustration of the vaults appears in Ramírez del Villar (1974, 94–95).

128. Will of Elena de Barrionuevo, Lima, December 1624?, AGN, PN, seventeenth century, Bernardo de Quiroz 222, f. 5.

129. Will of Domingo Benegas, Lima, April 15, 1626, AGN, PN, seventeenth century, Pedro López de Mallea 978, f. 295.

130. Will of Lucía Cusi, Lima, September 26, 1624, AGN, PN, seventeenth century, Antonio Tamayo 1851, f. 396.

131. Unfortunately the document does not indicate what these services were. Will of Inés Chumbe, Cuzco, February 25, 1638, ADC, PN, seventeenth century, Alonso Beltrán Luzero 5, f. 159.

132. Will of Francisco Rimasca, Cuzco, October 10, 1649, ADC, PN, seventeenth century, Martín López de Paredes 132, f. 399; and will of Don Pedro Gualpa, Cuzco, April 30, 1657, ADC, PN, seventeenth century, Martín López de Paredes 140, f. 1054.

133. Will of Miguel Quito, Cuzco, August 9, 1640, ADC, PN, seventeenth century, Joseph Navarro 236, f. 792. Sañoc or Sanoc was one of the Cuzco *ayllus* who were not members of royalty. In the celebration of the Citua festival, a massive pre-Hispanic purification ritual, members of this *ayllu* would come out shouting toward the Incan province of Antisuyo (Molina 1989 [1575?], 75). Bauer (2000, 45, 47, 50–51) maintains that the Sañoc *ayllu* was in charge of caring for the Antisuyo *guacas*.

134. Will of Joan Guamani, Cuzco, April 7, 1586, ADC, PN, sixteenth century, Pedro de la Carrera Ron 4, f. 668v.

135. Hinojosa was one of the conquistadors of La Plata, present-day Sucre in Bolivia (Puente Brunke 1992, 101, 370).

136. The link between the two was perhaps more complicated, given that Doña María's children were apparently not also the *cacique*'s: they were not named as heirs, as would have been their right as legitimate children. Both had the last name Hinojosa, which could indicate that their father was the *encomendero*. Will of Doña María Chimbo Ocllo, Cuzco, February 20, 1582, ADC, PN, sixteenth century, Antonio Sánchez 24, f. 215.

137. Will of Leonor Chimbo Ocllo, Cuzco, December 19, 1588, ADC, PN, sixteenth century, Alonso de Guerrero 5, f. 923. Pedro Arias de Ávila was the *encomendero* of Corca, Manaso, Vilque, Palpacalla, Pomacanchi, and Pomachape (Puente Brunke 1992, 351, 362, 368, 372).

138. Will of Mariana Urbina, Lima, September 6, 1636, AGN, PN, seventeenth century, Cristóbal Rodríguez 1647, f. 284; and will of Doña Isabel Chimbo Quipe, Cuzco, March 27, 1633, ADC, PN, seventeenth century, Luis Diez de Morales 75, f. 897.

139. Will of Miguel Mesquirán, Lima, September 20, 1637, AGN, PN, seventeenth century, Francisco de Bustamante 246, f. 329.

140. According to Covarrubias (2003 [1611], 271), the *calvario* was an ossuary that, in Spain, could eventually become a site of prayer. Juana Chumbi arranged to be buried in the Monte Calvario of the Santa Ana hospital "because I am poor, since the custom is to bury other poor people who die in said hospital." Will of Juana Chumbi, Lima, February 13, 1630, AGN, PN, seventeenth century, Antonio de Tamayo 1853, f. 46.

141. In 1649, for example, Joana Sulla requested that the low cross be carried at her burial because she was poor, but she wanted her grave to be in the main church. Cuzco, March 10, 1649, ADC, PN, seventeenth century, Juan Flores de Bastidas 94, f. 81. In 1651, Don Esteban Viracocha Ynga asked his executors to bury him wherever they deemed fit in the church of the hospital for natives, "given how poor I am." Cuzco, March 23, 1651, ADC, PN, seventeenth century, Juan Flores de Bastidas 94, f. 68.

142. See, for example, the funeral arrangements of Doña Francisca Ignacia de Carvajal, daughter of the *cacique* of Callao. In 1670 she instructed that her funeral procession be headed by the high cross, priest, and sacristan of her parish and six additional priests wearing surplices. Will of Doña Francisca Ignacia de Carvajal (see note 39).

143. Will of María Sánchez, Lima, July 12, 1589, AGN, PN, sixteenth century, Rodrigo Gómez de Baeza 49, f. 968.

144. AGN, PN, sixteenth century, Cristóbal de Pineda 1534, f. 102.

145. AGN, PN, seventeenth century, Francisco Holguín 953, f. 179. Without doubt, when a *cacique* or prominent figure was buried in his or her hometown, more elaborate rituals were possible. See, for example, the instructions for the funeral of Don Martín Chaucaguaman, *cacique* of Sisicaya (see note 102); and those in the will of Don Cristóbal Suna, *cacique* of Maras, Cuzco, April 23, 1655, ADC, PN, seventeenth century, Lorenzo de Messa Andueza 183, f. 759.

146. Apparently in burials of prominent Indians it was expected that the priest would wear a cope. See, for example, the wills of Joan Carlos Guaman, Cuzco, April 19, 1657, ADC, PN, seventeenth century, Martín López de Paredes 140, f. 1056; Don Baltazar Sona, Cuzco, February 14, 1667, ADC, PN, seventeenth century, Martín López de Paredes 149, f. 665; and Don Lorenzo Paucar, Cuzco, December 18, 1650, ADC, PN, seventeenth century, Lorenzo de Messa Andueza 176, f. 256.

147. Throughout the seventeenth century, testators generally requested that four clerics take part in their funeral procession, although some, such as

Luisa Mayguay, asked for ten. Will of Luisa Mayguay, Lima, April 9, 1620, AGN, PN, seventeenth century, Francisco de Bustamante 234, f. 151.

148. Will of Catalina Payco (see note 75).

149. Will of Ynés Quispe, Lima, September 16, 1623, AGN, PN, seventeenth century, Antonio de Tamayo 1851, f. 143. Others, such as Melchor Payta, a tailor, arranged for twelve poor men—probably evoking the Apostles—to attend his burial and for each one to be given a small sum. Will of Melchor Payta, Lima, August 11, 1631, AGN, PN, seventeenth century, Antonio de Tamayo 1854, f. 506.

150. Will of Catalina Carua, Lima, February 16, 1635, AGN, PN, seventeenth century, Antonio de Tamayo 1856, f. 84v.

151. The clause reads "all Indians." One assumes that it means "the poor."

152. In 1639, Don Francisco Mango Pongo, *cacique* and second-in-charge in the town of Caycay, in the diocese of Cuzco, arranged a funeral banquet as alms for the poor, in which ten sheep and quantities of *chuño* and corn were to be consumed. Cuzco, May 14, 1639, ADC, PN, seventeenth century, Alonso Beltrán Lucero 6, f. 428.

153. For example, Don Juan de Borja Manchipula, successor to the *cacicazgo* of Callao, included a clause in his will of 1622 directing that "among the best and most outstanding of my possessions be given to Father Fray Luis de Espinosa lay brother of Saint Francis two hundred pesos in eight-real coins so that he may do with them as I have instructed him. I command that they be turned over to him as soon as I die." Will of Don Juan de Borja Manchipula, Lima, November 9, 1662, AGN, PN, seventeenth century, Alonso Durán Vicentelo 422, n.p. Also, in her will written in Cuzco in 1624, Doña María Mañari Ñusta refers thus to arrangements known only to her confessor: "I declare that an account and record in the sum of four hundred pesos more or less is in the possession of the above-said Doña Magdalena my mother; I order that said sum and record be turned over to my confessor Father Fray Pedro de Vargas of the order of Saint Francis so that he may do with it as I have instructed him and ease my conscience's burden." Will of Doña María Mañari Ñusta (see note 92).

154. Will of Lucía Ruiz, Lima, July 21, 1613, AGN, PN, seventeenth century, Agustín de Atencia 168, f. 285; and will of Doña Ana Quispe Asarpay Coya (see note 46).

155. Will of Domingo de Cárdenas, Lima, October 1, 1601, AGN, PN, seventeenth century, Ramiro Bote 228, f. 497.

156. See chapter 3 on the idea of purgatory. See also Van Deusen (2004, 32–49). For a modern example, see Gudeman (1988).

157. AGN, PN, sixteenth century, Marcos Franco de Esquivel 33, f. 730. This does not seem to have been a simple notarial formula.

158. See, for example, the request that appears in 1602 in the will of Juana Siclla, a resident of Cuzco, ADC, PN, seventeenth century, Francisco de la Fuente 106, f. 57; the will of Diego Yucra, a native of Maras in Cuzco, written in 1624, ADC, PN, seventeenth century, Francisco Hurtado 119, n.p.; or that of the tailor Juan Alonso (see note 84).

159. Will of Doña María Cissa, Cuzco, July 24, 1633, ADC, PN, seventeenth century, Alonso Beltrán Luzero 4, f. 568.

160. Will of Pedro Guaman, Lima, March 31, 1629, AGN, PN, seventeenth century, Antonio de Givaja 733, f. 1150.

161. AGN, PN, seventeenth century, Antonio de Tamayo 1851, f. 485v.

162. AGN, PN, seventeenth century, Antonio de Tamayo 1853, f. 46.

163. Will of Lucía Matías, Lima, November 29, 1613, AGN, PN, seventeenth century, González de Balcázar 761, f. 1120.

164. See the will of Doña María Mallqui, Cuzco, March 30, 1642, ADC, PN, seventeenth century, Juan Flores de Bastidas 88, f. 559. Because of its individual nature, the "lonely soul" became an object of manipulation for those who desired protection through means such as witchcraft (Estenssoro 2003).

165. In his study of inheritances left to the soul in Spanish law, Maldonado y Fernández del Torco (1944, 96–97) denies a direct correlation in Spain between the portion of possessions retained by the deceased and the portion that, according to law, he or she should donate for the good of his or her soul, to which Maldonado ascribes an essentially spiritual value based on a "popular and widespread belief that recognizes the practice of an act of generosity toward a religious end as the accomplishment of a meritorious work." The author not only leaves hanging the analysis of the relationship between material goods and the benefits expected by donors but also omits the Christianizing phase of funerary offerings.

166. Will of Martín Orcoguaranca, Cuzco, May 12, 1586, ADC, PN, sixteenth century, Pedro de la Carrera Ron 4, f. 675v.

167. Will of Magdalena Caruayaco, Cuzco, September 19, 1586, ADC, PN, sixteenth century, Pedro de la Carrera Ron 4, f. 689.

168. Will of Diego Payco, Cuzco, February 24, 1586, ADC, PN, sixteenth century, Pedro de la Carrera Ron 4, f. 661. *Avasca* was a somewhat coarse fabric.

169. On the importance of fabrics in funerary offerings, see chapter 1. On the role of textiles in Andean societies, see Murra (1975).

170. Will of Luis Pérez, Lima, May 27, 1617, AGN, PN, seventeenth century, Cristóbal de Pineda 1533, f. 56.

171. Will of Doña Juana Ñusta, Lima, April 16, 1670, AGN, PN, seventeenth century, Nicolás de Ovalle Pizarro 1337, registro 3, f. 48. Santa Rosa was canonized the following year.

172. AGN, PN, seventeenth century, Gaspar de Monzón 1156, f. 66v. Doña Francisca Manchipula was the first mother superior of the Copacabana

beguinage, founded in 1676 to promote the religious life of indigenous women; it opened its doors in 1696 (García Irigoyen 1906, 1:213). On religious houses for women in Lima and other parts of the Spanish-American world, see the work of Nancy Van Deusen (2001).

173. Will of Doña Magdalena Quispe Sisa Ñusta (see note 48).

174. ADC, PN, seventeenth century, Juan Flores de Bastidas 91, f. 908.

175. Will of Doña Inés Chuqui Ñusta, Cuzco, November 29, 1646, ADC, PN, seventeenth century, Lorenzo de Messa Andueza 171, f. 2002.

176. Will of Don Lorenzo Paucar (see note 146).

177. Wills of María Panti, Cuzco, December 13, 1651, ADC, PN, seventeenth century, Lorenzo de Messa Andueza 177, f. 2005; and Cuzco, January 3, 1667, ADC, PN, seventeenth century, Lorenzo de Messa Andueza 203, f. 301.

Conclusion

1. See, for example, the complaint lodged by *caciques* and ordinary Indians from the town of Ccapi in the province of Chilques y Masques (the present-day province of Paruro, Cuzco) against their priest, the *bachiller* Juan Gutiérrez Censio. Among other charges, the *caciques* alleged that Gutiérrez refused to bury the poor, let several Indians die without the sacraments or confession, and did not come to collect and bury the body of a man who died outside the town (AAL, Apelaciones Cuzco, Leg. 6, 1645). For the Lima diocese, see the inquiry made into the case of the *bachiller* Joseph de Vargas, a priest's assistant in the Indian parish of San Mateo de Huánchor, who was accused of not helping those on their deathbed die properly and of not coming to collect and bury the bodies of Indians who died on the riverbank opposite the town (AAL, Visitas Pastorales, Leg. 9, Exp. XVIII, 1648).

2. On the work of Juan Pérez Bocanegra and its importance for the spread of Christian funerary ritual among Indian parish priests and the Quechua-speaking population, see chapter 4.

3. The donation deed can be found in ADC, PN, seventeenth century, Joseph de Solórzano 304, f. 429.

4. This statement excludes the status of children, which is still insufficiently understood in this period. Despite what we have asserted, the pattern of single burials was not the rule, for a person's remains could be placed on top of those of another, and the oldest could be moved to make space for new burials. The desire expressed by Diego de Almagro the Younger (see chapter 2) and the way in which bodies were arranged in the convent vaults corroborate this assertion (San Cristóbal 1988, 132–34).

5. Captain Domingo Francisco, a man described as an Indian, had been born in the Lima neighborhood originally known as the *reducción* El Cercado.

Domingo Francisco did not come from the Indian elite or from a family of *caciques*. He died a prosperous man, farmer, and landowner and also boasted a military title. Will and *fe de muerte* of Captain Domingo Francisco, Los Reyes, August 1653, AGN, Derecho Indígena, Leg. 7, Cuad. 130, f. 6.

   6. See chapter 6; Ramos (2005a).

BIBLIOGRAPHY

Abbott, Don Paul. 1996. *Rhetoric in the New World: Rhetorical Theory and Practice in Colonial Spanish America*. Columbia: University of South Carolina Press.

Acosta, José de. 1984–1987 [1588]. *De Procuranda Indorum Salute*. 2 vols. *Corpus Hispanorum de Pace*. Madrid: Consejo Superior de Investigaciones Científicas.

———. 1954 [1590]. Historia natural y moral de las Indias. In *Obras del P. José de Acosta,* edited by Francisco Mateos, S.J. Madrid: Atlas.

———. 2002 [1590]. *Historia natural y moral de las Indias*. Madrid: Dastin.

Adorno, Rolena. 1989. *Cronista y príncipe: La obra de don Felipe Guaman Poma de Ayala*. Lima: Pontificia Universidad Católica del Perú.

Alaperrine-Bouyer, Monique. 2007. *La educación de las elites indígenas en el Perú colonial*. Lima: Instituto Francés de Estudios Andinos, Instituto Riva Agüero, Instituto de Estudios Peruanos.

Albornoz, Cristóbal de. 1989 [1583?]. Instrucción para descubrir todas las guacas del Piru y sus camayos y haziendas. In *Fábulas y mitos de los incas,* edited by P. Duviols and H. Urbano. Madrid: Historia 16.

Alonso Sagaseta, Alicia. 1989. Las momias de los Incas: su función y realidad social. *Revista Española de Antropología Americana* 19:109–35.

Álvarez Posadilla, Juan. 1826. *Comentarios a las Leyes de Toro según su espíritu y el de la legislación de España*. Madrid: Imprenta de don Antonio Martínez.

El Amigo del Clero. 1909. Documentos para la historia, Nuestra Señora de Copacabana. Lima: Imprenta San Pedro.

Andrushko, Valerie A. 2007. The Bioarchaeology of Inka Imperialism in the Heartland: A Regional Analysis of Prehistoric Burials from Cuzco, Peru. Ph.D. dissertation, Anthropology, University of California, Santa Barbara.

Andrushko, Valerie A., Elva C. Torres Pino, and Viviana Bellifemine. 2006. The Burials at Sacsahuaman and Chokepukio: A Bioarchaeological Case

Study of Imperialism from the Capital of the Inca Empire. *Ñawpa Pacha* 28:63–92.

Angulo, Domingo. 1935. Notas y monografías para la historia del barrio de San Lázaro de la ciudad de Lima. In *Monografías históricas de la ciudad de Lima.* Lima: Librería e Imprenta Gil.

Anónimo Jesuita. 1968. Relación de las costumbres antiguas de los naturales del Pirú. In *Crónicas peruanas de interés indígena,* edited by F. Esteve Barba. Madrid: Atlas.

Anonymous. 1999 [1479?]. *Arte de bien morir y breve confesionario (Zaragoza, Pablo Hurus: c. 1479–84). Según el incunable de la Biblioteca del Escorial, Medio Maravedí,* edited by Francisco Gago Jover. Madrid: José J. Olañeta, Universitat de les Illes Balears.

Araníbar, Carlos. 1969. Notas sobre la necropompa entre los incas. *Revista del Museo Nacional (Lima, Perú)* 36:108–42.

Ares, Berta. 2005. "Un borracho de chicha y vino": La construcción social del mestizo (Perú, siglo XVI). In *Mezclado y sospechoso: Movilidad e identidades, España y América (siglos XVI–XVIII),* edited by G. Salinero. Madrid: Casa de Velázquez.

Ariès, Phillipe. 1977. *L'homme devant la mort.* Paris: Éditions du Seuil.

Arkush, Elizabeth, and Charles Stanish. 2005. Interpreting Conflict in the Ancient Andes: Implications for the Archaeology of Warfare. *Current Anthropology* 46 (1):3–28.

Armas, Fernando. 1953. *Cristianización del Perú (1532–1600).* Seville: Escuela de Estudios Hispanoamericanos.

Arriaga, Pablo Josef de. 1968 [1621]. Extirpación de la idolatría del Pirú. In *Crónicas peruanas de interés indígena,* edited by F. Esteve Barba. Madrid: Atlas.

Arriaza, Bernardo T., Felipe Cárdenas-Arroyo, Ekkehard Kleiss, and John W. Verano. 1998. South American Mummies: Culture and Disease. In *Mummies, Disease, and Ancient Cultures,* edited by T. A. Cockburn, E. Cockburn, and T. Reyman. Cambridge: Cambridge University Press.

Arrizabalaga, Jon. 1999. Poor Relief in Counter-Reformation Castile: An Overview. In *Health Care and Relief in Counter-Reformation Europe,* edited by O. P. Grell et al. London: Routledge.

Arrom, Silvia Marina. 2000. *Containing the Poor: The Mexico City Poor House, 1774–1871.* Durham, N.C.: Duke University Press.

Ashmore, Wendy, and Pamela L. Geller. 2005. Social Dimensions of Mortuary Space. In *Interacting with the Dead: Perspectives on Mortuary Archaeology for the New Millennium,* edited by G. F. M. Rakita et al. Gainesville: University of Florida Press.

Assadourian, Carlos Sempat. 1995. *Transiciones al sistema colonial andino.* Lima: Instituto de Estudios Peruanos.

Ávila, Francisco de. 1648. *Tratado de los evangelios que nuestra madre la iglesia nos propone en todo el año desde la primera dominica de adviento hasta la ultima missa de difuntos, santos de España y añadidos en el nuevo rezado. Explicase el evangelio y se pone un sermon en cada uno, en las lenguas castellana, y general destos indios deste reyno del Peru y en ellos donde da lugar la materia se refutan los errores de la gentilidad de dichos indios.* 2 vols. Lima: Imprenta de Pedro de Cabrera.

Azevedo, Paulo de. 1982. *Cusco ciudad histórica: Continuidad y cambio.* Lima: UNESCO, PNUD, Peisa.

Barnard, Alan, and Jonathan Spencer. 2002. *Encyclopedia of Social and Cultural Anthropology.* London: Routledge.

Barnes, Monica. 1992. Catechisms and Confessionarios: Distorting Mirrors of Andean Societies. In *Andean Cosmologies through Time: Persistence and Emergence,* edited by R. V. H. Dover, K. E. Seibold, and J. McDowell. Bloomington: Indiana University Press.

Barraud, Cécile. 1994. *Of Relations and the Dead: Four Societies Viewed from the Angle of Their Exchanges.* Translated by S. J. Suffern. Oxford: Berg. Original edition, Des relations et des morts.

Barriga, Víctor M. 1933–1954. *Los mercedarios en el Perú en el siglo XVI. Documentos inéditos del Archivo General de Indias.* 5 vols. Rome and Arequipa: Madre di Dio, La Colmena.

Bataillon, Marcel. 1950. *Erasmo y España. Estudios sobre la historia espiritual del siglo XVI.* Translated by A. Alatorre. 2 vols. México: Fondo de Cultura Económica.

Bauer, Brian. 1992. *The Development of the Inca State.* Austin: University of Texas Press.

———. 1998. *The Sacred Landscape of the Inca: The Cusco Ceque System.* Austin: University of Texas Press.

———. 2000. *El espacio sagrado de los incas: El sistema de ceques del Cuzco.* Cuzco: Centro de Estudios Regionales Andinos "Bartolomé de Las Casas."

———. 2004. *Ancient Cuzco: Heartland of the Inca.* Austin: University of Texas Press.

Bawden, Garth. 2004. The Art of Moche Politics. In *Andean Archaeology,* edited by H. Silverman. Oxford: Blackwell.

Beaudoin, Steven M. 2007. *Poverty in World History, Themes in World History.* London: Routledge.

Béjar, Raimundo. 1976. Un entierro en T'oqokachi, Cusco. *Revista del Museo Nacional* 42:145–51.

Benito, José Antonio, ed. 2006. *Libro de visitas de Santo Toribio de Mogrovejo (1593–1605), Colección Clásicos Peruanos.* Lima: Pontificia Universidad Católica del Perú.

Benson, Elizabeth P., and Anita G. Cook, eds. 2001. *Ritual Sacrifice in Ancient Peru*. Austin: University of Texas Press.

Benton, Lauren. 2002. *Law and Colonial Cultures: Legal Regimes in World History, 1400–1900*. Cambridge: Cambridge University Press.

Bernales Ballesteros, Jorge. 1972. *Lima, la ciudad y sus monumentos*. Seville: Escuela de Estudios Hispanoamericanos.

Bestard Camps, Joan. 1992. La estrechez del lugar. Reflexiones en torno a las estrategias matrimoniales cercanas. In *Poder, familia y consanguinidad en la España del Antiguo Régimen*, edited by F. C. Jiménez and J. H. Franco. Barcelona: Anthropos.

Betanzos, Juan de. 2004 [1551]. *Suma y narración de los incas*. Madrid: Polifemo.

Bible. *The New American Bible for Catholics*. Nashville: Thomas Nelson Publishers.

Bloch, Maurice, and J. H. Parry, eds. 1982. *Death and the Regeneration of Life*. 1st ed. Cambridge: Cambridge University Press.

Boone, Elizabeth H. 1994. Writing and Recording Knowledge. In *Writing without Words: Alternative Literacies in Mesoamerica and the Andes*, edited by E. H. Boone and W. D. Mignolo. Durham, N.C.: Duke University Press.

Boone, Elizabeth H., and Tom Cummins, eds. 1998. *Native Traditions in the Postconquest World*. Washington, D.C.: Dumbarton Oaks.

Borges, Pedro. 1960. *Métodos misionales en la cristianización de América, siglo XVI*. Madrid: Consejo Superior de Investigaciones Científicas.

Bossy, John. 1985. *Christianity and the West, 1400–1700*. Oxford: Oxford University Press.

Bourdieu, Pierre. 1977. *Outline of a Theory of Practice*. Cambridge: Cambridge University Press.

———. 1990. *The Logic of Practice*. Stanford: Stanford University Press.

Bourget, Steve. 2001. Children and Ancestors: Ritual Practices at the Moche Site of Huaca de la Luna, North Coast of Peru. In *Ritual Sacrifice in Ancient Peru*, edited by E. P. Benson and A. G. Cook. Austin: University of Texas Press.

———. 2006. *Sex, Death, and Sacrifice in Moche Religion and Visual Culture*. Austin: University of Texas Press.

Brading, David A. 1991. *The First America: The Spanish Monarchy, Creole Patriots, and the Liberal State, 1492–1866*. Cambridge: Cambridge University Press.

Brokaw, Galen. 2003. The Poetics of Khipu Historiography: Felipe Guaman Poma de Ayala and the Khipukamayuqs from Pacariqtambo. *Latin American Research Review* 38 (3):111–47.

Brown, Jonathan. 1998. *Painting in Spain, 1500–1700*. New Haven: Yale University Press.

Brown, Peter. 1981. *The Cult of the Saints: Its Rise and Function in Latin Christianity*. Chicago and London: University of Chicago Press.

———. 2000. The Decline of the Empire of God: Amnesty, Penance, and the Afterlife from Late Antiquity to the Middle Ages. In *Last Things: Death and the Apocalypse in the Middle Ages,* edited by C. W. Bynum and P. Freedman. Philadelphia: University of Pennsylvania Press.

Buikstra, Jane E. 1995. Tombs for the Living . . . or . . . for the Dead: The Osmore Ancestors. In *Tombs for the Living: Andean Mortuary Practices,* edited by T. D. Dillehay. Washington, D.C.: Dumbarton Oaks.

Buntinx, Gustavo, and Luis Eduardo Wuffarden. 1991. Incas y reyes españoles en la pintura colonial peruana: La estela de Garcilaso. *Márgenes: Encuentro y Debate* 8:151–210.

Burga, Manuel. 1988. *Nacimiento de una utopía: Muerte y resurrección de los Incas.* Lima: Instituto de Apoyo Agrario.

Burger, Richard L. 1992. *Chavín and the Origins of Andean Civilization.* London: Thames and Hudson.

Burger, Richard L., Craig Morris, Ramiro Matos Mendieta, Joanne Pillsbury, and Jeffrey Quilter, eds. 2007. *Variations in the Expression of Inka Power: A Symposium at Dumbarton Oaks, 18 and 19 October 1997.* Washington, D.C.: Dumbarton Oaks.

Burkhart, Louise. 1989. *The Slippery Earth: Nahua-Christian Moral Dialogue in Sixteenth-Century Mexico.* Tucson: University of Arizona Press.

———. 1996. *Holy Wednesday: A Nahua Drama from Early Colonial Mexico.* Philadelphia: University of Pennsylvania Press.

———. 1998. Pious Performances: Christian Pageantry and Native Identity in Early Colonial Mexico. In *Native Traditions in the Postconquest World : A Symposium at Dumbarton Oaks, 2nd through 4th October 1992,* edited by E. H. Boone and T. Cummins. Washington, D.C.: Dumbarton Oaks.

Burns, Kathryn. 1999. *Colonial Habits: Convents and the Spiritual Economy of Cuzco, Peru.* Durham, N.C.: Duke University Press.

———. 2005. Notaries, Truth, and Consequences. *American Historical Review* 110 (2): 350–79.

Burns, Robert I., ed. 2001. *Las Siete Partidas.* 5 vols. Philadelphia: University of Pennsylvania Press.

Bynum, Caroline Walker. 1995. *The Resurrection of the Body in Western Christianity, 200–1336. Lectures on the History of Religions.* New York: Columbia University Press.

Bynum, Caroline Walker, and Paul Freedman, eds. 2000. *Last Things: Death and the Apocalypse in the Middle Ages.* Philadelphia: University of Pennsylvania Press.

Cahill, David. 1995. Financing Health Care in the Viceroyalty of Peru: The Hospitals of Lima in the Late Colonial Period. *The Americas* 52 (2): 123–54.

Calancha, Antonio de la. 1974 [1638]. *Corónica Moralizada del orden de San Agustín.* 6 vols. Lima: Ignacio Prado Pastor.

Cañeque, Alejandro. 1996. Theater of Power: Writing and Representing the Auto de Fe in Colonial Mexico. *The Americas* 52 (3):321–43.

———. 2004. *The King's Living Image: The Culture and Politics of Viceregal Power in Colonial Mexico*. London: Routledge.

Canter, David. 2002. The Violated Body. In *The Body*, edited by S. T. Sweeney and I. Holder. Cambridge: Cambridge University Press.

Carmichael, Patrick H. 1995. Nasca Burial Patterns: Social Structure and Mortuary Ideology. In *Tombs for the Living: Andean Mortuary Practices*, edited by T. D. Dillehay. Washington, D.C.: Dumbarton Oaks.

Caro Baroja, Julio. 1985 [1978]. *Las formas complejas de la vida religiosa. Religión, sociedad y carácter en la España de los siglos XVI y XVII*. Madrid: Sarpe.

Carrithers, Michael, ed. 1985. *The Category of the Person: Anthropology, Philosophy, History*. Cambridge: Cambridge University Press.

Castañeda Delgado, Paulino. 1971. La condición miserable del indio y sus privilegios. *Anuario de Estudios Americanos* 28:245–335.

Caviedes, César N. 2001. *El Niño in History: Storming through the Ages*. Gainesville: University Press of Florida.

Celestino, Olinda. 1992. Les confréries religieuses à Lima. *Archives de Sciences Sociales des Religions* 37 (80):167–91.

Celestino, Olinda, and Albert Meyers. 1981. *Las cofradías en el Perú: región central*. Frankfurt am Main: Veuvuert.

Cerrón Palomino, Rodolfo. 1991. Un texto desconocido del quechua costeño (s. XVI). *Revista Andina* 9 (2):393–413.

Chapman, John. 2000. *Fragmentation in Archaeology. People, Places and Broken Objects in the Prehistory of South-eastern Europe*. London: Routledge.

Chara Zereceda, Oscar, and Viviana Caparó Gil. 1998. *Iglesias del Cusco: Historia y arquitectura*. Cuzco: Editorial Universitaria UNSAAC.

Charney, Paul. 1989. The Destruction and Reorganization of Indian Society in the Lima Valley, Peru, 1532–1824. Ph.D. dissertation, History, University of Texas, Austin.

———. 2001. *Indian Society in the Valley of Lima, Peru, 1532–1824*. Lanham, Md.: University Press of America.

Chiffoleau, Jacques. 1980. *La comptabilité de l'au-delà. Les hommes, la mort et la religion dans la région d'Avignon à la fin du moyen âge (vers 1320–1480)*. Rome: École Française de Rome.

Christian, William. 1981. *Local Religion in Sixteenth-Century Spain*. Princeton: Princeton University Press.

Cieza de León, Pedro de. 1984a. *Obras Completas*, edited by C. Sáenz de Santa María. 3 vols. Vol. 1. *La Crónica del Perú*. First, Second, and Third Parts. *Monumenta Hispano-Indiana*. Madrid: Consejo Superior de Investigaciones Científicas, Instituto Gonzalo Fernández de Oviedo.

———. 1984b [1553]. *Crónica del Perú*. First Part. 2d. ed. Lima: Pontificia Universidad Católica del Perú.

————. 1985. *Obras Completas,* edited by C. Sáenz de Santa María. Vol. 2. *Las guerras civiles peruanas.* First, Second, and Third Parts. Madrid: Consejo Superior de Investigaciones Científicas, Instituto Gonzalo Fernández de Oviedo.

————. 1986. *Crónica del Perú.* Second Part, edited by F. Cantù. 2d ed. Lima: Pontificia Universidad Católica del Perú, Academia Nacional de la Historia.

Cline, Sarah. 1986. *Colonial Culhuacán, 1580–1600: A Social History of an Aztec Town.* Albuquerque: University of New Mexico Press.

————. 1993. The Spiritual Conquest Reexamined: Baptism and Church Marriage in Early Sixteenth-Century Mexico. *Hispanic American Historical Review* 73:453–80.

————. 1998. Fray Alonso de Molina's Model Testament and Antecedents to Indigenous Wills in Spanish America. In *Dead Giveaways: Indigenous Testaments of Colonial Mesoamerica and the Andes,* edited by S. Kellogg and M. Restall. Salt Lake City: University of Utah Press.

Cline, Sarah, and Miguel León Portilla, eds. 1984. *The Testaments of Culhuacán.* Los Angeles: UCLA Latin America Center Publications.

Cobo, Bernabé. 1935 [1639?]. Historia de la fundación de Lima. In *Monografías históricas sobre la ciudad de Lima.* Lima: Librería e Imprenta Gil, S.A.

————. 1956 [1653]. *Historia del Nuevo Mundo.* Madrid: Atlas.

Cock, Guillermo. 2002. Inca Rescue. *National Geographic,* May, 78–91.

Cohen, Esther. 1989. Symbols of Culpability and the Universal Language of Justice: The Ritual of Public Executions in Late Medieval Europe. *History of European Ideas* 11:407–16.

————. 2000. The Animated Pain of the Body. *American Historical Review* 105 (1):36–68.

Cohn, Samuel. 1988. *Death and Property in Siena, 1205–1800: Strategies for the Afterlife.* Baltimore and London: Johns Hopkins University Press.

————. 2000. The Place of the Dead in Flanders and Tuscany: Towards a Comparative History of the Black Death. In *The Place of the Dead: Death and Remembrance in Late Medieval and Early Modern Europe,* edited by B. Gordon and P. Marshall. Cambridge: Cambridge University Press.

Conklin, Beth. 1993. Introduction: Visions of Death in Amazonian Lives. *Latin American Anthropology Review* 5 (2):55–56.

————. 2001. *Consuming Grief: Compassionate Cannibalism in an Amazonian Society.* Austin: University of Texas Press.

Conlee, Christina A., Jahl Dulanto, Carol F. Mackey, and Charles Stanish. 2004. Late Prehispanic Sociopolitical Complexity. In *Andean Archaeology,* edited by H. Silverman. Oxford: Bakewell.

Conrad, Geoffrey. 1982. The Burial Platforms of Chan Chan: Some Social and Political Implications. In *Chan Chan: Andean Desert City,* edited by M. Moseley and Kent C. Day. Albuquerque: University of New Mexico Press.

Contreras y Valverde, Vasco de. 1982–1983 [1649–1650]. *Relación de la ciudad del Cuzco, 1649.* Cuzco: Imprenta Amauta.

Cook, David N. 1976. Les indiens immigrés à Lima au début du 17e siècle. *Cahiers des Amériques Latines* 13–14:33–51.

———. 1981. *Demographic Collapse: Indian Peru, 1520–1620.* Cambridge and New York: Cambridge University Press.

———. 1992. Luis Jerónimo de Oré: Una aproximación. In *Symbolo Catholico Indiano,* edited by A. Tibesar. Lima: Australis.

Córdova y Salinas, Diego de. 1957 [1651]. *Crónica franciscana de las provincias del Perú.* [Original title: *Coronica de la Religiossisima Provincia de los Doce Apostoles del Peru de la Orden de N.P.S. Francisco, de la Regular Observancia . . . Compuesta por el R.P. Fr. . . . Con Licencia, en Lima, por Jorge Lopez de Herrera, Año de 1651.*] Edited by L. Gómez Canedo. Washington, D.C.: Academy of American Franciscan History.

Cordy-Collins, Alana. 2001. Decapitation in Cupisnique and Early Moche Societies. In *Ritual Sacrifice in Ancient Peru,* edited by E. P. Benson and A. G. Cook. Austin: University of Texas Press.

Cornejo, Miguel. 2004. Pachacamac y el canal de Guatca. *Bulletin de l'Institut Français d'Études Andines* 33 (3):783–814.

Covarrubias, Sebastián. 2003 [1611]. *Tesoro de la lengua castellana o española.* Edited by M. A. de Riquert. Barcelona: Alta Fulla.

Covarrubias Pozo, Jesús M. 1963. *Libro de cabildos de elección de alcaldes regidores y otros oficiales cabildantes yngas y yanaconas de las parroquias de San Geronimo y San Blas jurisdicción de la ciudad del Cuzco.* Cuzco: Instituto Interamericano de Arte.

Covey, Alan. 2006. *How the Incas Built Their Heartland: State Formation and Innovation of Imperial Strategies.* Ann Arbor: University of Michigan Press.

Crabbe, M. James C. 1999. *From Soul to Self.* London: Routledge.

Cuena Boy, Francisco. 1998. Utilización pragmática del derecho romano en dos memoriales indianos del siglo XVII sobre el protector de indios. *Revista de Estudios Histórico-jurídicos* 20:107–42.

Cummins, Tom. 1991. We Are the Other: Peruvian Portraits of Colonial Kurakakuna. In *Transatlantic Encounters,* edited by R. Adorno and K. Andrien. Berkeley: University of California Press.

———. 1993. La representación en el siglo XVI: La imagen colonial del Inca. In *Mito y simbolismo en los Andes: La figura y la palabra,* edited by H. Urbano. Cusco: Centro de Estudios Regionales Andinos "Bartolomé de Las Casas."

———. 1994. Representation in the Sixteenth Century and the Colonial Image of the Inca. In *Writing without Words: Alternative Literacies in Mesoamerica and the Andes,* edited by E. H. Boone and W. D. Mignolo. Durham, N.C.: Duke University Press.

———. 1998. "Let me See! Writing is for Them": Colonial Andean Images and Objects 'como es costumbre tener los caciques señores.' In *Native*

Traditions in the Post-Conquest World, edited by E. H. Boone and T. Cummins. Washington, D.C.: Dumbarton Oaks.

———. 2002. *Toasts with the Inca: Andean Abstraction and Colonial Images on Quero Vessels.* Ann Arbor: University of Michigan Press.

———. 2005. La fábula y el retrato: Imágenes tempranas del Inca. In *Los Incas, reyes del Perú,* edited by N. Majluf. Lima: Banco de Crédito del Perú.

D'Altroy, Terence. 2002. *The Incas.* Oxford: Blackwell.

Daggett, Richard. 1991. Paracas: Discovery and Controversy. In *Paracas Art and Architecture: Object and Context in South Coastal Peru,* edited by A. Paul. Iowa City: University of Iowa Press.

Dawson, Lawrence E. 1979. Painted Cloth Mummy Masks of Ica, Peru. In *The Junius B. Bird Pre-Columbian Textile Conference. May 19th and 20th, 1973,* edited by Ann Pollard Rowe, Elizabeth P. Benson, and Anne-Louise Schaffer. Washington, D.C.: Dumbarton Oaks.

Dean, Carolyn. 1999. *Inka Bodies and the Body of Christ: Corpus Christi in Colonial Cuzco.* Durham, N.C.: Duke University Press.

De la Vega Machicao, Edmundo, Kirk L. Frye, and Cecilia Chávez Justo. 2002. La cueva funeraria de Molino-Chilacachi (Acora) Puno. *Gaceta Arqueológica Andina* 26:121–37.

DeLeonardis, Lisa. 2000. The Body Context: Interpreting Early Nasca Decapitated Burials. *Latin American Antiquity* 11:363–83.

DeLeonardis, Lisa, and George F. Lau. 2004. Life, Death, and Ancestors. In *Andean Archaeology,* edited by H. Silverman. Oxford: Blackwell.

Delumeau, Jean. 1990. *L'aveau et le pardon. Les difficultés de la confession, XIIIe–XVIIIe siècles.* Paris: Fayard.

Des Chene, Dennis. 2000. *Life's Form: Late Aristotelian Conceptions of the Soul.* Ithaca, N.Y.: Cornell University Press.

Díaz Arriola, Luisa. 2004. Armatambo y la sociedad Ychsma. *Boletín del Instituto Francés de Estudios Andinos* 33 (3): 571–94.

Díaz Rementería, Carlos J. 1977. *El cacique en el virreinato del Perú. Estudio histórico-jurídico, Publicaciones del Seminario de Antropología Americana.* Seville: Universidad de Sevilla.

Diez de San Miguel, Garci. 1964 [1567]. *Visita hecha a la provincia de Chucuito.* Lima: Casa de la Cultura.

Dillehay, Tom D., ed. 1995. *Tombs for the Living: Andean Mortuary Practices.* Washington, D.C.: Dumbarton Oaks.

Discurso. 2004 [1542]. Discurso sobre la descendencia y gobierno de los incas. In *Suma y narración de los Incas,* edited by M. d. C. Martín Rubio. Madrid: Polifemo.

Doctrina. 1985 [1585]. *Doctrina Christiana y catecismo para instrucción de indios.* Facsimile of the trilingual text. Madrid: Consejo Superior de Investigaciones Científicas.

Domínguez Faura, Nicanor. 1989. Aguas y legislación de los valles de Lima: El repartimiento de 1617. *Boletín del Instituto Riva Agüero* 15:119–54.

———. 1993. Juan de Betanzos y las primeras cartillas de evangelización en la Lengua General del Inga (1536–1542). In *La venida del reino: Religión, evangelización y cultura en América, siglos XVI–XX*, edited by G. Ramos. Cuzco: Centro de Estudios Regionales Andinos "Bartolomé de Las Casas."

Donnan, Christopher B. 1978. *Ancient Burial Patterns of the Moche Valley, Peru*. Austin: University of Texas Press.

———. 1995. Moche Funerary Practice. In *Tombs for the Living: Andean Mortuary Practices*, edited by T. D. Dillehay. Washington, D.C.: Dumbarton Oaks.

Doyle, Mary E. 1988. The Ancestor Cult and Burial Ritual in Seventeenth and Eighteenth-Century Peru. Ph.D. dissertation, History, University of California, Los Angeles.

Doyon, Leon G. 2002. Conduits of Ancestry: Interpretation of the Geography, Geology, and Seasonality of North Andean Shaft Tombs. In *The Space and Place of Death*, edited by H. Silverman. Washington, D.C.: American Anthropological Association.

Duggan, Lawrence G. 1997. "For Force Is Not of God"? Compulsion and Conversion from Yahweh to Charlemagne. In *Varieties of Religious Conversion in the Middle Ages*, edited by J. Muldoon. Gainesville: University of Florida Press.

Dulanto, Jahl. 2002. Pampa Chica: Prácticas de culto a los ancestros en la Costa Central del Perú. *Gaceta Arqueológica Andina* 26:37–67.

Durán, Juan Guillermo, ed. 1982. *El catecismo del III Concilio Provincial de Lima y sus complementos pastorales (1584–1585)*. Buenos Aires: El Derecho.

Durston, Alan. 2004. Pastoral Quechua: The History of Christian Translation in Peru, 1550–1650, Ph.D. dissertation, Anthropology, University of Chicago, Chicago.

———. 2007. *Pastoral Quechua: The History of Christian Translation in Colonial Peru, 1550–1650*. Notre Dame, Ind.: University of Notre Dame Press.

Duviols, Pierre. 1971. *La lutte contre les religions autochtones dans le Pérou colonial: L'Extirpation de l'idolatrie entre 1532 et 1660*. Lima: Institut Français d'Études Andines.

———. 1978. Camaquen upani: Un concept animiste des anciens Péruviens. *Amerikanistische Studien. Festschrift für Hermann Trimborn* 1:132–44.

———. 1989. Introducción a la "Instrucción para descubrir todas las guacas del Piru y sus camayos y haziendas." In *Fábulas y mitos de los incas*, edited by P. Duviols and H. Urbano. Madrid: Historia 16.

———. 1994. Les Comentarios reales de los Incas et la question du salut des infidèles. *Caravelle* (62):68–80.

———. 2003. *Procesos y visitas de idolatrías: Cajatambo, siglo XVII con documentos y anexos*. Lima: Pontificia Universidad Católica del Perú, Institut Français d'Études Andines.

Duviols, Pierre, and Henrique Urbano, eds. 1989. *Fábulas y mitos de los incas.* Vol. 48, *Crónicas de América.* Madrid: Historia 16.

Dwyer, Jane Powell, and Edward B. Dwyer. 1975. The Paracas Cemeteries: Mortuary Patterns in a Peruvian South Coastal Tradition. In *Death and the Afterlife in Pre-Columbian America,* edited by E. P. Benson. Washington, D.C.: Dumbarton Oaks.

Eaton, George F. 1916. *The Collection of Osteological Material from Machu Picchu.* Vol. 5, *Memoirs of the Connecticut Academy of Arts and Sciences.* New Haven.

Eeckhout, Peter. 1999. *Pachacamac durant l'Intermediaire récent. Étude d'un site monumental préhispanique de la Côte centrale du Pérou.* Vol. 747. Oxford: Bar International Series.

———. 2004. Relatos Míticos y Prácticas Rituales en Pachacamac. *Bulletin de l'Institut Français d'Études Andines* 33 (1):1–54.

Egaña, Antonio de, S.I., ed. 1954–1974. *Monumenta Peruana.* 6 vols. Vol. 75 (I: 1565–1575); 82 (II: 1576–1580); 88 (III: 1581–1585); 95 (IV: 1585–1591); 102 (V: 1592–1595); 110 (VI: 1596–1599). *Monumenta Missionum Societatis Iesu, Missiones Occidentales.* Rome: Monumenta Historia Societatis Iesu.

Egaña, Antonio de, and Enrique Fernández, eds. 1981. *Monumenta Peruana.* Vol. 120 (VII: 1600–1602). *Monumenta Historica Societatis Iesu.* Rome: Institutum Historicum Societatis Iesu.

Eire, Carlos. 1995. *From Madrid to Purgatory: The Art and Craft of Dying in Sixteenth-Century Spain.* Cambridge: Cambridge University Press.

Escamilla-Colin, Michèle. 1997. L'art de ménager la violence dans la pratique inquisitoriale. In *La violence en Espagne et en Amérique (XVe–XIXe siècles). Actes du colloque international "Les raisons des plus forts,"* edited by J.-P. Duviols and A. Molinié-Bertrand. Paris: Presses de l'Université de Paris-Sorbonne.

Esquivel y Navia, Diego de. 1980. *Noticias Cronológicas de la gran ciudad del Cuzco.* 2 vols. Lima: Fundación Augusto N. Wiesse.

Estenssoro, Juan Carlos. 1992. Los bailes de los indios y el proyecto colonial. *Revista Andina* 10 (2):353–89.

———. 1996. Les pouvoirs de la parole. La prédication au Pérou: de l'evangelisation à l'utopie. *Annales* (6):1225–57.

———. 2003. *Del paganismo a la santidad: La incorporación de los indios del Perú al catolicismo, 1532–1750.* Lima: Institut Français d'Études Andines, Pontificia Universidad Católica del Perú.

———. 2005. Construyendo la memoria: la figura del inca y el reino del Perú, de la conquista a Túpac Amaru II. In *Los Incas, reyes del Perú,* edited by N. Majluf. Lima: Banco de Crédito del Perú.

Falcón, Francisco. 1918 [1567]. Representación hecha por . . . en concilio provincial, sobre los daños y molestias que se hacen a los indios. In *Informaciones acerca de la religión y gobierno de los incas,* edited by H. Urteaga. Lima: Imprenta y Librería Sanmarti y Cía.

Farriss, Nancy M. 1984. *Maya Society under Colonial Rule: The Collective Enterprise of Survival*. Princeton: Princeton University Press.

Fernández, Enrique, S.I., ed. 1986. *Monumenta Peruana*. Vol. 128 (VIII: 1603–1604), *Monumenta Historica Societatis Iesu*. Rome: Institutum Historicum Societatis Iesu.

Fernández de Palencia, Diego. 1963 [1571]. *Historia del Perú*. Madrid: Atlas.

Fleming, Stuart. 1986. The Mummies of Pachacamac: An Exceptional Legacy from Uhle's 1896 Excavations in Peru. *Expedition* 28 (3):39–45.

Flynn, Maureen. 1989. *Sacred Charity: Confraternities and Social Welfare in Spain, 1400–1700*. Basingstoke: Macmillan.

———. 1999. Baroque Piety and Spanish Confraternities. In *Confraternities and Catholic Reform in Italy, France, and Spain*, edited by J.P. Donnelly, S.J., and M.W. Maher, S.J. Kirksville, Mo.: Thomas Jefferson University Press.

Fortes, Meyer. 1965. Some Reflections on Ancestor Worship in Africa. In *African Systems of Thought*, edited by M. Fortes and G. Dieterlen. Oxford: Oxford University Press.

———. 1976. An Introductory Commentary. In *Ancestors*, edited by W.H. Newell. The Hague: Mouton.

Foucault, Michel. 1991 [1975]. *Discipline and Punish: The Birth of the Prison*. Translated by A. Sheridan. London: Penguin.

———. 2004 [1997]. *Society Must Be Defended. Lectures at the Collège de France, 1975–76*. London: Penguin.

Fowler, Chris. 2002. Body Parts: Personhood and Materiality in the Earlier Manx Neolithic. In *Thinking through the Body: Archaeologies of Corporeality*, edited by Y. Hamilakis, M. Pluciennik, and S. Tarlow. New York: Kluwer Academic/Plenum Publishers.

Frame, Mary. 2001. Blood, Fertility, and Transformation: Interwoven Themes in the Paracas Necropolis Embroideries. In *Ritual Sacrifice in Ancient Peru*, edited by E.P. Benson and A.G. Cook. Austin: University of Texas Press.

Frame, Mary, Daniel Guerrero Zevallos, María del Carmen Vega Dulanto, and Patricia Landa Cragg. 2004. Un fardo funerario del Horizonte Tardío del sitio Rinconada Alta, Valle del Rímac. *Bulletin de l'Institut Français d'Études Andines* 33 (3):815–60.

Gade, Daniel, and Mario Escobar. 1982. Village Settlement and the Colonial Legacy in Southern Peru. *Geographical Review* 72 (4):430–49.

García Gallo, Alfonso. 1972. *Estudios de historia del derecho indiano*. Madrid: Instituto Nacional de Estudios Jurídicos.

García Irigoyen, Carlos. 1906–1908. *Santo Toribio: obra escrita con motivo del tercer centenario de la muerte del santo arzobispo de Lima*. 4 vols. Lima: Imprenta y Librería de San Pedro.

Garcilaso de la Vega, Inca. 1945 [1609]. *Comentarios Reales de los Incas.* Edited by A. Rosenblat. 2d ed. 2 vols. Buenos Aires: Emecé Editores.

———. 1960 [1613]. *Historia general del Perú.* Second Part, *Comentarios Reales de los Incas.* Vols. 134–35. Madrid: Atlas.

———. 1991 [1609]. *Comentarios Reales de los Incas.* With analytical index and glossary by Carlos Araníbar. 2 vols. México: Fondo de Cultura Económica.

Garland, Beatriz. 1994. Las cofradías en Lima durante la colonia: Una primera aproximación. In *La venida del reino: Religión, evangelización y cultura en América, siglos XVI–XX,* edited by G. Ramos. Cuzco: Centro de Estudios Regionales Andinos "Bartolomé de Las Casas."

Garrett, David. 2005. *Shadows of Empire: The Indian Nobility of Cusco, 1750–1825.* Cambridge: Cambridge University Press.

———. 2008. "In Spite of Her Sex": The *Cacica* and the Politics of the Pueblo in the Late Colonial Andes. *The Americas* 64 (4):547–81.

Gasparini, Graziano, and Louise Margolies. 1980. *Inca Architecture.* Bloomington and London: Indiana University Press.

Geremek, Bronislaw. 1994. *Poverty: A History.* Oxford: Blackwell.

Gillespie, Susan D. 2002. Body and Soul among the Maya: Keeping the Spirits in Place. In *The Space and Place of Death,* edited by H. Silverman. Washington, D.C.: American Anthropological Association.

Girard, René. 2005 [1972]. *Violence and the Sacred.* London: Continuum.

Gisbert, Teresa. 1994. *Iconografía y mitos indígenas en el arte.* 2d ed. Original edition, 1980. La Paz: Línea editorial: Fundación BHN; Editorial Gisbert y Cía.

González Alonso, Benjamín, ed. 2006. *Las Cortes y las Leyes de Toro de 1505: Actas del congreso conmemorativo del V^e centenario de la celebración de las Cortes y de la publicación de las Leyes de Toro de 1505.* Valladolid: Cortes de Castilla y León.

González Holguín, Diego. 1989 [1608]. *Vocabulario de la lengua general de todo el Peru llamada Lengua Qquichua o del Inca.* Lima: Universidad Nacional de San Marcos.

González Pujana, Laura. 1982. *El libro de cabildo de la ciudad del Cuzco.* Lima: Instituto Riva Agüero.

———. 1993. *La vida y obra del licenciado Polo de Ondegardo.* Valladolid: Universidad de Valladolid.

González Sánchez, Carlos Alberto. 1996. Los libros de los españoles en el virreinato del Perú. Siglos XVI y XVII. *Revista de Indias* 56 (206):7–47.

Gordon, Bruce, and Peter Marshall, eds. 2000. *The Place of the Dead: Death and Remembrance in Late Medieval and Early Modern Europe.* Cambridge: Cambridge University Press.

Gorringe, Timothy. 1996. *God's Just Vengeance: Crime, Violence and the Rhetoric of Salvation.* Cambridge: Cambridge University Press.

Gose, Peter. 2003. Converting the Ancestors: Indirect Rule, Settlement Consolidation, and the Struggle over Burial in Colonial Peru, 1532–1614. In *Conversion: Old Worlds and New,* edited by K. Mills and A. Grafton. Rochester: University of Rochester Press.

Graubart, Karen B. 2007. *With Our Labor and Sweat: Indigenous Women and the Formation of Colonial Society in Peru, 1550–1700.* Stanford: Stanford University Press.

Grell, Ole Peter, A. Cunningham, and J. Arrizabalaga, eds. 1999. *Health Care and Relief in Counter-Reformation Europe.* London: Routledge.

Griffiths, Nicholas. 1996. *The Cross and the Serpent: Religious Repression and Resurgence in Colonial Peru.* Norman: University of Oklahoma Press.

Gruzinski, Serge. 1988. *La colonisation de l'imaginaire: Sociétés indigènes et occidentalisation dans le México.* Paris: Gallimard.

Guaman Poma de Ayala, Felipe. 1989 [1615]. *Nueva corónica y buen gobierno.* 2d facsimile ed. Original facsimile edition, 1936. Vol. 23, *Travaux et Mémoires de l'Institut d'Ethnologie.* Paris: Institut d'Ethnologie–Musée de l'Homme.

Gudeman, Stephen. 1988. The "Manda" and the Mass. *Journal of Latin American Lore* 14 (1):17–32.

Guillaume-Alonso, Araceli. 1990. Corps reclus et corps supplicié à travers les archives de la Santa Hermandad. In *Le corps dans la société espagnole des XVIe et XVIIe siècles,* edited by A. Redondo. Paris: Publications de la Sorbonne.

———. 1997. Justice sommaire dans les campagnes de Castille à l'aube du XVIe siècle (La Santa Hermandad). In *La violence en Espagne et en Amérique (XVe–XIXe siècles). Actes du colloque international "Les raisons des plus forts,"* edited by J.-P. Duviols and A. Molinié-Bertrand. Paris: Presses de l'Université de Paris-Sorbonne.

Guillén, Edmundo. 1974. *Versión inca de la conquista.* Lima: Milla Batres.

———. 1983. El enigma de las momias incas. *Boletín de Lima* 28 (5):29–42.

Guillén, Sonia E. 2005. Mummies, Cults, and Ancestors: The Chinchorro Mummies of the South Central Andes. In *Interacting with the Dead: Perspectives on Mortuary Archaeology for the New Millennium,* edited by G. F. M. Rakita et al. Gainesville: University of Florida Press.

Günther, Juan, and Guillermo Lohmann Villena. 1992. *Lima.* Madrid: Mapfre.

Gurevich, Aron. 1992. *Historical Anthropology of the Middle Ages.* Edited by J. Howlett. Cambridge: Polity Press.

Gutiérrez, Gustavo. 1992. *En busca de los pobres de Jesucristo: El pensamiento de Bartolomé de Las Casas.* Lima: Instituto Bartolomé de Las Casas.

Gutiérrez Noriega, Carlos. 1937. Ciudadelas chulparias de los Wankas. *Revista del Museo Nacional* 6 (1):43–51.

Hampe, Teodoro. 1982. Las momias de los incas en Lima. *Revista del Museo Nacional* 46:405–18.

Hanke, Lewis, and Celso Rodríguez, eds. 1978–1980. *Los virreyes españoles en América durante el gobierno de la Casa de Austria.* 7 vols. *Biblioteca de Autores Españoles.* Madrid: Atlas.

Hardoy, Jorge. 1969. Escalas y funciones urbanas en América Hispánica hacia el año 1600. In *El proceso de urbanización en América desde sus orígenes hasta nuestros días,* edited by J. Hardoy and R. Schaedel. Buenos Aires: Instituto Torcuato di Tella.

Hardoy, Jorge, and Richard Schaedel, eds. 1969. *El proceso de urbanización en América desde sus orígenes hasta nuestros días.* Buenos Aires: Instituto Torcuato di Tella.

Hardoy, Jorge, Richard Schaedel, and Nora Kinzer, eds. 1978. *Urbanization in the Americas from Its Beginnings to the Present.* The Hague: Mouton.

Harris, Olivia. 1982. The Dead and the Devils among the Bolivian Laymi. In *Death and the Regeneration of Life,* edited by M. Bloch and J. H. Parry. Cambridge: Cambridge University Press.

Hastorf, Christine A. 2001. The Xauxa Andean Life. In *Empire and Domestic Economy,* edited by T. D'Altroy, C. A. Harstof, and associates. New York: Kluwer Academic/Plenum Publishers.

Healey, Kevin. 1999. South America. Nord-West (Map). Montreuil: Blay-Foldex.

Hefner, Robert W., ed. 1993. *Conversion to Christianity: Historical and Anthropological Perspectives on a Great Transformation.* Berkeley: University of California Press.

Henderson, John. 2006. *The Renaissance Hospital: Healing the Body and Healing the Soul.* New Haven: Yale University Press.

Heras Santos, José Luis de las. 1992. *La justicia penal de los Austrias en la corona de Castilla.* Salamanca: Universidad de Salamanca.

Hertz, Robert. 1960. *Death and the Right Hand.* London: Cohen and West.

Herzog, Tamar. 2004. *Upholding Justice: Society, State, and the Penal System in Quito (1650–1750).* Ann Arbor: University of Michigan Press.

Hiltunen, Juha, and Gordon F. McEwan. 2004. Knowing the Inca Past. In *Andean Archaeology,* edited by H. Silverman. Oxford: Blackwell.

Homza, Lu Ann. 1999. The European Link to Mexican Penance: The Literary Antecedents to Alva's *Confessionario.* In *A Guide to Confession Large and Small in the Mexican Language, 1634,* edited by B. D. Sell, J. F. Schwaller, and L. A. Homza. Norman: University of Oklahoma Press.

Horton, Robin. 1972. African Conversion. *Africa* 41:85–108.

Horton, Robin, and J. D. Y. Peel. 1976. Conversion and Confusion: A Rejoinder on Christianity in Eastern Nigeria. *Canadian Journal of African Studies* 10 (3):481–98.

Hrdlicka, Ales. 1914. Anthropological Work in Peru in 1913, with notes on the pathology of the Ancient Peruvians. *Smithsonian Miscellaneus Collections* 61 (18):1–69.

Hsia, R. Po-Chia 1998. *The World of Catholic Renewal, 1540–1770.* Cambridge: Cambridge University Press.

Huertas, Lorenzo. 1981. *La religión en una sociedad rural andina (siglo XVII).* Ayacucho: Universidad Nacional de San Cristóbal de Huamanga.

Hyslop, John. 1985. *Inkawasi: The New Cuzco, Cañete, Lunahuaná, Peru.* Vol. 234, *BAR International Series.* Oxford.

Ifeka-Moller, Caroline. 1974. White Power: Social Structural Factors in Conversion to Christianity, Eastern Nigeria, 1921–1966. *Canadian Journal of African Studies* 8:55–72.

Iliffe, John. 1987. *The African Poor.* Cambridge: Cambridge University Press.

Iriarte, Isabel. 1993. Las túnicas incas en la pintura colonial. In *Mito y simbolismo en los Andes: La figura y la palabra,* edited by H. Urbano. Cuzco: Centro de Estudios Regionales Andinos "Bartolomé de Las Casas."

Isambert, François-A. 1975. Les transformations du rituel catholique des mourants. *Archives des Sciences Sociales des Religions* (20).

Isbell, William. 1997. *Mummies and Mortuary Monuments. A Postprocessual Prehistory of Central Andean Social Organization.* Austin: University of Texas Press.

———. 2004. Mortuary Preferences: A Wari Culture Case Study from Middle Horizon Peru. *Latin American Antiquity* 15 (1):3–32.

Itier, César. 1991. Lengua general y comunicación escrita: cinco cartas en quechua de Cotahuasi, 1616. *Revista Andina* 9 (1):65–107.

———. 1992a. La tradición oral quechua antigua en los procesos de idolatrías de Cajatambo. *Bulletin de l'Institut Français d'Études Andines* 21 (3): 1009–51.

———. 1992b. Un sermón desconocido en quechua general: La "plática" que se ha de hazer a los indios en la predicación de la Bulla de la Santa Cruzada. *Revista Andina* 10 (1):135–46.

———. 2003. Textos quechuas de los procesos de Cajatambo. In *Procesos y visitas de idolatrías. Cajatambo, siglo XVII,* edited by P. Duviols. Lima: Pontificia Universidad Católica del Perú.

Janusek, John Wayne. 2004. Collapse as Cultural Revolution: Power and Identity in the Tiwanaku to Pacajes Transition. In *Foundations of Power in the Prehispanic Andes,* edited by K. Vaughn, D. Ogburn, and C.A. Conlee. Washington, D.C.: American Anthropological Association.

Joyce, Rosemary. 2005. Archaeology of the Body. *Annual Review of Anthropology* 34:139–58.

Julien, Catherine. 1987–1989. Las tumbas de Sacsahuaman y el estilo Cuzco Inca. *Ñawpa Pacha* 25–27:1–126.

———. 1998. La organización parroquial del Cuzco y la ciudad incaica. *Tawantinsuyu* 5:82–96.

———. 2000. *Reading Inca History.* Iowa City: University of Iowa Press.

———. 2006. Introduction. In Titu Cusi Yupanqui, *History of How the Spaniards Arrived in Peru.* Indianapolis: Hackett.

Kagan, Richard, and Fernando Marías. 2000. *Urban Images of the Hispanic World, 1493–1793.* New Haven: Yale University Press.

Kaulicke, Peter. 1997. *Contextos funerarios de Ancón. Esbozo de una síntesis analítica.* Lima: Pontificia Universidad Católica del Perú.

———. 2000. *Memoria y muerte en el Perú Antiguo.* Lima: Pontificia Universidad Católica del Perú.

Kellogg, Susan. 1995. *Law and the Transformation of Aztec Culture, 1500–1700.* Norman and London: University of Oklahoma Press.

———. 1998. Indigenous Testaments of Early-Colonial Mexico City: Testifying to Gender Differences. In *Dead Giveaways: Indigenous Testaments of Colonial Mesoamerica and the Andes,* edited by S. Kellogg and M. Restall. Salt Lake City: University of Utah Press.

Kellogg, Susan, and Mathew Restall, eds. 1998a. *Dead Giveaways: Indigenous Testaments of Colonial Mesoamerica and the Andes.* Salt Lake City: The University of Utah Press.

———. 1998b. Introduction. In *Dead Giveaways: Indigenous Testaments of Colonial Mesoamerica and the Andes,* edited by S. Kellogg and M. Restall. Salt Lake City: University of Utah Press.

Kroeber, A. L., and William D. Strong. 1924. *The Uhle Pottery Collections from Chincha.* Vol. 21, *University of California Publications. American Archaeology and Ethnology.* Berkeley: University of California Press.

Kubler, George. 1946. The Quechua in the Colonial World. In *Handbook of South American Indians,* vol. 2, *The Andean Civilizations,* edited by J. H. Steward. Washington, D.C.: Smithsonian Institution, Bureau of American Ethnology.

La Fontaine, Jean. 1985. Person and Individual: Some Anthropological Reflections. In *The Category of the Person: Anthropology, Philosophy, History,* edited by M. Carrithers. Cambridge: Cambridge University Press.

Lalinde Abadía, Jesús. 1978. *Iniciación histórica al derecho español.* Barcelona: Ariel.

Las Casas, Bartolomé de. 1990. *De Unico Vocationis Modo.* Edited by P. Castañeda Delgado and A. García del Moral, O.P. Vol. 2, *Obras Completas.* Madrid: Alianza Editorial.

———. 1992a [1565]. *De Thesauris.* Edited by A. Losada. Vol. 11.1, *Obras Completas.* Madrid: Alianza Editorial.

———. 1992b [1565]. *Doce Dudas.* Edited by J. B. Lassègue. Vol. 11.2, *Obras Completas.* Madrid: Alianza Editorial.

Lassègue Morèles, Juan Bautista. 1987. Sínodos diocesanos del Cusco, 1591 y 1601. *Cuadernos para la historia de la evangelización en América Latina* 2:31–72.

Le Goff, Jacques. 1984. *The Birth of Purgatory*. Translated by A. Goldhammer. Chicago: University of Chicago Press.

Levillier, Roberto. 1921. *Gobernantes del Perú. Cartas y papeles. Siglo XVI. Documentos del Archivo de Indias*. 14 vols., *Colección de Publicaciones Históricas de la Biblioteca del Congreso Argentino*. Madrid: Sucesores de Rivadeneyra.

Libros de Cabildo de Lima 1534–1639. 1935–1964. Edited by J. Bromley. 23 vols. Lima: Imprenta Torres Aguirre.

Ligou, Daniel. 1975. L'Évolution des cimetières. *Archives des Sciences Sociales des Religions* 39:61–77.

Lissón Chávez, Emilio. 1943–1956. *La Iglesia de España en el Perú. Colección de documentos para la historia de la iglesia en el Perú*. 5 vols. Seville: Católica Española.

Lizárraga, Reginaldo de. 1908 [1591]. *Descripción y población de las Indias*. Lima: Imprenta Americana.

Llamas y Molina, Sancho de. 1827. *Comentario crítico-jurídico-literal a las ochenta y tres Leyes de Toro*. 2 vols. Madrid: Imprenta de Repullés.

Llanos, Luis A. 1941. Exploraciones arqueológicas en Quimsarumiyoc y Huaccanhuayco- Calca. *Revista del Museo Nacional* 10 (2):240–62.

Lobo Guerrero, Bartolomé, and Hernando Arias de Ugarte. 1987 [1613]. *Sínodos de Lima de 1613 y 1636, Tierra nueva e cielo nuevo; Sínodos americanos*. Madrid: Consejo Superior de Investigaciones Científicas.

Lockhart, James. 1992. *The Nahuas after the Conquest: A Social and Cultural History of the Indians of Central Mexico, Sixteenth through Eighteenth Centuries*. Stanford: Stanford University Press.

Lohmann, Guillermo. 1966. La restitución por conquistadores y encomenderos: Un aspecto de la incidencia lascasiana en el Perú. *Anuario de Estudios Americanos* 23:21–89.

Lopétegui, M. 1945. Apuros en los confesionarios. *Missionalia Hispánica* 2: 576–80.

Lounsbury, Floyd G. 1986. Some Aspects of the Inka Kinship System. In *Anthropological History of Andean Polities*, edited by J. V. Murra, N. Wachtel, and J. Revel. Cambridge: Cambridge University Press.

Lowry, Lyn B. 1991. Forging an Indian Nation: Urban Indians under Spanish Colonial Control (Lima, Peru, 1535–1765). Ph.D. dissertation, History, University of California, Berkeley.

Luebke, David, ed. 1999. *The Counter-Reformation: The Essential Readings*. Oxford: Blackwell.

Lugo Olín, María Concepción. 1998. La Bula de la Santa Cruzada . . . ¿un remedio para sanar el alma? *Secuencia. Nueva Época* 41:139–47.

MacCormack, Sabine. 1985. The Fall of the Incas: A Historiographical Dilemma. *History of European Ideas* 6:421–45.

————. 1988. Pachacuti: Miracles, Punishments, and Last Judgment: Visionary Past and Prophetic Future in Early Colonial Peru. *American Historical Review* 93 (Feb.–Dec.):960–1004.

————. 1991. *Religion in the Andes: Vision and Imagination in Colonial Peru.* Princeton: Princeton University Press.

MacCurdy, George Grant. 1923. Human Skeletal Remains from the Highlands of Peru. *American Journal of Physical Anthropology* 6:217–329.

Majluf, Natalia, ed. 2005. *Los Incas, reyes del Perú.* Lima: Banco de Crédito del Perú.

Málaga Medina, Alejandro. 1974. Las reducciones en el Perú. *Historia y Cultura* 8:141–72.

Maldonado y Fernández del Torco, José. 1944. *Herencias en favor del alma en el derecho español.* Madrid: Editorial Revista de Derecho Privado.

Mannarelli, María Emma. 1993. *Pecados públicos. La ilegitimidad en Lima, siglo XVII.* Lima: Ediciones Flora Tristán.

Mannheim, Bruce. 1991. *The Language of the Inka since the European Invasion.* Austin: University of Texas Press.

————. 1998. A Nation Surrounded. In *Native Traditions in the Postconquest World,* edited by E. H. Boone and T. Cummins. Washington, D.C.: Dumbarton Oaks.

————. 2002. Gramática colonial, contexto religioso. In *Incas e indios cristianos. Elites indígenas identidades cristianas en los Andes coloniales,* edited by J.-J. Decoster. Cuzco: Centro de Estudios Regionales Andinos "Bartolomé de las Casas."

Martínez-Burgos García, Palma. 1990. *Idolos e imágenes: La controversia del arte religioso en el siglo XVI español.* Valladolid: Secretariado de Publicaciones, Universidad de Valladolid/Caja Salamanca.

Martínez Cereceda, José Luis. 1995. *Autoridades en los Andes: Los atributos del Señor.* Lima: Pontificia Universidad Católica del Perú.

Martínez Gil, Fernando. 1993. *Muerte y sociedad en la España de los Austrias.* Madrid: Siglo Veintiuno de España Editores.

Martz, Linda. 1983. *Poverty and Welfare in Habsburg Spain: The Example of Toledo.* Cambridge: Cambridge University Press.

Marzal, Manuel. 1983. *La transformación religiosa peruana.* Lima: Pontificia Universidad Católica del Perú.

Matienzo, Juan de. 1967 [1567]. *Gobierno del Perú.* Lima: Institut Français d'Études Andines.

Mauss, Marcel. 1985 [1938]. A Category of the Human Mind: The Notion of Person, the Notion of Self. In *The Category of the Person: Anthropology, Philosophy, History,* edited by M. Carrithers. Cambridge: Cambridge University Press.

Mazet, Claude. 1976. *Population et société à Lima aux XVIe et XVIIe siècles: La paroisse San Sebastián (1562–1689)*. Paris: IHEAL.

McLynn, Neil. 2003. Seeing and Believing: Aspects of Conversion from Antoninus Pious to Louis the Pious. In *Conversion in Late Antiquity and the Early Middle Ages*, edited by K. Mills and A. Grafton. Rochester: University of Rochester Press.

Meléndez, Juan de. 1681. *Tesoros verdaderos de las Yndias en la Historia de la gran Provincia de San Juan Bautista del Peru de el Orden de Predicadores*. 3 vols. Rome: Nicolas Angel Tinassio.

Melling, David J. 1999. Suffering and Sanctification in Christianity. In *Religion, Health and Suffering*, edited by J. Hinnells and R. Porter. London: Kegan Paul.

Menzel, Dorothy. 1959. The Inca Occupation of the South Coast of Peru. *Southwestern Journal of Anthropology* 15:125–42.

———. 1976. *Pottery Style and Society in Ancient Peru: Art as a Mirror of History in the Ica Valley, 1350–1570*. Berkeley: University of California Press.

Merback, Mitchell B. 1999. *The Thief, the Cross, and the Wheel: Pain and the Spectacle of Punishment in Medieval and Renaissance Europe*. Chicago: University of Chicago Press.

Mesa, José de, and Teresa Gisbert. 1982. *Historia de la pintura cuzqueña*. 2 vols. Lima: Fundación Augusto N. Wiesse.

Metcalf, Peter, and Richard Huntington, eds. 1980. *Celebrations of Death: The Anthropology of Mortuary Ritual*. Cambridge: Cambridge University Press.

Mills, Kenneth. 1997. *Idolatry and Its Enemies: Colonial Andean Religion and Extirpation, 1640–1750*. Princeton: Princeton University Press.

Mills, Kenneth, and Anthony Grafton, eds. 2003a. *Conversion in Late Antiquity and the Middle Ages: Seeing and Believing*. Rochester: University of Rochester Press.

———, eds. 2003b. *Conversion: Old Worlds and New*. Rochester: University of Rochester Press.

Milton, Cynthia E. 2007. *The Many Meanings of Poverty: Colonialism, Social Compacts, and Assistance in Eighteenth-Century Ecuador*. Stanford: Stanford University Press.

Mirow, Matthew C. 2004. *Latin American Law: A History of Private Law and Institutions in Spanish America*. Austin: University of Texas Press.

Molina, Cristóbal de. 1989 [1575?]. Relación de las fábulas y ritos de los incas. In *Fábulas y mitos de los incas*, edited by H. Urbano and P. Duviols. Madrid: Historia 16.

Montalvo, Francisco Antonio. 1683. *El Sol del Nuevo Mundo*. Rome: Angel Bernavó.

Montesinos, Fernando de. 1906 [1642]. *Anales del Perú*. 2 vols. Vol. 2, *Juicio de Límites entre Perú y Bolivia*. Madrid: Imprenta de Gabriel L. y del Horno.

Morel D'Arleux, Antonia. 1993. Los tratados de preparación a la muerte: Aproximación metodológica. In *Estado actual de los estudios sobre el siglo de oro,* edited by García Martín, M. I. Arellano, J. Blasco, and M. Vitse. Salamanca: Universidad de Salamanca.

Moseley, Michael. 1997. Catástrofes convergentes: Perspectivas geoarqueológicas sobre desastres naturales colaterales en los Andes centrales. In *Historia y desastres en América Latina,* edited by V. García Acosta. Lima: Red de Estudios Sociales en Prevención de Desastres en América Latina, CIESAS.

———. 2002. Modeling Protracted Drought, Collateral Natural Disaster, and Human Responses in the Andes. In *Catastrophe and Culture: The Anthropology of Disaster,* edited by S. M. Hoffman and A. Oliver-Smith. Santa Fe, N.M.: School of American Research Press.

Moseley, Michael, and Eric E. Deeds. 1982. The Land in Front of Chan Chan: Agrarian Expansion, Reform, and Collapse in the Moche Valley. In *Chan Chan: Andean Desert City,* edited by M. Moseley and Kent C. Day. Albuquerque: School of American Research, University of New Mexico Press.

Mulcahy, Rosemarie. 1992. *La decoración de la Real Basílica del Monasterio de El Escorial: 'a la mayor gloria de Dios y el Rey.'* Translated by Consuelo Luca de Tena. Madrid: Patrimonio Nacional.

———. 1998. *The Decoration of the Royal Basilica of El Escorial.* Cambridge: Cambridge University Press.

Muldoon, James. 1979. *Popes, Lawyers, and Infidels: The Church and the Non-Christian World, 1250–1550.* Philadelphia: University of Pennsylvania Press.

———, ed. 1997. *Varieties of Religious Conversion in the Middle Ages.* Gainesville: University of Florida Press.

Murphy, Melissa. 2003. From Bare Bones to Mummified. *Expedition,* 5–7.

Murra, John V. 1975. *Formaciones económicas y políticas del mundo andino.* Lima: Instituto de Estudios Peruanos.

Murúa, Martín de. 1987 [1613]. *Historia general del Perú. Libro del origen y descendencia de los yngas.* Edited by Manuel Ballesteros, *Crónicas de América.* Madrid: Historia 16.

———. 2001 [1613]. *Historia General del Perú.* Madrid: Dastin.

Nalle, Sarah T. 1992. *God in La Mancha: Religious Reform and the People of Cuenca, 1500–1650.* Baltimore: Johns Hopkins University Press.

Niles, Susan. 1999a. *The Shape of Inca History: Narrative and Architecture in an Andean Empire.* Iowa City: University of Iowa Press.

———. 1999b. Book review of Isbell 1997. *Journal of Field Archaeology* 26 (4):475–78.

Olmedo Jiménez, Manuel. 1991. El hospital de Santa Ana de Lima durante los siglos XVI y XVII. In *Actas del III Congreso Internacional sobre los Dominicos y el Nuevo Mundo.* Madrid: Deimos.

Ondegardo, Polo de. 1906 [1561]. Informe del licenciado Polo de Ondegardo al licenciado Briviesca de Muñatones sobre la perpetuidad de las encomiendas en el Perú. *Revista Histórica (Lima, Perú)* 13 (1):125–96.

———. 1917 [1571]. *Informaciones acerca de la religión y gobierno de los Incas por el licenciado . . . seguidas de las Instrucciones de los Concilios de Lima.* Edited by H. H. Urteaga and C. A. Romero. Vol. 3, *Colección de libros y documentos referentes a la historia del Perú.* Lima: Imprenta y Librería Sanmarti y Cia.

———. 1982 [1585]. Instrucción contra las ceremonias y ritos que usan los indios conforme al tiempo de su infidelidad. In *El catecismo del III Concilio Provincial de Lima y sus complementos pastorales (1584–1585),* edited by J. G. Durán. Buenos Aires: El Derecho.

———. 1990. *El mundo de los incas.* Edited by Laura González Pujana and Alicia Alonso. Madrid: Historia 16.

Oré, Fray Luis Jerónimo de. 1992 [1598]. *Symbolo Catholico Indiano.* Lima: Australis.

Ortiz de Zúñiga, Iñigo. 1967–1972 [1562]. *Visita de la provincia de León de Huánuco.* 2 vols. Huánuco: Universidad Nacional Hermilio Valdizán.

Ortlieb, Luc, Anne-Marie Hocquenghem, and Alicia Minaya. 1995. Toward a Revised Historical Chronology of El Niño Events Registered in Western South-America. *Terra Nostra* 2.

Ots Capdequí, José María. 1921. *El derecho de familia y el derecho de sucesión en nuestra legislación de Indias.* Madrid: Imprenta Helénica.

———. 1943. *Manual de historia del derecho español en las Indias y del derecho propiamente indiano.* Buenos Aires: Universidad de Buenos Aires, Facultad de Derecho y Ciencias Sociales, Instituto de Historia del Derecho Argentino Ricardo Levene.

———. 1957. *El estado español en las Indias.* México: Fondo de Cultura Económica.

Owen, Bruce D., and Marilyn A. Norconk. 1987. Analysis of the Human Burials, 1977–1983 Field Seasons: Demographic Profiles and Burial Practices. In *Archaeological Field Research in the Upper Mantaro, Peru, 1982–1983: Investigations of Inka Expansion and Exchange,* edited by T. Earle, T. D'Altroy, C. Hastorf, C. Costin, G. Russell, and E. Sandefur. Los Angeles: Institute of Archaeology, University of California.

Pagden, Anthony. 1982. *The Fall of Natural Man: The American Indian and the Origins of Comparative Ethnology.* Cambridge: Cambridge University Press.

Pardo, Osvaldo F. 2004. *The Origins of Mexican Catholicism: Nahua Rituals and Christian Sacraments in Sixteenth-Century Mexico.* Ann Arbor: University of Michigan Press.

———. 2006. How to Punish Indians: Law and Cultural Change in Early Colonial Mexico. *Comparative Studies in Society and History* 48 (1):79–109.

Parsons, Jeffrey, Charles M. Hastings, and Ramiro Matos. 2000. *Prehispanic Settlement Patterns in the Upper Mantaro and Tarma Drainages, Junín, Peru.* 2 vols. Vol. 34, *Memoirs of the Museum of Anthropology, University of Michigan.* Ann Arbor: Museum of Anthropology, University of Michigan.

Pärssinen, Martti. 2003. *Tawantinsuyu. El Estado Inca y su organización política.* Lima: Institut Français d'Études Andines, Embajada de Finlandia, Pontificia Universidad Católica del Perú.

Pärssinen, Martti, and Jukka Kiviharju. 2004. *Textos andinos: Corpus de textos khipu incaicos y coloniales.* Madrid: Instituto Iberoamericano de Finlandia, Departamento de Filología Española, Universidad Complutense de Madrid.

Paxton, Frederick S. 1990. *Christianizing Death: The Creation of a Ritual Process in Early Medieval Europe.* Ithaca, N.Y.: Cornell University Press.

Pease, Franklin. 1965. El concepto de derecho entre los incas. B.A. dissertation, Law, Pontificia Universidad Católica del Perú, Lima.

———. 1984. Introducción. In Pedro de Cieza de León, *Crónica del Perú.* First Part. Lima: Pontificia Universidad Católica del Perú.

———. 1995. *Las crónicas y los Andes.* Lima: Fondo de Cultura Económica.

Peñaherrera del Águila, Carlos, ed. 1989. *Atlas del Perú.* Lima: Instituto Geográfico Nacional.

Peña y Montenegro, Alonso de la. 1995–1996 [1668]. *Itinerario para párrocos de indios.* 2 vols. *Corpus Hispanorum de Pace.* Madrid: Consejo Superior de Investigaciones Científicas.

Pereña, Luciano. 1984. Estudio Preliminar. Proyecto de sociedad colonial: Pacificación y colonización. In *De Procuranda Indorum Salute,* edited by L. Pereña. Madrid: Consejo Superior de Investigaciones Científicas.

Pérez Bocanegra, Juan. 1631. *Ritual formulario e institucion de curas, para administrar a los naturales de este reyno, los Santos Sacramentos del Baptismo, Confirmacion, Eucaristia y Viatico, Penitencia, Extremauncion, y Matrimonio, con advertencias muy necessarias.* Lima: Geronimo de Contreras.

Pérez Fernández, Isacio. 1988. *Bartolomé de Las Casas en el Perú. El espíritu lascasiano en la primera evangelización del imperio incaico.* Cuzco: Centro de Estudios Regionales Andinos "Bartolomé de Las Casas."

———, ed. 1995 [1571]. *El Anónimo de Yucay frente a Bartolomé de Las Casas: Edición crítica del Parecer de Yucay.* Cuzco: Centro de Estudios Regionales Andinos "Bartolomé de Las Casas."

Phipps, Elena. 2004. Garments and Identity in the Colonial Andes. In *The Colonial Andes: Tapestries and Silverwork, 1530–1830,* edited by E. Phipps, J. Hecht, and C. Esteras. New York and New Haven: Metropolitan Museum of Art/Yale University Press.

———. 2005. Rasgos de nobleza: Los uncus virreinales y sus modelos incaicos. In *Los Incas, reyes del Perú,* edited by N. Majluf. Lima: Banco de Crédito del Perú.

Pierce, Steven, and Anupama Rao, eds. 2006a. *Discipline and the Other Body: Correction, Corporeality, Colonialism.* Durham, N.C.: Duke University Press.
———. 2006b. Discipline and the Other Body: Humanitarianism, Violence, and the Colonial Exception. In *Discipline and the Other Body: Correction, Corporeality, Colonialism,* edited by S. Pierce and A. Rao. Durham, N.C.: Duke University Press.
Pizarro, Pedro. 1978 [1571]. *Relación del descubrimiento y conquista del Perú.* Lima: Pontificia Universidad Católica del Perú.
Pizzigoni, Caterina, ed. 2007. *Testaments of Toluca.* Stanford: Stanford University Press.
Porras Barrenechea, Raúl. 1937. *Las relaciones primitivas de la conquista del Perú.* Paris: Imprimeries Les Presses Modernes.
Protzen, Jean-Pierre. 1993. *Inca Architecture and Construction at Ollantaytambo.* New York: Oxford University Press.
Proulx, Donald A. 2001. Ritual Uses of Trophy Heads in Ancient Nasca Society. In *Ritual Sacrifice in Ancient Peru,* edited by E. P. Benson and A. G. Cook. Austin: University of Texas Press.
Puente Brunke, José de la. 1992. *Encomiendas y encomenderos en el Perú. Estudio social y político de una institución colonial.* Seville: Excelentísima Diputación Provincial de Sevilla.
Puente Brunke, José de la, and Fernando Janssen. 1997. Encomienda y riqueza en una zona marginal del Perú: El caso de Chinchaycocha, siglos XVI–XVII. *Histórica* 21 (1):111–34.
Pullan, Brian. 1999. The Counter-Reformation, Medical Care and Poor Relief. In *Health Care and Poor Relief in Counter-Reformation Europe,* edited by O. P. Grell. London: Routledge.
Quilter, Jeffrey. 1989. *Life and Death at La Paloma: Society and Mortuary Practices in a Preceramic Peruvian Village.* Iowa City: University of Iowa Press.
Quiroga, Pedro. 1922 [1563]. *Coloquios de la verdad.* Seville: Tipografía Zarzuela.
Rakita, Gordon F. M., and Jane E. Buikstra. 2005. Corrupting Flesh: Reexamining Hertz's Perspective on Mummification and Cremation. In *Interacting with the Dead: Perspective on Mortuary Archaeology for the New Millennium,* edited by G. F. M. Rakita et al. Gainesville: University of Florida Press.
Rakita, Gordon F. M., Jane E. Buikstra, Lane A. Beck, and Sloan R. Williams, eds. 2005. *Interacting with the Dead: Perspectives on Mortuary Archaeology for the New Millennium.* Gainesville: University of Florida Press.
Ramirez, Susan. 1997. *The World Upside Down: Cross-Cultural Contact and Conflict in Sixteenth-Century Peru.* Stanford: Stanford University Press.
———. 1998. Rich Man, Poor Man, Beggar Man, or Chief: Material Wealth as a Basis of Power in Sixteenth-Century Peru. In *Dead Giveaways: Indigenous Testaments of Colonial Mesoamerica and the Andes,* edited by S. Kellogg and M. Restall. Salt Lake City: University of Utah Press.

Ramírez del Villar, Roberto. 1974. *San Francisco de Lima, Tesoros del Arte Colonial Peruano*. Lima: Auge S.A.

Ramos, Gabriela. 1994. Diezmos, conflictos sociales y comercio a inicios del siglo XVII (Arzobispado de Lima, 1600–1630). In *La venida del reino: Religión, evangelización y cultura en América, siglos XVI–XX*, edited by G. Ramos. Cuzco: Centro de Estudios Regionales Andinos "Bartolomé de Las Casas."

———. 2005a. Funerales de autoridades indígenas en el virreinato peruano. *Revista de Indias* 65 (234):455–70.

———. 2005b. Los símbolos de poder inca durante el virreinato. In *Los Incas, reyes del Perú*, edited by N. Majluf. Lima: Banco de Crédito del Perú.

———. 2005c. Nuestra Señora de Copacabana: ¿Devoción india o intermediaria cultural? In *Passeurs, mediadores culturales y agentes de la primera globalización en el mundo Ibérico, siglos XVI–XIX*, edited by C. Salazar and S. O'Phelan Godoy. Lima: Institut Français d'Études Andines, Pontificia Universidad Católica del Perú, Instituto Riva-Agüero.

———. n.d. Los intérpretes de la lengua general en Lima y Cuzco, siglos XVI–XVII.

Ranger, Terence. 2003. Christianity and Indigenous Peoples: A Personal Overview. *Journal of Religious History* 27 (3):255–71.

Ravines, Rogger. 1977. Prácticas funerarias en Ancón. First Part. *Revista del Museo Nacional* 43:327–97.

———. 1981. Prácticas funerarias en Ancón. Second Part. *Revista del Museo Nacional* 45:89–166.

Rebillard, Eric. 2003. Conversion and Burial in the Late Roman Empire. In *Conversion in Late Antiquity and the Middle Ages: Seeing and Believing*, edited by K. Mills and A. Grafton. Rochester: University of Rochester Press.

Recopilación. 1982. *Recopilación de las leyes destos reynos, hecha por mandado de la Magestad Católica del Rey don Felipe Segundo nuestro señor; que se ha mandado imprimir, con las leyes que después de la ultima impressión se han publicado, por la Magestad Católica del Rey don Felipe Quarto el Grande nuestro señor*. 3 vols. Valladolid: Lex Nova. Original edition, 1640.

Redondo, Agustín, ed. 1988. *Les parentés fictives en Espagne, XVIe–XVIIe siècles*. Paris: Publications de la Sorbonne.

———, ed. 1990a. *Le corps dans la société espagnole des XVIe et XVIIe siècles*. Paris: Publications de la Sorbonne.

———. 1990b. Mutilations et marques corporelles d'infamie dans la Castille du XVIe siècle. In *Le corps dans la société espagnole des XVIe et XVIIe siècles*, edited by A. Redondo. Paris: Publications de la Sorbonne.

Reff, Daniel T. 2005. *Plagues, Priests, and Demons: Sacred Narratives and the Rise of Christianity in the Old World and the New*. Cambridge: Cambridge University Press.

Reiss, Wilhelm, and Alfons Stübel. 1880–1887. *The Necropolis of Ancon in Peru: A Contribution to Our Knowledge of the Culture and Industries of the Empire of the Incas.* 3 vols. Berlin: A. Asher & Co.

Resines, Luis. 1992. *Catecismos americanos del siglo XVI.* 2 vols. Salamanca: Junta de Castilla y León, Consejería de Cultura y Turismo.

Restall, Mathew. 1997a. Heirs to the Hieroglyphs: Indigenous Writing in Colonial Mesoamerica. *The Americas* 54:239–67.

———. 1997b. *The Maya World: Yucatec Culture and Society, 1550–1850.* Stanford: Stanford University Press.

Rey Hazas, Antonio, ed. 2003a. *Artes de bien morir: Ars moriendi de la Edad Media y del Siglo de Oro.* Madrid: Lengua de Trapo Ediciones.

———. 2003b. Introducción. In *Artes de bien morir: Ars moriendi de la Edad Media y del Siglo de Oro,* edited by A. Rey Hazas. Madrid: Lengua de Trapo Ediciones.

Riva Agüero, José de la. 1966. Sobre las momias de los Incas. In *Estudios de historia peruana. Las civilizaciones primitivas y el Imperio Incaico. Obras Completas,* vol. 5. Lima: Pontificia Universidad Católica del Perú.

Rivera, Mario A. 1995. The Preceramic Chinchorro Mummy Complex of Northern Chile: Context, Style, and Purpose. In *Tombs for the Living: Andean Mortuary Practices,* edited by T. Dillehay. Washington, D.C.: Dumbarton Oaks.

Rivera Serna, Raúl, ed. 1965. *Libro primero de cabildos de la ciudad del Cuzco.* Vol. 1, *Biblioteca de la Sociedad Peruana de Historia, serie Registro Histórico.* Lima: Universidad Nacional Mayor de San Marcos.

Robin, Valérie. 2004. La divine comédie dans les Andes ou les tribulations du mort dans son voyage vers l'au-delà. *Journal de la Société des Américanistes* 90 (1):143–81.

Rodríguez, Pedro, and Raúl Lanzetti. 1982. *El catecismo romano: Fuentes e historia del texto y de la redacción. Bases críticas para el estudio teológico del catecismo del Concilio de Trento.* Pamplona: Universidad de Navarra.

Rostworowski, María. 1978. *Señoríos indígenas de Lima y Canta.* Lima: Instituto de Estudios Peruanos.

———. 1982. Testamento de don Luis de Colán curaca en 1622. *Revista del Museo Nacional* 46:507–43.

———. 1983. *Estructuras andinas del poder. Ideología religiosa y política.* Lima: Instituto de Estudios Peruanos.

———. 1988. *Historia del Tahuantinsuyu.* Lima: Instituto de Estudios Peruanos.

———. 1992a. *Ensayos de historia andina: Elites, etnías, recursos.* Lima: Instituto de Estudios Peruanos.

———. 1992b. *Pachacamac y el Señor de los Milagros: Una trayectoria milenaria.* Lima: Instituto de Estudios Peruanos.

———. 1999. *El señorío de Pachacamac: El informe de Rodrigo Cantos de Andrade de 1573.* Lima: Instituto de Estudios Peruanos, Banco Central de Reserva del Perú.

———. 2002. Pachacamac. In *Obras completas*, vol. 2. Lima: Instituto de Estudios Peruanos.

———. 2004 [1970]. Mercaderes del valle de Chincha en la época prehispánica: Un documento y unos comentarios. In *Obras completas*, vol. 3. Lima: Instituto de Estudios Peruanos.

———. 2005 [1975]. La tasa de Chinchaycocha de 1549. In *Obras Completas*, vol. 5. Lima: Instituto de Estudios Peruanos.

Rowe, John H. 1948. The Kingdom of Chimor. *Acta Americana* 6 (1–2):36–59.

———. 1951. Colonial Portraits of Inca Nobles. In *The Civilizations of Ancient America. Selected Papers of the XXIXth International Congress of Americanists*, edited by S. Tax. Chicago: University of Chicago Press.

———. 1957. The Incas under Spanish Colonial Institutions. *Hispanic American Historical Review* (37):155–99.

———. 1981. Una relación de los adoratorios del antiguo Cuzco . *Histórica* 5 (2):209–61.

———. 1985. Probanza de los incas nietos de conquistadores. *Histórica* 9 (2):193–245.

———. 1990. El plano más antiguo del Cuzco: Dos parroquias de la ciudad vistas en 1643. *Histórica* 14 (2):367–77.

———. 1995. Behavior and Belief in Ancient Peruvian Mortuary Practice. In *Tombs for the Living: Andean Mortuary Practices*, edited by T. D. Dillehay. Washington, D.C.: Dumbarton Oaks.

Salazar, Lucy C. 2007. Machu Picchu's Silent Majority: A Consideration of the Inka Cemeteries. In *Variations in the Expression of Inka Power. A Symposium at Dumbarton Oaks, 18 and 19 October 1997*, edited by R. L. Burger et al. Washington, D.C.: Dumbarton Oaks.

Salomon, Frank. 1995. "The Beautiful Grandparents": Andean Ancestor Shrines and Mortuary Ritual as Seen through Colonial Records. In *Tombs for the Living: Andean Mortuary Practices*, edited by T. D. Dillehay. Washington, D.C.: Dumbarton Oaks.

———. 2004. *The Cord Keepers: Khipus and Cultural Life in a Peruvian Village*. Durham, N.C.: Duke University Press.

Sánchez, Ana. 1991. *Amancebados, hechiceros y rebeldes (Chancay, siglo XVII)*. Cuzco: Centro de Estudios Regionales Andinos "Bartolomé de las Casas."

Sancho, Pedro. 1917 [1534]. Relación para Su Majestad de lo sucedido en la conquista y pacificación de estas provincias de la Nueva Castilla. In *Las relaciones de la conquista del Perú*, edited by H. Urteaga and C. A. Romero. Lima: Librería e Imprenta Sanmarti.

San Cristóbal, Antonio. 1988. *Arquitectura virreynal religiosa de Lima*. Lima: Librería Studium.

Sandweiss, Daniel H. 1992. The Archaeology of Chincha Fishermen: Specialization and Status in Inka Peru. *Carnegie Museum of Natural History Bulletin* 29 (9).

Santolaria Sierra, Félix, ed. 2003a. *El gran debate sobre los pobres en el siglo XVI: Domingo de Soto y Juan de Robles, 1545.* Barcelona: Ariel.

———. 2003b. Estudio introductorio. In *El gran debate sobre los pobres en el siglo XVI: Domingo de Soto y Juan de Robles, 1545,* edited by F. Santolaria Sierra. Barcelona: Ariel.

Scarry, Elaine. 1985. *The Body in Pain: The Making and Unmaking of the World.* New York: Oxford University Press.

Schenone, Héctor H. 1992. *Iconografía del arte colonial. Los santos.* 2 vols. Buenos Aires: Fundación Tarea.

Schreiber, Katharina. 2001. The Wari Empire of Middle Horizon Peru: The Epistemological Challenge of Documenting an Empire without Documentary Evidence. In *Empires,* edited by S. Alcock, T. D'Altroy, K. Morrison, and C. Sinopoli. Cambridge: Cambridge University Press.

Schreuder, Deryck, and Geoffrey Oddie. 1989. What is "Conversion"? History, Christianity and Religious Change in Colonial Africa and South Asia. *Journal of Religious History* 15 (4):496–518.

Schwaller, John F. 2001. Book review of *Vida eterna y preocupaciones terrenales: Las capellanías de misas en la Nueva España, 1700–1821,* by Gisela von Wobeser. *Hispanic American Historical Review* 81 (1):154–55.

Segura Llanos, Rafael, María del Carmen Vega, and Patricia Landa. 2002. Recent Investigations at the Site of Cajamarquilla: Advances in the Study of Precolumbian Mortuary Practices on the Peruvian Central Coast. In *20th Annual Northeast Conference on Andean Archaeology and Ethnohistory.* London, Ontario, Canada.

Shepard, Glenn H., Jr. 2002. Three Days for Weeping: Dreams, Emotions, and Death in the Peruvian Amazon. *Medical Anthropology Quarterly* 16 (2):200–229.

Shimada, Izumi. 1991. Pachacamac Archaeology: Retrospect and Prospect. In Max Uhle, *Pachacamac.* Philadelphia: University Museum of Archaeology and Anthropology, University of Pennsylvania.

———. 2005. *Pachacamac Archaeological Project.* Available from http://www .pachacamac.net.

Shimada, Izumi, Ken-Ichi Shinoda, Julie Farnum, Robert Corruccini, and Hirokatsu Watanabe. 2004. An Integrated Analysis of Pre-Hispanic Mortuary Practices: A Middle Sicán Case Study. *Current Anthropology* 45 (3):369–402.

Sillar, Bill. 1996. The Dead and the Drying: Techniques for Transforming People and Things in the Andes. *Journal of Material Culture* 1 (3):259–89.

Sillar, Bill, and Emily Dean. 2002. Identidad étnica bajo el dominio Inka: Una evaluación arqueológica y etnohistórica de las repercusiones del *estado* Inka en el grupo étnico Canas. *Boletín de Arqueología PUCP* 6:205–64.

Silverman, Helaine. 2002. Introduction: The Space and Place of Death. In *Anthropological Papers of the American Anthropological Association,* edited by H. Silverman. Washington, D.C.: American Anthropological Association.

————, ed. 2004. *Andean Archaeology.* Blackwell Studies in Global Archaeology. Oxford: Blackwell.

Silverman, Helaine, and William H. Isbell, eds. 2002. *Andean Archaeology I: Variations in Sociopolitical Organization. II: Art, Landscape, and Society.* Vol. 1. London: Kluwer Academic/Plenum Publishers.

Solórzano y Pereyra, Juan de. 1972 [1648]. *Política Indiana.* 5 vols. Madrid: Atlas.

Spierenburg, Pieter. 1984. *The Spectacle of Suffering: Executions and the Evolution of Repression: From a Preindustrial Metropolis to the European Experience.* Cambridge: Cambridge University Press.

Squier, E. George. 1877. *Peru. Incidents of Travel and Exploration in the Land of the Incas.* London: Macmillan and Co.

Stastny, Francisco. 1983. El arte de la nobleza inca y la identidad andina. In *Mito y simbolismo en los Andes: La figura y la palabra,* edited by H. Urbano. Cusco: Centro de Estudios Regionales Andinos "Bartolomé de las Casas."

Stothert, Karen E. 1979. Unwrapping an Inca Mummy Bundle. *Archaeology* 32 (4):8–17.

Straw, Carole. 2000. Settling Scores: Eschatology in the Church of the Martyrs. In *Last Things: Death and the Apocalypse in the Middle Ages,* edited by C. W. Bynum and P. Freedman. Philadelphia: University of Pennsylvania Press.

Strocchia, Sharon T. 1992. *Death and Ritual in Renaissance Florence.* Baltimore: Johns Hopkins University Press.

Stumer, Louis M. 1954. Population Centers of the Rimac Valley of Peru. *American Antiquity* 20 (2):130–48.

Suardo, Juan Antonio. 1935. *Diario de* Lima *(1629–1639).* Edited by R. Vargas Ugarte. Lima: Imprenta Vázquez.

Suárez, Margarita. 2001. *Desafíos transatlánticos: Mercaderes, banqueros y el estado en el Perú virreinal, 1600–1700.* Lima: Pontificia Universidad Católica del Perú/Instituto Riva Agüero, Instituto Francés de Estudios Andinos, Fondo de Cultura Económica.

Sweeney, Sean T., and Ian Hodder, eds. 2002. *The Body.* Cambridge: Cambridge University Press.

Tabío, Ernesto. 1965. *Excavaciones en la costa central del Perú (1955–58).* Havana: Academia de Ciencias de Cuba, Departamento de Antropología.

Taylor, Gerald. 1985. Un documento quechua de Huarochirí, 1608. *Revista Andina* 3 (1):157–85.

————, ed. 1987. *Ritos y tradiciones de Huarochirí. Manuscrito quechua de comienzos del siglo XVII.* Lima: Instituto de Estudios Peruanos, Instituto Francés de Estudios Andinos.

————, ed. 1999. *Ritos y tradiciones de Huarochirí.* 2d rev. ed. Lima: Instituto Francés de Estudios Andinos, Banco Central de Reserva del Perú, Universidad Particular Ricardo Palma/Centro de Investigación.

———. 2000a. Camac, camay y camasca en el manuscrito quechua de Huarochirí. In *Camac, camay y camasca y otros ensayos sobre Huarochirí y Yauyos.* Lima: Instituto Francés de Estudios Andinos.

———. 2000b. Supay. In *Camac, camay y camasca y otros ensayos sobre Huarochirí y Yauyos.* Lima: Instituto Francés de Estudios Andinos.

———. 2003. *El sol, la luna y las estrellas no son dios . . . La evangelización en quechua, siglo XVI.* Lima: Instituto Francés de Estudios Andinos.

Terraciano, Kevin. 1998. Native Expressions of Piety in Mixtec Testaments. In *Dead Giveaways: Indigenous Testaments of Colonial Mesoamerica and the Andes,* edited by S. Kellogg and M. Restall. Salt Lake City: University of Utah Press.

Thomas, Julian. 2002. Archaeology's Humanism and the Materiality of the Body. In *Thinking through the Body: Archaeologies of Corporeality,* edited by Y. Hamilakis et al. New York: Kluwer Academic/Plenum Publishers.

Thompson, Donald. 1972. La ocupación incaica en la sierra central. In *Pueblos y culturas de la sierra central del Perú,* edited by D. Bonavia. Lima: Cerro de Pasco Corporation.

Tibesar, Antonino, O.F.M. 1991. *Comienzos de los franciscanos en el Perú.* Translated by Jorge Narváez Muñoz, O.F.M.P. Iquitos: Centro de Estudios Teológicos de la Amazonía (CETA).

Toledo, Francisco de. 1986. *Disposiciones gubernativas para el virreinato del Perú.* 2 vols. Vol. 1 (1569–1574), edited by María Justina Sarabia Viejo. Seville: Escuela de Estudios Hispanoamericanos.

———. 1989. *Disposiciones gubernativas para el virreinato del Perú.* 2 vols. Vol. 2 (1575–1580), edited by María Justina Sarabia Viejo. Seville: Escuela de Estudios Hispanoamericanos.

Tomás y Valiente, Francisco. 1966. La sucesión de quien muere sin parientes y sin disponer de sus bienes. *Anuario de Historia del Derecho (España)* 36:189–254.

———. 1969. *El derecho penal de la monarquía absoluta (siglos XVI–XVII–XVIII).* Madrid: Tecnos.

———. 1997. *Manual de historia del derecho español.* 4th ed. Madrid: Tecnos. Original edition, 1983.

Torero, Alfredo. 1974. *El quechua y la historia social andina.* Lima: Universidad Particular Ricardo Palma.

———. 1995. Acerca de la lengua Chinchaysuyo. In *Del Siglo de Oro al Siglo de las Luces: Lenguaje y sociedad en los Andes del siglo XVIII,* edited by C. Itier. Cuzco: Centro de Estudios Regionales Andinos "Bartolomé de Las Casas."

Torres Saldamando, Enrique, Pablo Patrón, and Nicanor Boloña. 1888. *Libro primero de cabildos de Lima.* 3 vols. Paris: Paul Dupont.

Trujillo Mena, Valentín. 1981. *La legislación eclesiástica en el virreynato del Perú durante el siglo XVI.* Lima: Imprenta Editorial Lumen.

Uhle, Max. 1924. *Explorations at Chincha.* Edited by A. L. Kroeber. Berkeley: University of California Press.

———. 1988 [1913]. Acerca de la cronología de las antiguas culturas de Ica. In *Max Uhle y el Perú Antiguo,* edited by P. Kaulicke. Lima: Pontificia Universidad Católica del Perú.

———. 1991 [1903]. *Pachacamac.* Philadelphia: University Museum of Archaeology and Anthropology, University of Pennsylvania.

Urton, Gary. 2003. *Signs of the Inka Khipu: Binary Coding in the Andean Knotted-String Records.* Austin: University of Texas Press.

Urton, Gary, and Jeffrey Quilter, eds. 2002. *Narrative Threads: Accounting and Recounting in Andean Khipu.* Austin: University of Texas Press.

Van Deusen, Nancy. 2001. *Between the Sacred and the Worldly: The Institutional and Cultural Practice of Recogimiento in Colonial Lima.* Stanford: Stanford University Press.

———, ed. 2004. *The Souls of Purgatory: The Spiritual Diary of a Seventeenth-Century Afro-Peruvian Mystic, Ursula de Jesús, Diálogos.* Albuquerque: University of New Mexico Press.

Van Oss, Adrian. 2002. *Catholic Colonialism: A Parish History of Guatemala, 1524–1821.* Cambridge: Cambridge University Press. Original edition, 1986.

Varela, Javier. 1990. *La muerte del rey: El ceremonial funerario de la monarquía española (1500–1885).* Madrid: Turner.

Vargas Ugarte, Rubén, ed. 1951. *Concilios limenses (1551–1772).* 3 vols. Lima.

———. 1953–1962. *Historia de la Iglesia en el Perú.* 5 vols. Burgos: Imprenta de Aldecoa.

———. 1963. *Historia de la Compañía de Jesús en el Perú.* 3 vols. Burgos: Imprenta de Aldecoa.

Varón, Rafael. 1982. Cofradías de indios y poder local en el Perú colonial: Huaraz, siglo 17. *Allpanchis* (20):127–46.

———. 1997. Surco, Surquillo y Miraflores. La gente y sus recursos entre los siglos XVI y XX. In *Arqueología, antropología e historia en los Andes. Homenaje a María Rostworowski,* edited by R. Varón and J. Flores. Lima: Instituto de Estudios Peruanos/Banco Central de Reserva del Perú.

Vega, Juan José, ed. 1974. *Relación de la descendencia, gobierno y conquista de los incas.* Lima: Biblioteca Universitaria.

Venegas, Alexo. 1911 [1537]. Agonía del tránsito de la muerte con los avisos y consuelos que cerca della son provechosos, dirigida a la muy ilustre señora doña Ana de la Cerda, condesa de Mélito, etc. In *Escritores místicos españoles,* edited by M. Mir. Madrid: Casa Editorial Bailly Baillière.

Verano, John W. 1995. Where Do They Rest? The Treatment of Human Offerings and Trophies in Ancient Peru. In *Tombs for the Living: Andean Mortuary Practices,* edited by T. D. Dillehay. Washington, D.C.: Dumbarton Oaks.

————. 2001. The Physical Evidence of Human Sacrifice in Ancient Peru. In *Ritual Sacrifice in Ancient Peru*, edited by E. P. Benson and A. G. Cook. Austin: University of Texas Press.

Verdery, Katherine. 1999. *The Political Lives of Dead Bodies: Reburial and Postsocialist Change*. New York: Columbia University Press.

Villarejo, Avencio. 1965. *Los agustinos en el Perú (1548–1965)*. Lima: Ausonia.

Voragine, Santiago de la. 1987. *La leyenda dorada*. 1st ed. 2 vols. Vol. 2. Madrid: Alianza Editorial.

————. 1990. *La leyenda dorada*. 2 vols. Vol. 1. Madrid: Alianza Editorial.

Vovelle, Michel. 1983. *La mort et l'Occident*. Paris: Gallimard.

Vreeland, James. 1978. Prehistoric Andean Mortuary Practice: Preliminary Report from Peru. *Current Anthropology* 19 (1): 212–14.

————. 1998. Mummies of Peru. In *Mummies, Disease, and Ancient Cultures*, edited by T. A. Cockburn, E. Cockburn, and T. Reyman. Cambridge: Cambridge University Press.

Walker, Phillip L. 2001. A Bioarchaeological Perspective on the History of Violence. *Annual Review of Anthropology* 30:573–96.

Ward, Kerry. 2006. Defining and Defiling the Criminal Body at the Cape of Good Hope: Punishing the Crime of Suicide under the Dutch East India Company. In *Discipline and the Other Body: Correction, Corporeality, Colonialism*, edited by S. Pierce and A. Rao. Durham, N.C.: Duke University Press.

Weiner, Annette. 1985. Inalienable Wealth. *American Ethnologist* 12 (10):210–27.

Wightman, Ann. 1990. *Indigenous Migration: The Forasteros of Cuzco, 1570–1720*. Durham, N.C.: Duke University Press.

Wobeser, Gisela von. 1999. *Vida eterna y preocupaciones terrenales: Las capellanías de misas en la Nueva España, 1700–1821*. México: UNAM.

Wuffarden, Luis Eduardo. 2005. La descendencia real y el 'renacimiento inca' en el virreinato. In *Los Incas, reyes del Perú*, edited by N. Majluf. Lima: Banco de Crédito del Perú.

Xerez, Francisco de. 1985 [1534]. *Verdadera relación de la conquista del Perú. Crónicas de América*. Madrid: Historia 16.

Yupanqui, Titu Cusi. 1992 [1570]. *Instrucción al licenciado don Lope García de Castro*. Edited by Liliana Regalado. Vol. 9, *Clásicos Peruanos*. Lima: Pontificia Universidad Católica del Perú.

Zárate, Agustín de. 1995 [1555]. *Historia del descubrimiento y conquista del Perú*. Lima: Pontificia Universidad Católica del Perú.

Zavala, Silvio. 1971. *Las instituciones jurídicas en la conquista de América*. México D.F.: Porrúa.

Zevallos Quiñones, Jorge. 1994. *Huacas y huaqueros en Trujillo durante el virreinato*. Trujillo: Normas Legales.

Zuidema, R. Tom. 1964. *The Ceque System of Cuzco: The Social Organization of the Capital of the Inca*. Leiden: E. J. Brill.

————. 1980. Parentesco inca. In *Parentesco y matrimonio en los Andes,* edited by E. Mayer and R. Bolton. Lima: Pontificia Universidad Católica del Perú.

————. 1986. *The Inca Civilization of Cuzco.* Austin: University of Texas Press.

————. 1995. *El sistema de los ceques del Cuzco: La organización social de la capital de los incas con un ensayo preliminar.* Lima: Pontificia Universidad Católica del Perú.

INDEX

Spanish power established in, 5
wills
—author demographics, in this
text, 126–27
—doubts about sincerity of conversion, 122–23
—parish information recorded in,
130
Lima diocese, 5, 27
Lima sierra, 18
lineage, legitimacy, and succession,
163–64, 166–68, 177–79
Llaca, Antonio, 168
Llapa, Ana, 168
Llavin, María, 171
Lloque Yupanqui, 52
Loayza, Jerónimo de
hospital founding, 102, 104–5
Instrucción in furtherance of conversion, 66, 71, 79
parish organization, 98
report on idolatries for, 265n17
suppressing the Jajua rituals,
256n51
Lobo Guerrero, Bartolomé, 108–9,
137, 151, 276n33
Loja, Ecuador, 18
"lonely soul," idea of, 208
Lowry, Lyn B., 127
Luna Atoc, Cristóbal, 192
Lupaqa, 17, 252n28
Lurín valley, 16, 17

MacCormack, Sabine, 27, 32, 250n7,
266n25
machayes, 188
Machiguenga, 257n62
Machumbi, Diego, 293n80
Machu Picchu, 17
Magdalena village, 108
Maldonado y Fernández del Torco,
José, 302n165
Manchipula, Pedro, 165, 171, 210
Manco Inca, 53, 56, 59
Mango Pongo, Francisco, 301n152
Mannarelli, María Emma, 287n8
Mannheim, Bruce, 281n19
Mantaro valley, 19

Manuscript of Huarochirí, 87, 272n73,
273n77
Marcatampu shrine, 93
Marian devotions, 112, 123
Martín de Porres, Saint, 295n88
martyrdom, of Atahualpa, 46–47
Matías, Lucía, 208
Matienzo, Juan de, 69
Matsigenka, 29
Maya, 254n35
mayordomos, 172–73, 185, 195, 197
Mayz, Pedro, 191–92
memory
Christianizing, 194
churches as spaces guarding and
refining, 188
concept of the ancestor in, 10, 28
creating, 203–4, 211–12
destroying through fire, 50, 53
maintaining, 203–13
memory, reproducing and prolonging
confraternities' role in, 174, 216
family tombs for, 169
tombs as means of, 65
will arrangements for
—alms-giving, 202–3
—care of the family tomb, 169
—funeral processions, 201–3
—obligations of the living, 180–81,
192–93, 206–7, 212
—vigil masses, 201
Mena, Cristóbal de, 39
Mena, Trujillo, 274n5
Mendoza, Hurtado de, 93, 265n16
Menzel, Dorothy, 14, 23, 31, 251n10,
252n16
Mercedarians, 138, 194–95
La Merced monastery, 56, 138, 197
Mesa, Gerónimo de, 179
Mesquirán, Miguel, 198
mestizas/os, 76, 121, 151, 179, 198
Mexico, 2, 280nn6–7
Mexico-Peru compared, 126
Middle Ages, 59, 60
military, social mobility through,
171–73
the missionary project, 2–4, 60–63,
67–69, 89–91

wills (*cont.*)
  encomenderos and, 122, 140, 168
  history of, 115
  indigenous scribes, composing of,
    120–21
  information found in, 122, 130,
    136
  language of, 119, 121
  notaries of, 116–19, 121, 123
  Otra exhortación más larga on, 83
  for the poor, 116–17
  priests and
  —executors of, 124, 140, 185, 186
  —requirements for, 116, 118
  —witnesses of, 168
  provoking reflection through, 124
  reinforcing family ties, 212
  structure of
  —annotating details of death, 220
  —conventions for, 121–22, 123
  —division of property, 124
  —funeral ceremonies, instructions
    pertaining to, 124
  —gravesite, instructions pertaining
    to, 124, 129
  —invocations in, 123
  —manuals used for preparing, 123
  —meditation on death section,
    123–24
  —payment of debts and restitu-
    tions, 124
  as teaching documents, 124
  universal heir, appointment of,
    177–84, 192

witnesses of, 124–26, 168, 196
written in indigenous languages,
  280n6
women
  as *cacicas*, 170–71, 192, 288n13,
    290n35
  certifying documents, 126
  on choice of executors, 186–87
  role in funerary rituals, 257n57
  spouses as universal heirs,
    180–81
  virtuous, bequest supporting, 210

Xerez, Francisco de, 38–39, 259n7

Yacovleff, Eugenio, 255n41
Yarise, Felipe, 282n30
Ychsma
  deity, 251n14
  province, 94
Ynga, Esteban Challco Viracocha, 170,
    295n93, 300n141
Ynga, Fernando, 169, 175, 194, 211
Ynga, Joan Pascac, 298n121
Ynga, Juan Gualpa Sucso, 167, 190
Ynga, Lázaro Quispe Topa, 170
Ynga, Luis Chalco Yupanqui, 169
Yungas, 28, 30
Yupangui, Francisco Chalco, 204

Zárate, Agustín de, 30, 40, 42–43,
    74
Zuidema, R. Tom, 287n3
Zúñiga, Diego Mesia de, 97

GABRIELA RAMOS is University Lecturer in Latin American
History, University of Cambridge.